WAREZ

Before you start to read this book, take this moment to think about making a donation to punctum books, an independent non-profit press,

@ https://punctumbooks.com/support/

If you're reading the e-book, you can click on the image below to go directly to our donations site. Any amount, no matter the size, is appreciated and will help us to keep our ship of fools afloat. Contributions from dedicated readers will also help us to keep our commons open and to cultivate new work that can't find a welcoming port elsewhere. Our adventure is not possible without your support.

Vive la Open Access.

Fig. 0. Hieronymus Bosch, *Ship of Fools* (1490–1500)

First published in 2021 by dead letter office, BABEL Working Group, an imprint of punctum books, Earth, Milky Way.
https://punctumbooks.com

The BABEL Working Group is a collective and desiring-assemblage of scholar–gypsies with no leaders or followers, no top and no bottom, and only a middle. BABEL roams and stalks the ruins of the post-historical university as a multiplicity, a pack, looking for other roaming packs with which to cohabit and build temporary shelters for intellectual vagabonds. We also take in strays.

ISBN-13: 978-1-68571-036-1 (print)
ISBN-13: 978-1-68571-037-8 (ePDF)

DOI: 10.53288/0339.1.00

LCCN: 2021951510
Library of Congress Cataloging Data is available from the Library of Congress

Work on this book was made possible through the award of a Philip Leverhulme Prize from the Leverhulme Trust.

LEVERHULME
TRUST

Book design: Vincent W.J. van Gerven Oei
Cover image: Ahmed Adly via Unsplash

punctumbooks
spontaneous acts of scholarly combustion

HIC SVNT MONSTRA

WAREZ

The Infrastructure and Aesthetics of Piracy

Martin Paul Eve

p.

Contents

Acknowledgements

Many individuals have helped me in the writing of this book. My thanks at punctum to Eileen Joy, Vincent W.J. van Gerven Oei, and Lily Brewer. For her brilliantly helpful suggestions on the manuscript, my thanks to Virginia Crisp. Notably, thanks also to Jamie Harries, Ronald Snijder, Paul Tavner, Jake Bickford, James Baker, and John Fink for responding to my queries on degenerative DRM. I owe a debt to Ben Garrett for assembling the DeFacto2 archive that underpins this work. My thanks go also to Iñigo Quilez for permission to include images of his DemoScene productions. With thanks to my friends, in no particular order: Joe Brooker, John and Caroline Matthews, Caroline Edwards, Iain Robert Smith, James and Holly Crow, Helen and Duncan Stringer, Alyson Jakes, Duncan Gray, Richard Hall, Hazel and Michael Vanderhoeven, Siân Adiseshiah, Ernesto Priego, Ben Johnson, Lianne de Mello, Julian Cottee, Doireann Lalor, Mark Blacklock, Peter Christian, Roland Clare, Kay Mendlson, Warren Young, Andy Byers, Mauro Sanchez, Rose Harris-Birtill, Paula Clemente Vega, Tom Grady, Jon Fugler, Bryan Cheyette, Stephen Curry, Don Waters, Ross Mounce, Tobias Steiner, and Sam Moore. Everyone at A Love From Outer Space. *Friendship* has sustained me through the writing of this book under difficult global circumstances. I hope to see you all on the other side of the coronavirus pandemic. My final thanks, as ever, go to my family — Gill Hinks, Rich Gray, Alyce Magritte, Nova Gray, Mina Gray, Susan Eve, Juliet Eve, Lisa Holloway, Carin Eve, Anthony Eve, Julia Eve, Sam Jones, and Toby Eve — but especially, with all my love, to my wife, Helen.

For Nova and Mina,
who will not know, for some time, what this book is about

and for James,
who already does.

Terminological Notes

Throughout this book, the terms "Warez Scene" and "the Scene" are capitalized in order to denote the underground movement. Other terms, such as NukeNets have some capitalisation where there are CamelCase formulations, while some roles do not. User nicknames are specified in the case used by the holder.

Glossary

0day. Refers to the most bleeding-edge access to pirate **releases**. Its derivation is that access comes "0 days" since its release.

Addline. The command that will add a user to a topsite. This command contains the user's Internet Protocol (IP) details, **ident** mask, and other security features.

Affiliate. An arrangement whereby a **release group** is associated with a **topsite** and "pres" its **releases** on that site. It can also refer to the affiliation of **courier** groups with a site.

ASCII art. An artistic mode in which graphics are constructed from textual characters using the American Standard Code for Information Interchange.

Autotrader. A **courier** who uses software to transfer **releases** between **topsites** automatically without any human intervention. It is also used to refer to such software itself. It is generally frowned upon but is also a seemingly widespread practice.

Bittorrent. A protocol for the distribution of content between peers. It is often but not exclusively used in the lower echelons of the piracy hierarchy.

Bouncer (BNC). A proxy to which users connect. These mechanisms hide or cloak a **topsite**'s actual IP address. Bouncers can handle either just the **File Transfer Protocol (FTP)** command channel or can also take the form of "traffic bouncer" that also masks the data stream. There are also IRC bouncers that keep users connected to an **Internet Relay Chat** server, which means that they do not have to reconnect to the server every time and that their connecting IP address remains hidden.

Bulletin Board System (BBS). A precursor to the internet that offered dial-in access to a single machine. The Scene originated in BBS cultures and moved to the internet in the 1990s.

Courier. An individual who moves **releases** between sites to build ratio credit for download and to participate in courier charts. The act of transferring a release, in competition with other couriers, is called "**racing.**" Previously, in earlier BBSs, a courier was also referred to as a "broker."

Courier Charts. Competitive scoring systems that rank couriers. Based on **weektop scorecards**.

Crack. A modification to a piece of software that removes its copyright protection routines. Often bundled with **releases**.

Daemon. A piece of server software that runs as a background process, rather than interactively. Examples include web servers and FTP servers that serve remote users. **Topsites** use FTP daemons.

DRM. Digital Rights Management. Programming routines that aim to make it impossible, illegally, to copy an artefact. **Cracks** aim to circumvent DRM/TPM.

Dupecheck. A database of previous scene **releases**, allowing a **release group** to ascertain whether a **release** is a duplicate of a previous work.

Eggdrop. A piece of software for running IRC bots. It is frequently used to run **topsite** bots.

Exif. Exchangeable image file format. An image file format that may contain metadata exposing the original source.

File eXchange Protocol (FXP). The use of FTP to transfer files between two remote servers rather than the more common client-server architecture.

File Transfer Protocol (FTP). A protocol for storing and retrieving files from a remote server.

FLAC. The Free Lossless Audio Codec. A lossless music compression format.

FXP board. A bulletin board or forum site where pirated **releases** are disseminated through hacked servers. It is a lower level of the Warez Scene that is strictly frowned upon by the **topsite** scene.

Ident. A protocol specified in the specification document "RFC 1413" (Request for Comment) that identifies the user of a particular TCP (Transmission Control Protocol) connection. It is used in the Scene to determine whether a user connecting to the **topsite** is authorized.

Internal. A **release** designed only for dissemination among members of the release group itself. Such **releases** are not beholden to the same standards (e.g., **dupecheck**) as public **releases**.

Internet Relay Chat (IRC). A distributed online chat system used by Sceners to communicate with one another. Site bots also post updates to the IRC channels of **topsites**.

Keygen. A "key generator." A piece of software that will produce a valid, but counterfeit, serial key or license for software that requires it. Often distributed with a **release**.

Leet-speak. A contraction of "elite speak"—a form of slang communication that uses text and numbers. Often, the numbers "1337" or "31337" are used to mean "leet" of "eleet" for the digits' resemblance to "e," "l," and "t."

MP3. The MPEG-2 Audio Layer III codec. A music compression format.

NFO Files. Short for iNFOrmation file. A text file that contains information about a **release**. Usually also populated with **ASCII art**.

Nuke. Both a noun and a verb. In its noun form, this refers to a "bad" **release** that has been marked as a rule violation at either the **topsite**-level (a violation of individual site rules) or Scene-level (a violation of release rule standards). Nuke as a verb refers to the act of marking a **release** as bad using the "site nuke" command.

NukeNet. An inter-site system for **nuking** releases.

Nuker. A person with the role of **nuking** releases.

Pre. A noun and a verb. It is the moment at which a **release** is made available.

Pre-spam. The act of posting **pre** announcements in order to convey a message rather than to advertise the true availability of a **release**. They are also used to catch autotraders.

Race. The competitive transfer of **releases** between **topsites** by **couriers**. The goal is to earn credits and to score highly enough to retain one's account on the site. Statistics from this contribute to the **weektop scorecard**.

RAID. A Redundant Array of Independent Disks. This is a storage schema that makes additional copies of data locally, spread across many different hard-disk drives ("striping"), in order to protect against the risk of catastrophic drive failure and data loss. **Topsites** use RAID to protect their archives.

Release. A pirate artefact, be it music, movies, software, games, etc.

Release Group. A set of individuals working together to create **releases**.

SceneBan. A lifetime ban instated on an individual for a serious infraction, such as being a law enforcement officer.

Site. Short for **topsite**.

Siteop. A site operator. The administrator who runs a **topsite**. These users may not be the site owner (i.e., the physical owner of the server).

Topsite. An FTP server with a high-speed internet connection and vast amounts of storage space. It has **affiliates**, **couriers**, **siteops**, **nukers**, and other user categories. It is ranked according to various criteria for participation in **courier charts**.

TPM. Technical Protection Measures (TPM). See **DRM**.

Weektop Scorecard. Also referred to as wkup or wktop. The weekly positional ranking of **couriers** and **release groups** by the volume uploaded to a particular **topsite**. Used to create a competitive ambiance and Scene-wide scoring systems such as **courier charts**.

Zipscript. A software routine that executes on a **topsite** while a **release** is being uploaded. This provides integrity checking, release tagging, and other "race" features.

ONE

Original Pirate Material

Some men rise, some men fall
I hear ya call, stand tall now
Has it come to this?
Original pirate material

— The Streets, "Original Pirate Material"

This is the first scholarly research book about the "Warez Scene." The Warez Scene is a worldwide, underground, organized network of pirate groups specializing in obtaining and illegally freely releasing digital media before their official sale dates.[1] This underground subculture, which began life in the pre-internet-era Bulletin Board Systems (BBSs), moved to File Transfer Protocol (FTS) servers (also known as "topsites") in the mid-to-late 1990s.[2] The "Scene," as it is known, is highly illegal in almost every aspect of its operation. The term "warez" itself refers to

1 This definition is derived from Virginia Crisp, *Film Distribution in the Digital Age: Pirates and Professionals* (Basingstoke: Palgrave Macmillan, 2017), 186. Alf Rehn, "Electronic Potlatch: A Study on New Technologies and Primitive Economic Behaviors" (PhD diss., Royal Institute of Technology, 2001), 57–58, refuses to use the term "pirate" to refer to Scene groups. I dispute this decision, though, and use the formulation here throughout.

2 Patryk Wasiak, "'Illegal Guys': A History of Digital Subcultures in Europe during the 1980s," *Zeithistorische Forschungen/Studies in Contemporary History* 9 (2012): 267.

pirated media, a derivative of "software." This Warez Scene is an underground culture with its own norms and rules of participation, its own forms of sociality, and its own artistic outputs. This book describes and analyses what we know about this underground culture, its operations, and its infrastructures.

Before I turn to this network, I want to talk about another criminal enterprise: the stock exchange. In early 2012, a company called Knight Capital developed a software system designed to make them millions of dollars. The software worked at timescales lower than those possible for humans with a sophisticated high-frequency trading algorithm. For instance, when the software detected that shares had begun to dip, it would sell its stock before price drops could do any financial damage. Likewise, searching for patterns in the data that people cannot perceive within an actionable timeframe, the software looked for shares that appeared to be on the up and made purchases at a tremendous rate. It was a clever piece of software engineering and part of a broader societal obsession with acceleration that recognizes how speed is among the defining characteristics of contemporary capital. It was also a startling example of what a computational approach could do to accelerate traditional, stock-market trading in the service of profit.[3]

The only problem was that the trading software did not work as intended. In fact, Knight Capital's software worked exceptionally badly. Losing value at approximately $10 million per minute, it took almost an hour for a supervisor to realize the damage and for the company to shut the system down. After losing $460 million in forty-five minutes, the software destroyed Knight Capital's reputation and actual value. Yet, the damage went far beyond this. Reputational waves spread quickly through the stock exchange. The algorithm's unusual trading activities caused a loss of confidence in the 150 or so companies affected by its operations. This disruption heralded the birth of the automated flash crash, the now periodic incursion of soft-

3 For more on speed, see also Rehn, "Electronic Potlatch," 141.

ware system failure into social systems of corporate value and share circulation.[4]

My story of high finance points to an obsession with speed and competition in contemporary computation, but it also gestures towards another structure: a competitive game. High-frequency traders situate their servers immediately adjacent to the stock exchange so that they can race against one another on millisecond timescales. Recent advances in high-frequency trading have sought speed advantages of less than a billionth of a second at substantial cost.[5] These traders use sophisticated software algorithms to trade automatically and much more quickly than would be possible in a system overseen by human reactions. The top traders gain reputational supremacy for the success of their algorithms and the sophistication of their hardware. They put in many hours per week, usually excessively so, trading stocks and shares. They live a high-octane yet digitally mediated life. They also, of course, take home more wealth than they could ever hope to spend, hence my quip on the moral "illegality" of such undertakings.

This is not a book about the stock market. But this tale of high finance's obsession with computational speed and automation, using light-speed hardware, deploying algorithmic transfers, and featuring reputational predominance, is an obsession that resonates strongly with the pirates of the Warez Scene. For, as ironic as it may sound for a covert, illegal network, the Scene thrives on fierce competition for cultural capital and prestige among its members. For instance, as far back as 1997, journalists recognized that the primary sphere in which this Warez Scene

---

4 Tim Harford, "High-Frequency Trading and the $440m Computer Glitch," *BBC News*, August 11, 2012, https://www.bbc.co.uk/news/magazine-19214294.

5 Alexander Osipovich, "High-Frequency Traders Push Closer to Light Speed with Cutting-Edge Cables," *Wall Street Journal*, December 15, 2020, https://www.wsj.com/articles/high-frequency-traders-push-closer-to-light-speed-with-cutting-edge-cables-11608028200.

operated was prestige rather than money.[6] In this way, the Scene appears strange to outsiders. Most people assume that pirates conduct their activities to gain access to pirate material. They may even believe that pirates work for financial gain. While this may be true of the lower-level, pirate spaces of public peer-to-peer (P2P) sharing sites, it is not the case of the Scene to which this book is devoted. The structures of the Scene and the motivations of its participants are very different from those widely studied paradigms of public file trading.[7] The piracy on which this book trains its gaze is piracy for piracy's sake rather than for the actual access to the material gains of that digital piracy.

What could link this Warez Scene with high-frequency trading on the stock market? Strangely, the two groups have converging histories and parallel mechanisms of action that sit symbiotically as frames for understanding the paradigms of their birth. This link is odd because they would seem divided across the political spectrum and the line of legality. Commentators usually consider digital piracy in anti-capitalist terms (whatever that might mean, given the complexities and polyvalences of the term "capitalism"). Indeed, it is an illegal activity in which supposed "free riders" seek to get "something for nothing" at the expense of artists and developers, an aspect continually decried by many cultural producers and their representatives.[8] Conversely, stock trading is the epitome of capital; its high mass. Participants in this game seemingly invest their hard-earned cash into other businesses to see a commensurate return on investment, which supposedly benefits all parties:

---

6 David Pogue, "Some Warez over the Rainbow," *MacWorld*, October 1997, https://cdn.preterhuman.net/texts/computing/macintosh/Macintosh.txt.

7 Clyde W. Holsapple et al., "Parameters for Software Piracy Research," *The Information Society* 24, no. 4 (2008): 199–218; Andrew Sockanathan, "Digital Desire and Recorded Music: OiNK, Mnemotechnics and the Private BitTorrent Architecture" (PhD diss., Goldsmiths, University of London, 2011), 187.

8 For instance, see Nico van Eijk, Joost Poort, and Paul Rutten, "Legal, Economic and Cultural Aspects of File Sharing," *Communications & Strategies* 77, no. 1 (2010): 35–54.

the company gains capital, the investor gains wealth, and society gains the services of the corporation in question, under the invisible-handed "supervision" of price-pressure and markets.[9]

However, this caricature of two pugnacious spheres of activity squaring up against one another is little more than a stereotype and betrays a superficiality of understanding. In actuality, the motivations within each field are far more complex than this initial evaluation can countenance. Both sides actually share a common goal — the automation of their various practices in order competitively to outflank other players for a capital return based on speed within a game-like environment; that is, algorithmic stock traders and high-level pirates both engage in games with an economic character. In the financial arena, this takes the form of algorithmic, high-frequency trading, in which the software, situated on high-bandwidth, low-latency servers directly adjacent to the major stock exchanges, conducts trades with only minor human interaction. However, an identical phenomenon has developed at various levels of the Warez Scene, in which couriers, as they are known, use similar techniques to ensure that they beat their rivals in the near-instantaneous transmission of copyrighted material from server to server. Both spheres of activity use the same term to refer to this rise of algorithmically controlled transaction — autotrading.

Most important for the central argument that I will advance in this book is that the Warez Scene has economic competition and aesthetic styling at its heart, just like high-frequency trading. This parallel is none so evident in that there was even at one time a topsite called "The World Trade Center."[10] While the po-

---

9 Although, see William Davies, *The Limits of Neoliberalism: Authority, Sovereignty and the Logic of Competition* (Thousand Oaks: SAGE Publications, 2014) for a history of this supervisory terminology with respect to markets. Wendy Brown, *Undoing the Demos: Neoliberalism's Stealth Revolution* (New York: Zone Books, 2015) also provides a worthwhile critique of such cultures.

10 WTC, "World Trade Center Topsite (WTC-world.trade.center.1998.07.07.nfo)," July 7, 1998, DeFacto2, warez.scene.nfo.collection.v1.0.24351.shroo.ms.zip.

litical motivations of stock-market traders, as opposed to pirate groups, will vary in line with the type of capital with which they deal, that is, the symbolic versus the actual respectively, there is an economic logic that underwrites the cultural and aesthetic practices of the Warez Scene.[11]

How can we understand the culture of this Warez Scene as economic, and why should we? Certainly, Alf Rehn has already taken one approach to this in his unpublished PhD thesis, detailing the Scene as a fractional economy.[12] Yet as we will see, most of the announcements put out by members of this subculture are keen to stress the importance of the non-pecuniary nature of their activities. Under such circumstances, it doesn't seem very easy to imagine how this space, which is devoid of money, might be considered economic. To understand this characterization, it is necessary to turn briefly to the ideas of economics and capital that make such a statement possible. The sociologist Pierre Bourdieu devoted a substantial part of his career to studying how various forms of capital — cultural, social, symbolic, and material — can become interchangeable. For instance, the possession of multiple forms of social and cultural capital (whom and what one knows, respectively) can translate into symbolic capital (prestige). Based on this prestige, one may, for example, be employed and thereby generate material capital (money).[13] As a parallel example, consider that most academic publishing works on this basis of capital exchange. Academics are rarely paid directly for the journal articles that they publish. Instead, they accumulate reputations based on the quality of their published work. In turn, such reputation translates into being hired

11 The economic character of the Warez Scene, on which this book expands, has already been addressed by Alf Rehn, "The Politics of Contraband: The Honor Economies of the Warez Scene," *The Journal of Socio-Economics* 33, no. 3 (July 2004): 359–74. I do not radically depart from the analysis in this paper but instead broaden and deepen our understanding by more explicitly setting out the activities undertaken in this subculture.

12 Rehn, "Electronic Potlatch," 24.

13 See, for example, Pierre Bourdieu, *Outline of a Theory of Practice*, trans. Richard Nice (Cambridge: Cambridge University Press, 1977), 180.

or being promoted. We can then perceive a system where a symbolic or reputational capital (prestige) transmutes into actual, material capital (money and wealth, albeit not as extensively as some may imagine).

We can perceive such fungibility of capital in the two spheres of activity with which I opened this book. It is, of course, utterly uncontentious to argue that the accumulation of material capital and wealth is the primary aim of stock exchange autotrading. However, it is not the only form of capital at play here, and this activity relies on the exchange of and negotiations for other types of capital. A trader's reputation for speed and good algorithms will breed opportunities to tap into information networks that will likely influence future success, a kind of "Matthew Effect" in which the rich become richer.[14] By contrast, but also somehow in parallel, in the Warez Scene on which this book focuses, material capital is distinctly not the most critical form. Instead, that honor falls on the forms of prestige and social capital accumulated at significant personal and legal risk. In turn, however, these reputational capitals bring material advantages to pirates as they will need never to purchase the media to which they have access.

Why should we think of this high-level piracy Scene in these terms of economics and capital? My fundamental argument is that we need to reconceptualize the Warez Scene to understand the psychology of those who participate within it. Douglas Thomas offers the traditional, and, as I argue, insufficient, account of the Warez Scene and its grounding in BBS cultures. He notes the emergence of a new "logic of reproduction" in which we erase the distinction between the original and the copy in the digital world. "Unlike aesthetic representation," writes Thomas, "the logic of code does not exalt the original over the copy."[15]

14 I have written previously about the Matthew Effect in Samuel Moore et al., "'Excellence R Us': University Research and the Fetishisation of Excellence," *Palgrave Communications* 3 (2017): 6, https://www.nature.com/articles/palcomms2016105.

15 Douglas Thomas, "Innovation, Piracy and the Ethos of New Media," in *The New Media Book*, ed. Dan Harries (London: British Film Institute, 2004),

That is, in the digital space, we usually presume that once we have crafted the original, its reproduction can occur ad infinitum without any detrimental loss. This reasoning leads to various open-source software logics and the open-access movement in academic publishing. As I have argued, it can also lead to a type of digital commodity fetishism, where people mistake the near-zero cost of reproduction with a near-zero cost of producing the first copy.[16] In the piracy space, it has led to the canonical formulation that pirates are merely taking advantage of the infinite reproducibility of the internet to copy things "in the way the internet intended." Information wants, commentators tell us, to be free. In the conventional understanding, pirates simply use the internet to get things free of charge.

My argument is different. I argue that the Warez Scene is an aesthetic subculture and an alternative reality game, fixated on originality.[17] Members engage for enjoyment and the accumulation of reputational capital rather than for the outcome of material wealth. I draw on several evidential bases to make this case. As one example of this alternative lineage, consider the aesthetic cultures of skill in pirates' cracking systems for software. The 1980s cracking Scene was born alongside the legal, computer-art subculture known as the DemoScene, which continues today. In fact, software cracking was not illegal when it began, as my later history of the group Fairlight shows; it was a legal hobby.[18] It is, in fact, the DemoScene with which the Warez Scene shares its name. The DemoScene is a subculture where computer programmers, artists, and musicians build short but increasingly complex, procedural animations called "demos" to showcase their technological mastery. Often, crackers would

---

84.

16 Martin Paul Eve, "The Great Automatic Grammatizator: Writing, Labour, Computers," *Critical Quarterly* 59, no. 3 (October 2017): 39–54.

17 I use the term "alternative reality game" rather than "alternate reality game," the preferred formulation in some of the secondary literature, purely out of a British English preference.

18 See Bryan Clough and Paul Mungo, *Approaching Zero: Data Crime and the Computer Underworld* (London: Faber & Faber, 1992), 61–84.

distribute these aesthetic showcases alongside their pirate works to demonstrate their "cool" credentials and technical ability. At the same time, the Warez Scene also disseminates information about releases. Such information consists most often of credits for the cracking and dissemination, inside NFO (pronounced "info") files. These files usually contain ASCII art alongside their information that provides a decorative context and shows off the artistic skills of the creator. In other words, core to the Warez Scene is a set of aesthetic artifacts that allow participants to showcase their "cred" and cool — forms of social capital.

In this book, I argue that to understand the mentality of those who participate in the Warez Scene, it is first necessary to grasp the textual-artistic histories and cultures from which they emerged. To do so, I turn to the background contexts of the DemoScene and chart a history of ASCII Art that pays attention to computational colonialism hidden within its walls, alongside a lineage of concrete poetry and information aesthetics. One of the most curious aspects of the contemporary Scene is that aesthetic practices have always been core to its makeup, particularly among the class of users known as "crackers." To understand the Scene in its most recent iterations, we must look back to previous eras of home computer hobbyist culture beginning in the late 1980s.

While the ethos that Thomas suggests of personal accumulation and greed may be true for the development of widespread P2P networks, such as the famed history of Napster, the second part of my fundamental argument is that such a view is incorrect for the Warez Scene.[19] This is because many philosophies of piracy focus on the primacy of the copy, that is, the notion that it is the copy in which pirates are interested. I argue that this is not true in the Scene. It is, in fact, ideas of originality and craft that

19 For just a couple of sources on the role of Napster and the growth of P2P sharing, see Raymond Shih Ray Ku, "The Creative Destruction of Copyright: Napster and the New Economics of Digital Technology," *The University of Chicago Law Review* 69, no. 1 (2002): 263–324, and Peter J. Alexander, "Peer-to-Peer File Sharing: The Case of the Music Recording Industry," *Review of Industrial Organization* 20, no. 2 (2002): 151–61.

participants in this space value. As Rehn puts it, the Scene "is a meritocracy based on primacy, and the game of proving primacy is never-ending."[20] Ironically, coming first must happen again and again and again. As I will show, the rules and strictures of the Scene centrally reinscribe such notions of originality and the importance of being the first to release the liberated copy. There is a fundamental valorization of the speed to a "new original." A pirate release exalts the craft of the crack or the quality of media encoding. A pirate release showcases the business logic of swiftness and scarcity in a group's supply chain. Hence, be it in the programming skill of cracking software, the care in ensuring the quality of a film release, or in the business acumen of a supplier who can obtain music before its release date, the Warez Scene values specific types of originality and skill, a far cry from most descriptions of pirate activity.

If one is to comprehend this ethos of software piracy as a skilled aesthetic form, in which credit and authorship attribution is sought—as pirate material and with originality—we must think of the Warez Scene more broadly than a culture in which individuals are merely "ripping others off."[21] Certainly, there are adverse, economic effects from the Scene upon those who create art forms and software. But the artifacts created by the Scene are probably best considered as remix productions, an aspect to which I will later return in more detail. In the case of software, for instance, these are code-based modifications that exhibit skill and technicality in a surface reproduction that is identical to a commercially available artifact but that behave differently under the hood. In many ways, this is similar to the traditional reading of other subcultures that appropriate mainstream objects and give them a fresh spin. The famed punk aes-

---

20 Rehn, "Electronic Potlatch," 152.

21 This is akin to the pirate function that Kavita Philip outlines in her "What Is a Technological Author? The Pirate Function and Intellectual Property," *Postcolonial Studies* 8, no. 2 (2005): 199–218.

thetic is a canonical example of how commercially produced objects were taken and repurposed.[22]

The challenge for this parallel with the punk scene is that the appropriated artifacts of the Warez Scene do not exhibit any external semiotic difference from the originals. Crackers have modified the underlying code so that the software behaves in the same way as the original. They are fabrications that act as perfect copies, "posing," Hillel Schwartz tells us, as good copies do, "au naturel."[23] By way of an analogy: sophisticated cracking outfits in the software space seek to reverse engineer, for instance, the oil painting, the *Mona Lisa,* only to recreate its exact form except with acrylic paints. Of course, in one sense, the originality of pirate artifacts nonetheless remains "parasitic" on the "host" object and particularly the labor structures that enable original artistic production.[24] At the same time, this yields the paradoxical formulation that I call the "warez aesthetic." Appropriating a line from the British hip-hop group The Streets, the warez aesthetic is a sense of original, pirate material. The warez aesthetic gives precise surface mimesis of an original, an "exact copy," while valuing a new original construction behind the scenes — a construction that differs from the original; hence, original pirate material.

Reputations in the Scene are made or broken by the artistic successes of crackers, the business fluency of covert suppliers, and the skill and connectedness of their couriers. Those who debate the originality of these works have had their day in court and won. There is no disputing the Scene's illegality. But one has only to look at the development of various sampling music

22 Johan Kugelberg and Jon Savage, *Punk: An Aesthetic* (New York: Rizzoli, 2012).

23 Hillel Schwartz, *Culture of the Copy: Striking Likenesses, Unreasonable Facsimiles* (New York: Zone Books, 2014), 268. A parallel is also made by Maria Eriksson, "A Different Kind of Story: Tracing the Histories and Cultural Marks of Pirate Copied Film," *Tecnoscienza: Italian Journal of Science & Technology Studies* 7, no. 1 (2016): 100.

24 Alexander Sebastian Dent, "Introduction: Understanding the War on Piracy, Or Why We Need More Anthropology of Pirates," *Anthropological Quarterly* 85, no. 3 (2012): 667.

cultures to see how the appropriation of existing work, remade into a new artifact, can have significant artistic merit and demonstrate skill despite the courts' injunctions. The problem for the Scene with this argument, and the unfairness to those musical cultures, is that the Scene remakes artifacts that already exist, resituating them outside the sphere of monetary exchange. The fundamental question then becomes: where is the line of originality inscribed? To what extent does the situation play a key role here? The readymade artifacts of the Modernist period, such as Marcel Duchamp's famous urinal *Fountain* (1917), asked this question long before the digital era. Is art artistic merely because it is in a museum? The Scene prompts similar meta-critical reflections. Can originality be derived from the resituation of an artifact within a new distribution context and, especially, an illegal context?

At the same time, the Scene nonetheless has its own cultures of exchange, that is, a currency that attempts to situate itself outside of monetary transactions but that functions economically. It does not matter, as Thomas notes, that the Warez Scene deems itself beyond money and refuses to operate on any paysite basis. The basic fact of the matter is that Sceners compete for prestige, which translates into site access, which translates into access to warez—about which they care relatively little—but also into reputation, esteem, and prestige—about which they care a great deal. This misunderstanding of the Scene's psychological profile and behavioral characteristics has rendered most law-enforcement efforts ineffectual.[25] Tracing the Scene's roots to aesthetic practices that value scarcity, primacy, originality, skill, craft, elitism, organization, rankings, prestige, reputation, and even trustworthiness, honor, and loyalty, allows us much better to get inside the mind of the high-level pirate.

It is also the case that the Scene is composed of many discrete sub-Scenes that carry different levels of prestige. Being able to access retail music at the same time as the general public will

25 Eric Goldman, "A Road to No Warez: The No Electronic Theft Act and Criminal Copyright Infringement," *Oregon Law Review* 82 (2003): 371.

hardly confer the same degree of reputation as someone who can obtain PlayStation games five months before launch. As I will go on to discuss, each of these sub-Scenes has its own set of rules, norms, cultures, procedures, and senses of humor, among other elements. Given this, why do I focus on the Scene as a whole as though it were a total, coherent entity? First, because there is overlap. Sections for MP3, for example, exist on the same topsites as those specializing in games and films. Sites wish to offer their users a range of pirate media forms. So the MP3 Scene touches on the movie Scene and the console Scene. (That said, because those working in the ISO Games Scene may look down on MP3 suppliers, it is sometimes the case that music sections are isolated from other areas.) Second, because the evidential bases for each sub-Scene are themselves relatively small. We know about the Scene only through leaks and pirate archives. If we subdivided down and saw no commonality between different sub-Scenes working in different media forms, there would be barely sufficient documentation to understand its working as a whole. So treating the Scene as a whole means that I can study several cultures under one bracket and use more evidence, albeit with some loss of resolution and specificity.

This framing of a prestige-accumulation operation, which spans all of these sub-Scenes, leads to the other novel lens through which I analyze the Warez Scene in this book: As an alternative (or alternate) reality game. Alternative reality games (ARGs), as set out by Antero Garcia and Greg Niemeyer, are challenging to define. Still, they have the broad characteristics of being world-making exercises that feature competitive/play-like or gamified activities in which the essence of the world "only exists when [the games] are played, and there really is very little to hold on to at the end of the game, save for the transformative experiences of the players."[26] ARGs, therefore, can be "broadly understood as digitally-mediated games that transpire within the

26 Antero Garcia and Greg Niemeyer, "Introduction," in *Alternate Reality Games and the Cusp of Digital Gameplay*, eds. Antero Garcia and Greg Niemeyer (New York: Bloomsbury Academic, 2017), 1.

'real,' physical world."[27] ARGs consist of three components: They are alternative; they are realities; and they are, in some senses, games. The Scene has all of these characteristics.

An essential component of the last of these fronts — that ARGs are, in some ways, games — is that they have rules. ARGs contain a structured mediation between a set of rule-like principles and players pushing against those boundaries. "In ARGs," write Garcia and Niemeyer, "the rules of the game superimpose a novel, subversive order on the grid of a city."[28] In the case of the Warez Scene, this city is the internet and its legitimate channels of sale and distribution. As Chapter Four shows, the Warez Scene overlays a set of subversive but binding rules and quality standards as a quasi-judicial principle over the everyday norms of the net. "Every ARG," continue Garcia and Niemeyer, "enacts that fundamental political power of bringing many individuals into an articulated organized community."[29] These are core activities of the rule-making elements of the Scene. Their function is to create a bound virtual communitarian space.

At the same time, though, there is a temptation to see transgressive potential in this rule-enforced aspect of ARGs. It is easy to imagine that whenever users test the bounds of the rules to modify their reality, this is evidence that the "game is a meaningful, vox populi alternative to corporate order."[30] This is not the case in the Scene, as it is not in many ARGs. Instead, "[c]orporate order is often camouflaged," and that which seemed "diverse, approachable, and horizontal, is in fact often highly centralized."[31] Bearing more than a passing resemblance to the formulation of a "community of dissensus" that Bill Readings once used to characterize the contemporary university, the systems of rule formation in the Scene are nonetheless often

27 Ibid., 10.
28 Ibid., 4.
29 Ibid.
30 Ibid.
31 Ibid.

hierarchically determined.[32] This is a continual refrain of this book: the Warez Scene is not genuinely transgressive. Piracy at this level does not, as Michael Strangelove has claimed, undermine the very definitional aspects of capitalism.[33] It is, in reality, a system that reproduces the logics of contemporary capital and exchange within its own competitive frameworks. For this very reason, I opened by comparing the Scene to the world of high-finance trading systems. The game part of ARGs is evident in the Scene because it sets up a playing space with ultra-competitive rules. And the specific game is an exchange of different forms of capital.

The gamified nature of the Scene may not always be evident to its participants. Indeed, many ARGs deliberately seek to obscure their game-like basis and the sense of playing that goes with it. As Montola and Stenros document, an early ARG called *The Beast*—a tie-in with Steven Spielberg's film *A.I.* (2001)—went under the slogan "TINAG," This Is Not A Game. As they note for *The Beast,* "[t]he total denial of the gameness was the design principle. Everything had to look and feel as much as possible like it was real and believable."[34] That said, it is not universally the case that ARGs deny their game-like natures. *Reality Ends Here* and *Ingress* both operate on the premise of being other spaces, while Virtual Reality (VR) games such as *Superhot* feature interlude cut-scenes where the user dons a VR headset in the VR space. Yet, the denial that one is playing a game has been central to these modes from the start.[35]

32 Bill Readings, *The University in Ruins* (Cambridge: Harvard University Press, 1996), 19–20.

33 Michael Strangelove, *The Empire of Mind: Digital Piracy and the Anti-Capitalist Movement* (Toronto: University of Toronto Press, 2005).

34 Markus Montola and Jaakko Stenros, "Case B: The Beast," in Markus Montola, Jaakko Stenros, and Annika Wærn, *Pervasive Games: Theory and Design* (Boston: Morgan Kaufmann Publishers, 2009), 27.

35 On *Reality Ends Here,* see Jeff Watson, "Games Beyond the ARG," in *Alternate Reality Games and the Cusp of Digital Gameplay,* eds. Antero Garcia and Greg Niemeyer (New York: Bloomsbury Academic, 2017), 187–210. On *Ingress,* see Thaiane Moreira de Oliveira, "'Ingress': A Restructuring of the ARG or a New Genre? An Ethnography of Enlightened and Resistance

It is in the denial of game-like-ness that ARGs begin to become realities. As Rehn notes, "[w]hat goes on in the [S]cene can be and obviously feel like 'just' a computer game, but the involved are at least to some extent aware of how seriously outsiders take their activities."[36] Players of ARGs often take their alternative worlds somewhat too seriously and end up blurring the boundaries between their game space and the real world, either mistaking the game for reality or reality for the game. There is, writes Jane McGonigal, "a tendency to continue seeing games where games don't exist."[37] That said, as Stephen Kline, Nick Dyer-Witheford, and Greig De Peuter put it, pirating material is a kind of fun game. "We may," they write, "even get a charge out of cracking the various technological systems while Microsoft or Sony try to keep us out: hell, it's just another level to the game." Even while corporate organizations attempt to gamify work, a model in which "work-as-fun" becomes a dominant business principle, I contend that the Scene's organization of "piracy-as-play" is the logical counterpoint to this.[38]

It is also hard to find one's way into the Scene. This hiddenness is characteristic of ARGs, which often have obscure entry points and are conventionally referred to as "rabbit holes"—points of ingress that lure in new users searching for

---

Factions in Brazil," in *Alternate Reality Games and the Cusp of Digital Gameplay,* eds. Garcia and Niemeyer, 288–310. For more on computer games that have computers in them, see Ian Bogost, "Persuasive Games: Process Intensity and Social Experimentation," *Gamasutra,* May 23, 2012, https://www.gamasutra.com/view/feature/170806/persuasive_games_process_.php.

36 Rehn, "Electronic Potlatch," 235.

37 Jane McGonigal, "'This Is Not a Game': Immersive Aesthetics and Collective Play," in *Melbourne DAC 2003 Streamingworlds Conference Proceedings* (Melbourne: Royal Melbourne Institute of Technology University, 2003), 5.

38 Stephen Kline, Nick Dyer-Witheford, and Greig De Peuter, "Workers and Warez: Labour and Piracy in the Global Game Market," in *Digital Play: The Interaction of Technology, Culture, and Marketing,* eds. Stephen Kline, Nick Dyer-Witheford, and Greig De Peuter (Montreal: McGill-Queen's University Press, 2003), 198.

clues.[39] For Garcia and Niemeyer, "a 'good' rabbit hole is one that, for those not *looking* for clues, blends into the background and noise of the world."[40] Much of the Scene's structure focuses on ensuring that points of entry, its rabbit holes, are obscure. The question with which the Scene must wrestle, of course, is: How does one recruit new talent to one's illegal underground group without making it obvious to law enforcement how to get in touch? The usual solution is advertorial NFOs with tantalizing mentions of "you know where to find us" and similar bread-crumbs. Even the Scene's esoteric naming conventions appear to present an intriguing rabbit hole where a user may question why the piece of music they have illegally downloaded carries such an overloaded folder structure (e.g., "Aeon_Zen-Inveritas-WEB-2019-ENTiTLED," which is the naming structure of a Scene music release). Of course, a genuinely enterprising user would begin to read, trying to learn where to find the Scene. But the entrances to such rabbit holes are few and far between, deliberately made obscure both for operational safety and to retain the mystique and exclusivity of the Scene.

The type of game rubric under which we can categorize the Warez Scene has been provided most succinctly by Ian Bogost.[41] Bogost refers to and delineates a subset of ARGs that "create their unique open social-code-driven play experiences" through "means of very small system designs, using just enough multimedia materials to glue the whole thing together." These are games that "are neither multimedia games nor are they games without system design." But they do have a minimal aesthetic and they do also have design principles. However, "[w]e might," writes Bogost, "call such works *games of social experimentation*, for their primary aesthetic force arises from social behavior inspired by a specific system." That is to say that, for Bogost, there is a whole set of ARGs "in which players can devise their own ac-

39 Dave Szulborski, *This Is Not a Game: A Guide to Alternate Reality Gaming* (Macungie: New-Fiction Publishing, 2005), 49.

40 Garcia and Niemeyer, "Introduction," 15.

41 The quotes in this paragraph are attributed to Bogost, "Persuasive Games."

tivities within the confines of the simulation." This is very much how the Warez Scene works. There are codified norms of behavior (e.g., system design) in which users interact socially in different ways from the world at large. A low-grade aesthetic (e.g., ASCII art and DemoScene executables) provides an alternative context of retro multimedia "cool," even while this does not appear central. And players operate in a reality where their own aesthetic stylings and systems of respect are of the utmost import. The Warez Scene sets up a gaming environment and asks users to compete within that structure. Perhaps the difference in this space to other ARGs is that the penalties for failing at the game are severe: Jail time. At this point, the real world intersects with the alternative reality of the Scene.

Yet, we should also not neglect the "alternative reality" portion of ARGs. The curious thing about this book is that I have to talk about an entire online world or community of practice that does not exist for most readers. "To play an ARG," write Garcia and Niemeyer, "is to dive into a counter-narrative *in medias res,* and to co-generate story, strategy, and collaboration in real time, in real place."[42] The reality of this alternative world, though, is unassailable for those who exist within it. This extra-geographic yet territorial nature of the Scene leads Rehn to refer to it as though it were somehow a separate country of "Warezonia."[43] Yet the Scene does exist in our reality. Topsites, dupe databases, and the releases themselves are very much real.

However, the world I describe will seem alien and foreign to most readers. For instance, the rules of this subculture seem incomprehensibly hypocritical: a release group may not steal the work of a rival release group, even as the goal is to steal the original artifact from the creator. A release group may not duplicate the releases of another group, even while the very goal is duplication of the original. Sites specializing in giving material away for free, seemingly in an egalitarian spirit, have hierarchical structures of exclusion. "Lamers" will not be tolerated. The

42 Garcia and Niemeyer, "Introduction," 5.
43 Rehn, "Electronic Potlatch," 32.

Scene will scorn "newbies." Authority will accrue to those who have been longest in the Scene. That is, authority will stick to those who have spent the most extended period defying the authority of the law. Consistency is not the motto of the Scene. Yet, these hypocritical norms have been internalized and are just a way of life for those on the inside. They are unassailable bounds of daily operations, the Scene's business as usual.

There are other characteristics of the Scene that look like an ARG. For instance, Markus Montola, Jaakko Stenros, and Annika Wærn describe a system of "onion"-layered participation in such games, where there are those on the fringes and those at the core.[44] Participants interact with one another and work as a whole to structure the world. However, in the Scene, some participants are disposable compared to others. For instance, traders and couriers are easily replaced, even though they participate heavily, often for hours and hours per week. On the other hand, software crackers, who are highly skilled, are indispensable and irreplaceable. Their skillsets are in demand and not easy to replicate. Just as "[d]ifferent players have unequal levels of participation within an ARG," the Scene is hardly a flat hierarchy.[45]

Paul Virilio's formulation of a split, stereoscopic or stereophonic reality is a helpful framework for understanding the Scene's existence as an alternative reality within an alternative reality game.[46] In a culture of digital globalization, Virilio suggests, it becomes necessary "to split the reality of the world in two."[47] "As," he writes, "with *stereoscopy* and *stereophony,* which distinguish left from right, bass from treble, to make it easier to perceive audiovisual relief, it is essential today to effect a split in primary reality by developing a *stereo-reality,* made up on the one hand of the actual reality of immediate appearances and, on the other, of the *virtual reality* of media trans-appearances."[48]

44 Montola, Stenros, and Wærn, *Pervasive Games,* 120–21.
45 Garcia and Niemeyer, "Introduction," 6.
46 This is gestured to by McGonigal, "'This Is Not a Game.'"
47 Paul Virilio, *The Information Bomb,* trans. Chris Turner (London: Verso, 2005), 15.
48 Ibid.

The Scene is of this nature, existing in two spaces at once, producing the requirement to "read two different worlds at the same time."[49] A world within a world, separate from ours, with different rules and codes of conduct, the Scene is like a game but nonetheless a reality, albeit an alternative one.

```
 #     #
   # #
#######
   # #
 #     #
```

The high-level Warez Scene has existed for several decades now and has taken various guises, although research into it is often said to be relatively scarce. It has been called "one of the least researched" fields of cybercrime.[50] As Sigi Goode puts it, "[t]here has been comparatively little research into the behaviour and makeup of piracy groups."[51] That said, having completed work on this book, I now think this oft-repeated assertion to be untrue. The belief that the Scene is unresearched stems from the fact that there is relatively scant, popular knowledge of its activities. However, this is not the same as a field being unresearched. In reality, as my bibliography attests, there is a substantial volume of research material on the Warez Scene. The work of Bodó Balázs, Virginia Crisp, David Décary-Hétu, Nick Dyer-Witheford, Eric Goldman, Maria Eriksson, Alf Rehn, Andrew Sockanathan, and others, all point to a disaggregated community of scholarship that has investigated this subculture. The approaches have been diverse and range from legal analyses to

49 Garcia and Niemeyer, "Introduction," 9.

50 David Décary-Hétu, Carlo Morselli, and Stéphane Leman-Langlois, "Welcome to the Scene: A Study of Social Organization and Recognition among Warez Hackers," *Journal of Research in Crime and Delinquency* 49, no. 3 (2012): 361.

51 Sigi Goode, "Exploring the Supply of Pirate Software for Mobile Devices: An Analysis of Software Types and Piracy Groups," *Information Management & Computer Security* 18, no. 4 (2010): 220.

socio-technical studies via economic appraisals. This work remains, nonetheless, the first book solely about the Scene.

The knowledge of the Warez Scene that I describe in this book arises from the study of pirate archives, garnered from the open web, but in general terms, it handles material from around the turn of the millennium. Certainly, others such as David Tetzlaff have worked to chart different epochs of the Scene's development, such as an era of Hotline chats and so forth.[52] The period and practices that I map cover the time when the topsite Scene came of age — a point of significant capacity scaling and strange formalization despite the distributed and somewhat anarchic nature of the Scene. In other senses though, the historicization of this book is not rigorous and precise. The artifacts to which I had access cover a relatively broad duration of several decades. In particular, topsite NFOs tend to come from an earlier period and may now be grossly outdated, while contemporary release NFOs are still available and reflect current Scene practice. These are analyzed herein as though they were a single historical unit, produced from the same time period. This may be too much of a simplification, but it is the only way to handle such breadth of material while presenting a coherent narrative.

It is also worth noting upfront that there are challenges of legality in reporting on the Warez Scene, which is obviously a space in which the participants are conducting illegal activities. The Internet Relay Chat (IRC) channels within which most discussions have taken place have a strict honor code that entails a "no logging" principle. Only through the violation of these codes is the material on which I report brought to light. Further, there is no way the participants in this environment, none of whose true identities were ever known to me, would consent to be studied. While I handle this question of ethics more thoroughly below, this book avoids most ethical problems by focusing on the structures of the Scene in total, read out of

52 David Tetzlaff, "Yo-Ho-Ho and a Server of Warez," in *The World Wide Web and Contemporary Cultural Theory: Magic, Metaphor, Power,* eds. Andrew Herman and Thomas Swiss (New York: Routledge, 2000), 99–126.

the documents that have surfaced into the public realm, rather than examining individuals. In this respect, this book differs greatly from other anthropological studies of hacker cultures, such as those charted in the recent digital ethnographic work of Gabriella Coleman.[53] I do not interview Sceners, and I have not tracked down their channels online, although I have received the occasional email from purported members of this culture interested in this book. Instead I work within a framework for the ethnographic study of the documentary emergence of institutions and practices.

DIGITAL ARCHIVES AND ETHICS

How do we know, then, what we know about the Warez Scene? If this space is so secret and closely guarded, how can I write a book about it? What kind of documentary evidence could serve to back up readings and understandings of practice?

Although the Scene is highly private, participants leak information, and there are now specific archives dedicated to its documentation. One of the core features that makes this possible is that the Scene thrives on word of mouth and bragging documents. Participants balance the secrecy of topsites against a need to show off and to declare how powerful a site is. Given the nostalgic investment that many Scene users have — after all, it is frequently, although not always, an activity conducted in participants' teenage years — it is not surprising that archives have emerged that chart the workings of the Scene.

An excellent example of this documentation is how sites have zipscripts that generate NFOs. While these are covered in more detail later, the point is that when release groups upload pirate releases to sites, these servers add a file that documents their existence. Usually, this file states that the release was at the site before a user had it. For instance, the NFO of "Distorted Illusions"

53 Gabriella Coleman, *Coding Freedom: The Ethics and Aesthetics of Hacking* (Princeton: Princeton University Press, 2012).

adds, as a note, "remember we had it first!"[54] These site NFO files sometimes boast of the hardware, speed of internet connection ("Powered by 155Mbits"), and affiliated release groups.[55] These documents also often reveal the location of the sites. For example, the file may specify that, for a particular release group, the site is the "European HQ" or "Polish HQ." The Appendix in this book details the sites known to us via the so-called "shrooms.ms site.nfos" pack from the DeFacto2 archive. Of course, such NFO files are a serious security risk. A true, security-conscious environment would not risk disseminating a site's name, location, siteops' names, and other information. It would, instead, lie low. As we shall see, the problem is that the fun of the Scene, the reason most of its participants invest in this alternative reality game, comes from competition and bragging. These files, a risk, are how Sceners earn street cred.

Every release also has an NFO that specifies details of the release group, information about the release itself, and other assorted snippets of information. These documents can help us garner a picture of the interlocking relationship between groups. They also demonstrate their practices (e.g., the types of affiliation that release groups request reflects an evolution of software and hardware setups in the topsite network).

Furthermore, "Scene magazines" report on activities in this underground network. Articles in these magazines cover "courier reports" (i.e., ranking courier groups), reviews of pirated software and films, and various interviews and pieces of "Scene history."[56] These documents, somewhat hard to come by, chart a selective but informative path to understanding the practices of the Warez Scene. In a knowing wink to future historians, many

---

54 DI, "Distorted Illusions Topsite (DI-distorted.illusions.XXXX.XX.01.nfo)," n.d., DeFacto2, warez.scene.nfo.collection.v1.0.24351.shroo.ms.zip.

55 VDR, "Virtual Dimension Research Lake Topsite (VDR-vdr.lake.1998.02.09.nfo)," February 9, 1998, DeFacto2, warez.scene.nfo.collection.v1.0.24351.shroo.ms.zip.

56 See, for instance: lester, "Which Ftpd Is Right for You?" *Netmonkey Weekly Report (Nwr36.Txt),* February 22, 1999.

of these magazines specifically refer to their reports as "biased" (e.g., "Lester's biased courier report").

Various documentation projects have sought to build centralized archives of these files. Among the most prominent of these at the time of writing is the DeFacto2 archive, which aims to host "FTP session captures and user logs," "[o]ld daemons from the 1990s and 2000s," "[c]racktros, crack-tros, intros," and "[m]agazines and publications."[57] This archive hosts many of these file types and offers insight into the practices — pragmatic, cultural, and aesthetic — of the Scene. However, it is unclear to what extent the archive operators have filtered the records. Most of the material in DeFacto2 comes from around the turn of the millennium. In soliciting material, the operators write, "[d]on't worry if you feel the files are too new or irrelevant, send them up anyway."[58] They also note though that they "will filter through what [they] can use."[59] While this does not provide us with any information about why they would filter through records, we can surmise that it is concerned with legality. The archive does not host any copyright-infringing material, except for the NFO files, which themselves are under copyright, albeit a copyright that the authors will never enforce. It must also have something to do with non-incrimination. By detailing the Scene's history from twenty years ago, the chance of an indictment resulting from the files is meager. After all, the statute of limitations period will have passed in many cases, although this will vary by international jurisdiction. Conversely, it is essential to note that the DeFacto2 archive does refer pseudonymously to siteops, nukers, couriers, and other individuals who, at one time, operated an illegal network of topsites.

I should broach one final question at this point: how reliable are the DeFacto2 archive and other Scene archival sources? Most of the sources I draw upon in this book are of an in-world,

57 DeFacto2, "Wanted Uploads," *GitHub*, March 25, 2019, https://github.com/Defacto2/defacto2.net.

58 Ibid.

59 Ibid.

or even in-game, nature. They describe an online reality that is unfamiliar to outsiders, from the inside. Authors, as in any context, modify their statements to portray themselves in the best light possible. Therefore, I take all Scene documentary sources with a pinch of salt. While Sceners do not have any reason to hide the illegality of their actions, they frequently engage in internecine conflicts and other factional activities that may shape their writing.

Tying in with my earlier observations on the alternative reality structure of the Scene, it is also notable that Sceners tend to write as though the world in which they operate is the world as a total. They are usually so inside the system that they take for granted its norms, rules, regulations, procedures, processes, and rhythms. But in many ways the Scene is a fantasy land. It is an artificial construct that members have made. This does not mean that it is less real, but it lends a slightly strange character to these documents.

The nearest analogy to this situation is the work chronicling the virtual space of the computer game *Minecraft* and, especially, the oldest-running "anarchy server," *2builders2tools* (*2b2t*). This server is essentially a multiplayer *Minecraft* environment where there are no rules. This anarchy has led to a whole swathe of media coverage and the assertion from at least one participant that "[e]xploring *2b2t* is like archaeology. [...] There's so much that it says about the nature of Minecraft itself and about the design of the game. *2b2t* deserves a book."[60] It seems that *2b2t* serves as a crucible for studying unchecked, anonymous, human behavior. The server has seen Nazi propaganda and cultures of destruction, and it is generally highly nihilistic. While *Minecraft* was designed for children, *2b2t* is an R-rated experience. As one write-up put it, it is "a place of hostile users who drop the N- and F-words in chat, and build landscape-dominating swastikas."[61]

60 Roisin Kiberd, "The Minecraft Server That Will Kill You 1,000 Times," *Newsweek*, September 15, 2016, https://www.newsweek.com/2016/09/23/minecraft-anarchy-server-2b2t-will-kill-you-498946.html.

61 "2b2t Photodiary: Inside Minecraft's Most Offensive Server," *PCGamesN*, October 17, 2016, https://www.pcgamesn.com/minecraft/2b2t-photodiary-

Most notably, while *Minecraft* is supposed to be a game about cooperative building, in the *2b2t* landscape, so-called "griefers" travel the landscape destroying the work of others. Rival factions gather to build and protect their landscape against enemies. The server is the computer-Lego equivalent of Cormac McCarthy's dystopian, post-apocalyptic environment in *The Road* (2006).

Yet what is perhaps most useful about the world of *2b2t* for the analysis in this book is how users themselves chronicle an in-game history. The *2b2t* Wiki offers a history of the server over its decade of existence, charting an "Age of Unrest," followed by "The Great Decay Period," an "Age of Resurgence," the "Pre-Hype Period," an "Age of Hype," followed by the current "Automation Period." Users chart the constructions and usually destructions of various monuments in the game within a historical framework.[62] The feature I wish to draw attention to is how they cover in-game events. Consider, for instance, the article on "Imperator's Base." The Wiki states that "Imperator's Base, usually shortened to Imp's Base and also known as Viking Base and the Ungriefable Base, is one of the largest bases in *2b2t,* built by Imperator's group in 2012. It was home to the most well-known build on *2b2t,* the Jesus Statue, and was griefed by jared2013 in 2015."[63] Other articles give biographies and histories of players that refer to the in-game universe as though it were a totality: "[o]n a supply run through the nether, Judge met up with Offtopia to recruit willyroof and marksman77, both friends of elecdrof, from Shitpit City. They returned to Old Town finding jdw and Elecdrof adding builds to Old Town. One of the new recruits wanted to build outside of the base and Judge said fine."[64]

Much of the reporting on the Warez Scene in this book is similar; a huge alternative reality game that spins a social web within which people can almost wholly exist. Most of the ac-

inside-minecrafts-most-offensive-server.

62 "Timeline," *2b2t Wiki,* 2020, https://2b2t.miraheze.org/wiki/Timeline.

63 "Imperator's Base," *2b2t Wiki,* 2020, https://2b2t.miraheze.org/wiki/Imperator%27s_Base.

64 "THEJudgeHolden," *2b2t Wiki,* 2020, https://2b2t.miraheze.org/wiki/THEJudgeHolden.

counts given in NFO documents from the archives that I here consult talk about the in-world mechanics of the Scene as though "the Scene is all that is the case," with apologies to Wittgenstein. They relate histories of sites, FTPDs, individuals, nukewars, and other esoteric phenomena in ways that will engender little external understanding or empathy. Studying documents from the Scene is like coming across a new world with a different history to the external one and trying to make sense of what it says. There are entire unexplained vocabularies, histories, jokes, codes of conduct, and principles. Reading accounts of the Scene is like exploring a language without referents. I will never see most of the artifacts and practices detailed in this book — only the leaked traces. It is a little like trying to understand the Battle of Hastings without knowing what "France" and "England" are (although proponents of the imagined communities theories of nationhood might argue that we do not have solid and shared conceptions of what these nations actually are).

What does this mean for the comprehensiveness of this book? It seems to me beyond doubt that Sceners who read this book will find elements with which they disagree, that are incorrect, that have mislabelled a practice, and that mischaracterize some of the ethos of their world. I will, certainly, be labeled a "lamer," in Scene parlance.[65] By contrast, I am also relatively confident that most of the high-level outline that I here piece together is correct. The surfaced archive is too extensive, with enough already written to give some confidence in much of the history. It is also the case that chroniclers can never resist writing about these subcultural spaces, even though it poses a security risk. Creating an alternative reality is not enough. One must, it seems, cement it with magazines, documentation, and other persistent artifacts that perpetuate the game.

Studies such as this fall under the rubric of "netnographies," or works that attempt to examine the principles and characteristics of various online cultures ethnographically. A fundamental challenge of working in this space is ethics. Most of the

65 See also a similar disclaimer in Rehn, "Electronic Potlatch," 91.

documents and conversations in the DeFacto2 archive, in Scene magazines, and in site wktop charts (weekly rankings of user upload volumes) were thought, by the conversation participants and authors, to have been held or published privately.

Indeed, the study of underground pirate cultures presents a set of ethical issues that have been best covered, in recent days, by Robert V. Kozinets. The first question is: does studying the Warez Scene constitute the study of human subjects? In this book, I do not conduct interviews with participants nor do I intervene. The primary research model is textual and archival. I have read many documents from the Scene and used this to reconstruct its operating procedures. This methodology places the research in this book in the category of "archival research" that involves the downloading "of existing posts," which "does not strictly qualify as human subjects research. It is only where interaction or intervention occurs that consent is required."[66]

Because their doings are illegal, a separate but related question pertains to the risk of harming those whose activities I document in this book. Kozinets notes that "studying illicit [...] communities" constitutes studying a vulnerable group, a group who are vulnerable to law enforcement action.[67] This appraisal of harm applies to interventions and interactions, of which there are none here. Under their pseudonyms in these documents, the individuals about whom I am writing have bragged openly of their illegal activities. As well, law enforcement agencies already have access to the records that I study in this volume.

A further question surrounds the ethics of harm. When the harm that may result from research that reveals illegal practices is the bringing to justice of criminals, is this a harm that should stop research? There may be borderline cases. The example that Kozinets gives is drug users, who should undoubtedly not be exposed to prosecution through research interviews if we wish to study the phenomena of drug addiction. Exposing drug us-

66 Robert V. Kozinets, *Netnography: Ethnographic Research in the Age of the Internet* (Thousand Oaks: SAGE Publications, 2010), 151.

67 Ibid., 153.

ers would lead, in the end, to a situation where no user of illicit drugs would ever speak to a researcher. Though does the same apply in cases where freely available, online material reveals criminal activities? Taken to the extreme, if my reading of these open, online documents revealed a murder, should I not publish the research because it might bring a murderer to justice? (Probably I should go to the police first.) Such reasoning generates only further questions about the severity of the crime and the need to protect sources from the harm of being prosecuted. Is it, and should it be, a matter for the individual researcher to decide who should be prosecuted and who should be protected?

In this light, I needed a policy about using pseudonyms and real names and whether the material should be attributed. Indeed, the politics of citation and online pseudonymity is a tricky subject. As Amy Bruckman notes, "[n]orms for presentation vary for different sites."[68] In the Warez Scene, participants go by IRC usernames and site nicknames, which do not necessarily correspond to one another. That is, it is possible to use a different alias on topsites than on IRC. The two are linked only by a site invite script. Participants who have been arrested, tried, and convicted are "decloaked" in official legal documents, which are publications of record (e.g., the site operator of "The Ratz Hole"). While in other online cultures participants "may also routinely disclose information linking their pseudonym and real name," this is not commonly the case in the Warez Scene where such disclosures would carry genuine risks of law enforcement penalties.[69]

The secondary literature's advice on handling pseudonyms is challenging to navigate. In works such as Kozinet's, it is said that "online pseudonyms function exactly like real names and should be treated as real names."[70] Yet, in the case of the DeFacto2 archive, the pseudonyms are up to two decades old, and many or

68 Amy Bruckman, "Teaching Students to Study Online Communities Ethically," *Journal of Information Ethics* 15, no. 2 (2006): 89.

69 Kozinets, *Netnography,* 145.

70 Ibid., 144.

most are no longer in use. In fact, some may now be used by different, entirely innocent individuals. Further, were this book to treat Warez pseudonyms as real names that contain confidential data, it would also be impossible to cite material directly from the archive. This is due to "the fact that a direct quote can be accessed through a full-text search in a public search engine."[71] Hence, the dilemma for this volume is: should I present pseudonyms and quotations that are in the public sphere online verbatim? There is minimal risk of linking these pseudonyms to a real-world identity, unless the user has already been convicted in a court of law.

Finally, this citation situation is complicated even further by the fact that many of the documents that I cite are so-called Warez "magazines." With titles such as the *NetMonkey Weekly Report, The Marshall Mussolini Show,* and many others, these documents contain articles written by Scene members and are signed as such. In other words, these are magazine sources like any other, even though the authors are people who have likely conspired to violate copyright law. These are instances where "culture members or culture leaders would like credit for their work."[72] The authors of these magazine documents put their names at the end and wished to be viewed as the authors of these sentiments, though they perhaps did not realize where the documents would appear on the open web. In any case, we can draw a parallel with the writings of the Mexican insurgent, Subcomandante Marcos. A prolific writer of anti-neoliberalist literature and military leader of the Zapatista Army of National Liberation, Marcos is still cited using his pseudonym; because he wanted the credit.

As this book argues, the Warez Scene is, at its core, about seeking credit. Groups vie for status and reputation in their releases. Other groups jostle to recruit defecting reputed rippers and crackers. Couriers want to be the best, to make it to the top of the weekly upload charts, and to be known to outpace all of

71 Ibid., 145.
72 Ibid.

their rivals. The Scene is made and broken on individual reputation and notoriety. At the same time, this fame is deliberately limited. It is an internal system of prestige, and many Warez documents decry the spreading of information about the Scene beyond the inner sanctum.

I have had, then, to take a stance on whether to reveal or not pseudonyms and sometimes real names. I am guided in this decision by one of Kozinets's core principles: "should we not consider some message posters, gatekeepers, and community members to be 'public figures,' and accord them less power to control information about themselves (and more direct credit for their work) than so-called 'private people' who are not seeking power, influence, or attention in the same way?"[73] I cite the authors of Warez magazines using the pseudonyms that they have signed on their work. I take them to have indicated a desire for credit for their writing by signing their work. In this way, I see Warez magazines as no different from any other form of electronic publication channel in that it is a medium that requires attribution. Group names, which are public signoffs, I likewise use without redaction. In other cases, when analyzing courier charts and site wkup/wktop figures leaked outside of their original intended venues, I nonetheless retain pseudonyms as these figures wished to receive credit within their culture for their efforts. Similarly, in the instances where site NFO files list the names of siteops, I retain these, as these were advertorial documents. These all appear to be requests for credit. I note that it is also possible, with some ease, to view these original documents, thanks to archives such as DeFacto2; redaction would also have been inefficacious. I also name those convicted or charged in a court of law as their names are matters of public record.

These principles allow me to take a relatively neutral stance. They are unlikely to give any additional assistance to law enforcement officers, who already possess these documents. At the same time, they facilitate the validation of the truth claims in this subcultural ethnography. For, as Anthony Grafton has put

73 Ibid.

it, "the culturally contingent and eminently fallible footnote offers the only guarantee we have that statements about the past derive from identifiable sources. And that is the only ground we have to trust them."[74]

In an earlier draft of this book, I had intended to provide a pack of the NFO files and other documents on which I draw. The purpose of distributing these files in a companion archive would have been to make it easy to ascertain the sources from which I have derived information. My footnotes to Scene documents, for instance, contain filenames that would allow lookup in such an archive. As in the Appendix, they would provide a list of extant sites at one point in the Scene's history. They could show the competitive history of courier racing through wktop charts. They might demonstrate the rules and meta-rules of various sub-Scenes and the overarching Nuke Council. They are the artifacts that prove the existence of the sub-surface, alternative reality of the Warez Scene.

However, I have opted not to distribute this archive with the work in light of the above discussion of ethics and redaction. The work is slightly impoverished because the archive on which it draws will inevitably decay and fall out of sight. The verification of my claims will become much more demanding over time as this archive fades. However, this is the ethical choice for this study, that is, to maintain the only-ever partial anonymity of attributional pseudonymity in the Scene.

STRUCTURE

By way of orientation, I will close this introduction with some notes on the structure of this book. This introductory first chapter has opened by setting the stage and the arguments of this book. It has given high-level background and has described the archives that document the Warez Scene and the ethics of using them for academic research.

---

74 Anthony Grafton, *The Footnote: A Curious History* (Cambridge: Harvard University Press, 1999), 233.

The rest of this book features five other chapters. The second chapter covers theoretical conceptions of piracy and details the forms of piracy that are not the Scene. It also considers the crafts and skills of the pirates who make up this Scene. Chapter Three then introduces the technical infrastructures of the Scene. This chapter opens with a methodological analysis via Susan Leigh Star's well-known article, "The Ethnography of Infrastructure," which outlines the "tricks of the trade" used in this book. Among these tricks of the trade are examinations of the Scene's "embeddedness," for instance: how it is sunk inside university structures for high-speed server links; that the membership of the Scene takes for granted its infrastructural provisions but that these appear opaque and unclear to outsiders; that the embodiment of standards are shown in Scene rules and other types of procedural rule documents; that the Scene becomes visible on breakdown, especially when law enforcement operations are put into place; and that there are vast quantities of hidden labor used to support the infrastructure of the Warez Scene. This chapter then moves to examine the architectures of topsites—the high-capacity, high-bandwidth FTP servers that underlie the Scene—in both hardware and software terms. Finally, this chapter turns to the communication channels, bots, IRC networks, and other quasi-social spaces surrounding the Scene.

The fourth chapter of this book looks at structures of organization and rule-following. An essential characteristic of the Scene is that it is a highly regulated space, governed by interacting systems of rules that sit in perpetual tension with its distributed and anarchic decentralization. It is this rule system that allows me to frame the Scene as an alternative reality game. This chapter opens by examining the principles and histories of the term "organized crime," which oscillates between the designation of activities as criminal, as opposed to the branding of individuals and gangs as organized criminals. From here, the rest of this chapter examines how the Scene's guiding documents resemble quasi-judicial frameworks. For instance, through an extensive analysis of the FLAC Scene Rules v3, and the dissenting counter-document, I show how these rulesets mirror legal contracts, with recitals, binding natures, and free entry.

At the same time, however, Chapter Four also examines quality control systems on the ground. In particular, by analyzing dupechecking I aim to show one of the core contradictions of the Scene — that a culture dedicated to stealing other people's work would have a strict set of rules and principles that determine the right of groups to release their pirate material. This chapter ends by studying the systems of nuking in the Scene, that is, the processes by which releases are marked invalid or bad. By looking at the Nuke Council's guiding documents, I unearth the tensions between local implementations of rules on topsites themselves, which remain autonomous entities, against Scene-wide decisions on the permissibility, or otherwise, of a release.

Chapter Five turns to the aesthetics of the Warez Scene. A fundamental argument of this book is that we should consider the alternative reality game of the Scene as an aesthetic subculture. That is to say that the stylings of "cool" that attract members who can build a reputation in this space are crucial but, too, that much of the Scene has an aesthetic character in which artforms play a role. This chapter examines two related computer-art phenomena that converge in the Warez Scene, the DemoScene and ASCII Art communities. Tracing back the origins of the Scene to the early computer-art DemoScene, and the commensurate levels of skill involved in creating cracks and demos, this section is among the most important for those who wish to understand the motivations of Warez Sceners. This chapter also examines how the Scene's cracking practices have influenced mainstream cultural production, noting the feedback loops of innovative Digital Rights Management (DRM) mechanisms that, for example, alter gameplay within cracked videogames.

The sixth and final chapter examines the Scene's interactions with law enforcement over a two-decade period. Covering the early busts of Operation Cyber Strike in 1997 right through to the 2020 SPARKS raid, this chapter details the different operational strategies that law enforcement has used to clamp down on the Scene. The chapter closes with an appraisal of the success of law enforcement agencies and notes the whack-a-mole style of operations in which takedowns appear only shortlived before the many-headed hydra resumes its operations.

```
#     #
  # #
#######
  # #
#     #
```

This book asks the fundamental question: what is the Warez Scene? The answer is complicated and multi-faceted, but I have arrived at a different definition from other scholars. From all my work on this book, I conclude that the Warez Scene is an illegal, online, alternative reality game with aesthetic subcultural stylings that operates on a quasi-economic basis. It is an anarchically governed free-for-all that has nonetheless developed its own codes of behavior, ethics, activities, and, most importantly, hierarchies of prestige.[75]

Why should we ask this question? Aside from the intrinsic interest in studying a fascinating subcultural space, there are arguments that a failure to understand these cultures results in a legal inability to regulate them. In his study of historical pirate networks, Adrian Johns posits, there is a clear moral of the story, that publishers and legal mechanisms in the past have only succeeded by understanding that which they faced. "The best way," writes Johns, "to counter piracy is to appreciate the culture of the pirates themselves — and to understand it better than they do."[76] We should also ask these questions to answer Alexander Sebastian Dent's "plea for more anthropology of piracy."[77] It is clear that Dent is right to note that "the precise nature and con-

---

75 For more on Scene ethics, see Alf Rehn, *Ordered Misbehavior: The Structuring of an Illegal Endeavor* (Stockholm: Royal Institute of Technology, 2003).

76 Adrian Johns, "Pop Music Pirate Hunters," *Daedalus* 131, no. 2 (2002): 77.

77 Dent, "Introduction."

sequences of the upcoming implosion of draconian anti-piracy measures will be best understood through localized treatments that the ethnographically aware are in the best position to provide."[78] Before we can delve into the localized instantiations of pirate cultures and their demonizations, we must understand the operations of the global distribution network, the Scene, that undergirds these.

A penultimate note on typography and sourcing is worth propounding here. Throughout this book I cite works created by an underground subculture with its own standards of writing and speech. It is fair to say that correct English is not high on the agenda of these writers. Throughout this book I have opted to retain the original spelling and grammar of the sources, rather than to correct this or to add pedantic "sic" markings after every technically incorrect usage. From this, readers will also glean a sense of the communication style of the Scene and come to greater familiarity with its discourses and language registers.

What, then, of the financial "scene" with which I opened? I contend that finance and stock-trading are the best analogies to how the Warez Scene operates. A highly technical infrastructure that thrives on speed and reputation, with material reward possible, but by no means guaranteed, or even valued beyond reputation, it is the cut-throat, competitive nature that defines the Warez Scene. Yet, in contradictory fashion, the Scene is also a space of sociality and friendship, amid this competition. The Scene is an alternative reality game, and its players are addicted. Until we recognize that members of the Scene are not, at heart, really interested in pirate media but in the process of the competition itself, it is unlikely that law enforcement will be able to control this anarchic darknet.

---

78 Ibid, 669.

Two

Setting the Scene

PIRATE PHILOSOPHY AND IMAGERY

What is digital piracy? Is it freedom fighters campaigning for the open liberation of digital material? Or is it simply the high-seas equivalent of buccaneers, extorting victims economically while hiding, coward-like, behind their screens? Of course, the very term "piracy" implies that there is a cut-throat nature to the act in its metaphor. It also implies that there must be personal gain at the illicit expense of another. However, piracy's terminology places this activity within various imaginaries and optics that condition how we understand its motivational frames.[1]

The domineering propaganda campaigns of the Motion Picture Association of America are, by now, familiar to most home-video audiences in the twenty-first century. The advertisement begins, "you wouldn't steal a car." The comparison they make is that one should not download pirated material because such an action would be analogous to theft. Ironically, given its deceptively simple logic, it is on such framing that one of the core philosophical debates around piracy rests: is digital piracy

1 For more, see James Meese, "The Pirate Imaginary and the Potential of the Authorial Pirate," in *Piracy: Leakages from Modernity*, eds. Martin Fredriksson and James Arvanitakis (Sacramento: Litwin Books, 2014), 19–38.

a form of theft? Can intellectual property be stolen? Further, it turns out that these questions have answers that are not addressable in simple terms of property relations but that sit within debates about labor in the digital world.

The terms of piracy and theft require upfront debate because there are significant differences. Theft is the act of deceptively appropriating someone else's property and thereby depriving the legitimate owner of access to it. UK law, for example, is explicit in stating that to steal something means that the original owner must lose access: "[a] person is guilty of theft if he dishonestly appropriates property belonging to another with the intention of permanently depriving the other of it."[2] US law varies by state, but all larceny-theft provisions contain at least two components: 1.) dishonest appropriation of property; 2.) with the intent to deprive the original owner of it.[3] Digital piracy does not deprive the original owner of the item in question because the act of copying has no impact on the original artifact. While a campaign by the Federation Against Software Theft (FAST) in the UK used the slogan "piracy is theft," the legal reality is very different.[4]

In the digital world, what we are discussing when we speak of piracy as theft is the unauthorized reproduction of an infinitely re-copyable artifact—not a "theft" in the traditionally understood sense. The transmission of a digital artifact from one party to another does not, in most cases, result in a loss of access for the original owner; although the recent craze for non-fungible tokens (NFTs) is an attempt to introduce such rivalry

2 United Kingdom, "Theft Act 1968," http://www.legislation.gov.uk/ukpga/1968/60/crossheading/definition-of-theft.

3 I have previously covered this topic in a similar fashion in Martin Paul Eve, *Password* (New York: Bloomsbury Academic, 2016), 84–85.

4 For more on this, see Matthew Yglesias, "Piracy Is a Form of Theft, and Copyright Infringement Is Neither," *Slate Magazine*, December 15, 2011, https://slate.com/business/2011/12/piracy-is-a-form-of-theft-and-copyright-infringement-is-neither.html, and Michał Krawczyk et al., "'Piracy Is Not Theft!' Is It Just Students Who Think So?" *Journal of Behavior and Experimental Economics* 54 (2015): 32–39.

in the digital world. However, this ability to copy without deprivation is why various thinkers have branded digital artifacts as "non-rivalrous." There is no rivalry for their ownership, and it is possible to share these objects without losing the original.[5] What is instead eroded in the realm of piracy is the coercive, scarcity relationship between ownership and purchase inherent in physical objects. In short, the supposition is that if an identical copy of an artifact is available for free, the underlying labor that created the first copy will go unremunerated. People will not pay for something they can get for free.

Digital rights management technologies, intellectual property laws, blockchain ledgers, and the comeback of physical media (e.g., vinyl records) are all attempts to reintroduce rivalry and scarcity into the world of digital objects and to stem the tide of piracy.[6] While the former three approaches use software systems, including cryptographic proof of work/space/stake, to reinscribe scarcity into the digital realm, the latter links a digital purchase to real-world ownership — albeit at significant ecological cost in the case of vinyl and blockchain — and conspicuous consumption.[7]

There is an irony in these attempts to halt piracy. In one sense, the entire purpose of anti-piracy initiatives is to ensure that the creators of digital artifacts are remunerated for their labor, thus ensuring, under capital, the continued production of such objects. There is often a focus in such initiatives on the im-

---

5 See, for instance: Peter Suber, *Open Access* (Cambridge: MIT Press, 2012). On the tricky terminology of digital objects, see Yuk Hui, *On the Existence of Digital Objects* (Minneapolis: University of Minnesota Press, 2016).

6 Marc Hogan, "Is Vinyl's Comeback Here to Stay?" *Pitchfork*, January 22, 2018, https://pitchfork.com/features/article/is-vinyls-comeback-here-to-stay/. Richard Stallman famously argues against the use of the term "intellectual property" in Richard M. Stallman, "Did You Say 'Intellectual Property'? It's a Seductive Mirage," *gnu.org*, April 20, 2015, https://www.gnu.org/philosophy/not-ipr.en.html.

7 Kyle Devine, "Nightmares on Wax: The Environmental Impact of the Vinyl Revival," *The Guardian*, January 28, 2020, http://www.theguardian.com/music/2020/jan/28/vinyl-record-revival-environmental-impact-music-industry-streaming.

age of the "starving" musician or artist. This figure is swindled of a livelihood by the copying power of the digital realm, even as it is more likely to be the intermediary large corporate record labels that stand to lose the most. In another sense, though, these attempts to halt piracy deflect attention away from this labor through what Marx called commodity fetishism.[8] Commodity fetishism is the principle that people believe that, when they buy something, they are paying for the object rather than paying for the labor that created the object. By emphasizing the relationship in a commercial transaction as purchasing an object rather than underwriting the labor that produced the object, anti-piracy initiatives devalue labor. "You wouldn't steal a car" is the framing rather than "you wouldn't steal the work time that produced a car." In their imagery of the starving artist, such efforts at once glorify labor and its remuneration but do so by erasing labor from any visibility within an economic transaction.

Piracy is also potentially a highly offensive term for unauthorized, digital reproduction. Why? The ICC International Maritime Bureau reported in its annual piracy report for 2004 that seaborne pirates murdered thirty crew members that year.[9] Every year, real sailors are kidnapped, threatened, and murdered by real, seafaring pirates. However, the typical imagery of the pirate has been subject to a romanticization that downplays violence and habilitates piracy. The Disney-fied images of pirates that have become routinized viewing for infants the world over, for instance, do not usually include AK47s and other contemporary weapons systems. Captain Hook may be the baddie, but the maiming and murder of his victims remain offscreen. As C.R. Pennell puts it, "[t]here was," and still is, "in reality, nothing attractive about pirate violence, except for sadists and

8 Karl Marx, *Capital: A Critique of Political Economy,* trans. Ben Fowkes (London: Penguin Books, 1992), 1:1–146.

9 "Annual Death Toll from Piracy Rises," *ICC Commercial Crime Services,* 2004, https://www.icc-ccs.org/index.php/405-annual-death-toll-from-piracy-rises.

voyeurs, and those who held pirates to be heroes skated quickly over this thin ice."[10]

The widespread romanticization of piracy is, at least in part, linked to an idea of resistance to capitalism. More often than not, commentators tie this view to the idea of the commons. As Peter Linebaugh and Marcus Rediker highlight, the history of maritime piracy intertwines with various understandings and practices of the commons and "commoning."[11] But the idea of the commons has also played a vital role in the study of digital technologies. It even shares an etymological root with "communication."[12] Indeed, perhaps the most distinct feature of the digital landscape is the possibility of sharing all digital artifacts in common; the cost-per-perfect copy is nearly zero. It seems it should be possible to share all digital files in common. In such a light, digital piracy appears to resist capitalistic flows, a type of digital communism.

Given this well-known romanticization, it is surprising that Virginia Crisp writes that "[w]ithin popular and much academic discourse it is hard to escape the understanding that pirates are nothing more than deviant thieves."[13] Certainly, this is the discourse that operates within industry-sponsored, anti-piracy, advertisement campaigns. However, as Crisp goes on to note, "another construction of the 'pirate' is as a 'subversive radical' engaged in a power struggle with the cultural industries."[14] In-

10 C.R. Pennell, "Introduction," in *Bandits at Sea: A Pirates Reader,* ed. C.R. Pennell (New York: New York University Press, 2001), 5.

11 See, for instance, Peter Linebaugh and Marcus Rediker, *The Many-Headed Hydra: Sailors, Slaves, Commoners, and the Hidden History of the Revolutionary Atlantic* (Boston: Beacon Press, 2003), 140.

12 Raymond Williams, *Keywords: A Vocabulary of Culture and Society* (Oxford: Oxford University Press, 2014), 36–37.

13 Virginia Crisp, "To Name a Thief: Constructing the Deviant Pirate," in *Piracy,* eds. Fredriksson and Arvanitakis, 39. A good counter-point to this can also be found in Janice Denegri-Knott, "Sinking the Online 'Music Pirates': Foucault, Power and Deviance on the Web," *Journal of Computer-Mediated Communication* 9, no. 4 (2004), https://academic.oup.com/jcmc/article/9/4/JCMC949/4614489, which uses Foucauldian principles to take apart notions of deviant power.

14 Crisp, "To Name a Thief," 43.

deed, the worldwide emergence of political "Pirate Parties" and various ambivalent pirate philosophies is evidence of the docility of pirate imagery.[15] We can feel at home with the idea of pirates as friendly renegades, fighting against the global corporate hegemony, liberating material from those who had wrongly seized it from the hands of the people. We link piracy as resistance in such contexts to ideas of helping people in common, an almost-communism, a lineage perhaps best explored in Eric Hobsbawm's relatively well-known analysis of social banditry and noble robbers.[16] This is a far cry from murder on the high seas.

This metaphor of the commons, though, has featured heavily in digital spaces. On a superficial level, it seems to be a helpful analogy for what is happening in the digital world when resources are shared, and copies are co-owned. However, figures such as Sam Moore and Stuart Lawson have recently pointed out that the commons is a somewhat vague and imprecise analogy that buries historical detail in favor of an idealized, and generalized, notion of the commons.[17] The commons, in other words, becomes a floating signifier onto which every participant projects their own take.

At its heart, much of the digital landscape looks more like the thirteenth-century period of enclosure in England when there was mass consolidation of previously common land into larger farms. As Nick Dyer-Witheford notes, enclosure was a multi-sided mass societal upheaval, one that required

15 Mariacristina Sciannamblo, "The Internet between Politics and the Political: The Birth of the Pirate Party," in *Piracy*, eds. Fredriksson and Arvanitakis, 177–94; United States Pirate Party, *No Safe Harbor: Essays about Pirate Politics* (n.p.: CreateSpace, 2012); Gary Hall, *Pirate Philosophy: For a Digital Posthumanities* (Cambridge: MIT Press, 2016); Virginia Crisp, "The Piratical Is Political," *Soundings* 55 (2013): 71–80.

16 Eric Hobsbawm, *Bandits* (New York: Pantheon Books, 1981).

17 Samuel Moore, "Common Struggles: Policy-Based vs. Scholar-Led Approaches to Open Access in the Humanities" (PhD diss., King's College London, 2019); Stuart Lawson, "Open Access Policy in the UK: From Neoliberalism to the Commons" (PhD diss., Birkbeck, University of London, 2019).

> a new regime of social discipline, surveillance, and criminalization including the witch-hunting of commons dwellings and using women, poor laws, antivagrancy legislation, workhouses, and the first steps in the formation of an internal state apparatus of thief-taking and policing to monitor, confine, and punish the potentially unruly population evicted from the land.[18]

Certainly, the produce of these newly enclosed spaces can remain available to consume without paying. However, the practices of commoning, in which common-pool resources are shared, worked over together, and communally governed, are rarely present in these new digitally enclosed cultures that large multinational corporations often own. Again, piracy can present itself as though it is a resistance to such practices of enclosure.

However, the history of the internet is much more complex than a simplistic, historical analogy to England's enclosure can show. For instance, it is naïve to believe that the origins of the internet lie in common spaces where users disseminated everything for free for the good of everyone, as if it were some form of utopian commons that was later enclosed. Instead, it is worth remembering that the US military's Advanced Research Projects Agency originally developed the internet, known as ARPANet. As Janet Abbate writes, "[i]n the years since the Internet was transferred to civilian control, its military roots have been downplayed [… but] [t]he Internet was not built in response to popular demand […]. Rather, the project reflected the command economy of military procurement."[19] The academic

---

18 See Nick Dyer-Witheford, "E-Capital and the Many Headed Hydra," in *Critical Perspectives on the Internet,* ed. Greg Elmer (Lanham: Rowman & Littlefield Publishers, 2002), 129–31; Silvia Beatriz Federici, *Caliban and the Witch: Women, the Body, and Primitive Accumulation* (New York: Autonomedia, 1997); Fiona Jeffries, "Reading 'Caliban and the Witch' Politically," *Gender, Place & Culture* 25, no. 9 (2018): 1322–28; Jane Humphries, "Enclosures, Common Rights, and Women: The Proletarianization of Families in the Late Eighteenth and Early Nineteenth Centuries," *The Journal of Economic History* 50, no. 1 (1990): 17–42.

19 Janet Abbate, *Inventing the Internet* (Cambridge: MIT Press, 2000), 144–45.

side of the early internet was secondary to its military history. As Leonard Kleinrock, an early internet engineer specified, "[e]very time I wrote a proposal I had to show the relevance to the military's applications."[20] Hence, there is no precise movement from open, digital commons to enclosed, network platforms, with piracy as an intervening resistance movement.

That said, there are histories of enclosure in the digital world at a very material level, to which Dyer-Witheford directs us. For instance, the 1993 introduction of domain name sales was a clear incursion of commerce into the inter-networked world rather than the first-come, first-served system that had preceded this. The analogies to physical space and sale here were prominent, including the idea that those who sit on domains with no intention of using them are so-called "cyber-squatters." Also, from 1991 to 1995 the architecture of the internet backbone was transferred from the National Science Foundation, a US government agency, to a group of telecommunications companies. The US government billed this as a democratic move, purportedly to ensure that they did not have permanent and final governance of a vital, trans-national infrastructure. However, it was also an enclosure of sorts where previously public-owned technology was transferred into private ownership.[21]

It is against this mode of enclosure that some narratives romantically situate "hackers, pirates, free-software creators, universal and open access movements, cyberactivists, and hacktivists."[22] As is clear from the diverse figures in this list, there are many spaces where one can see resistance to capital in the digital arena. This resistance has also spanned many different media types over history. As has been bolstered by the recent historical work of John Willinsky and Adrian Johns, piracy, as a form of resistance to commercial practices, is not unique to

20 Ibid., 77. This is a genealogy I have previously explored in Martin Paul Eve, *Pynchon and Philosophy: Wittgenstein, Foucault and Adorno* (London: Palgrave Macmillan, 2014), 155.

21 Dyer-Witheford, "E-Capital and the Many Headed Hydra," 132.

22 Ibid., 135.

digital media.[23] However, digital piracy is far more widespread now than the unauthorized duplication of books in the early years of print. If digital piracy is a form of resistance, then it is omnipresent. The (admittedly, extremely partisan) Software & Information Industry Association and Business Software Alliance at one point estimated that 38 percent of software worldwide was pirated.[24]

The responses to these enclosures have been categorized differently, depending on the perspective of the classifier. As Sarah Coleman and Dyer-Witheford point out, "[d]istinguishing between political and criminal responses to enclosure is not always easy."[25] On the one hand, it is difficult to conceptualize digital piracy as a radical, economic proposition when its analogous material metaphor is essentially one that involves murder for personal gain. On the other hand, decrying digital pirates as equivalent to seafaring killers is likewise obviously problematic and renders piracy's definition nebulous. For example, "pirate" covers a broad swathe of copyright infringement activities, to which the next section of this chapter will turn. However, it also extends to a swath of ongoing illicit, naval activity. As Dawdy and Bonni put it: "[a]lthough many definitions of piracy have been offered, no authors we came across were willing to venture an explanatory model that would link diverse types of so-called piracy."[26] Pirates have, at various times, been "predators, parasites, criminals, outlaws, rebels, heroes, heroines, evildoers, buffoons, opportunists, armed robbers, raiders, plunderers,

23 Adrian Johns, *Piracy: The Intellectual Property Wars from Gutenberg to Gates* (Chicago: University of Chicago Press, 2011); John Willinsky, *The Intellectual Properties of Learning: A Prehistory from Saint Jerome to John Locke* (Chicago: University of Chicago Press, 2017).

24 Dyer-Witheford, "E-Capital and the Many Headed Hydra," 139.

25 Sarah Coleman and Nick Dyer-Witheford, "Playing on the Digital Commons: Collectivities, Capital and Contestation in Videogame Culture," *Media, Culture & Society* 29, no. 6 (2007): 937.

26 Shannon Lee Dawdy and Joe Bonni, "Towards a General Theory of Piracy," *Anthropological Quarterly* 85, no. 3 (Summer 2012): 674.

bandits, brigands, liberators, rogues, robin hoods, rapscallions, and bloodthirsty killers."[27]

Truly, piracy is diffusely defined. Piracy is "a substitute for declared war," a form of "violent maritime predation in that it is not part of a declared or widely recognized war."[28] It has also been seen in economic terms as the taking of "tributes," as "unrequited, systematic exactions effected by force or threat of force," and as the activity of "commerce raiders."[29] Importantly, though, it is a mode of illicit violence in which — at least in the Graeco-Roman era — the idea of a "base" was key. As Philip de Souza notes, the maritime nature of piracy and the hefty equipment toll that this brought meant that pirates required an anchor point, a lair, or a hideout. As de Souza puts it, "[s]hips also need harbours or anchorages, so that the pirates' bases become an important factor in their success, and the suppression of piracy requires the control of such bases."[30]

These definitions all go some way towards understanding the concept of piracy. However, Dawdy and Bonni point to perhaps the most salient feature of piracy as it applies in the digital and seafaring worlds when they propose a definition of "a form of morally ambiguous property seizure committed by an organized group."[31] While I have already covered how the notion of "property seizure" does not hold water for digital piracy, Dawdy and Bonni's definition contains an even more critical element: a

---

27 Ibid., 674; Pennell, "Introduction"; Lawrence E. Babits, Joshua B. Howard, and Matthew Brenckle, "Pirate Imagery," in *X Marks the Spot: The Archaeology of Piracy,* eds. Russell K. Skowronek and Charles R. Ewen (Gainesville: University Press of Florida, 2006), 271–81; Russell K. Skowronek, "X Marks the Spot — Or Does It?," in *X Marks the Spot,* eds. Skowronek and Ewen, 282–98.

28 Fernand Braudel, *The Mediterranean and The Mediterranean World in the Age of Philip II,* trans. Siân Reynolds (New York: Harper and Row, 1972), 2:865; John L. Anderson, "Piracy and World History: An Economic Perspective on Maritime Predation," in *Bandits at Sea,* ed. Pennell, 82.

29 Anderson, "Piracy and World History," 84, 92; David J. Starkey, "Pirates and Markets," in *Bandits at Sea,* ed. Pennell, 110.

30 Philip de Souza, *Piracy in the Graeco-Roman World* (Cambridge: Cambridge University Press, 1999), 11.

31 Dawdy and Bonni, "Towards a General Theory of Piracy," 675.

pirate needs a crew. For, as they note, "[o]ne thing that many of the [extant] definitions lack is an emphasis on the *social* quality of piracy [...]. No pirate works alone. This is an important fact that has not been sufficiently appreciated in the literature on piracy due to a leap to legally classify piracy with individually-motivated criminality."[32]

It is impossible to underemphasize the importance of a group, or as we might call it a Scene, for piracy. It is no coincidence that P2P networks that connect individuals, forming ad hoc temporary groups, have thrived at the lower end of the piracy food chain. Nevertheless, as we will go on to see, the tension between individualism and collectivity runs through the heart of the Warez Scene. The environment prizes elitism and individual skill above all else. Exclusivity of access — to computer hardware, computational skill, a supply chain for various media forms — is rewarded with even further exclusivity and admission to elite grounds far from the public view.

Conversely, Sceners are almost all part of groups. For instance, Sceners dub couriers in the iND (individual) group "lamers." A pirate without a team is scarcely a pirate at all. Nevertheless, the groups are fractious. They bicker, argue, attack one another, compete, and generally take a no-holds-barred approach. Hence, we have the contradiction at the heart of piracy: individualism and elitism run to its core, but at the same time no person is an island. A community spirit, of sorts, is crucial.

At various levels, online pirates have also been conceptualized in terms of publishing and distribution modalities, as an informal distribution mode.[33] That is, some have taken piracy to be a form of publishing, a distribution channel like any other with a dissemination role. As Balázs Bodó and Zoltán Lakatos note of Hungarian P2P sites, for example, administrators and uploaders fulfill "the same function in P2P piracy as publish-

---

32 Ibid., 675.

33 Ramon Lobato and Julian Thomas, "An Introduction to Informal Media Economies," *Television & New Media* 13, no. 5 (2012): 379–82.

ing does in the book industry."[34] As Virginia Crisp also shows, these shadow, publishing cultures mirror the practices of mainstream distribution, with the highest value placed upon pirating the most famous works in licit channels.[35] While it may be true to state that piracy is a form of distribution and that it does constitute part of the contemporary ecology of media distribution, the ways in which it can act to filter, frame, and amplify material—the functions that Michael Bhaskar ascribes to the activity of "publishing"—are conditioned by mainstream, legal methods.[36] That is to say that if we conceive of piracy as a publishing and dissemination activity, it is one that is closely linked to mainstream cultures of licit dissemination.

It is relatively easy to see how piracy fulfils some of these functions of publishing. Certainly, pirate cultures amplify the material that passes through their halls, although this may not operate in the ways that audiences, producers, or even pirates anticipate.[37] In providing another route to obtaining the material, albeit in a way that undercuts the legal market with a free offering, piracy amplifies. However, the functions of filtering and framing are somewhat different here than in conventional, permitted distribution channels (such as sales through Amazon).

In terms of filtering, as Crisp notes, the material that sails through pirate channels is conditioned by the material produced in legal streams. To return to my original formulation of "original pirate material," this is a model in which the Scene emphasizes uniqueness and originality, despite it being a copy

34 Balázs Bodó and Zoltán Lakatos, "Piracy Cultures| P2P and Cinematographic Movie Distribution in Hungary," *International Journal of Communication* 6 (2012), https://ijoc.org/index.php/ijoc/article/view/1261.

35 Virginia Crisp, "Access and Power: Film Distribution, Re-Intermediation and Piracy," in *The Routledge Companion to World Cinema*, eds. Rob Stone et al. (London: Routledge, 2018), 449.

36 Michael Bhaskar, *The Content Machine: Towards a Theory of Publishing from the Printing Press to the Digital Network* (New York: Anthem Press, 2013).

37 Virginia Crisp, "'BLOODY PIRATES!!! *Shakes Fist*': Reimagining East Asian Film Distribution and Reception through Online Filesharing Networks," *Journal of Japanese and Korean Cinema* 3, no. 1 (2012): 65–72.

culture. There are sets of rules, covered extensively in Chapter Four, that determine what is allowed to be "published" in the Scene. Although these rules are a type of filtering, allowing both local (i.e., topsite-level) and Scene-wide prescriptions and proscriptions, they are conditioned by the material put out by Hollywood studios. The Scene rules are secondary filtering systems for a series of preproduced artifacts that have, already once before, been through various filtering mechanisms.

In terms of framing, the Scene certainly takes on this publishing activity. The framing of the pirate artifact as being subject to quality control and rigorous scrutiny mechanisms is clear. This manifests, for instance, in the obscure, directory naming conventions that mark out a Scene "release" (the term used for a pirate artifact, be it a movie, TV show, computer game, or music recording). The Scene designation is meant to frame pirate publication as high-standard and high-speed.

Understanding pirate practices through the lens of publishing is also apt as there are parallels between contemporary digital piracy and earlier phases of book publishing history. As Bodó Balázs puts it:

> a longer historical lens suggests that the current crisis of copyright, piracy, and enforcement has much in common with earlier periods of change and conflict among cultural producers. From the early days of the book trade in the fifteenth century, cultural markets were shaped by deals within the publishing trade and with political authorities over who could reproduce works and on what terms. Broadly speaking, pirate publishers then played two roles in this early history. In the first mode, "they printed censored texts" and in the second "they introduced cheap reprints that reached new reading publics."[38]

38 Balázs Bodó, "Coda: A Short History of Book Piracy," in *Media Piracy in Emerging Economies,* ed. Joe Karaganis (New York: Social Science Research Council, 2011), 399.

As we shall see, these pirate cultures are not brilliantly placed to circumvent censorship. However, they certainly reach new audiences who would not have paid for the original works. In the digital space, the mass publics who wish to download material without paying make an audience for this material. Ironically, members of the Scene decry the mass circulation of their work. While we can understand the high-level, piracy Scene in relation to histories and practices of publishing, it also sits in an uneasy and ambivalent tension with such modes.

Nevertheless, if we consider piracy as a form of publication or dissemination, then it is vital to consider the role and mythologies of the original author or artist. Let us return to the starving artist figure, who plays a role in the appropriation and habilitation of piracy as a metaphor for digital copying outside the circuit of capital.[39] The parallel here is that nonparticipation in consumer monetary exchange equates to starving someone. The logic is made causative, and the starving takes on the active voice. It is claimed in this case that it is from the artist that you are stealing the car.

The romanticized mythology of the starving artist is problematically deployed within discourses on digital piracy. It is true that, in some senses, copyright law places extreme restrictions on artistic freedom. For example, proponents of remix culture, in some ways central to the argument in this book, note how contemporary copyright law impedes the interplay between tradition and the individual talent, forbidding the reuse of in-copyright works within radically new spaces, even for artistic purposes.[40] At the same time, as Matthew Barblan points

39 For just a couple of the many studies that have looked at the economic effects of widespread, peer-to-peer piracy at lower tiers than the Scene to which I turn in this book, see Nico van Eijk, Joost Poort, and Paul Rutten, "Legal, Economic and Cultural Aspects of File Sharing," *Communications & Strategies* 77, no. 1 (2010): 35–54; Gilbert B. Rodman and Cheyanne Vanderdonckt, "Music for Nothing or, I Want My MP3: The Regulation and Recirculation of Affect," *Cultural Studies* 20, nos. 2–3 (2006): 245–61.

40 Lawrence Lessig, *Remix: Making Art and Commerce Thrive in the Hybrid Economy* (New York: Penguin Books, 2008); David Shields, *Reality Hunger: A Manifesto* (London: Hamish Hamilton, 2011); Charlotte Higgins,

out, "[a]s popular as the 'starving artist' cliché may be, real artists need food. Meeting artists' basic needs goes a long way towards empowering them to create their art. Copyright's role in giving artists the economic freedom to meet their basic needs — by generating income from their art — is an important part of the relationship between copyright and creative freedom."[41] In turn, this is linked to the tricky intersections between commerce and art. As Tyler Cowen controversially put it, "[e]conomic circumstances influence the ability of artists to express their aesthetic aspirations. Specifically, artistic independence requires financial independence"; a sentiment that echoes Virginia Woolf's earlier feminist pronouncements on the need for a room of one's own.[42]

The problem with the myth of the starving artist as a target of anti-piracy campaigns is that one is not supposed to challenge this stereotype. Instead, regardless of its truth, the myth is that the artist's starvation is the factor that allows him or her to produce "great art" — a troubling assertion, to say the least. That is, anti-piracy campaigns summon the assertion that, in some ways, great artists should be starving. Although industry proponents may say that they are working to alleviate this situation, anti-piracy campaigns that invoke the figure of the starving artist present at once a character that is to be pitied from their impoverishment while, simultaneously, painting a persona that relies on impecunity for artistic creation. Great art, this myth seems to say, can only come from those who are starving.

Such a stance draws attention to precisely which figures we make out to be victims in anti-piracy campaigns. In some cases, the call to "support the artists" clarifies that it is creators whom digital pirates economically damage. This feeds and is fed by the myth of the starving artist. In other senses, more systemic, capi-

"China Miéville: Writers Should Welcome a Future Where Readers Remix Our Books," *The Guardian,* August 21, 2012, http://www.theguardian.com/books/2012/aug/21/china-mieville-novels-books-anti-piracy.

41 Matthew Barblan, "Copyright as a Platform for Artistic and Creative Freedom," *George Mason Law Review* 23, no. 4 (2016): 794.

42 Tyler Cowen, *In Praise of Commercial Culture* (Cambridge: Harvard University Press, 2000), 16.

talistic damage is posited to the consumer. The logic goes that if people refuse to pay for games, music, and movies, eventually these artifacts will not be manufactured, thereby damaging the consumer. As James Newman puts it: "[c]oncerted anti-piracy campaigns from the 1980s onwards, such as the "Don't copy that floppy" television campaign, have consistently sought to discursively construct the legally-paying consumer as the real victim."[43] This context switching between harm to the creator and harm to the consumer calls into question the tricky interrelationship between art and commerce, between autonomy and utility. For even as the myth of the starving artist posed the use of commerce as a way of supporting artistic genius, such niche, arthouse productions are often not those upon which digital piracy trains its sights. The popular artforms that pirates most frequently target are those with mass appeal — the products of what first-generation Frankfurt School thinkers such as Theodor W. Adorno and Max Horkheimer would call "the culture industry."[44] While, as Maria A. Slowinska has pointed out, there are ways in which many "contemporary art and contemporary commercial strategies" converge to form a new hybrid figure of art and commerce, the fact that there is a populism in the targets of digital piracy should make us question the role of the starving artist within such discourses.[45] It should also lead us to question how revolutionary piracy is if it just serves up the same culture industry products. Is it the same figure hiding behind the moniker of "creator" when one summons Vincent van Gogh and the Disney corporation? Both are "starving" artists under some anti-piracy rhetorics.

43 James Newman, *Videogames* (London: Routledge, 2013), 145.

44 See Max Horkheimer and Theodor W. Adorno, "The Culture Industry: Enlightenment as Mass Deception," in *Dialectic of Enlightenment: Philosophical Fragments,* ed. Gunzelin Schmid Noerr, trans. Edmund Jephcott (Stanford: Stanford University Press, 2002), 95–136; Deborah Cook, *The Culture Industry Revisited: Theodor W. Adorno on Mass Culture* (Lanham: Rowman and Littlefield, 1996).

45 Maria A. Slowinska, *Art/Commerce: The Convergence of Art and Marketing in Contemporary Culture* (Bielefeld: Transcript Verlag, 2014), 17.

Then, piracy is at once both an attack on and a replicative function within capital. Like theft, piracy is an attack on capital accumulation within circuits of commerce. It is a disruptive mechanism that blocks the intended flow of finance. This is why there are laws against it. At the same time, piracy has an often-neglected function of replicating popular media forms, with personal accumulation at the lowest possible price point — zero. Digital piracy accrues personal gain to the perpetrators and practitioners, even if it does not entail loss in the same sense as theft for the original owner. In this book, I demonstrate that this gain need not even be the item that is pirated but a form of cultural cachet within the subcultural Warez Scene. In short, there are economic logics within the alternative reality game of the Scene that replicate the macro-economics of contemporary capital. Thus, while piracy may wreck certain economic systems, it does so by reimplementing its own micro-logics of capital and redistributing the culture industry's homogenized outputs.

The fact that piracy operates on its own logic of capital was recognized in the 1997 "No Electronic Theft Act" (NET) in the US. As Eric Goldman notes, "[t]he NET Act modified criminal copyright law [...] in two principal ways: first, it expanded the definition of 'financial gain' to cover bartering implicit in warez trading, and second, it created a new basis of criminal infringement based only on a minimum quantum of infringement (irrespective of motive)."[46] The former is essential since criminal copyright infringement is "the willful infringement of a copyright (a) for purposes of commercial advantage or private financial gain [...] or (b) by the reproduction or distribution (including by electronic means), during any 180 day period, of copyrighted works with a total retail value of more than $1,000."[47] Of course, one could argue that legal frameworks such as the NET Act are merely bringing piracy to be understood within an economic frame of reference, rather than the piratical activities themselves

46 Eric Goldman, "Warez Trading and Criminal Copyright Infringement," SSRN *Electronic Journal* (2004): 3.

47 Ibid., 4.

possessing an economic character. Certainly the NET Act has the obvious benefit of making warez trading a form of criminal activity that can be successfully prosecuted, as had happened in over eighty cases by 2004.[48]

But digital piracy is also not one, single thing. As Goldman puts it, "[t]he generic term warez trading imprecisely lumps together disparate activities."[49] In this book, I deal with the subset of piracy that takes place in elite circles behind closed doors rather than the mass systems of P2P sharing that may cause large-scale, economic damage through their broad accessibility. That said, these two spheres are not entirely separable; releases from the Scene leak into the public sphere and are usable by anyone who stumbles across them.[50] For this reason, the next section of the book deals with the forms of piracy that are not the Scene. This tension between the desire to share and the desire to remain hidden runs through the analyses of this book and reveals the curious and conflicting motivations that drive people to participate within these subcultures.

Finally, if piracy is often romanticized, as much of this section has suggested, then we should pay close attention to whose piracy is romanticized. In the West or Global North,[51] piracy is often romanticized through an exoticization, or orientalization, of racial mythology. Historically, as Kavita Philip notes, "[t]he pirate figure has commonly functioned as a raced, gendered subaltern who effects the inversion of hegemonic power relations."[52] This seafaring imaginary of deviant, racial servitude

---

48 Ibid., 3.

49 Eric Goldman, "The Challenges of Regulating Warez Trading," *Social Science Computer Review* 23, no. 1 (2005): 24.

50 Goldman, "Warez Trading and Criminal Copyright Infringement," passim.

51 There are many problems with the homogenizing move of referring to the Global North or the West, but I nonetheless use these terms as challenging yet useful groupings through which to explore briefly various racial imaginaries of piracy. See Dimiter Toshkov, "The 'Global South' Is a Terrible Term. Don't Use It!," *RE-DESIGN*, November 11, 2018, http://re-design.dimiter.eu/?p=969.

52 Kavita Philip, "What Is a Technological Author? The Pirate Function and Intellectual Property," *Postcolonial Studies* 8, no. 2 (2005): 199.

runs from St. Augustine through Bertolt Brecht, but it has also evolved to match the contemporary digital world. In the digital space, the fear of pirate Others, particularly bootleggers in "Eastern" nations, has arisen as a specter to haunt Hollywood studios and record labels. The ways in which this can be understood lie in the "world-shaping," "ideological work" that involves "naming the original as 'real' and the copy as 'fake'"; a way for corporations to re-mark damaging piracy as the efforts of foreign agents, as dominant forces have done through history.[53] Consider that "good piracy," which is romanticized as political freedom fighting, often takes the form, of, for instance, free-culture pioneers such as Lawrence Lessig arguing before the US Supreme Court for the right of consumers to copy their own media and to transform it. By contrast, as Philip goes on to argue, "[b]ad piracy is Asian piracy"; the cheap resale of "counterfeit" DVDs on the street corner.[54]

This is to say that while certain forms of piracy are romanticized, racial or ethnic biases drive these choices. Ironically, as we will go on to see, the Scene actually reproduces some of these (post-)colonial logics itself. The geo-segmentation of Warez networks into the US, European, and Asian sites, with poor intercontinental routing speeds, led to a hierarchy of topsites in which different racing charts were produced for different regions.[55] In turn, this drove a valorization of specific geographic site locations, mostly centered in the US and Europe. It is also notable that, as the Scene deals with almost every digital media format available, pornography is also prominent within this space. Given that pornography has well-known racial characteristics and that pornographic works have titles that denote genre through racial labels, the Scene is a space that is flooded with a stream of textual, racial epithets. Even if it has been argued, then, that "pornography often promises difference, but actually

53 Ibid., 208.

54 Ibid., 212.

55 Alf Rehn, "Electronic Potlatch: A Study on New Technologies and Primitive Economic Behaviors" (PhD diss., Royal Institute of Technology, Stockholm, 2001), 102.

culminates in a universalizing sex act which overcomes difference," the Scene is a world where announcement bots daily sexualize and objectify Black and Asian people.[56]

The geographic and linguistic centers of the Scene that I cover seem to have an Anglo-European bias. As English remains the dominant language of intercultural exchange in most spaces, this is hardly surprising. As we will see, many Scene rules specify that only the Latin character set (i.e., a–z) are valid in release filenames, thereby requiring the transliteration of non-anglophone releases. That said, there are groups that specialize in releasing material from non-English cultures. For instance, many release names reflect the Japanese pop music genre (JPOP) (e.g., "4TE-More_Ippo_Zutsu-JPOP-WEB-2015-POWDER"). While this shows that the Scene does work internationally, it is also the case that such releases must set themselves aside, using the JPOP or KPOP (Korean pop) tags. Given that this text appears in the release name, many topsites also likely ban such releases. The marker of distinction and diversity here also serves as a marker by which releases may be excluded. The majority of this book is concerned with the functions of the Anglophone Scene. This is due to a combination of factors, including but not limited to the composition of the archives to which I had access and my ability to read only European languages. It is possible that other more geographically specific Scenes would merit further attention and research.

PIRACY OUTSIDE OF THE SCENE

If we are not to conceive of digital piracy in romanticizing anti-capitalist terms, yet we are also to value or, at least, to understand the craft and novelty of original pirate material that constitute my claimed warez aesthetic, then we need to consider the different levels of the piracy ecosystem and the differing

56 See the description of Celine Parreñas Shimizu's work in Jennifer C. Nash, *The Black Body in Ecstasy: Reading Race, Reading Pornography* (Durham: Duke University Press, 2014), 132.

motivations of actors within that web.[57] Often constructed as a hierarchical "piracy pyramid," online copyright violation can be broken down into a hierarchy as follows, from top to bottom:

1. Topsites, or the Scene
2. File eXchange Protocol (FXP) boards
3. Private torrent trackers
4. Public torrent trackers, or XDCC and other P2P mechanisms
5. Bootleggers.[58]

The remaining chapters of this book primarily focus on the top level of this environment — the topsites and release groups that constitute the network known as the Warez Scene. But it is worth unpacking the lower hierarchies to understand each level's motivations and conceptualize piracy within these spaces. As Jonas Andersson and Stefan Larsson note, motivations and justifications for participation vary hugely between different types of actors within these areas.[59] But the Warez Scene can only really be understood by its distinction from other types of piracy, by its differentiation from other forms.

57 For more on avoiding the romanticising terms, see You Jie, "Cultural Resistance or Corporate Assistance: Disenchanting the Anti-Capitalist Myth of Digital Piracy," in *Piracy,* eds. Fredriksson and Arvanitakis, 195–215. See also Francesca da Rimini and Jonathan Marshall, "Piracy Is Normal, Piracy Is Boring: Systemic Disruption as Everyday Life," in *Piracy,* eds. Fredriksson and Arvanitakis, 323–44.

58 For more on the pyramid terminology, see Andrew Sockanathan, "Digital Desire and Recorded Music: OiNK, Mnemotechnics and the Private BitTorrent Architecture" (PhD diss., Goldsmiths, University of London, 2011), 188–93. For another pair who use the pyramid terminology and set this out in visual form, albeit confined only to the virtual space, see Ard Huizing and Jan A. van der Wal, "Explaining the Rise and Fall of the Warez MP3 Scene: An Empirical Account from the Inside," *First Monday* 19, no. 10 (2014).

59 Jonas Andersson and Stefan Larsson, "The Justification of Piracy: Differences in Conceptualization and Argumentation Between Active Uploaders and Other File-Sharers," in *Piracy,* eds. Fredriksson and Arvanitakis, 217–40.

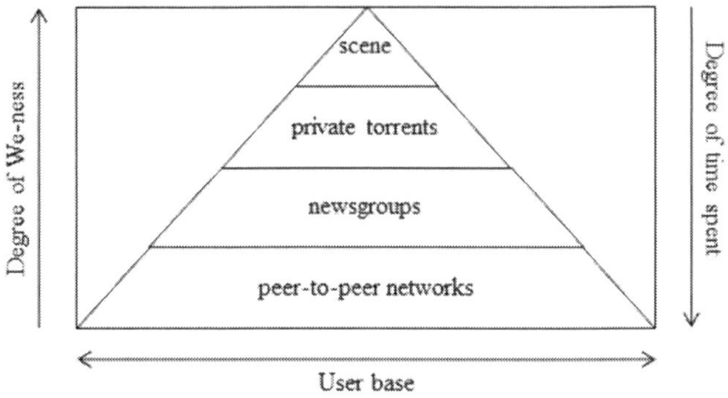

Figure 1. Huizing and van der Wal's pyramid. Reproduced under a Creative Commons License.

Different scholars have painted the pyramid differently at different times and with diverse structuring motivations for the hierarchy. Ard Huizing and Jan A. van der Wal, for instance, compare the Scene to private torrents, newsgroups, and public P2P networks (shown in Figure 1).[60] The structuring logic that Huizing and van der Wal employ is across the axes of "community" or "We-ness," as they term it. They also use the level of time investment made by members of each tier with a final dimension indicating the relative proportion of users within each segment. That is, for Huizing and van der Wal, the Scene can be characterized as a space of a small userbase, where participants spend a lot of their time as part of a tight-knit community. By contrast, public P2P networks represent the precise opposite on every single one of these traits. The descending area coverage of each tier of the pyramid makes it an excellent metaphorical form for this representation.

As Virginia Crisp has aptly shown, this diagram and all such pyramids are reductive. Her own schema of the formal and informal movie distribution ecology aptly shows the bottlenecks

60 Huizing and van der Wal, "Explaining the Rise and Fall of the Warez MP3 Scene."

and entry points when filtering through these systems.[61] It is clear that, in reality, a simple pyramid is reductive of the flows between official and non-official distribution. Despite this, for reasons of concision in this explanatory portion of the book, I stick to a simplified pyramid and hierarchical structure, albeit one that also encompasses non-digital piracy (e.g., bootleggers selling material on street corners). Such an approach confounds, to some extent, Huizing and van der Wal's setup. Bootleggers likely spend a significant amount of time in their pirate activities, and they profit from it, even if they are not a closely bonded group and even if they are a broader userbase. Starting at the bottom of my structure, it is perhaps easiest to understand the motivations of these bootleggers.[62]

"Bootleggers" are people who sell pirated material, be it on the streets or online. We should take note that there is sometimes a racialized demonization of the idea of bootlegging, as it often takes place within less economically developed nations.[63] Nonetheless, such individuals will have a variety of supply chains for their material, which will range from full Scene releases — with the Scene sometimes billed as the key distribution route — right down to home-made copies of media that they legally own but have illegally duplicated.[64] The motivation of these individuals is crystal clear: they are into piracy in order to make money.[65] Bootleggers are often confused, as Lee Marshall notes, with "tape traders," who have, for example, recorded a live gig of jambands such as Phish, the Dave Matthews Band, and the Grateful Dead, who all encourage this practice. Indeed, tape trading is a licit activity in which such bands "permit their audiences to record their live concerts and then let fans trade

61 Virginia Crisp, "Release Groups & The Scene: Re-Intermediation and Competitive Gatekeepers Online," *Cinéma & Cie* 17, no. 29 (Fall 2017): 77.

62 The definitive study of music bootleggers, on which I draw here, is Lee Marshall, "For and Against the Record Industry: An Introduction to Bootleg Collectors and Tape Traders," *Popular Music* 22, no. 1 (2003): 57–72.

63 Philip, "What Is a Technological Author?" 207.

64 Crisp, "Release Groups & The Scene," 78.

65 Marshall, "For and against the Record Industry," 58.

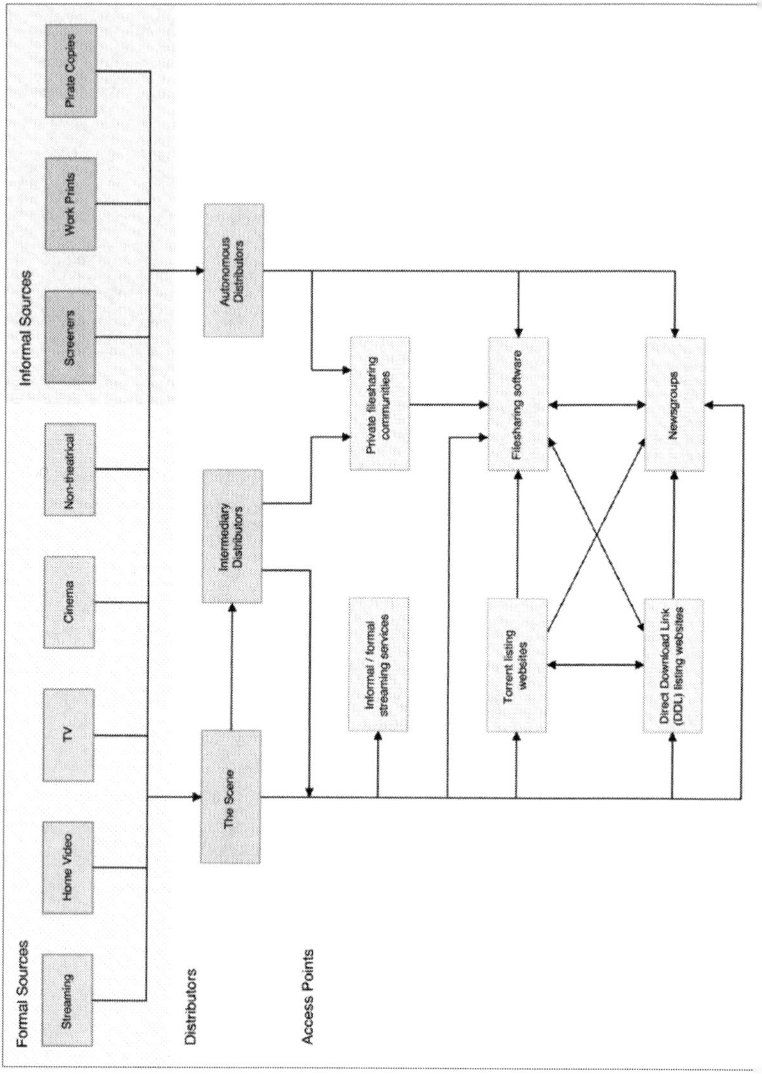
Formal Sources
Informal Sources
Streaming
Home Video
TV
Cinema
Non-theatrical
Screeners
Work Prints
Pirate Copies
Distributors
The Scene
Intermediary Distributors
Autonomous Distributors
Access Points
Informal / formal streaming services
Private filesharing communities
Torrent listing websites
Filesharing software
Direct Download Link (DDL) listing websites
Newsgroups

Figure 2. Virginia Crisp's more thorough diagram of distribution sources. Copyright Virginia Crisp, reproduced by kind permission of the author.

these recordings amongst themselves on the condition that no money is involved."[66] Tape trading is legitimate, as long as it is noncommercial. Bootleggers, by contrast, reintroduce commercial motive into piracy and, as a result, are hated in common both by anti-piracy outfits and, as we shall see, the Scene itself.

Importantly, as I note in several contexts throughout this book, most Scene releases come with strict prohibitions against selling their pirated warez. To be caught bootlegging or selling warez outputs will, in most cases, merit a lifetime "SceneBan." This has caused a great deal of confusion in the secondary literature. Some work, such as S.M. Furnell's taxonomy of cybercrime, has totally misread the motivations of Sceners. For while he correctly ascribes "challenge," "ego," and "ideology" to Sceners, he also writes erroneously that they operate for "money."[67] This goes directly against the vast body of evidence in, say, Scene notices and announcements that decry those who sell warez or access.[68]

While this spurning of commercial motive could lead us back to romantic ideals of piracy, it is not truly linked to any deep-seated ethical principle. It is rather because selling pirate material is likely to attract unwanted legal attention. However, anti-piracy campaigns, such as the aforementioned notorious "You Wouldn't Steal a Car" campaign, have often targeted this bootlegging level of pirates, accusing the practice of funding terrorism.[69] For instance, a report commissioned by the RAND Corporation accuses the Warez Scene of supplying ma-

66 Ibid.

67 S.M. Furnell, "Categorising Cybercrime and Cybercriminals," *Journal of Information Warfare* 1, no. 2 (2020): 42.

68 For instance, RUHEBITTE, "The Truth About Warez Seller Since aka Kartus aka Styler (The.truth.about.warez.seller.Since.aka.Kaktus.aka.Styler-RUHEBITTE)," c. 2006–2010, DeFacto2, warez-scene-notices-2006-2010.

69 Steve Cisler, "Pirates of the Pacific Rim," *Leonardo* 39, no. 4 (August 2006): 377–80.

terial that is used by "many more people further downstream" (e.g., the bootleggers) to fund terrorism. These accusations are even made while, "as far as can be determined," Warez Scene groups themselves "do not engage in other forms of organized crime, such as drug or human trafficking" and "are driven by the challenge, by wanting access to free goods, and by the thrill of 'living on the edge,' not to mention 'street cred[it]' among the groups."[70] Crisp's distribution diagram seems to confirm that the Scene is one of the few routes by which, for example, films enter lower pirate markets. Even when it is claimed that "the true warez culture is a non-profit venture," an aspect to which I will return, this is problematic given that the Scene does likely feed bootlegging markets.[71] As a result, even though the Scene has a strict ethos of prohibiting the distribution of their releases on public P2P media[72] and membership bases who "strongly object to commercial piracy," commerce springs from their activities, downstream in bootlegging.[73]

Bootleggers pose a genuine threat to the economics of various media industries. As I have already noted, there is a geo-specificity to this. As Kline et al. point out, "the major breeding-grounds for contraband games are probably in the black markets of the world, China, the Russian Federation, Southeast Asia, and other emerging, or declining, markets."[74] While Hong Kong is lined with markets selling the latest contraband Play-

70 Gregory F. Treverton et al., "The Shape of Counterfeiting and the Example of Film Piracy," in *Film Piracy, Organized Crime, and Terrorism* (Santa Monica: RAND Corporation, 2009), 38.

71 Stephen Kline, Nick Dyer-Witheford, and Greig De Peuter, "Workers and Warez: Labour and Piracy in the Global Game Market," in *Digital Play: The Interaction of Technology, Culture, and Marketing* (Montreal: McGill-Queen's University Press, 2003), 212.

72 WALMART, "WALMART Anti-P2P Statement (tairlthan-walmart.nfo)," 2007, DeFacto2.

73 Goldman, "Warez Trading and Criminal Copyright Infringement," 11.

74 Kline, Dyer-Witheford, and De Peuter, "Workers and Warez," 213. For an exploration of cultural differences in music piracy between the US and Japan, see Ian Condry, "Cultures of Music Piracy: An Ethnographic Comparison of the US and Japan," *International Journal of Cultural Studies* 7, no. 3 (2004): 343–63.

Station titles, by some estimates 98 percent of titles are pirated in Russia and Ukraine. However, it is a mistake to see this as entirely localized. The Interactive Digital Software Association "accuses more than fifty countries of either aiding counterfeiters or failing to establish or seriously enforce adequate protections against theft of intellectual property." Despite Sceners trying to keep releases in the family, their work finds its way down to bootleggers who are spread worldwide. "If the interactive game industry is now globalized," write Kline et al., then "so too is the shadow world of pirate enterprise that haunts it."[75]

In my hierarchy, the level above bootleggers is the set of public torrent trackers that have been a thorn in the side of criminal enforcement agencies for almost two decades. The most notorious of these in the West, The Pirate Bay, has proved virtually impossible to close, despite massive ongoing legal efforts, police raids, and state interventions.[76] These sites are public, open depositories of pirated material in which end users use protocols such as Bittorrent, a fast P2P distribution algorithm, to disseminate the material among themselves. The actual torrent files, hosted by sites such as The Pirate Bay, do not contain the pirated material itself. Instead, the torrent files are pointers that coordinate peers to communicate and to share the files. The initial seeder is the person who has infringed, not the intermediate hosting site. Therefore, when these sites are raided there is no actual pirate material on their servers, despite their clear, ongoing intent to violate copyright law. Instead, the central servers

---

75 Kline, Dyer-Witheford, and De Peuter, "Workers and Warez," 215.

76 There is a large, secondary literature that focuses on The Pirate Bay and other public trackers, their influence on politics, and crime. For just a selection, see Patrick Burkart, *Pirate Politics: The New Information Policy Contests* (Cambridge: MIT Press, 2014); Joost Poort et al., "Baywatch: Two Approaches to Measure the Effects of Blocking Access to The Pirate Bay," *Telecommunications Policy* 38, no. 4 (May 2014): 383–92; Felix Oberholzer-Gee and Koleman Strumpf, "File Sharing and Copyright," *Innovation Policy and the Economy* 10, no. 1 (2010): 19–55; Astra Taylor, "Serfing the Net," *The Baffler* 2, no. 1 [18] (2010): 20–26. Again, I note here the geographical specificity of my claim, using the slightly problematic, but nonetheless helpful catch-all of the "West."

themselves merely have the indexing files. Such a torrent system is akin to having the table of contents to a book that points to where you can get the chapter but not the chapter itself. This referential characteristic of torrenting has made it difficult, in legal terms, to shut down sites like The Pirate Bay.

While this type of torrent site is open to the public, a tier of activity above this works on an invitation-only basis — private Bittorrent trackers. These sites require users to be active in uploading and participating. They usually have strict rules and quality assurance processes. These, in turn, lead to well-seeded torrents and high-quality material, shared between a limited but still relatively large userbase.

To date, the most notorious, private Bittorrent trackers have been Oink's Pink Palace and its successor, What.CD. These websites were private music trackers funded by donations from the userbase, which provided a clear legal route to their prosecution. Specializing in lossless distribution formats where the sound quality of the music is identical to the original on the recording (i.e., is not compressed in a way that loses any quality), Oink's Pink Palace was eventually raided and shut down in 2007 having run for three years. The founder of the site, Alan Ellis (the eponymous "Oink"), was prosecuted for copyright fraud but was not found guilty even though he did not deny running the site, demonstrating the difficulty of legally pursuing torrent website operators (siteops).[77]

Oink's Pink Palace was succeeded by What.CD, which ran from 2007 until 2016, when it preemptively shut down to avoid a raid.[78] Perhaps the most notable feature of this site was the introduction of its own custom server software and its highly slick tracker website, Ocelot and Gazelle, respectively. The professionalism of these software developments, which could handle up to five million connected peers with just three gigabytes

77 "Music File-Sharer 'Oink' Cleared of Fraud," *BBC News,* January 15, 2010, http://news.bbc.co.uk/1/hi/england/tees/8461879.stm.

78 For more on these trackers, see Blake Durham, "Circulatory Maintenance: The Entailments of Participation in Digital Music Platforms," *American Music* 38, no. 2 (Summer 2020): 197.

of RAM, has many similarities to the custom FTP daemons of the Scene, covered below.[79] Although undeniably and totally illegal, such was the extent and organizational prowess of What.CD that it was hailed, even in professional journalism circles, as "[t]he greatest music collection in the world," ever.[80] Just as Library Genesis is painted as the illegal equivalent of the Library of Alexandra in the digital-book, piracy space, so What.CD was for music.[81] Clearly, requiring that users remain active, upload material at a ratio to their download, and have strong cataloguing and metadata principles led to the creation of what can only be described as a professional piracy outfit, despite the fact that the site administrators did not profit financially from their dealings. It is clear that the Scene is a much more tightly knit group, and that private Bittorrent trackers are much more spread out than this; however, there are distinct parallels between the "best" outfits at this level, and the work of the top-level Scene.

The motivations of those who participate in Bittorrent "communities" are varied.[82] Most people who use public trackers, it can be assumed, are primarily interested in acquiring the end content free of charge. As there are no motivational structures, such as a requirement to upload, the focus is on the material

79 Ernesto Van der Sar, "'What.CD' Debuts Lightweight Tracker for Its 5 Million Peers," *TorrentFreak,* October 14, 2010, https://torrentfreak.com/what-cd-debuts-lightweight-tracker-for-its-5-million-peers-101014/.

80 Nikhil Sonnad, "A Eulogy for What.CD, the Greatest Music Collection in the History of the World—Until it Vanished," *Quartz,* November 18, 2016, https://qz.com/840661/what-cd-is-gone-a-eulogy-for-the-greatest-music-collection-in-the-world/.

81 Balázs Bodó, "The Genesis of Library Genesis: The Birth of a Global Scholarly Shadow Library," in *Shadow Libraries: Access to Educational Materials in Global Higher Education,* ed. Joe Karaganis (Cambridge: MIT Press, 2018), 25–52; Balázs Bodó, "Library Genesis in Numbers: Mapping the Underground Flow of Knowledge," in *Shadow Libraries,* ed. Karaganis, 53–78; Martin Paul Eve, "Lessons from the Library: Extreme Minimalist Scaling at Pirate Ebook Platforms," *Digital Humanities Quarterly* (2022), forthcoming.

82 Mark Cenite et al., "More Than Just Free Content: Motivations of Peer-to-Peer File Sharers," *Journal of Communication Inquiry* 33, no. 3 (2009): 206–21.

itself on these sites. Furthermore, there is often less of a "cult of the uploader" around releases, compared to, for instance, private torrent sites, where user classes and hierarchies reward those who upload quality releases, which I cover in Chapter Four..

On occasion, proponents have nonetheless argued that such pirate sites act as cultural depositories, preserve media for the longer term, and motivate broad participation — "shadow libraries" as "dark archives." This is an extension of my earlier argument that piracy is a type of publishing activity. Certainly, there was a direct campaign to preserve the illegal archive in the case of the Library Genesis torrent collection.[83] However, there is a problem with this argument: the robustness of these illegal sites as a preservation system is dubious at best. Hence, those who believe that such activities constitute "a grand subaltern repository for access and preservation" are overlooking the fact that recent studies show preservation robustness of not more than 40 percent.[84] Certainly, this may be better than nothing, and we cannot ignore these so-called "shadow economies" of illicit distribution, but it is hardly a solid infrastructural basis on which to found the perpetuation of our cultures.[85]

One of the challenges in understanding the motivations of various actors in these spaces is that different media types may come with different motivations. Suppose we assume that participation in public, torrenting communities occurs primarily

83 See, for example, u/shrine, "Charitable Seeding Update: 10 Terabytes and 900,000 Scientific Books in a Week with Seedbox.Io and UltraSeedbox," *Reddit,* 2019, https://www.reddit.com/r/seedboxes/comments/e3yl23/charitable_seeding_update_10_terabytes_and_900000/; u/shrine, "Library Genesis Project Update: 2.5 Million Books Seeded with the World, 80 Million Scientific Articles Next," *Reddit,* 2020, https://www.reddit.com/r/DataHoarder/comments/ed9byj/library_genesis_project_update_25_million_books/.

84 John D. Martin, "Piracy, Public Access, and Preservation: An Exploration of Sustainable Accessibility in a Public Torrent Index," *Proceedings of the Association for Information Science and Technology* 53, no. 1 (2016): 1–6

85 For more on the use of the term "shadow economy," see Ramón Lobato, *Shadow Economies of Cinema: Mapping Informal Film Distribution* (London: Palgrave Macmillan, 2012).

in order to obtain illegally copied objects. In that case, there are many reasons why an agent may do so. However, the reasons vary with the artifact in question. For instance, it is plausible that some software piracy takes place within a business context. Pirate copies of, for instance, Microsoft's Office suite might be obtained by those working within professional office cultures. By contrast, the motivations in obtaining the latest Marvel Cinematic Universe superhero film are less likely to be professional, and it is more likely that such a user would participate to enhance their own leisure time. Likewise, the motivations in obtaining pirate copies of academic books may be very different to the reasons for obtaining the latest heavy metal album, and it would be different ethically too, given that education is an eleemosynary purpose.

Moreover, motivations for acquiring digital artifacts for free through public torrenting and its precursors are often relational to the user and their financial circumstances. For example, consider a 1994 study that found that the individual benefits of pirating software pertained to financial gain, overcoming the challenge of copying, and not having to go out to buy the software.[86] Likewise, a 1997 study found that the most frequent argument for software piracy was that software was too expensive, and end users said that they could not afford to purchase it.[87] The personal circumstances of an individual appear to play a crucial role in why they may download copyrighted material without paying. Generalizing to entire spheres of activity may paint a false picture.

It is possible to speculate near-endlessly about the motivations for participating in the acquisition of illegally copied artifacts, and there have been many studies examining such behav-

---

86 Penny M. Simpson, Debasish Banerjee, and Claude L. Simpson, "Softlifting: A Model of Motivating Factors," *Journal of Business Ethics* 13, no. 6 (1994): 431–38.

87 Hsing K. Cheng, Ronald R. Sims, and Hildy Teegen, "To Purchase or to Pirate Software: An Empirical Study," *Journal of Management Information Systems* 13, no. 4 (1997): 49–60.

ior.[88] However, what seems clear is that, at the crossover point from public to private Bittorrent trackers, there is the beginning of a shift in generalized motivation. While many private Bittorrent users participate because they wish to have access to pirated artifacts, it is also at this step in the pyramid hierarchy that piracy begins to take on a life of its own. That is, some of the structures of private Bittorrent trackers encourage pirates to participate for the sake of piracy, rather than to gain access to new music, films, and software. Whether public or private, while Bittorrent trackers are not formally considered to be part of the Warez Scene, we can begin to see motivational congruence at this point.[89]

The motivational and rule-based structures of such private trackers reveal this shift. Private Bittorrent trackers have strict rules about participation, and they structure participants' ability to download according to a ratio system. For example, the user must have uploaded a certain amount in a ratio to download. Hence a ratio of 1.5 means that the user has uploaded 1.5 times the amount they have downloaded. At first glance, there does not seem to be any particular significance to this, and the motivation remains a desire to have enough upload credit to download new releases. However, it goes further than that. The Project Gazelle tracker that powered What.CD has support for in-built user classes. These range from "Member" through "Elite" and up to "Torrent Master."[90] These user classes sometimes have extraordinary criteria. The default number of uploads, for instance, to become a "Torrent Master," is set in the

88 Moez Limayem, Mohamed Khalifa, and Wynne W. Chin, "Factors Motivating Software Piracy: A Longitudinal Study," *IEEE Transactions on Engineering Management* 51, no. 4 (November 2004): 414–25.

89 For more on this, see Sockanathan, "Digital Desire and Recorded Music," 194; b-bstf, "Guide to Internet Piracy," *2600: Hacker Quarterly* (Summer 2004).

90 What.CD, "Project Gazelle," *GitHub*, 2020, https://github.com/WhatCD/Gazelle.

codebase to 500 uploads.[91] As we will see, ratio and lifetime upload statistics also play a core role in Scene couriering practices.

Given that each upload to a private torrent tracker has significant and rigorous metadata input requirements, and given that running a client setup with 500 local torrents requires substantial computational resource, the existence of these user classes suggests more than simply a desire to earn credits for download.[92] Instead, there is a prestige economy at work here, where users seek recognition, albeit pseudonymous, from their pirating peers. The promotions system used by these private trackers gamifies the uploading process. It makes the activity an end in itself with similar prestige pursuit as the alternative reality game of the Warez Scene. As Blake Durham puts it, private trackers are structured as "prestige econom[ies] primarily organized around the exchange of digital audio files."[93] However, they also animate "a vibrant social ecology in which users regard upload statistics and musical-technical knowledge as symbolic capital."[94] That is, knowledge and ownership play a role in the systems of symbolic exchange and respect.

This system also introduces scarcity to ensure competition and fair play with a strict one-account-per-lifetime rule and an insistence that they will severely punish any rule-breaking. In a similar fashion to the so-called "SceneBan" of the Warez Scene, the idea is that members have one chance, and, if they blow it, they are out. Particularly relevant to private trackers is the default rule, built into the Gazelle codebase, that insists that users "do not trade, sell, give away, or offer accounts."[95] As we will go on to see, this mirrors the language used in the NFO files of the Warez Scene that repeatedly stipulate the noncommercial nature of the enterprise and on which we have already touched.

---

91 What.CD, "Project Gazelle: Sections/Schedule/Index.php," *GitHub*, January 8, 2016, https://github.com/WhatCD/Gazelle.

92 Durham, "Circulatory Maintenance," 205–6.

93 Ibid., 199.

94 Ibid.

95 What.CD, "Project Gazelle: Classes/Rules.Class.php," *GitHub*, November 8, 2016, https://github.com/WhatCD/Gazelle.

On the other hand, private trackers such as What.CD did operate a donation system. The reason for this is clear, for "[o]ne of the principal ironies of the study of extralegal, apparently non-monetary exchange systems such as What.CD is the fundamental necessity of monetary expenses dedicated to maintaining the technical infrastructure of the ecology."[96] With costs of approximately several thousand dollars per month, the infrastructural spending of private Bittorrent trackers precludes an exchange strictly outside the financial sphere, as does the purchase and ongoing maintenance of topsites in the Scene.

To return to our pyramid, in the contemporary digital piracy ecology it is the users who enjoy the game of piracy for its own sake on private Bittorrent trackers who begin to show us the motivations of the higher-level actors. Private Bittorrent trackers are the point at which the participatory but exclusionary prestige regimes of the actual Scene kick in. That said, high-level Warez Scene figures do not recognize the same motivational structure at play in these lower echelons. There is, writes at least one study, "a unanimous anti-P2P feeling amongst Scene members, with all those interviewed making a distinction between 'piracy,' where reliability, quality, and security are protected by the accountability of membership to FXP boards and release groups, and 'filesharing,' seen as an irresponsible quest for 'free content' where users are not invested in the reciprocal exchange of information."[97]

Before returning to the top of the pyramid to which this book is dedicated, there is one further intermediate layer between Bittorrent trackers and the Scene, just mentioned, FXP boards. These secretive boards were especially prominent early in the twenty-first century. However, there is barely any scholarly literature that covers their operations and most of the information that I have managed to garner comes from informal reports, such

96 Durham, "Circulatory Maintenance," 207.
97 Sockanathan, "Digital Desire and Recorded Music," 198.

as Reddit posts.[98] One of the only academic mentions is in Sander Gellaerts's doctoral thesis from Tilburg University in 2015. This is based on legal cases heard in The Hague in 2013, under docket number "ECLI:NL:GHDHA:2013:BZ6496" and in Rotterdam under docket number "ECLI:NL:RBROT:2011:BR5610" in 2011.[99] Andrew Sockanathan's doctoral thesis from Goldsmiths in 2011 likewise contains a section on the history of the Scene that details the operations of these boards.[100] Finally, Mercè Molist Ferrer also writes about FXP boards in her 2014 book, *Hackstory.es: La Historia Nunca Contada del Underground Hacker en la Península Ibérica.* Ferrer's main sources, though, are Wikipedia and the Pub-Crackin 101 Tripod Site, to which I also refer.[101] However, Ferrer also spoke privately with a man called Lluís Ridao, who claimed to be a former FXP board member who corroborates Gellaerts's legal analysis. Finally, some of the below comes from the "Guide to Internet Piracy" published in the Summer 2004 edition of *2600: Hacker Quarterly*.[102]

FXP boards are sites where users post warez on hacked servers. With private membership rosters, the FXP board Scene is in fact even more illegal than almost any of the other levels of the warez pyramid, and it may also be more secretive. Unlike the other levels, FXP board participation involves hacking (i.e., cracking) into computers to establish them as distribution systems without their owners' consent. Specifically, FXP boards operate through four classes of users: administrators (who run the boards), scanners (who seek out vulnerable servers), hack-

98 u/skoyern, "R/Networking—What Happened to FXP?," *Reddit,* 2016, https://www.reddit.com/r/networking/comments/499d1z/what_happened_to_fxp/.

99 ECLI:NL:RBROT:2011:BR5610, voorheen LJN BR5610, 10/600129-08 (Rechtbank Rotterdam, August 24, 2011); ECLI:NL:GHDHA:2013:BZ6496, voorheen LJN BZ6496, 22-004070-11 (Gerechtshof Den Haag, April 8, 2013).

100 Sockanathan, "Digital Desire and Recorded Music," 190.

101 Mercè Molist Ferrer, *Hackstory.es: La Historia Nunca Contada del Underground Hacker en la Península Ibérica* (Spain: published by the author, 2014), 103–4.

102 b-bstf, "Guide to Internet Piracy."

ers (who break into these machines), and fillers (who put warez on the servers). Then, there are two models of FXP boards. One model is a space where boards would find publicly accessible FTP servers that are improperly secured and fill these with warez for others to download. The second is one where members would hack servers to install their own FTP daemons. The process in that second, more common model, usually looks as follows. First, in consultation with hackers, scanners identify a remotely exploitable computer-software vulnerability. Usually, this means finding a piece of vulnerable software and then working out how remotely to identify that software. As a hypothetical example, let us say that a remote-control system called "Vulnerable RC" contains, by mistake on the part of the programmers, an exploitable vulnerability. However, the vulnerability only exists in version 1.24 of the software. Scanners would establish a process that searched the entire range of Internet Protocol (IP) addresses for this software. They would do this by sequentially trying to connect to the default port of this server on every machine address on the internet, sometimes attempting to avoid the IP ranges of known governmental agencies. Once connected, they would only report success if the machine replied with the opening response banner, "Welcome to Vulnerable RC v 1.24," or similar. Often these scanning processes, which take a long time, would run on remote machines. (After all, there are 4.3 billion theoretically accessible IPV4 addresses in the world, even if many of these are reserved and not publicly assignable in reality). These remote machines were hacked themselves but were found not to have sufficient bandwidth to act as a warez store. These remote systems for scanning were known as "scanstros."[103]

Once a scanner has successfully identified a vulnerable server, they pass the details over to a hacker. Hackers then exploit the vulnerable software and install a covert FTP daemon on the machine. As Gellaerts puts it: "[i]n the FXP board case, sus-

103 MantiCore, "AW: SQL scannen lohnt sich das noch?," *raid.rush,* May 3, 2010, https://raidrush.net/threads/sql-scannen-lohnt-sich-das-noch.711040/.

pects were convicted of participating in a criminal organization with the aim of hacking and exchanging copyrighted works. [... T]he Public Prosecution here focused on the forum whose purpose was to hack into computer systems to make use of the disk space and bandwidth so that copyrighted works could quickly be uploaded and downloaded."[104] In keeping with the paradoxical ethical formulations of other Scene levels, there appears to have been a code of honor among this class of otherwise highly illegal actors that forbade them from re-hacking machines that another Board had already compromised. The resulting FTP site is called a "pubstro," which we might speculate to mean "public store" in "leet speak," (more on this later). The hacker then posts the empty box to a section on the Board for "empty stros."

Hackers around the turn of the millennium seemed to favor vulnerabilities on the Windows operating system. These were easier to come by and exploit than their Unix and Linux cousins. For many years, the most common vulnerabilities were a weak Netbios Password that would allow remote execution, a similar setup in DameWare NT Utilities (i.e., a popular remote administration client), or a blank password on a Microsoft SQL Server. Once hackers had found a vulnerability, they would create a batch file on the remote machine, using the "echo" command. This command writes lines to a file. In this case, the hacker would write a series of lines to a file that instructs the server to download new software and to install it. To download the files, the hacker would use the Trivial File Transfer Protocol (TFTP) and then use psexec.exe (a lightweight remote shell program) to execute this file remotely, which would typically then install Serv-U FTP server (an FTP server program) or an IRC bot, giving further access to the machine.[105]

104 Sander Gellaerts, "Watermerken als juridisch bewijsmiddel: Een onderzoek naar de effectiviteit van digitale watermerken als juridisch bewijsmiddel" (PhD diss., Tilburg University, 2015), 188. My translation.

105 b-bstf, "Guide to Internet Piracy."

Hackers sound like an exotic species of computer literati who know what they are doing. It is certainly true that being a hacker at this level involves some computational ability that is beyond most people's competence. However, it would be an overstatement to believe these figures to be supremely competent, able to break into any machine at will. Instead, FXP board hackers appear to have been opportunists who ride on the back of existing exploits. They are unlikely to have crafted their own exploits and instead used prefabricated tools to crack into computers that were already vulnerable. Indeed, some of the higher-level FXP board hackers may have gained access to rare exploits that were not publicly available, giving them an edge on the competition. But most hackers in this area are better defined as "script kiddies" or "tricky kids," as one source puts it.[106] Certainly, being a hacker on an FXP board is nowhere close to the technical skill required of software crackers in the high-level Scene.

Finally, fillers ride in at the last minute and transfer pirate material across to the hacked servers. Usually, fillers seek boxes with large hard-drive capacity and extreme bandwidth. For this reason, scanners usually targeted IP ranges that were on high-speed university links and so forth. Fillers need good warez access, which could be from the topsite Scene or other FXP boards. As with couriering in the Warez Scene itself, FXP board fillers receive praise for beating the competition on speed. Once a filler has populated a stro, they post the resulting hacked server to all of their Boards, credit the hacker and scanner, and bask in the glory of having created a release site.

FXP boards usually ran on vBulletin, an extensible (Hypertext Preprocessor) PHP-based internet forum system. The boards would generally run a modified version of this software, including add-ons such "ShavedApe's Fxp-Pack 3.0.1," packaged within releases with revealing names such as "Vbulletin_3.6.8_Pre_Modded_FXP_Edition_v.1.5." These plugins appear to have added functionality to the base software, such as monitoring

---

106 TonikGin, "IRC XDCC Hacking Exposed," September 11, 2002, http://www.madchat.fr/reseau/IRC_XDCC_Hacking_Exposed.htm.

the uptime of the posted hacked servers, checking whether the login credentials work, and so forth. They also appear to contain discoverability features, such as allowing posters to specify the contents of the stro, thereby making it possible for the board to show all servers that contain a specific release. Of course, the software on which the boards themselves ran was itself pirated. Due to the extreme illegality of FXP boards, which involve hacking or cracking on top of regular pirating activities, membership of such boards was and is not encouraged among those in the actual, high-level Scene.

Nonetheless, the history of FXP boards marks a critical point beyond the threshold of private torrenting in the piracy hierarchy. Membership of FXP boards was confined to an elite cadre of individuals. Competition between boards was fierce. As with the topsite Warez Scene, FXP board members were bound by a code of secrecy about their boards and a code of honor concerning the rules of participation, and it was not permitted to give out information about these sites. Further, sharing pubstros outside of these boards was frowned upon and would cause a user to be banned.

At the same time, an entire culture on IRC developed precisely around sharing the fruits of FXP boards. An example of this is the subculture in FDFNet's oompah list. FDFNet was an IRC network that ran a channel, #warez, in the early years of the twenty-first century. As the name implies, the theme of this channel was clear. The name of the group that ran this channel was "oompah," presumably after Roald Dahl's orientalized, candy-production workers in *Charlie and the Chocolate Factory* (1964).[107] This channel provided users with a downloadable list of warez FTP sites when they entered the channel and typed the command "!list." Most of the sites on the list were from FXP boards.

"The list" is worth a brief detour here as the sociality and interactions around it work in the same way as does much of the

107 *Urban Dictionary*, s.v. "oompah," April 9, 2003, https://www.urbandictionary.com/define.php?term=OOmpah.

piracy ecology, including FXP boards themselves. Those in the true Scene scorned FXP boards. Those on FXP boards scorned the oompah list. In both cases this was due to the threat of exposure of secret cultures to public scrutiny which can also carry legal penalty. Yet the list also exhibits similar motivational characteristics and rewards as FXP boards and the Scene. First, it is notable that while access to the oompah list was open to all, non-contributors experienced "a 6-hour time delayed version of [the] complete list."[108] Access to the full list was available only to those who contributed, thereby gamifying participation. The list also exhorts users: "Don't be a leech. Contribute!" and gives instructions as to how users can add their own sites to the index ("To add a site /msg Balthor SITE xxx.xxx.xxx.xxx /dirs L: & P:").

Further, as with high-level, warez groups, the oompah list put out hardware requests with bounty offers attached: "OOmpah is also looking for shell accounts to run eggdrop bots from. If you can provide a LEGIT eggable shell, please contact manoman. We will reward you."[109] The emphasis on "LEGIT" here is telling because it is clear that the operators of the #warez channel were keenly aware that they would likely receive hacked shells in response to this inquiry. Accepting these could have placed them in legal jeopardy. Like the nuking system in the high-level Scene, covered below in more extensive detail, the oompah list also had a quality-control mechanism: "[i]f you notice any bad sites please help us out by typing '!bad sitenum reason' in #warez. Thanks."[110] A team of moderators then worked to verify whether the claim for "badness" was accurate.

The list provided an overview of content on each site and a rating, but a brief survey of just one of the list outputs clearly shows the link to FXP boards. Consider this site entry:

---

108 oompah, "Site list (sites.txt)," May 3, 2003.
109 Ibid.
110 Ibid.

[92186] <18 Apr 2003 15:37> Rated: 1 rossx

203.251.32.102 / l:ENVY-FXP p:ENVY-FXP port:50000

bridge 3000-eph, chess 2003-eph, fim speedway grand prix-flt, indiana jack-flt, pet racer-flt, pet soccer-flt

The site in question here is running on the IP address 203.251.32.102 on port 50000. It contains the games Bridge 3000, Chess 2003, and some racing and sports games. Notably, though, the login and password are both "ENVY-FXP." While no public trace record remains of ENVY FXP, apart from the oompah list, it is safe to assume that ENVY FXP was an FXP board. The high port, the login and password, and the fact that the warez resides at the root ("/") on this server are giveaways of its hacked status.[111]

The oompah list also contains public, anonymous FTPs with warez hidden on them, that is, the first type of FXP board output that I mentioned. Consider the following site entry:

[92636] <20 Apr 2003 09:02> Rated: 1 RaouL

137.68.225.12 /leebt/homepage/icon/ / %;^^;% /AUX/PUB/ l:anonymous p:i.test.ca port:21

discreet 3dsmax v4.2-tfl, fifa 2002-flt, magix video deluxe v1.02-mage, mechwarrior 4 black knight expansion-flt, shrek game land activity-eph

While this site looks similar to the previous example, several interesting characteristics are not present in the preceding case. First, the login name here is "anonymous." The password appears to be simply a generic email address (i.e., the user could login to the anonymous account using any password). Most significant, though, is the pathname that is given: "/leebt/home-

111 Ibid.

page/icon/ / %;^^;% /AUX/PUB/." Instead of the pirated material living at the precise directory where one logs in ("/"), this site hides its warez inside a directory maze. The space in the filename, the special character "%," "^," and ";" as well as the restricted system keyword "AUX" means that it is not possible directly to navigate this tree using an FTP client. It is also likely that the site will contain hundreds of directories at every level, meaning that someone who stumbles upon the site is unlikely ever to find this directory by chance. In short, the only way that an end-user would find the warez on this server is by knowing the exact location where it is stored—a common tactic used by FXP boards when filling public servers and that the oompah list reveals.[112]

As noted before, the oompah list and others like it were deemed "pub stealers"—ironically, for a culture that thrives on taking the work of others without permission. However, a whole, lower system developed that fed off the illicit activities of the FXP board scene. Tools such as user clown's "locksmith" emerged that would allow a user to crack the directory mazes on public FTP servers, find other boards' work, and allow sharing against their wishes.[113] Given the commensurate damage of computer hacking compounding the existing illegality of multimedia piracy and although the FXP board scene's risks seem higher, I have found very few references to criminal prosecution for participation apart from the listed cases above.

However, to close this section on motivations, it should be noted that the FXP board scene, like the private torrent tracker scene, was highly organized and coordinated. However, hierarchies of FXP board memberships lent a different motivational structure to participation. Forum posts from purported members list a vast network of underground FXP boards, including: Rosevalley, MB-FXP, Riverndale, Innovation of Darkness, IllusionFXP, DFF, Saccon, Undieable Warriors, Enter by Force, eVolite, Legends of the Unspoken Minds, Voice of the Scene,

112 Ibid.
113 "Pub-Crackin 101," *PC-FXP*, http://pc-fxp.tripod.com/pc101.htm.

VoCHT, WDRC, equinox, Aurora, Tension, Peace'n'Warez, Jinxed, Sentinels of Light, Skilled, phoenix, UnderGround Council, Apocalypse, DupeFXP, Evolution, eMOTiONDVD, iGNiTiON, TMC StormFXP, Spuitkak-FXP, and others.[114]

It can be assumed that FXP board Sceners participated in their activities with the same zeal and abstract motivation as their analogs in the topsite Scene. It is clear that if one simply wanted access to the latest pirated materials, there are far easier ways to go about this than to join an FXP board. The latter involves learning its rules and codes of conduct and engaging in highly illegal scanning and hacking activities. Instead, it seems evident that those who participated in FXP board cultures sought status and respect among their peers. Who would be the best-known hacker? Who had access to more elusive exploits? Which scanners could consistently turn up new, fast, and exploitable ranges? And which fillers had genuine courier access to topsites, that would then allow them to filter down their warez from the topsite scene? Far from being an effort to ensure the broadest, public dissemination of pirated material, the FXP board scene should be considered another closed enclave, driven by elitist principles rather than any altruistic benefit. It is, then, hard to make the analogy of the "digital commons" work here, as it was hard to see this at many other levels of the piracy pyramid. In this sense, while many wish to romanticize digital piracy and to view it as a liberatory phenomenon, piracy goes through the same cycles of enclosure as any other digital space.

UNDERGROUND CRAFT

The etymology, history, and development of piracy and pirate imagery are far more convoluted than its most contemporary appropriation by digital copyright lobbyists can countenance. As Gary Hall notes, the etymological root of "pirate" in ancient Greece is one where "the pirate is someone who tries, tests, teas-

---

114 Bliendbos, "Zijn hier ook nog ouwe fxp-ers ?," *FOK!forum*, November 19, 2016, https://forum.fok.nl/topic/1831163/1/999.

es, and troubles, as well as attacks."[115] I here take from Hall's work his broader sense in which piracy "is not opposed to capitalism" but is instead "fundamental to it," embracing the negative critique of piracy's replicative potential.[116] Models of capital replicate themselves within subcultures of digital piracy.

When most people think of digital piracy, they think of the public-facing sources that I have just covered—the popular manifestations and accessible incarnations of home copyright violation. However, this is a poor reflection of the Scene's submerged and elite culture that has operated on a secretive and hierarchical basis of suppliers, couriers, release groups, and topsites for several decades.[117] Even existing books that detail the cultures of internet piracy in quite some depth sometimes misunderstand, mischaracterize, and overlook this high-level, elite core. For instance, John Gantz and Jack B. Rochester's *Pirates of the Digital Millennium: How the Intellectual Property Wars Damage Our Personal Freedoms, Our Jobs, and the World Economy* runs to 294 pages. The text is high on didactic questions: "[w]hat did you think about downloading copyrighted media when you began reading this chapter? [...] What new information have you gleaned from reading it?"[118] But this work, like many others, is low on coverage of the inner mechanisms of piracy, its supply chains, its political economies, and its aesthetics.[119]

Before moving to detail its actual workings, in this penultimate section of my second chapter I want to set out how the upper echelon of the piracy pyramid is a site of skill and craft. These may sound odd terms to apply to those who spend their time working illegally to disseminate material to which they do

115 Hall, *Pirate Philosophy,* xiv.

116 Ibid., 140.

117 Virginia Crisp, *Film Distribution in the Digital Age: Pirates and Professionals* (London: Palgrave Macmillan, 2017), 105–6.

118 John Gantz and Jack B. Rochester, *Pirates of the Digital Millennium: How the Intellectual Property Wars Damage Our Personal Freedoms, Our Jobs, and the World Economy* (Upper Saddle River: Prentice Hall, 2005), 88.

119 There are a few sporadic mentions of Scene activities in this book but for the most part they go unmentioned. Ibid., 211.

not own the copyright. However, until we grasp the considerable level of proficiency in this space, we will fail to understand why individuals choose to participate in these activities across both technical and artistic zones. Without this distinction, we will also incorrectly posit a simple lineage between those working to release pirated material and those who merely consume such outputs on social media.

While Chapter Three examines in detail the technical infrastructures and social roles of individuals within the Warez Scene, a few upfront examples will demonstrate the multiple levels of expertise present at the top of this pyramid. Take, for instance, the crackers — the individuals tasked with removing the protection systems on pirated games and apps in the space of the software piracy Scene. To understand the skill and craft involved in the cracking process, one must first know a little about how computer programs work. Most code for contemporary games and software applications is written in a high-level language such as C. Computer programming languages, like C, allow programmers to write code more comprehensibly than lower-level languages, such as assembly. For instance, the C statement "int x = 133;" assigns the number "133" to an integer ("int") variable called "x." However, computers cannot understand the instructions in the forms given in languages such as C. Instead, they work on lower-level instruction sets that might, for instance, be equivalent to: "move the number 133 into a memory location" ("mov DWORD PTR [rbp-0xc],0x85"). It should instantly be evident that the C incarnation of this statement is far easier to read and to understand than is the assembly instruction, which is, in fact, not even itself the lowest level language.

When programmers write their code in C or other high-level languages, it must be translated into an executable format. This is a process called compilation. This usually takes the form of producing a byte or object code that can be switched back to a set of assembly instructions, but that cannot easily be retranslated back into the original language, C. That is, the version of the program that will be distributed to users can, albeit with some difficulty, be turned back into assembly language. But it cannot be translated back into the more user-friendly form of C.

Crackers aim to modify the logic of program flow to circumvent copy control measures. A typical, digital rights management protection routine might be to evaluate a set of conditions (e.g., "are the checksums on the binaries as they should be?," "is the serial code valid?," "is anyone else in the world using the same serial code?") and then to switch execution to the anti-piracy code. That is, the code will follow this type of logic:

> IF [GAME HAS BEEN PIRATED], GO TO 2: [ANTI-PIRACY FUNCTION]
>
> ELSE, GO TO 1: [NORMAL EXECUTION]
>
> 1: [NORMAL EXECUTION]
>
> 2: [ANTI-PIRACY FUNCTION]

Typically, this logic will be extremely convoluted and made deliberately difficult to understand. Crackers seek to modify this logic so that, regardless of whether the "IF [GAME HAS BEEN PIRATED]" statement evaluates to true, it is always the "1: [NORMAL EXECUTION]" function that is run, rather than the anti-piracy function.

However, to make this modification, crackers only have access to the compiled version of the code, not the original C version.[120] This means that they must work to understand the code at the lowest possible of levels and then patch this version for general consumption. Even worse, anti-piracy detection often seeks to ascertain whether this type of reverse-engineering and patching has been performed, which I cover more extensively in Chapter Five. Therefore, crackers must be aware of the un-

120 Sigi Goode and Sam Cruise, "What Motivates Software Crackers?" *Journal of Business Ethics* 65, no. 2 (May 2006): 174.

intended consequences of modifying binary executables. Every change that they make risks triggering another booby trap.

This is all to say that being a cracker in a release group is an incredibly demanding job. As David Tetzlaff puts it, "[t]here aren't that many true crackers" and "[f]or every true cracker or hacker there are countless numbers of mere pirates."[121] Crackers are in short supply because cracking is one of the most challenging programming tasks that it is possible to imagine: to work against the flow with a decompiled binary file to enable an alternative desired execution flow. As with other types of computer information security roles, this type of breakage is akin to an incredibly elaborate puzzle that the cracker must solve to succeed. The escalating war between ever-more elaborate forms of Digital Rights Management (DRM) and the growing skill of crackers makes for a fascinating standoff. It also demonstrates to some extent the intellectual respect, if not legal or moral respect, that we should accord to such individuals.

Likewise, one might wish to consider the operational skill of siteops. Perhaps the number one condition desired by those participating in the Warez Scene is that law enforcement cannot detect their activity. Siteops, therefore, deploy a range of technologies and social mechanisms to protect themselves from the police, covered more thoroughly in the next chapter. These include addlines that specify the ident protocol, which will tie a user to a particular IP address; site "bouncers" that mask or cloak the true IP address of a warez topsite; and, of course, generally ensuring best practices for information security (e.g., patching software on the server, using encryption protocols, and so on).

Siteops, although slightly separate from hardware providers, must also work to ensure that their sites are of a high technical capacity. In the period studied by this book and surfaced in the DeFacto2 archive, gigabit symmetrical connections were the norm with multiple terabytes of storage space in Redundant Ar-

121 David Tetzlaff, "Yo-Ho-Ho and a Server of Warez," in *The World Wide Web and Contemporary Cultural Theory: Magic, Metaphor, Power,* eds. Andrew Herman and Thomas Swiss (New York: Routledge, 2000), 107.

ray of Independent Disks (RAID) configurations. As this type of hardware, particularly the high-capacity network connections, was hard to come by at a reasonable price, many topsites resided on university premises where this infrastructure was readily available.[122] For instance, Pirates with Attitude (PWA)'s flagship topsite ran at the University of Sherbrook, undoubtedly without permission.[123] This in turn meant that siteops required extensive skills to mask the site's presence on campus from the watchful eyes of legitimate systems administrators.[124]

As will become apparent in Chapter Six, siteops are not always successful in keeping their activities hidden. Hence, the stakes are high in this game. After all, the coordinated nature of the Warez Scene usually pushes its activities into the category of criminal conspiracy to violate copyright rather than mere civil wrongs of copyright violations against individuals and corporations. The prison sentences for such conspiracies can be lengthy, so the skill and craft of siteops are a matter of crucial import. Furthermore, Sceners routinely shame insecure sites, and a negative reputation for information security is likely to lose the site affiliates.

The crafts and skills of the Scene are also what make studies like this possible. Archives such as DeFacto2 exist because participants seek credit for their work and ability. Were there no skill and no seeking of credit, it is unlikely that the Warez Scene would be as known as it is.

---

122 Huizing and Wal, "Explaining the Rise and Fall of the Warez MP3 Scene."

123 Goldman, "Warez Trading and Criminal Copyright Infringement," 25.

124 The tell-tale sign of a topsite on campus is short, sporadic bursts of high-speed data transfers both incoming and outgoing from a limited subset of IP addresses. However, as bandwidth capacity has increased and P2P networks have become increasingly common, in the period between that covered by the documentation to which I have access and the contemporary Warez Scene, it is not clear whether or not such sites have become harder to detect.

THREE

Infrastructures of the Scene

In Chapter Two, I examined the portions of the piracy world that are not the Warez Scene. In a more positive vein, this chapter now turns to outline the systems that do make up this highest level of the piracy pyramid. In reverse engineering the functions of various elements of the Scene, I explore the set of technical infrastructures that underpins the social interactions constituting this alternative reality game. Infrastructures are a set of interlocking technical architectures. Yet what is infrastructure at its core and how does it help us to understand the Scene? How do we recognize it? And how might we study it?

In her well-known article, "The Ethnography of Infrastructure," the sociologist Susan Leigh Star famously made a call to study infrastructures, which at the same time was a call to study "boring things."[1] In this phrasing Star is of course being a little coy. The first examples that she gives are the International Classification of Diseases (ICD) and the telephone book, both of which can seem mundane and ordinary or even "boring" but both of which can tell us several interesting things. For instance, Star points out that a telephone book reveals a great deal about the demographics of an area through how businesses present themselves, for example, restaurants and ethnicity. The ICD is

1 Susan Leigh Star, "The Ethnography of Infrastructure," *American Behavioral Scientist* 43, no. 3 (1999): 377.

likewise essential and exciting because it shows precisely what is considered a disease or illness and what lies outside of that purview. Given the degree of controversy around medical diagnoses of psychiatric complaints and volumes such as the Diagnostic and Statistical Manual of Mental Disorders (DSM), Star knows that the ICD tells us a lot too about that most socially studied of fields: medicine. While these objects appear tedious and routinized — "boring things" — we can learn things through their study.

The same is true of the software and hardware infrastructures of the Scene. These are the architectures that, although impressive in themselves, exist merely to support the social structures of the Scene. However, they form the core interface point that most individuals have when interacting with this underground piracy network. Indeed, the software and hardware facilities run by Scene operatives can be described according to the taxonomy that Star sets out in her article. We can describe elements of the Scene in terms of their

- Embeddedness: the servers and networks are "sunk into and inside of other structures." This is especially the case with the ways in which existing, public architectures are often repurposed in the Scene, such as university high-speed connections or public Internet Relay Chat (IRC) networks, running private chat channels for Scene activities.

- Transparency: the infrastructure that "invisibly supports" the tasks of Scene operatives.

- Reach or scope: these infrastructures have "reach beyond a single event or one-site practice." The diversity of materials disseminated among Scene members, ranging from music, to films, to software, to games often comes with different requirements from the infrastructure, which is adaptive to such needs. The generic model of File Transfer Protocol

(FTP) servers is one that can easily be repurposed when new media formats come along.

- Learned as part of membership: communities of practice, such as the Scene, take their infrastructures for granted. No member of the Scene will be willing, in most circumstances, to explain how things work to a "noob" (i.e., a "newbie" or someone who has just entered the space). Either you know, or you don't. Of course, this is not actually strictly the case or nobody new would ever join. It simply means that the level of tacit knowledge among Scene members is great and transmission takes place through private channels of mentorship alongside observational practices.

- Links with conventions of practice: there is a type of path dependency on past conventions. Star gives the example of the QWERTY keyboard but the naming scheme for Scene releases (e.g., "Aeon_Zen-Inveritas-WEB-2019-ENTiTLED") is a good example of something that developed over time but that has now become established practice, for reasons that will become clear. It appears very hard to change existing Scene practices. Once norms of practice have been embedded and validated, they become widespread and inflexible. A good example of this, to which I will turn, is the development of custom FTP daemons in the earlier years of the Scene, later replaced by the widespread adoption of glftpd, a piece of server software.

- Embodiment of standards: infrastructures work with other infrastructures through common interfaces. As we will see, the FTP servers of the Scene are no different, and, while sites isolate themselves from one another for security reasons, they also take advantage of the File eXchange Protocol (FXP) hack to allow direct transmission between servers. The rulesets that form the standards for each type of release (analyzed in more detail in Chapter Four) are further evidence of the importance of standardization for Scene practices.

- Becomes visible upon breakdown: the invisibility of infrastructure fades away when it breaks. The legal busts of the Scene are good examples of the failures of Scene infrastructure but also its social patterns. Sites that have unreliable uptime or that behave erratically reveal infrastructural fault lines that draw attention to the quotidian nature of much of the technical architecture.[2]

Bearing these points in mind throughout this chapter, the infrastructural components of the Warez Scene to which I will now turn can be subdivided into several discrete levels: topsites, IRC channels, bouncer systems, and command-and-control systems. Throughout, I will refer to the characteristics of the Scene's infrastructures toward which Star's framework points in order to understand how the technical components of the Scene facilitate its operation. As a point of note, most of the specifications that I detail come from around the turn of the millennium, the year 2000, gleaned from the DeFacto2 archive. It is likely and possible that many specific technological elements are now changed and work under different systems.

TOPSITE ARCHITECTURES

A topsite ("site") is a high-bandwidth (by now at least gigabit), high-storage (tens to hundreds of terabytes) FTP site with affiliated release groups. Topsites are usually named and also given a two to three-letter abbreviation that identifies the site with greater safety than the full name (e.g., TWH is "The Wolves House").[3] The abbreviation is, in some cases, phonetic rather than an acronym (e.g., SLR is "The Cellar").[4] Mentioning the

---

2 All references ibid.

3 For an example of site name abbreviations see CWS, "Courier Weektop ScoreCard 001 (cws001.txt)," February 9, 1998, DeFacto2; TWH, "The Wolves House Topsite (TWH-the.wolves.house.1999.12.30.nfo)," December 30, 1999, DeFacto2, warez.scene.nfo.collection.v1.0.24351.shroo.ms.zip.

4 SLR, "The Cellar Topsite (SLR-the.cellar.1998.11.08.nfo)," November 8, 1998, DeFacto2, warez.scene.nfo.collection.v1.0.24351.shroo.ms.zip.

full name or even sometimes just the abbreviation of a site to a user not on the site is usually an offence that will incur deletion ("deluser").[5] Topsites are the core infrastructure of the Warez Scene. They are the places where pirate artifacts are released and traded. They are the archives that contain the files and the history of the Scene. Topsites are the sacred spaces of this world. It is hard to get into them, and it is hard to keep one's account.

Before the FTP era of the Scene, pirates would dial in to a particular Bulletin Board System (BBS) site to upload or download material and communicate with others.[6] Such BBS sites have been labeled the origins of virtual community by the Communication Studies scholar Fred Turner, and they provided the first truly virtual social space, rooted in the background of the American 1960s counterculture.[7] Despite this framing, it is also clear that the BBS scene was geographically dispersed, with segmented underground cultures in countries as diverse as Italy, Portugal, and Uganda.[8] Although BBSs were a revolution in terms of international communication, such systems also had the disadvantage of monopolizing a telephone line while a user was connected. This exclusivity made connecting to more than one board a painful process.[9] The switch to FTP took place as a move to embrace the interconnectedness of the internet during the general demise of BBS in the period between 1994 and

5 "Topsite Rules," *ReScene*, 2020, http://rescene.wikidot.com/topsite-rules#toc4.

6 Andrew Sockanathan, "Digital Desire and Recorded Music: OiNK, Mnemotechnics and the Private BitTorrent Architecture" (PhD diss., Goldsmiths, University of London, 2011), 175–76; Patryk Wasiak, "Telephone Networks, BBSes, and the Emergence of the Transnational 'Warez Scene,'" *History and Technology* 35, no. 2 (2019): 177–94.

7 Fred Turner, "Where the Counterculture Met the New Economy: The WELL and the Origins of Virtual Community," *Technology and Culture* 46, no. 3 (2005): 485–512.

8 "International Scenes," *Phrack Magazine*, January 9, 1996, http://phrack.org/issues/65/15.html.

9 Douglas Thomas, *Hacker Culture* (Minneapolis: University of Minnesota Press, 2002), 118.

1996.[10] Ben Garrett, the maintainer of the DeFacto2 archive, describes how the BBS Scene faded after the closure of New York's Park Central system in 1996. This central communication board was, as he puts it, "the ring and the referee" of deciding which groups had won a particular race to release a piece of software, a phrasing that chimes with my later analysis of the quasi-judicial nature of Scene rule documents.[11]

It is beyond the scope and remit of this book to give a comprehensive history of the BBS pirate Scene, which has already been covered elsewhere.[12] Importantly for the subject at hand, from 1994 to 1996, there emerged two parallel Scenes, with the BBS Scene existing alongside the emergent internet Scene. As Garrett describes it, this bifurcation led to challenges for the official status of releases. With the parallel Scenes in operation, a confusing situation emerged "where there was one group winning the release on the BBS scene and another winning on the internet."[13] This duality was unsustainable and, after Operation Cyber Strike shut down a number of significant BBS sites (an event that I cover in Chapter Six), the Scene decided to transfer to a series of secretive internet FTP servers.[14]

The rival standard into which the Scene could have branched is the ubiquitous Hypertext Transfer Protocol (HTTP) and Hypertext Markup Language (HTML) combination that forms the contemporary web. That is, the Scene could have become based on the web. As was covered in Chapter Two, the FXP board Scene went in this direction, although this subset nonetheless uses the web-facing component to share hacked FTP sites. In many ways, this structure makes sense as a path from BBS sites: the logical successor of BBSs is online forums. For instance, the

10 Wasiak, "Telephone Networks, BBSes, and the Emergence of the Transnational 'Warez Scene.'"

11 Ben Garrett, "Online Software Piracy of the Last Millennium," April 27, 2004, 4, DeFacto2, http://www.defacto2.net/file/download/a53981.

12 See, for instance, Wasiak, "Telephone Networks, BBSes, and the Emergence of the Transnational 'Warez Scene.'"

13 Garrett, "Online Software Piracy of the Last Millennium," 4.

14 Ibid.

leading provider of forum software is called vBulletin. At first, some warez topsites likely did move to HTML forums, but, for protocol reasons, FTP won out. While one lower portion of the piracy world moved over onto internet forum boards, albeit still using FTP, the other, the portion to which this book is dedicated, instead went down the route of FTP and IRC.

In any case, FTP proved to be a valuable tool for the Scene. Given that the nature of the Scene involves the transfer of files, a protocol that is designed purely for file transfer made sense. Indeed, basic knowledge and understanding of the FTP protocol are critical to comprehend the Scene's transfer systems and "racing," covered below. In turn, understanding FTP also requires some comprehension of network socket communications, which I will roughly attempt to convey here.

In the TCP/IPV4 protocol, on which most of the internet operates, every server (i.e., computer) is assigned an address.[15] These generally take the following form: 192.168.0.1.[16] Server software "listens" on a port on these addresses, so a web server might listen on port 80. This would mean that if I connected to 192.168.0.1 at port 80, I could expect to find a web server. FTP is implemented by FTP server software (i.e., a "daemon"). As there are 4,294,967,296 possible IPV4 addresses in the world (though many are reserved for special purposes and a figure that has been drastically superseded by the 340 trillion trillion trillion addresses in IPV6), and as each IPV4 address has 65,535 ports, FTP on the internet seemed an excellent way for the Scene to hide its activities while allowing those in the know to connect.

15 Some servers share addresses and use translation technologies such as Network Address Translation (NAT) to route the packet to the correct machine on a local network, but for the purposes of simple explanation, the generalization that "every machine on the internet has an IP address" is fine.

16 The address that I use as an example here is in a reserved range for local networks. That is, the 192 range that I here use as an example can in reality only be used for local addresses and not on the global internet. Another example of a reserved IPV4 address is 127.0.0.1, the address that a computer can always use to refer to itself.

Finding Scene operations by chance, Sceners reasoned, would be like locating a needle in a haystack.

FTP was born in 1971 in RFC 114, the "Request for Comment" system that the Internet Engineering Task Force uses to discuss new proposed specifications.[17] It died, to some extent, in 2020, when major web browsers deprecated support for the protocol.[18] FTP, as it exists today, uses a command channel to specify client-server interactions and various data channels to transfer the contents of files. The protocol begins, as with all network operations, with a server daemon listening on a port. In conventional or legitimate FTP servers, this port is usually 21, but for stealth, Scene topsites usually run on much higher port numbers, making it harder to guess their location. Next, a client connects and is presented with a banner message while the server then awaits authentication. A typical connection and authentication process for a regular FTP daemon and client might look as follows:

Server: 220 FTPD ready
Client: USER mpeve
Server: 331 Password required for mpeve.
Client: PASS password
Server: 230 User mpeve logged in.

In the File Transfer Protocol, responses are prefixed by a number that indicates the server's state. This makes it easier for clients to ensure that they issue the correct directives at the right time. Each digit in the response indicates a different status. The leftmost digit, for instance, indicates the success or failure of the command (1xx = positive preliminary reply; 2xx = positive completion reply; 3xx = positive intermediate reply, etc.). The middle digit shows to what the status pertains (e.g., x3x indicates

17 A.K. Bhushan, "File Transfer Protocol," *Internet Engineering Task Force,* April 16, 1971, https://tools.ietf.org/html/rfc114.

18 Catalin Cimpanu, "Chrome 87 Released with Fix for NAT Slipstream Attacks, Broader FTP Deprecation," *ZDNet,* November 17, 2020, https://www.zdnet.com/article/chrome-87-released-with-fix-for-nat-slipstream-attacks-broader-ftp-deprecation/.

that the status relates to authentication and identification). The final digit specifies the precise status. Hence, the "331" response is a positive, intermediate reply pertaining to authentication and means the server needs the password for the specified account.

When a user wishes to transfer a file to or from an FTP server, they use a set of commands that instruct the server either to listen for a data connection or to initiate a data connection to a remote system. These two commands are called, respectively, "PASV" (passive mode) and "PORT" (active mode). In PASV mode, the server listens on an additional port and returns a response to the user's client, telling them what this port is. A typical response to the PASV command might read "227 Entering Passive Mode (192,168,0,1,216,4)." This would mean that the server was now listening on the IP address 192.168.0.1 on port 55300. (For reasons that are too complicated to explain, the port is calculated from the last two digits through this formula: 216 x 256 + 4.) Usually, the client would then connect to this address and port and begin receiving or sending data on this second channel.

FTP can also work the other way around. The active PORT command is the inverse of PASV. In this case, the client listens on a port (let us use 55300 again) and tells the server to connect to its own address. So let us say that a client's address was 192.168.0.2. A typical PORT command might read, "PORT 192,168,0,2,216,4." Once this command has been issued, the FTP server will attempt to connect to 192.168.0.2 on port 55300 and then send or receive data on that channel.

As noted, usually in FTP, when a PASV or PORT command is opened, the client either connects to the server to send or receive data, or the server connects to the client. That is, normally, the parties using the data connection will be the same as on the command channel: The server and the client. However, although some servers do enforce this, ensuring that only an authorized party can connect, much of the Warez Scene exploits a vulnerability here to enact high-speed transfers between FTP servers without needing to download the file to the client machine and then upload it to the second site. This site-to-site transfer is called File eXchange Protocol (FXP).

How does this work? The simple answer is that a client can instruct one server to listen (PASV) and then issues a PORT command to another server telling it to connect to that server. In this way, two remote FTP servers can directly transfer files to one another. Consider the following example situation: we have a client (192.168.0.1), a server (192.168.0.2), and another server (192.168.0.3). The client connects to both servers and, at the appropriate moment, issues the following commands:

Client to Server 1: PASV
Server 1: 227 Entering Passive Mode (192,168,0,2,216,4)
Client to Server 2: PORT 192,168,0,2,216,4
Server 2: 200 PORT command successful.

When the client then initiates a transfer command ("RETR" [retrieve] or "STOR" [store]), the servers will connect to each other, rather than to the client, and the file will be transferred from server to server.

Why is this important? Warez topsites are extremely high-bandwidth servers. They have powerful connections that far outstrip the capacity of clients using residential internet systems (see the Appendix for known hardware links among a range of millennial-era topsites, indicating far-above-average connection speeds, usually of the "T1," "T3," "OC48" types and other high-capacity lines). The user class called "couriers" or "traders," descended from the brokers of the antecedent BBS Scene, "race" releases from one site to another in exchange for download credit.[19] To do so, couriers must transfer the files in new releases as fast as they can (and before others) from servers that already have the release to those that do not, provided the rules permit the release on the destination. Were this conducted by downloading each file to the local machine, using a home connection,

19 "A Day in the Life of a Warez Broker," *Phrack Magazine*, 1995, http://phrack.org/issues/47/20.html.

and then uploading it to the second server, the race would unfold at tortoise pace. Instead, the high-speed, high-octane nature of trading from site-to-site is enhanced using FXP.[20]

That said, some couriers instead use a method called shell trading—using high-speed remote boxes to move the files. This consists of using their local storage as an intermediary and then uploading to multiple sites.[21] This latter method has the advantage, first, of using download credits only on a single source, and second, of leaving slots open on other sites. That is, in traditional sites, one may not download using two accounts at the same time. FXP locks a download slot from a site. Hence, if one is trying to upload to multiple sites, there are several ways of doing this, but shell-trading is the most efficient in leaving slots open (see Figures 3 and 4). Nonetheless, FXP couriering is still an efficient manipulation of the FTP standard as couriers can chain their sites together; for instance, in Figure 3, it would be possible to move the file from Site 1 to Site 2, then to Site 3, and so on. However, the speed at which races take place means that the shell trader who can lock the files during the transfer, using a shell trade, will have a distinct advantage.

Scene servers leverage other enhanced features of the FTP protocol. For instance, Scene FTP servers are additionally secured through multiple levels of authentication and authorization, on top of that provided by regular FTP. The foremost of these is the "AUTH TLS" extension to FTP specified in RFC 2228 (another Request for Comment document) to provide transport layer security to the site's command channel.[22] This means

20 For instance, see lester, "The Art of Good Trading," *Netmonkey Weekly Report* (nwr28.txt), December 22, 1998, DeFacto2.

21 See Lord Rameses, "Interview with hodd of VOLiTiON," *Courier Weektop Scorecard* (CwS-116.txt), September 3, 2000, DeFacto2; Lord Rameses, "Interview with Seraph of XCRYPT," *Courier Weektop Scorecard* (CwS-118.txt), September 17, 2000, DeFacto2.

22 Steven J. Lunt, "FTP Security Extensions," *Internet Engineering Task Force,* October 1997, https://tools.ietf.org/html/rfc2228. See also greyline, "glftpd-LNX-2.04_1.0.1e-glFTPD TLS README (2+deb7u3_x86_docs/README.TLS.txt)," *mewbies.com,* 2014, http://mewbies.com/glftpd-LNX-2.04_1.0.1e-2+deb7u3_x86_docs/README.TLS.txt.

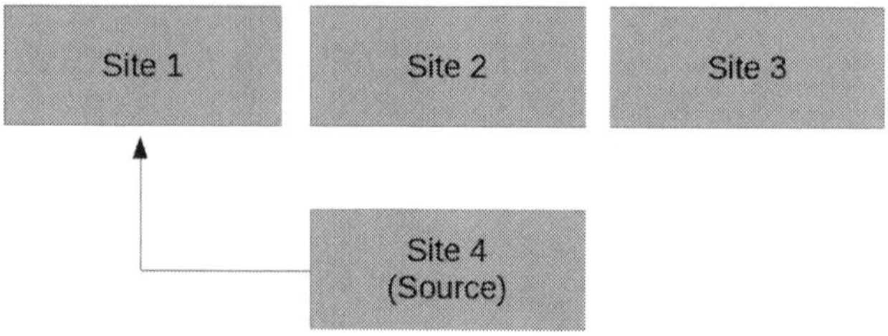

Figure 3. FXP showing single site to site transfer.

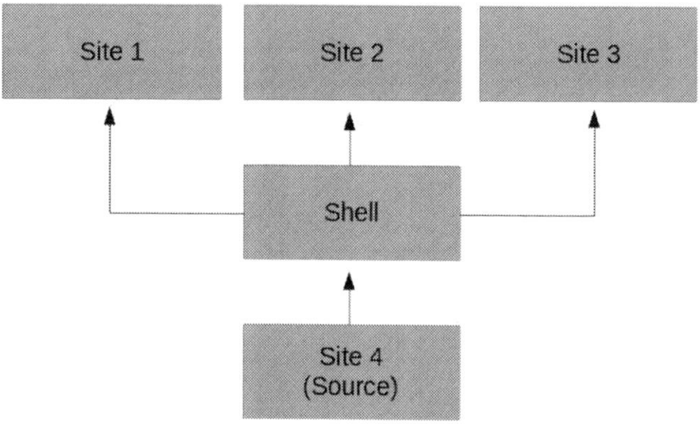

Figure 4. Shell trading showing transfer to multiple sites from single source.

that all communication between the server and the client is encrypted and cannot be intercepted (i.e., end-to-end encryption). The same is true of the data channel in FXP transfers between servers, which clients can initiate through the "PROT" command, ensuring that data transferred between sites cannot be intercepted.

Scene servers and members additionally use the IDENTD protocol alongside IP authentication to identify users.[23] This protocol allows the user's identification by a string of text in front of their IP address. So, for instance, my ident might be "martin@192.168.0.1." The "martin" part is specified by the daemon listening on my IP address on port 113 for incoming requests. Specifically, the IDENT protocol distinguishes between users on a single machine or network who share an IP address. So let us say that I share the IP 192.168.0.1 with my brother, Richard. When I connect, my IDENTD tells the server that it is me, "martin," and not "richard," who is connecting, which serves as an additional, albeit potentially spoofable, level of authentication. Topsites will typically not send a 220 banner until a user with a correct IDENT and IP connects, thereby concealing that an FTP server exists at an address and port. Evidence for the use of IDENTD is prevalent in Scene magazines, such as the interview with Redbone of RTS in the *Courier Weektop Scorecard* issue 130. Here it is noted that tight IDENT and IP-based authentication are required and that "lame" (i.e., insecure) "ip masks like *@xxx.xxx* and ident@xxx.xxx.* are no longer accepted."[24] Once a user has passed the IP mask check and the IDENTD check, and it is known that there is a possible user matching, the server initiates a standard FTP

23 For an instance of mistaken identity using the ident protocol, see Rebel Chicken, "That Wasn't You?" *Reality Check Network* (RCN-20.txt), 1996, DeFacto2; Brian Baskin et al., *Netcat Power Tools,* ed. Jan Kanclirz (Burlington: Syngress Publishing, Inc, 2008), 119.

24 skimp, "Interview with Redbone of RTS," *Courier Weektop Scorecard* (CwS-130.txt), December 16, 2000, DeFacto2.

authentication process, which then places the user in the appropriate role-based authorization.[25]

When users are invited to a site, they must give the site operator or group administrator their "addline." This command will add the user to the site, specifying their login name, password, and ident. In theory, common security precautions should pertain to addlines. For instance, users are encouraged to have only a temporary password in their addline that they later change. According to many of the "Scene notice" packs that contain warning announcements, the reason for this is the presence of "addline stealers." One of these documents, for instance, cautions that "when someone just pm you to add you to his leet gigabit.nl [a site in the Netherlands with a gigabit connection] or something like that, he just want your addline."[26] These documents warn that users should "use [a] temp password and change it in first login" and "use [a] diffrent [*sic*] password for each site."[27] Indeed, the threat of a security breach is high. Further Scene notices speak of how "some people got weird msges about a guy asking their addline and they gave it and he hacked their user on sites" while others detail instances of site operators being compromised.[28] Of course, such a "ploy to steal ppls addlines" is also dependent on IP address masking via ident.[29] That is, in order to benefit from knowing someone's addline, even if the password is shared between sites, a would-be hacker would still need to obtain an address within the IP mask, thereby miti-

---

25 greyline, "glFTPD Configuration File Examples (glftpd-LNX-2.04_1.0.1e-2+deb7u3_x86_docs/glftpd.conf-EXAMPLES.txt)," *mewbies.com*, 2014, http://mewbies.com/glftpd-LNX-2.04_1.0.1e-2+deb7u3_x86_docs/glftpd.conf-EXAMPLES.txt.

26 Site.Info.Leaker.READ.NFO.Updated-iND (screamia.updated.nfo)," n.d., DeFacto2, warez-scene-notices-2006-2010.

27 Ibid.

28 "Scene.Ban.SCR.and.RiDERz.Leader.READNFO-iND (Scene.Ban.SCR.and.RiDERz.Leader.READNFO-iND.nfo)," n.d., DeFacto2, warez-scene-notices-2006-2010; "Scene.Notice.FiNaLe (finale.nfo)," n.d., DeFacto2, warez-scene-notices-2006-2010.

29 "Security.Warning.take.note.ppl-BwaRe (security.warning.take.note.ppl-bware.nfo)," n.d., DeFacto2, warez-scene-notices-2006-2010.

gating, though not eliminating, many of these risks. This is not, however, impossible. Many high-speed shells used for trading are bought from commercial providers. These all sit within similar IP ranges. Therefore, it is not beyond the bounds of possibility for a dedicated hacker to obtain an addline and then to be able to obtain an IP address that matches the requisite IDENTD mask.

Once a user has been added to a site, they will next be given the details on how to connect. This usually takes the form of an IP address or a hostname that resolves to an IP address. Because IP addresses of servers can identify the location of a machine on the internet, most Scene sites use bouncers (BNCs) to cloak their true location. BNCs are secondary machines that sit between an end-user and the site itself. The user connects to the BNC, not to the site. This means that the site's main IP address, in many cases, can remain hidden from the view of any of the site's users. It also provides an additional layer of security because the site can specify that only its bouncers are allowed to connect to the server, thereby making it harder to portscan for the site itself. A site will usually close any connection that does not come from one of its recognized bouncers. All the above authentication and authorization mechanisms must be routed through a BNC.[30]

Typically, the point of the bouncer is to serve not only as a technical protection measure but also as an un-prosecutable legal intermediary. The BNC itself will not store any incriminating files and will simply forward on connections. If the police raid a site's BNC — as happened in 2000 to the site, MS, whose "bouncer was narqed"[31] — it is assumed that there will be insufficient evidence to prosecute the bouncer operator for copyright infringement. However, this may be a flawed supposition. There have been prosecutions of individuals for running IRC bots that did not serve any illegal files themselves but that aided and abetted the group in running its operations. For this reason, a topsite

30 Paul Craig, *Software Piracy Exposed* (Rockland: Syngress, 2005), 111.

31 LS, "SCENE NEWS," *Courier Weektop Scorecard* (CwS-102.txt), June 3, 2000, DeFacto2.

may wish to move location rapidly if a bouncer is busted as the configuration will reveal the true site IP address, which can often be geolocated to give a physical location. Further, bouncers introduce another point of failure that can cause anxiety among Scene members — a place at which infrastructural breakage may be introduced and that exposes the otherwise seamless infrastructure, as per Star's schema. For instance, in 1999 there was speculation that law enforcement officers had raided the site ATX ("Atomic-X") because it had gone offline. In reality, it was merely that the "site was temporarily down due to bouncer problems."[32] Despite the infrastructural fragility that this introduces, many Scene figures believe that "if the site doesn't use a ip bouncer or firewall" there is a much greater risk of a police raid.[33]

Due to the nature of FTP, bouncers come in two flavors: command-channel bouncers and traffic bouncers. A command-channel bouncer is extremely easy to implement and passes commands directly between the client and the server. Notably, when the PORT or PASV command is initiated, the actual site server IP will be revealed, and all data traffic will be routed directly to the server. That is, because a command-channel bouncer simply relays commands between a user and the site, when the FTP server is instructed to open its port, the server will report its actual IP. On the other hand, a traffic bouncer gets around this problem by routing all traffic through its own system but at the cost of much greater complexity and bandwidth requirements. A traffic bouncer must process every command and response sent to and from the server and rewrite the output IPs for data channels when negotiated. In turn, this involves opening a channel to the specified remote address and forwarding the data. Finally, this comes with difficult setbacks in negotiating end-to-end encryption as the BNC must read the com-

32 ndetroit, "ndetroit's sites and stats section," *Netmonkey Weekly Report* (nwr47.txt), May 11, 1999, DeFacto2.

33 Saint Tok, "Interview with The Crazy Little Punk," *DeFacto2* (df2-02.txt), February 1997, DeFacto2.

mands sent to the server and transparently pass the encrypted data channel, breaking end-to-end encryption. In this case, if a traffic bouncer is compromised, it becomes possible to intercept usernames, passwords, and other sensitive information sent to the site. For an example of a traffic bouncer and its complexities, see the Yet Another Traffic Bouncer project part of the glftpd repository[34] Traffic bouncers are of similar complexity to FTP servers and are not trivial pieces of software.

Indeed, support for such bouncers must be baked into the FTP daemon (i.e., server) software itself and regular (i.e., non-warez) server software does not usually feature such support. In the 1990s, this need for custom security implementations and other features led to the development of several Scene-specific FTP server daemons, the histories of which are documented in the *Netmonkey Weekly Report,* issue XXXVI from February 22, 1999.[35] Beyond bouncer support, these daemons contain features not found in regular, FTP server software. These include:

- ident-based authentication;
- logging of user statistics;
- a userbase separate from accounts on the server's operating system;
- group management functionality;
- ratio and leech accounts;
- private directories;
- the "pre" functionality that moves a directory from a private area of the site to a public space;
- interaction with bots and IRC.

In the early days of the shift from BBS to FTP, Sceners competed to develop FTP daemons that provided the richest feature-set.[36]

---

34 glftpd, "Yet Another Traffic Bouncer," *Github,* 2020, https://github.com/glftpd/yatb.

35 lester, "Which Ftpd Is Right for You?" *Netmonkey Weekly Report* (Nwr36.Txt), February 22, 1999.

36 There is brief coverage of the history of Scene daemons in Alf Rehn, "Electronic Potlatch: A Study on New Technologies and Primitive Economic

The first of these noted in the *Netmonkey Weekly Report* was xftpd, called "probably the first major wide-scale [S]cene daemon that every site ran for years." The challenge with this daemon is that it required custom coding "for pretty much anything," leading to high maintenance/sysop requirements. This criticism indicates some of the hidden labor structures in maintaining the Scene's infrastructure, one more of Star's premises for studying infrastructure. Just as crackers are adept software engineers, writing secure custom FTP server software requires a level of sophisticated software development that verges on professional standards.

bleachboy's bftpd, written for "The Bleach Box" (BBX) topsite, overcame some of xftpd's weaknesses. "This daemon," writes the *Netmonkey* report, not only "successfully merged the dying BBS scene with the fledgeling FTP [S]cene" but would "revolutionize the way the [S]cene viewed ftp sites." Specifically "coded for warez, by someone who knew what he was doing," bftpd eventually died out when development stopped. The *Netmonkey* report also notes the difficulty in installing this daemon, one more instance of infrastructural breakage due to technical complexity. Nonetheless, this daemon appears to mark the start of a competitive phase among sites, where the software itself was a selling point for different servers. This proliferation of daemons meant that different sites were able to offer different user experiences. At the same time, this was a slight problem because, in each case, the authors were reinventing the wheel, starting from scratch whenever they coded a new daemon.

Alongside bftpd sat Reanimator's rftpd. According to Netmonkey, around 1998, "[n]early every site that didn't have a custom daemon used rftpd."[37] Evidence for this can be found in the list of software run by various historic sites in the Appendix; for instance, "The Rising Sun." This daemon featured "[b]uilt in support for weektops, groupop, flags, nuking, and a bot .tcl,"

Behaviors" (PhD, Royal Institute of Technology, Stockholm, 2001), 107.

37 lester, "Which Ftpd Is Right for You?"

which "made this THE daemon of choice for everyone."[38] As we will see, these features are key determinants of Scene hierarchies to this day. Wkups (weektops) refer to the weekly upload levels of participants on the site — to be "#1 wkup" is to have uploaded the most on any topsite in a given week, which is vital for courier chart scoring. Groupops refers to the ability for groups on the site to manage their own slots and is the equivalent of permitting a group owner to administer people in their group as they see fit. That is, a groupop will have permission to add and delete users, up to their slot allowance for the group. Nuking, as covered more extensively in Chapter Four, is a system of quality control and credit revocation when a release is found to be bad. Finally, as covered further below, the reference here to "bot.tcl" shows support for IRC daemon bots. These allow the site's activities to be relayed to a secret channel, giving an overview of what is happening inside the FTP daemon, such as, for instance, new releases.

Although rftpd was purported to be in widespread use, a daemon called ftp4all was also apparently used by several Scene sites, including "The Raging Monkey" (TRM) and "Narkos" (NKS).[39] An interesting characteristic of this daemon was that it was released under the open-source GPL license (The GNU Public License, which is an open source CopyLeft license). It may seem a strange quirk, but many of the FTP servers used by the Warez Scene are not open source. Hiding the source code is sometimes billed as a security feature, although information security professionals have thoroughly rejected security by obscurity.[40] In any case, the customization allowed by ftp4all was a leading feature in its adoption.

---

38 Ibid.

39 NKS, "Narkos Topsite (NKS-narkos.XXXX.XX.00.nfo)," n.d., DeFacto2, warez.scene.nfo.collection.v1.0.24351.shroo.ms.zip.

40 Karen Scarfone, Wayne Jansen, and Miles Tracy, *Guide to General Server Security: Recommendations of the National Institute of Standards and Technology* (Gaithersburg: National Institute of Standards and Technology, 2008).

Furthermore, the open license meant that others could study the source code to ensure that it was free of any vulnerabilities or deliberate backdoors. As the so-called "Linus's Law" puts it, in software development, "given enough eyeballs, all bugs are shallow."[41] It was reasoned that with more people looking at the source code of ftp4all, it should be possible to craft a more secure daemon. Notably, however, ftp4all did not seem to attract the widespread adoption that one would expect from such an open-source project.

The most widespread daemon in the period under study was glftpd, authored by greyline. A closed-source daemon that is still maintained as of 2021, the *Netmonkey* report notes that "[n]early _every_ site uses" glftpd. Clearly, this homogeneity poses a challenge for sites to distinguish themselves from one another: "your site will have to have some other reason to stand out, as it will look JUST LIKE every other site out there."[42] Nonetheless, siteops are advised by *Netmonkey* that "[t]his is the daemon if you want the best, but can't code your own."[43] Notably, some release groups began specifically requesting sites that run on glftpd.[44]

This heavy dependence in the Scene on a single FTP daemon comes with both benefits and drawbacks. The benefits include centralized bug fixes, peer support for setup and operations, familiarity, and ensured interoperability between servers. The major negative, aside from the lack of aesthetic and functional distinction between sites, is that any security breach in the software will affect the whole Scene. As of November 2020, there have been six disclosed vulnerabilities in glftpd.[45] The sever-

---

41 Eric S. Raymond, *The Cathedral and the Bazaar: Musings on Linux and Open Source by an Accidental Revolutionary* (Cambridge: O'Reilly Media, 2001), 30.

42 lester, "Which Ftpd Is Right for You?"

43 Ibid.

44 VERTEX, "1000 Password Plus v1.1.0 (vertex.nfo)," November 1, 2007, DeFacto2.

45 "Glftpd: Security Vulnerabilities," *CVE Details,* November 16, 2020, https://www.cvedetails.com/vulnerability-list/vendor_id-346/Glftpd.html.

ity of these vulnerabilities ranges from trivial to significant. At the lowest end of the spectrum, a vulnerability in glftpd 1.23, disclosed in 2001, allowed a connecting user to overwhelm the server's Central Processing Unit (CPU) resources. This vulnerability "allows remote attackers to cause a denial of service (CPU consumption) via a LIST command with an argument that contains a large number of * (asterisk) characters."[46] Given that users needed to be connected to the server to perform this action, though, the remedy would be fairly simple: to ban the user causing the denial of service attack.

There have been two critical severity vulnerabilities in glftpd. The first of these, in glftpd 1.18, allows attackers to enter a directory to which they should not have permission. This vulnerability relies on the fact that glftpd uses path completion. So, if there is a hidden directory called /private/test, attempting to change directory to /private/t will enter the /private/test directory, provided there are no other directories under "private" beginning with "t." The problem here was that glftpd checked permissions against /private/t rather than /private/test. Therefore, the site mishandled access management. Such management is essential for the Scene as release groups have private folders on affiliated topsites, where they store their releases before they are "pred" (i.e., released) simultaneously on all of their servers. Others who have unauthorized access to these directories could therefore steal releases from different groups or gain an advantage in trading at speed.

The most serious vulnerability in glftpd to date was present in version 1.17.2, disclosed in 1999. This vulnerability allowed for total system takeover by connected users. As the description of this exploit puts it:

> [t]here are three known serious vulnerabilities in GlFtpd. The first problem is an account which is created by default upon installation of the software. The username and password for this account are both "gltftpd" and the uid is 0 (root). This

46 Ibid.

> account can only be used by users connecting from localhost. This is a problem because "local users" can log into a host's glftpd with root privileges (and compromise the entire system). The second problem is world writeable ~/site directory. The last problem is the possibility to execute arbitrary commands on the target host. Glftpd comes with a feature called ZIPCHK, which is a command sent to the ftpd to check the integrity of a zip file on the server remotely. ZIPCHK executes "unzip" on the file without validating the filename input. With a special filename such as " ; ls," it is possible to execute arbitrary commands as the uid of glftpd.[47]

While the first two of these vulnerabilities causes challenges, it is the last of these, the ZIPCHK script, that is the worst. For example, when one names a file " ; a_linux_command" and then executes "SITE ZIPCHK ' ; bash a_linux_command'," the file "a_linux_command" will be executed. This can contain malicious code that will open a backdoor on the server. As this leads to arbitrary command execution, the consequences for a server could be dire. At the same time, because glftpd runs as root — the most privileged account on Linux- and Unix-based systems — a compromise of the main account in glftpd can have system-wide repercussions.

Coupled with a network forensics investigation in 1999, the closed-source nature of glftpd led a later issue of *The Netmonkey Weekly Report* to declare that the software featured a deliberate backdoor that would allow the developers to login without valid accounts. The claimed implications of this were considerable, with the report's authors noting that "[i]f ppl take this seriously (and they should), then 50 sites need to go down tonight, and stay down until they are 100% confident in their daemon."[48] Again, there is a bitter irony in the fact that a sizeable subset of the infrastructure running this underground darknet

47 Ibid.

48 ndetroit, "The Truth about GLFTPD," *Netmonkey Weekly Report* (nwr39.txt), March 17, 1999, DeFacto2.

uses closed-source FTP daemons speculated to contain security holes. Using Star's notion of looking for the hidden labor that undergirds infrastructure provision, it could be that the authors of this software felt that their efforts were not duly rewarded and so took steps to reward themselves. That said, later in 1999 it was claimed, as a rumor, that "greyline is going to release the full source code to his much celebrated (maligned?) daemon, GLFTPD."[49] At the same time, regardless of this, it "will not be an open-source project however, and the 'official' version will be maintained by greyline."[50] The report jokingly noted that there was "[n]o word on whether or not a certain infamous feature [the backdoor] will be included."[51] This is all to say that glftpd has had a controversial and somewhat checkered history. While it appears that the disclosed vulnerabilities were genuine coding errors, there have also been allegations of deliberate tampering to allow insiders to login to servers to which they should not have permission. The fact that the source code is unavailable helps provide fuel for such speculative fires. Nonetheless, it appears that glftpd remains in widespread use to this day and is the "daemon of choice" for most system operators.

The *Netmonkey Weekly Report* also details three private FTP daemons explicitly developed for certain sites or affiliations. For instance, eftpd was run exclusively on a site called E. Its "features include 'enigma cookies,' and an 'anti-restarters' feature."[52] The latter likely pertains to FTP's "REST" command that allows resumption of uploads and downloads and prohibiting this as a technique to stop couriers simply hogging a file. As to just what "enigma cookies" are, this remains aptly opaque to an outsider. It could be some form of game on the site that features "fortune cookie" type messaging, or it could refer to "cookies" in the technical sense used in contemporary web parlance (used to track users and to maintain information across a single brows-

49 lester, "Stories from the Watercooler," *Netmonkey Weekly Report* (nwr47.txt), May 11, 1999, DeFacto2.

50 Ibid.

51 Ibid.

52 lester, "Which Ftpd Is Right for You?"

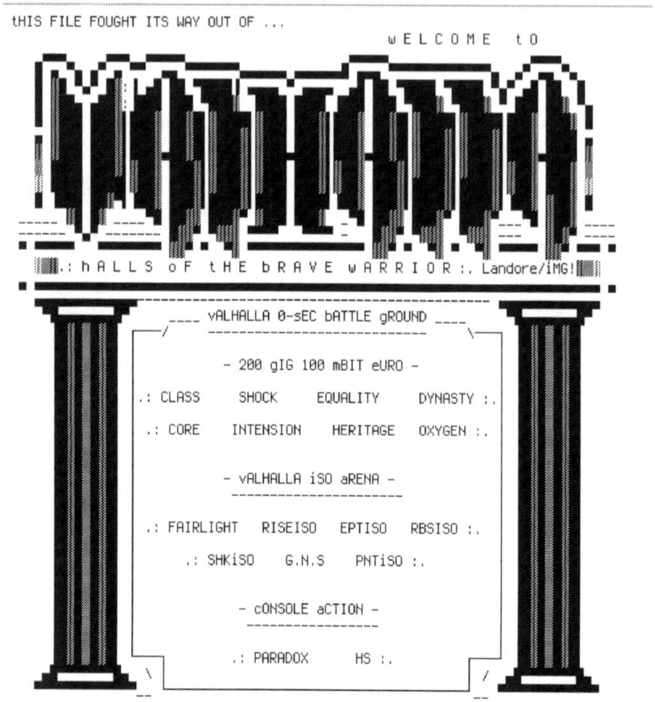

Figure 5. The distinctive NFO art for the site Valhalla (V) by Landore/iMG.

ing session). From the outside, it is impossible to tell. Another private daemon, eqlftpd, was run on "EQUALITY-affilled sites." EQUALITY was a courier group, which I cover below, and this daemon worked on a distributed basis: "[o]ne eqlftpd site shares its cpu and HD load seamlessly across 7 different machines."[53] The *Netmonkey* report notes that this daemon was a very closely guarded secret and that it is "unlikely it will ever become public."[54] Finally, the daemon hftpd (HADES FTPD), run on the site "HADES," is described as a feature-rich daemon "coded by

53 Ibid.
54 Ibid.

exile" that has "the ability to break down releases by groupname and disk-size."[55]

The purpose of these custom daemons is to give a topsite an identity that helps to distinguish it from others. This quest for identity continues into topsite aesthetics. Topsites are usually themed according to their name. For instance, the NFO ASCII art for "Valhalla" (V), shown in Figure 5, has a temple or giant hallway theme as indicated in Norse legend.[56] "Camelot" (CAM), shown in Figure 6, has a theme that conflates the court of King Arthur with a crusade-like feel, akin to Chrétien de Troyes's ironic retrospective mapping of crusade imagery onto Arthurian legend in his poem *Cligès*.[57] While the culture and aesthetics of NFO files are detailed in Chapter Five, customizing artwork and a sitebot theme are all considered part of what makes for a high-quality site "experience."[58]

Notably, many topsites carry adult themes (e.g., "Titty Twister" (TT) and "Wet Dreams" (WD) in the Appendix) but also racist tropes. "Camelot," for instance, bears the worrying hallmarks of crusade appropriation, which is common among contemporary far-right movements.[59] It also features the Celtic cross in the NFO, which has become one of the most common white supremacist symbols in circulation, alarmingly coupled with human skull iconography.[60] Other sites also have distress-

---

55 Ibid.

56 Also analysed by Rehn, "Electronic Potlatch," 132.

57 Anthony Bale, "Introduction," in *The Cambridge Companion to the Literature of the Crusades,* ed. Anthony Bale (Cambridge: Cambridge University Press, 2018), 1–8.

58 [S]peedy, "What Was the Best Site of Alltime?" *Netmonkey Weekly Report* (nwr-19.txt), October 5, 1998, DeFacto2.

59 See, for instance, Amy S. Kaufman and Paul B. Sturtevant, *The Devil's Historians: How Modern Extremists Abuse the Medieval Past* (Toronto: University of Toronto Press, 2020); Rory MacLellan, "Far-Right Appropriations of the Medieval Military Orders," *The Mediaeval Journal* 9, no. 1 (2019): 175–98; Catherine E. Karkov, Anna Kłosowska, and Vincent W.J. van Gerven Oei, eds., *Disturbing Times: Medieval Pasts, Reimagined Futures* (Earth: punctum books, 2020).

60 Sierra Lomuto, "White Nationalism and the Ethics of Medieval Studies," *In the Middle,* December 5, 2016, https://www.inthemedievalmiddle.

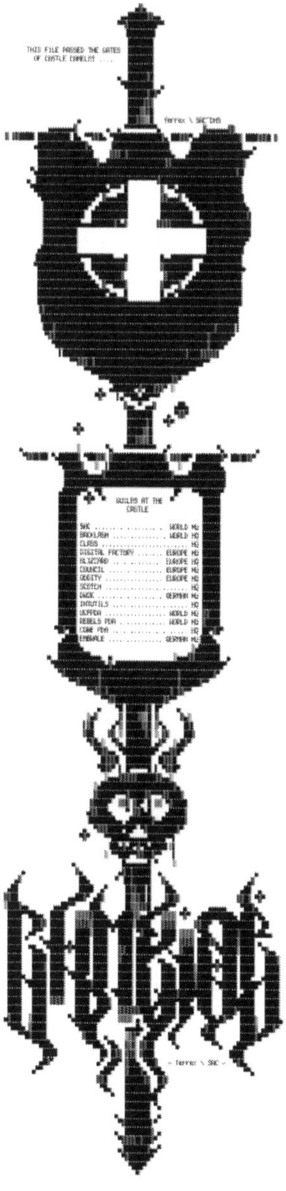

Figure 6. "Camelot" (CAM) ASCII Art depicting crusade imagery by ferrex\SAC.

ing racist traits, some even more explicit. For example, the NFO for the site "Dixieland" (DXL), which I will not reproduce here, is outrightly and incredibly racially offensive, depicting the Ku Klux Klan and using the terminology of lynching. Notably, in the site NFO, there is no indication that this site was specifically dedicated to racist content. Indeed, the affiliations listed include the prominent and respected mainstream Scene group, Drink or Die. However, the theme for the site is exceptionally racially offensive, and it sits alongside the many instances of hate speech, usually homophobia, found in Scene publications.

INFORMATION CHANNELS AND COMMUNICATION

Topsite theming continues into a site's affiliated IRC channels, or sometimes even entire IRC networks, that alert users of on-site activities through a sitebot and give updates on the site status. Access to topsite channels is restricted to hardware providers, site operators ("siteops"), their friends, moderators ("nukers"), release groups ("affiliates"), and couriers ("traders" or "racers"). Site channels are protected by invitation-only scripts on the site, password keys on the channels to ensure that unauthorized users are not invited by mistake, and encryption using a variety of protocols.[61]

IRC presents the risk of exposure to those who connect to servers. A direct connection can be used to incriminate an individual based on their internet protocol address. The usual output of the IRC "whois" command will show the connecting IP of the user. It is also the case that, since each site has its own channel or even server, users are often connected to multiple networks with many invitation-only and passworded channels. In order to mitigate the hassle of connecting on every startup to each network and channel and to protect the user's identity, users typically connect through a third-party IRC bouncer. These are different from the bouncers used by sites. However, they

com/2016/12/white-nationalism-and-ethics-of.html.

61 Rehn, "Electronic Potlatch," 82.

perform a similar set of functions: the first is that they cloak the user's actual connection source, and the second is that they provide an ongoing stable connection to the server, which negates the need to re-invite oneself to every channel all of the time.

These bouncers are typically provided by third parties or on secure servers elsewhere. For example, for some time the *Netmonkey Weekly Report* advertised www.socalsys.com as being a "Scene-friendly" provider of "shells, bounces, vhosts, and web space."[62] This provider was also one of the server providers for the LinkNet IRC network. Likewise, *Courier Weektop Scorecard* advertised a "ShellBox Y2K Special- $100/yr 3bg + personal vhost under shellbox.org, payment must be recieved [*sic*] by Midnight, Jan6 <http://www.shellbox.org>."[63] These shells are used to remain permanently connected to an IRC server and channels without ever exposing the end-user's IP address. Instead, typically, a vhost, which is short either for "vanity host" or "virtual host," is used to hide a user's actual address. These vhosts, though, also often reveal the "friendliness" of a server to these types of activity, although it is no guarantee. For instance, as of August 2020, Jeah.net had an available vhost, "hangs.out.at.the.warezcafe.com." (For example, a user's "whois" result if someone queried it could appear as "martin@hangs.out.at.the.warezcafe.com.") At the same date, xzibition.com's "lost" server had "user.glftpd.org" as an available host, while "Endurance" offers "pirates.illegal-warez.net" and "has.9-million.gigs.of.illegal-warez.net."

Different IRC bouncers provide different functionalities. The most commonly mentioned bouncer in the DeFacto2 warez-scene-notices-2006-2010 pack is "psyBNC," described as a "way to have a hostname that doesn't tie you to your IP" by one very basic scene security document.[64] psyBNC is a legitimate piece of

62 ndetroit, "The Scene News," *Netmonkey Weekly Report* (nwr55.txt), August 2, 1999, DeFacto2.

63 LS, "CWS News," *Courier Weektop Scorecard* (CWS-80.txt), January 1, 1999, DeFacto2.

64 "Site.Security.READNFO-acksyn (Site.Security.for.Users.Windows.XP.1.3-acksyn.nfo)," n.d., DeFacto2, warez-scene-notices-2006-2010.

software, with many users beyond the Scene. In its own words, it acts as "an easy-to-use, multi-user, permanent IRC-Bouncer with many features. Some of its features include symmetric ciphering of talk and connections (e.g., using the Blowfish and IDEA encryption schemes), the possibility of linking multiple bouncers to an internal network including a shared partyline, vhost- and relay support to connected bouncers and an extensive online help system."[65] As should be clear, many of these features, such as encryption, are highly valuable to the Scene for security purposes.

Within site channels, sitebots produce information about topsite activity in human-readable formats. For instance, a typical pre-line might appear thus: "<c***dealr> New Util-PRE! on '*' by fjorre/AOD : COREL.PAINTER.V8.0.PROPER.RIP-CALiMERO."[66] This tells us the name of the release and the section, "Util," alerting interested users to the presence of a new output on the site. However, site announcements also often contain additional information that is of use to traders, including in this case the name of the person and group who has created the release. For instance, consider the test pre line shown in issue 171 of *The Marshall Mussolini Show*: "->PRE<-- Woot_a_releaze-trujd-CD-2006-AMRC from AMRC_PRE_MACHINE (1 file(s), 140kB, genre: ??)."[67] In addition to giving the name of the release, this line also provides information about the number of files, the size, and, although missing here, the musical genre in the case of an MP3 release.[68] Regarding the later discussion of trading, this information dissemination channel allows for the automated discovery and transfer of releases between sites. This release happens in fact to be a trap though. It is not an ac-

---

65 "About," *psyBNC*, 2008, https://psybnc.org/about.html.

66 "SCENE QUOTES," *Ketchup* (ketchup_issue_19-2003.nfo), April 2003, DeFacto2.

67 "RELEASES OF THiS WEEK," *The Marshall Mussolini Show* (tmms_issue_171-2006_19.nfo), April 2006, DeFacto2.

68 This information is deduced by the site from the associated SFV file, which provides checksums and a file list, and from the ID3 metatag information embedded in the music files themselves.

tual music release and Sceners would recognize that "trujd" is a leetspeak synonym for "trade." (Leetspeak is a sub-language of scene discourse to which I will turn later in this chapter.) The trap is set to catch traders who are automatically moving everything from one site to another — the autotrading to which I gestured in the introduction.

Sitebots also provide updates on the status of races on the site, that is, they do not just cover information about releases being pred, but about the particular state of the release on the site. For instance, consider the example provided by Craig:

> <COGBoT> (COG-NEW) -0519- Flamingpear.Flexify.v1.98.for.Adobe.Photoshop.Incl.Keygen-SCOTCH by xxxxxx(RTS)
>
> <COGBoT> (COG-UPD) Flamingpear.Flexify.v1.98.for.Adobe.Photoshop.Incl.Keygen-SCOTCH (1 files expected)
>
> <COGBoT> (COG-COMPLETE) Flamingpear.Flexify.v1.98.for.Adobe.Photoshop.Incl.Keygen-SCOTCH (total: 1MB / avg. 2909kB/s) 1. xxxxxx/RTS [1.0M/1F/100.0%/2909KB/s][69]

While the intricacies of racing and trading are complex, this site log from COG demonstrates many of the basic principles. The trader, whose pseudonym redacted by Craig to "xxxxxx" of the group RTS, creates a new release directory and uploads, first, a Simple File Verification (SFV) file. This file, which contains a list of files in the release and their checksums, allows the site to ascertain the release structure. This structure includes:

- the number of files it contains;
- the size of files;
- and, once the files are uploaded, whether there has been any corruption during the transfer.

69 Craig, *Software Piracy Exposed*, 122.

The site can then infer which files to expect and report on the race conditions. New racers generate speed reports on the bot, which also alerts couriers that there is a competition underway. For instance, "[20:25] <|Azrael|> [flashi] starts punishing the new victim [WHITEOUT-DEViANCE] with a speed of [3398k/s]."[70]

IRC channels are more than just information-dissemination mechanisms. They also form the core areas of sociality for the Scene. As Alf Rehn puts it, one "could write a monograph on warez chatting alone."[71] As such, and as one would expect, IRC channels are protected by various security mechanisms. As mentioned earlier, site channels are both password protected and invitation only, with the sitebot issuing invitations in response to a "site invite" command.[72] While the latter aspect, the invitation-only feature, ensures that a user has access to the site itself and cannot gain admittance without passing all of the checks thereon, the former, the password, ensures that a user does not accidentally invite a user who is not themselves (for instance, through a nickname typo). In addition, sitebots and ops enforce access on an ongoing basis, with users who are deleted (for instance, "site deluser") removed from the channel.

Typically, the IRC networks on which the millennial Scenes operated enforced a secure connection to prevent interception and eavesdropping. LinkNet, which specialized in encrypted connections, appears to have been a common network used for scene activities.[73] The nature of IRC networks is curious for this setup, though. The "R" in IRC stands for "relay," which is there because an IRC network comprises multiple servers that connect to one another. When a user connects to one of these servers, it relays any messages sent to it to the other servers. There is

---

70 "Busted.allstarz.net.logs (Logs_Mandmore_4.txt)," n.d., DeFacto2, warez-scene-notices-2006-2010.

71 Rehn, "Electronic Potlatch," 125.

72 David McCandless, "Warez Wars," *Wired*, April 1, 1997, https://www.wired.com/1997/04/ff-warez/; "LAMURGH QUOTES," *The Marshall Mussolini Show* (tmms_issue_190-2006_38.nfo), September 24, 2006, DeFacto2.

73 "The truth about depax (xdd22245.nfo)," n.d., DeFacto2.

a chain of connection between a user, a bouncer, a server, and a network in the Scene. Each of these adds hop, lag, and time delay to message relay. Top traders will attempt to connect to the same server as the sitebot to minimize latency for new site updates about releases.

Notably, however, this multi-server approach combines both decentralization and risk. The fact that servers are decentralized means that the network can still stand if a single server is compromised. This decentralization is a fundamental principle of the Scene in general: it seeks to disaggregate risk from any central points of failure or security compromise. However, at the same time, such decentralization means that it may be easier for the network to be infiltrated by a bad server, which can then parse the entire logs of a site. For this reason, sitebots and channels also often had a blowfish encryption key to protect eavesdropping by the servers themselves.[74] Essentially, the Scene attempts to operate on as low of a trust basis as is possible. Sites attempt to protect themselves from IRC servers. IRC servers can then operate on a zero-knowledge basis and can effectively claim plausible deniability. As ever, the weakest link remains individual users who can compromise a site, its IRC channel, or any other of its routes. Beyond maintaining a tightly knit community of totally trusted actors, there is little that the Scene can do to mitigate the risks of individual users.

Scene discourse, which takes place in these IRC channels, has its own conventions of humor and standards of interaction. Indeed, courier charts and Scene magazines nearly always feature a section of quotes of the week. As the courier raanu put it, there is a "community to goof around with on channels while waiting for pres."[75] Some Scene members such as turn|| claim that "chatting in site chans sux anyway" and that "it will only help you get into some lame quote bots," suggesting that the sole purpose of

74 See, for instance ndetroit and lester, "Interview with metaray," *Netmonkey Weekly Report* (nwr56.txt), September 8, 1999, DeFacto2.

75 "Interview with raanu ('Interviewk')," *The Marshall Mussolini Show* (tmms_issue_082-2004_33.nfo), August 2004, DeFacto2.

such discourse is recursively to feed the quote sections of those very magazines.[76]

Scene humor is frequently adult in nature yet immature in its content. Sometimes this is not the case. Indeed, some groups have deliberate rules that demand maturity and codes of decorum. For instance, RiSC demands that its members act "maturely" as they "get a lot of respect because of it."[77] It was important to this courier group's image to project the impression that "[w]e're not children here," although the demand of members was only that they "NOT be rude or inconsiderate to other RiSC members."[78] It seems fine to be rude to members of other groups or to use crudity in humor.[79] Not all Scene humor is crude, though. Some Scene comedy, for instance, is just zany or related to extremely niche practices that will not be familiar to those on the outside. For instance, the courier magazine, *The Marshall Mussolini Show* (*TMMS*), had a running in-joke in the issue header where many, but not every, issue after issue 120 was mislabelled "i S S U E . F i F T Y . E i G H T." "Issue fifty-eight comming at yall," as issue 124 claims.[80]

Some of the humor is also related to trading and scene activities themselves. For instance, in *TMMS* 174 the quote joke reads,

> <jack> btw, sidenote… i know you're trading for stats, not creds
> stats? I trade to pass quota[81]

The joke here is that while trading allows couriers to acquire credits ("creds") on the site at a usual ratio of 1:3 (for every 1MB

76 "LAMURGH QUOTES," *The Marshall Mussolini Show* (tmms_issue_082-2004_33.nfo), August 2004, DeFacto2.
77 RiSC, "Guidelines (risc.guidelines.txt)," n.d., DeFacto2.
78 Ibid.
79 RiSC, "Ethics (risc.ethics.txt)," n.d, DeFacto2.
80 "iSSUE FiFTY EiGHT," *The Marshall Mussolini Show* (tmms_issue_124-2005_23.nfo), June 2005, DeFacto2.
81 "LAMURGH QUOTES," *The Marshall Mussolini Show* (tmms_issue_174-2006_22.nfo), June 2006, DeFacto2.

uploaded the trader receives 3MB of download), many couriers do not trade for the sake of credits. In fact, they often have more credits than they can use. Instead, they trade in order to compete in the upload-chart statistics that are produced weekly and demonstrate their couriering skill, thereby showcasing their elite access. Indeed, one "releases of the week" section in *TMMS* reads: "[s]orry i'm not into listening [to] music. Trading is my passion!"[82] However, sites also have quotas for couriers, who must ensure that they upload a certain volume each month, or they will be automatically deleted from the site.[83] Usually, for top couriers, passing quota is a trivial matter. Hence, the joke here is that jack says to sidenote that he knows that he is not trading for credits, only for the glory of the statistics, to which sidenote responds that he was, in fact, only trading in order merely to make the quota. Certainly, it's not a very good joke, but this is the essence of Scene humor. It "might," as a later issue of *TMMS* puts it, "also be that you're just not funny."[84]

Indeed, many aspects of Scene humor are, to be blunt, just not as funny as its proponents like to imagine. As Jimmy Maher notes, with the Scene foreshadowing later in even more outlandish corners of the internet such as *4chan* and *8chan*, "[m]uch about this underground culture, made up as it was almost entirely of adolescent males, is distasteful, even shocking to adult sensibilities of both its time and our own."[85] For instance, a great deal of the humor revolves around a casual homophobia of this ilk:

---

82 "RELEASES OF THiS WEEK," *The Marshall Mussolini Show* (tmms_issue_293-2008_36.nfo), September 2008, DeFacto2.

83 For more on quota vs. leech accounts see Justin Keery, "Special Report on Electronic Gifts: Teenage Pirates and the Junior," *The Independent,* December 11, 1992, https://www.independent.co.uk/news/science/special-report-on-electronic-gifts-teenage-pirates-and-the-junior-underworld-parents-should-know-that-children-can-buy-or-sell-illegal-copies-of-video-games-and-sex-writes-justin-keery-1562928.html.

84 "LAMURGH QUOTES," *The Marshall Mussolini Show* (tmms_issue_563-2013_44.nfo), November 2013, DeFacto2.

85 Jimmy Maher, *The Future Was Here: The Commodore Amiga* (Cambridge: MIT Press, 2012), 182.

<daneboy> <-- goin to san fran 20 days! :D
<daneboy> got any suggestions for things to see?
<weirdnick> gay people?[86]

Such offhand aggression and homophobia that pervades Scene magazines and quotes sections are emblematic of a hyper-masculine, geek environment. That said, it is not fair to characterize all Scene participants as adolescent men as Maher does. After all, the topsite environment requires sophisticated access to high-speed links, expensive computer hardware, and in-depth knowledge of system administration. These skills and levels of access are typically not available to teenagers. Instead, it might be better to characterize these slanging matches as childish or immature, with a male slant to the banter. Without excusing either, the notorious language of "locker room chat" might be the nearest parallel. Though, it is also clear from records of Scene busts and raids that women do participate. For instance, there is the case of Stacey Nawara, who used the handle "avec" and who was a courier for Razor 1911, although she was also the only woman arrested during this raid.[87] Indeed, of those arrested and charged in Operation Buccaneer, detailed in Chapter Six, the age range was 20 to 34, and the breadth of professions included "corporate executives, computer network administrators at major universities, employees of large hi-tech companies, students, and government workers."[88] This represents a substantial diversity of participants. Nonetheless, as one ex-Scener put it in an interview elsewhere:

86 "LAMURGH QUOTES," *The Marshall Mussolini Show* (tmms_issue_394-2010_32.nfo), July 2010, DeFacto2.

87 Paul J. McNultey, "Warez Leader Sentenced to 46 Months," *US Department of Justice*, May 17, 2002, https://www.justice.gov/archive/criminal/cybercrime/press-releases/2002/sankusSent.htm.

88 Gregor Urbas, "Cross-National Investigation and Prosecution of Intellectual Property Crimes: The Example of 'Operation Buccaneer'," *Crime, Law and Social Change* 46, nos. 4–5 (December 2006): 209.

> [t]he thing that struck me when re-reading this 20 year old text was the level of aggression and gorilla chest thumping. Clearly I owe a lot of apologies. This was more apparent after I penetrated deep into my garage and dug out the old C64. Re-reading some of the scroll texts and *Reason 4 Treason* articles made me cringe. It appears I took aim at any dork, nerd, drop-out, non-music listener, anti-graffiti, pro-establishment, unfashionable person out there. I'm not sure why, perhaps it was because I occasionally copped a bit of flak myself for being a "computer head" at school. Being a Dungeons & Dragons geek and using a briefcase as a school bag didn't do me any favours either.[89]

As Maher continues, much of Scene discourse demonstrates an "adolescent need for acceptance and validation" and "a crude social Darwinism ruled the [S]cene, with the most skilled and connected crackers almost worshipped and lesser lights cruelly excluded and dismissed as 'lamers.'"[90]

This concept of "unfunny humor" at the expense of certain demographic groups has come under intense scrutiny from ethicists.[91] However, I believe that explaining Scene humor as funny or unfunny misses its actual function. The jokes in NFO files are not present in order to make participants laugh. They are, instead, intended as demarcations of insider-outsider status. Scene humor is not supposed to be funny; it is supposed to provoke a knowing nod or smirk among those who get it. Further, it often depends on being able to identify the individual in question. While names are sometimes censored in the weekly quotes sections of courier charts, this allows Sceners who saw the original dialogue to show off their privileged levels of access to others. The affect that humor typically intends to pro-

89 Jimmy Maher, "A Pirate's Life for Me, Part 2: The Scene," *The Digital Antiquarian,* January 1, 2016, https://www.filfre.net/2016/01/a-pirates-life-for-me-part-2-the-scene/.

90 Maher, *The Future Was Here,* 182.

91 Oliver Conolly and Bashshar Haydar, "The Good, The Bad and The Funny," *The Monist* 88, no. 1 (2005): 121–34.

voke is transformed into a performed esoteric epistemology, an opportunity for Sceners to flaunt their insider status. Knowing someone who appears in the weekly quotes, or being able to identify them, and understanding what is faintly amusing about the context are all part of the elaborate ritual of insider-ness that permeates Scene life.

At the same time, there is a danger inherent in Scene humor and its quotes to the participants. While courier charts and other documents are supposed to remain interior to the Scene, they inevitably leak out into archives such as DeFacto2. When these documents contain the Sceners' IRC nicknames, they expose these people to law enforcement officers as targets for investigation. Although some Scene-quotes segments anonymize participants, this represents a dangerous form of humor with inherent risk. Likewise, there is the danger that law enforcement will investigate any document that names sites, sitebots, Sceners, channels, and IRC networks. While it is probably not thought through enough to constitute a deliberate act, Scene humor nonetheless remains a risky business.

The other distinctive element of IRC and communication cultures in the Scene since the 1980s is the informal language development known as leetspeak ("elite-speak").[92] Leetspeak, in which words such as "hacker" becomes "h4xxor" and so forth, initially developed to allow phreakers (old-school telephone hackers) to avoid detection by the FBI, who were monitoring connections for particular words and phrases. That is, law enforcement agents were searching for words that they believed to pertain to piracy and cracking. Leetspeak is thus a basic form of encryption that allowed BBS users to evade surveillance.[93] It is, indeed, also from this linguistic culture that the term "warez"

---

92 Manuel Perea, Jon Andoni Duñabeitia, and Manuel Carreiras, "R34D1NG W0RD5 W1TH NUMB3R5," *Journal of Experimental Psychology: Human Perception and Performance* 34, no. 1 (2008): 237.

93 Sockanathan, "Digital Desire and Recorded Music," 181; Tamás Polgár, *Freax: The Brief History of the Computer Demoscene* (Winnenden: CWS-Verlag, 2008), 70.

emerges, that is, as a shortened and modified form of "software." As Maher puts it:

> like so many subcultures, the cracking scene developed its own distinct vocabulary of odd phrasings, distorted spellings, and portmanteau words that are still used in some segments of Internet culture today. They allegedly replaced the word software with warez, hacker with haxxor, and elite with eleet to circumvent electronic law enforcement filters that might be tracking their activities, but one senses that such constructions were in reality more important to these "[S]ceners" as markers of inclusion and exclusion.[94]

While the vocabulary and syntax vary hugely, Bruce Sterling characterized many features of this discourse in his 1992 book *The Hacker Crackdown*, noting that "[s]pecialized orthography, especially the use of 'ph' for 'f' and 'z' for the plural 's,' are instant recognition symbols. So is the use of the numeral 'Ø' [zero] for the letter 'O'—computer-software orthography generally features a slash through the zero, making the distinction obvious."[95] This orthography can work because the cognitive overhead of parsing numbers as though they were letters is very low. As Perea et al. write, "the cognitive system regularizes the shape of the leet digits (and letter-like symbols) embedded in words with very little cost."[96]

Far from being an unreflective discourse, in its hyperbolic overloading, leetspeak is also deliberately ironic. For instance, the quotes sections of *TMMS* are titled "LAMURGH QUOTES," meaning "lamer quotes," with "lamer" being the term used to deride other participants. The almost but not quite homophonic "lamurgh" is emblematic of a culture in which the ridiculousness of the language is understood by participants, even while

94 Maher, *The Future Was Here*, 182.

95 Bruce Sterling, *The Hacker Crackdown: Law and Disorder on the Electronic Frontier* (New York: Bantam Books, 1992), 85.

96 Perea, Duñabeitia, and Carreiras, "R34D1NG W0RD5 W1TH NUMB3R5," 240.

they use it. An example of the self-knowingness of this system can be seen in the *Netmonkey Weekly Report* #78, in which dennison writes that he "will be mailing them [his system specs] over to my great pal JEFFK after I type this report so he can 'haxxxxor' [hack] my 'computrar' [computer]."[97] That said, despite the knowing wink in the use of such forms, many Sceners take aliases that include leetspeak, such as LiV3D, bl44t, tom, and others.[98]

In all, though, these communication infrastructures of IRC provide two core functions to the Scene. First, they provide information channels about the internal working of topsites, which allows members to see new releases, monitor race statuses, and keep track of vital stats. Second, they provide the spaces of sociality and humor that make the Scene fun.

FACILITATING INFRASTRUCTURES

If the alternative reality game of the Scene did not have topsites, there would be no place for pirated warez to reside. However, if there were no IRC servers and channels for these sites, there would be no enjoyment. The game of the Scene works well because participants can socialize with one another in a related but separate space to the site, bantering and jostling, even as those spaces relay the competitive economic data about races that are taking place on the site itself.

Hence, technology in the Scene, while nonetheless being core to the illicit activities, is there to facilitate social interaction and play. We cannot understand the Scene purely in terms of its technologies. We need to comprehend the technologies' purposes in order to grasp their role within the overall function of the Scene.

---

97 dennison, "DENNISON'S GAME REVIEW," *Netmonkey Weekly Report* (nwr78.txt), March 29, 2000, DeFacto2.

98 "stats," *The Marshall Mussolini Show* (tmms_issue_105-2005_04.nfo), January 2005, DeFacto2.

It is to this functional, organizational element to which the next chapter is devoted. Here I turn to the organizational principles that govern the activities of releasing and racing warez on topsites. This will cover how the Scene's organization can be conceptualized, examining Scene standards and rules, the principles of dupes and dupechecking, the roles of nukes and nukers, and the interaction between local site rules and Scenewide standard rules.

FOUR

Organization

THE CASE OF COURIER CHARTS

The Scene is highly organized, but it achieves that organization in a distributed fashion. The Scene appears as an organized phenomenon that has emerged without hierarchical leadership or a self-organizing paradigm. In this chapter I examine aspects of Scene organization and operation. Before we turn to the formal structures, I want to give a few examples of Scene organizational paradigms as seen in site hierarchies, in release group affiliations, and in courier scoring systems.

In this organizational paradigm, consider foremost that not all topsites are created equal. Indeed, topsites are organized into a hierarchy. This hierarchy of topsites is determined based on its affiliated release groups, link speed, hardware setup and capacity, and other factors, such as linked courier groups.[1] Indeed, the term "topsite" implies a hierarchy, but not every "site" is "top." The ranking and judgment around what constitutes a topsite is a devolved matter decided by those who produce various types of charts and rankings. Sometimes, this can be decided democratically (i.e., "I pick a few weektop traders from the top groups to

1 [S]peedy, "What was the best site of Alltime?" *Netmonkey Weekly Report* (nwr-19.txt), October 5, 1998, DeFacto2.

vote on ranks each week"[2]), but this is not always the case. For instance, the *Courier Weektop ScoreCard* issue 001 from February 1998 used the sites in Table 1. The sources I used here are as close to the date of the ScoreCard as I was able to ascertain, with additional information from other NFOs cited where used to populate other details.

Sitename	Known Affils	Known Hardware/ Software	Location	Siteops and Nukers
AiR Force One (AF1)[3]	RiSE, ViCE, Game Group		Hungary[4]	Bandido[5]
Ambiquous (AMB)[6]	Renaissance, RiSE, GPF, Divine Canadian, RTN, GCRACK NA		Canada	
Camelot (CAM)[7]	Backlash, Rebels		Germany[8]	

2 LS, "SiTE OPS AND TRADERS READ BELOW," *Courier Weektop Scorecard* (CwS-137.txt), February 3, 2001, DeFacto2.

3 AF1, "AiR Force One Topsite (AF1-air.force.one.1998.02.12.nfo)," February 12, 1998, DeFacto2, warez.scene.nfo.collection.v1.0.24351.shroo.ms.zip.

4 "opfastlink.txt," 2002, http://144.217.177.36:1421/EBooks/paraZite/opfastlink.txt.

5 "SceneBusts10 (scenebusts10.htm)," 2000, paraZite.

6 AMB, "Ambiquous Topsite (AMB-ambiquous.1998.02.18.nfo)," February 18, 1998, DeFacto2, warez.scene.nfo.collection.v1.0.24351.shroo.ms.zip.

7 CAM, "Camelot Topsite (CAM-camelot.1998.11.13.nfo)," November 13, 1998, DeFacto2, warez.scene.nfo.collection.v1.0.24351.shroo.ms.zip.

8 CAM, "Camelot Topsite (CAM-camelot.XXXX.XX.02.nfo)," n.d., DeFacto2, warez.scene.nfo.collection.v1.0.24351.shroo.ms.zip.

Sitename	Known Affils	Known Hardware/ Software	Location	Siteops and Nukers
Digital Corruption (dC)[9]	Renaissance, PWA, UCF		Europe	Ico, Sinister, SirMagik, Iceb, Novocaine, Toth, Vorteqz, Trade
DaFat of the Land (DF)[10]	Request To Send, Sodom, Revolution		USA	"Powered by 34mbit T3 Ethernet" "24 Gigs"[11]
DreamLand (DL)[12]	DiMENSiON, RAZOR 1911, The Corporation		USA[13]	
Enigma				
Etirnity (ET)[14]	DEVOTiON, MORTALITY			
FalseHood (FH)[15]	RAZOR 1911, RiSC, GRS			Gollie, Morbid16

9 Note that there are several sites with the acronym dC and it may be that this does not refer to this specific site, which is my best guess. DC, "Digital Corruption Topsite (DC-digital.corruption.1998.02.12.nfo)," February 12, 1998, DeFacto2, warez.scene.nfo.collection.v1.0.24351.shroo.ms.zip.

10 DF, "DaFat of the Land Topsite (DF-da.fat.1998.02.23.nfo)," February 23, 1998, DeFacto2, warez.scene.nfo.collection.v1.0.24351.shroo.ms.zip.

11 DF, "DaFat of the Land Topsite (DF-da.fat.1998.09.16.nfo)," September 16, 1998, DeFacto2, warez.scene.nfo.collection.v1.0.24351.shroo.ms.zip.

12 DL, "DreamLand Topsite (DL-dream.land.1999.01.21.nfo)," January 21, 1999, DeFacto2, warez.scene.nfo.collection.v1.0.24351.shroo.ms.zip.

13 DL, "DreamLand Topsite (DL-dream.land.1999.04.27.nfo)," April 27, 1999, DeFacto2, warez.scene.nfo.collection.v1.0.24351.shroo.ms.zip.

14 ET, "Etirnity Topsite (ET-etirnity.1996.08.10.nfo)," August 10, 1996, DeFacto2, warez.scene.nfo.collection.v1.0.24351.shroo.ms.zip.

15 FH, "FalseHood Topsite (FH-false.hood.1998.02.26.nfo)," February 26, 1998, DeFacto2, warez.scene.nfo.collection.v1.0.24351.shroo.ms.zip.

16 FH, "FalseHood Topsite (FH-false.hood.1998.08.27.nfo)," August 27, 1998, DeFacto2, warez.scene.nfo.collection.v1.0.24351.shroo.ms.zip.

Sitename	Known Affils	Known Hardware/ Software	Location	Siteops and Nukers
Fortress of Solitude (FOS)[17]	RiSC, Drink or Die, RAZOR 1911, UCF, BLH, TRG		Europe[18]	
Lunatic Asylum (LA)[19]				
PRimaryLink20			Europe[21]	
Quadcon (QC)[22]	RiSCiSO, Ranaissance, SHOCK, CoNCePT, RNG, GPF	"2 Separate T1 Systems" "43gb Main/ ISO" "7gb Release"	USA	Katman, GaL, BanDiDo, Koyote, Poo, CorrupT
The ROCK[23]	PWA, Phrozen Crew		USA[24]	

17 FOS, "Fortress of Solitude Topsite (FOS-fortress.of.solitude.1998.02.10.nfo)," February 10, 1998, DeFacto2, warez.scene.nfo.collection.v1.0.24351.shroo.ms.zip.

18 FOS, "Fortress of Solitude Topsite (FOS-fortress.of.solitude.1998.12.23.nfo)," December 23, 1998, DeFacto2, warez.scene.nfo.collection.v1.0.24351.shroo.ms.zip.

19 LA, "Lunatic Asylum Topsite (LA-lunatic.asylum.1995.04.21.nfo)," April 21, 1995, DeFacto2, warez.scene.nfo.collection.v1.0.24351.shroo.ms.zip.

20 PL, "Primary Link Topsite (PL-primary.link.1997.12.19.nfo)," December 19, 1997, DeFacto2, warez.scene.nfo.collection.v1.0.24351.shroo.ms.zip.

21 PL, "Primary Link Topsite (PL-primary.link.1996.11.03.nfo)," November 3, 1996, DeFacto2, warez.scene.nfo.collection.v1.0.24351.shroo.ms.zip.

22 QC, "QuadCon Topsite (QC-quadcon.1998.02.09.nfo)," February 9, 1998, DeFacto2, warez.scene.nfo.collection.v1.0.24351.shroo.ms.zip.

23 TR, "The Rock Topsite (TR-the.rock.1998.08.14.nfo)," August 14, 1998, DeFacto2, warez.scene.nfo.collection.v1.0.24351.shroo.ms.zip.

24 TR, "The Rock Topsite (TR-the.rock.1999.03.13.nfo)," March 13, 1999, DeFacto2, warez.scene.nfo.collection.v1.0.24351.shroo.ms.zip.

Sitename	Known Affils	Known Hardware/ Software	Location	Siteops and Nukers
Silly Symphonies (SS)[25]	MiLLENNiUM, Drink or Die, DARK SiDE		Finland	
Stairway to Heaven (STH)[26]	VENGEANCE, PREMIERE, CELEBRE			
Total Technology				
The Rising Sun (TRS)[27]	SiEGE, CLASS	"T3 Speed" "10 GiGS" "RFTPD"	USA	
The Wolves House (TWS)[28]	Equality, Shock, Parasite, Core, Backlash		The Netherlands	
Virtual Dimension Research Lake (VDR)[29]	Devotion, Sodom, CLASS	"Powered by 155Mbits"	Europe	

25 SS, "Silly Symphonies Topsite (SS-silly.symphonies.1998.05.13.nfo)," May 13, 1998, DeFacto2, warez.scene.nfo.collection.v1.0.24351.shroo.ms.zip.

26 STH, "Stairway to Heaven Topsite (STH-stairway.to.heaven.1998.03.04.nfo)," March 4, 1998, DeFacto2, warez.scene.nfo.collection.v1.0.24351.shroo.ms.zip.

27 TRS, "The Rising Sun Topsite (TRS-the.rising.sun.1998.01.18.nfo)," August 18, 1998, DeFacto2, warez.scene.nfo.collection.v1.0.24351.shroo.ms.zip.

28 TWH, "The Wolves House Topsite (TWH-the.wolves.house.1998.02.15.nfo)," February 15, 1998, DeFacto2, warez.scene.nfo.collection.v1.0.24351.shroo.ms.zip.

29 VDR, "Virtual Dimension Research Lake Topsite (VDR-vdr.lake.1998.02.09.nfo)," February 9, 1998, DeFacto2, warez.scene.nfo.collection.v1.0.24351.shroo.ms.zip.

Sitename	Known Affils	Known Hardware/ Software	Location	Siteops and Nukers
Watch Tower (WT)30	Pirates Gone Crazy, Teenagers in Crime, 2000AD, Revolt, Real Time Pirates		USA	Txxxxxx Cxxxxxxx, Mxxxxxxx, Ixxxx, Vxxxxx xxxxx, Kxxxxxxx
xquziit (XQZ)31	RAZOR 1911, X-Force		"Southern" USA	"XQZ Staff"

Table 1: The details of ranked sites in the *Courier Weektop ScoreCard* issue 001 from February 1998.

As shown in Table 1, release groups — the basic social units into which pirate operations are organized — are often affiliated with sites, contributing to their status. Remember, release groups are those who obtain software, films, television shows, music, pornography, and other digital artifacts that they obtain through a supplier, someone who works within the media industry and can obtain these items before they are on general sale. Skilled technicians within the group (i.e., crackers) then disassemble the software or otherwise circumvent the Digital Rights Management (DRM) restrictions on the media and prepare this material for release. There is an organized division of labor. After this, the release is uploaded to the groups' dump — a high-bandwidth private server. From there, usually by an automated process called a prebot, the material is distributed to the private areas that the groups are assigned on topsites. Release groups are affiliated to multiple sites because different sites hold differ-

30 WT, "Watch Tower Topsite (WT-watch.tower.1998.03.02.nfo)," March 2, 1998, DeFacto2, warez.scene.nfo.collection.v1.0.24351.shroo.ms.zip.

31 XQZ, "Xquizit Topsite (XQZ-xquizit.1998.03.25.nfo)," March 25, 1998, DeFacto2, warez.scene.nfo.collection.v1.0.24351.shroo.ms.zip.

ent types of content; because different sites are situated at different geographical locations thereby affecting possible speeds due to internet routing; and because this redundancy acts to militate against any single point of failure. Sites award a negotiable number of affilslots (i.e., affiliation slots) to release and courier groups when they take up affiliation, which is the effective rate of pay for affiliation within the Scene's organized economics.[32] Some of these have upload and download traffic ratio restrictions, and some allow unlimited download, or "leech."[33] This works because most accounts on topsites run on a ratio-credit basis at a rate of 1-to-3; for every one megabyte uploaded, the user is given three megabytes of credit to download. Suppliers, crackers, and other functionaries within the group will receive slots on sites in exchange for their services. However, the slots on every single site will likely not stretch far enough to reward all group members, so multiple sites are needed.

Release groups upload their releases to their private areas on their affiliated topsites and, when the material is present on all of these sites and has been dupechecked, the release is pred (pronounced "preed," a verb referring to the prerelease nature of the material) in an organized and coordinated fashion. This action moves the content from the staging area to the publicly accessible area of the site. Dupechecking is, as the neologism suggests, a mechanism for ensuring that the release is not a duplicate of material that has already been released by another group, showing Scene-wide coordination. Duplicate releases are not allowed and, if found, will incur a nuke by a site's nuker. A nuke marks the release as problematic — this can be for duplication or contravention of the site's content rules — and comes with a multiplier credit penalty on the site. Therefore, a nuke multiplier of 3× means that the user loses credit to the tune of three times the size of that release. Higher multipliers, therefore, incur a nega-

32 "Stats for CFL (CONTiNUOUS FLOW)," The Marshall Mussolini Show (tmms_issue_196-2006_44.nfo), October 2006, DeFacto2.

33 For more on leech slots, see skimp, "Interview with glimerman of RiSC," *Courier Weektop Scorecard* (CwS-137.txt), February 3, 2001, DeFacto2.

tive penalty. There are various dupecheck mechanisms in place, but the most reputable databases are private and, in turn, affiliated to sites in exchange for ratio-free slots.

The release process is a time-critical, synchronized, organized operation. At any time, many release groups will be racing to be the first to put out a high-quality release as multiple suppliers tend to proffer their material simultaneously. There can sometimes be only seconds between releases and only the latter, the duplicate, will be nuked. Each topsite has multiple groups affiliated to it, and these sites will be the first to receive all the material that they release. It is therefore imperative that the operation to make a release public is executed at the same time on all the sites to which a group is affiliated. A siteop will usually become extremely unhappy if a group does not ensure coordination between all its affiliated sites for the public release of material.

Sites are then guaranteed to receive the content released by the groups affiliated with them. However, this will not ensure that they will hold all the content that is generally available. Release groups who are not on the site may still release material that siteops want to be present in their archive and available to their users. Therefore, to ensure full coverage, sites employ couriers to bring them material from unaffiliated release groups. Siteops also set specific rules that determine content that is allowed. For example, siteops might permit only the most recent material, only particular genres of music, and only certain high-quality release groups. The role of the courier is to earn credit by transferring releases from one site to another. This is accomplished by one of two routes. Either the trader uses the File Exchange Protocol (FXP) to transfer from site to site, or they use a shelltrading method, which I cover in the previous chapter. When a release is pred, couriers determine on which sites the release was pred and copy the release to the sites on which they have accounts and whose rules allow the release.

This courier race is supposed to be a game of reflexes, but in reality it boils down to sophisticated, automated algorithms — in a process known as autotrading[34] — and high-bandwidth trading boxes. A variety of technological measures are deployed to make this possible. Firstly, the IRC channels for each site will announce new releases, as covered in the previous chapter. Successful couriers write custom clients, rarely shared with others, that integrate with this system. This likely contains several discrete components:

- a regular expression engine integrated with an IRC client that matches the sitebot announce and parses the release name and associated components into its discrete elements;
- a rule or status engine that determines the sites to which the release may be transferred and monitors the sites on which the release is already complete;
- a routing engine that determines the optimum route to trade the release;
- a server-based File Transfer Protocol (FTP) client component that remains connected to the sites in question and initiates File eXchange Protocol (FXP) transfers between sites from the routing engine, or using shelltrading approaches, usually initiated by a UDP (User Datagram Protocol) signaling mechanism.

This software may or may not prompt the trader for verification that it has made the right decisions. When it does so, it is deemed a legitimate tool in the arsenal of the site courier. However, when it is completely automated, the system is an autotrader and therefore problematic. Often siteops will lay traps for unsuspecting autotraders in the hopes of catching them, which is called prespam. For instance, a user named "trader" might be found out if they traded the following release:

34 See "iSSUE FiFTY EiGHT," *The Marshall Mussolini Show* (tmms_issue_533-2013_14.nfo), 2013, DeFacto2 for an extensive discussion of bans on autotrading.

Figure 7. Rankings in *The Marshall Mussolini Show* from 2003. Source: "Rank," *The Marshall Mussolini Show* (tmms_issue_054-2003_48.nfo), December 2003, DeFacto2.

> <sitebot> NEW PRE! Hello.Trader-Are.You.A.Bot-2014-Prepare.For.Deluser was just pred by Group. It is 357mb of Electronic.

A human would quickly identify that this release was a decoy solely designed to snare the unsuspecting user. A poorly designed, regular expression engine that did not operate without a blacklist would see this as entirely legitimate, and would trade it to all applicable sites, incurring the user's deletion on all of these sites. The tradeoff that couriers must make, then, is either to sacrifice their time to accruing the necessary levels of upload per month to remain on their sites, or to develop a successful autotrading strategy that will not get them caught. The organization of sophisticated, trading-client software is quite astounding.

This situation is further complicated by the system of organized rankings and prestige awarded to couriers through the various wkup chart systems in operation. These charts, which are often combined with commentary, and which form the basis on which I have surmised most of the information in this section, go under names such as *Courier Weektop Scorecard, The Game Scene Charts, Weekly Wanking Stats, Scene Charts, Retarded Courier Scores, Ketchup,* and *The Marshall Mussolini Show.* As above, in each chart, sites are ranked. In the above example of Courier Weektop Scorecard, every site was ranked on a 1x multiplier. However, different charts use different rules. Consider, for instance, at random, the rank section of *The Marshall Mussolini Show* issue 54 from 2003, shown in Figure 7.

In this chart, points are awarded based on where a courier has placed in the weekly uploaded volume for the site. However, the multiplier for the site, which is based on how difficult it is to trade to that site, determines the points. Hence, scoring first on NB, TR, or XTM is better than scoring first on LC or T, which in turn trump DOT, FEO, etc. The wkup scores are shown in Figure 8.

Where a courier places depends upon having slots on each of the sites and then scoring within the top twenty wkup. Scoring twentieth awards one point, scoring nineteenth two points, and so on. These site scores are then combined with the multiplier to give a points score. For example, WHiTEHEAT came ninth in the wkup solely on the site LC. This means an award of twelve points. However, because LC is a site ranked 2×, the total points awarded are 24.00, which led to a final placement of position 35 in the charts, having transferred a total of 2,435 megabytes. By contrast, junk scored extremely highly across many sites (for instance, first on NB, T, FEO, MD, RSN), transferring 66,126 megabytes and placing first on the chart in total, with 348.5 points. Indeed, most of the couriers who scored in the top ten appear to be on most sites. sekk1 in position two, for instance, scored in the top twenty on every site. As we move further down the chart, we find couriers who did not place within the top twenty on every site, although it is unclear whether this is because the couriers do not have a slot on these sites or simply failed to score. Other charts use this same approach. *Ketchup,* for instance, writes that "[t]he points are gathered by taking the spot of the site the user achieved, and multiply it with the ranking of that particular site. Example; if the user gets #1 at a 3.0× ranked

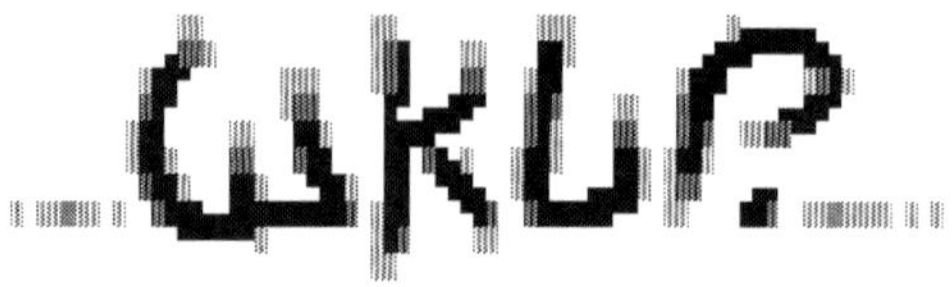

200-	+/-	Spot	Courier	Group	Points	Mbytes	2.5 NB	2.5 TR	2.5 XTM	2.0 LC	2.0 T	1.5 DOT	1.5 FEO	1.5 MD	1.5 RSN	1.0 ACX	1.0 B1
200-	+19	1.	junk	PR	348.5p	66,126mb	1	2	3	6	1	3	1	1	1	2	.
200-	+13	2.	sekk1	PR	305.0p	52,263mb	3	6	4	10	2	2	6	4	8	5	13
200-	-1	3.	fain	BRZ	286.5p	45,403mb	8	5	7	5	6	4	9	3	2	3	29
200-	+7	4.	chiller	AMNMP3	251.5p	40,230mb	.	4	5	3	7	11	5	5	13	6	6
200-	+2	5.	danjuls	BRZ	247.0p	50,334mb	2	3	2	30	3	1	7	.	55	1	.
200-	-3	6.	turntablz	PR	241.5p	36,132mb	6	7	8	11	4	9	8	7	17	8	16
200-	+1	7.	drkev	EQMP3	207.5p	34,645mb	7	18	12	8	12	5	12	9	5	9	14
200-	-3	8.	theadde	PR	199.0p	34,792mb	5	10	11	15	5	14	10	12	19	4	19
200-	+3	9.	igloo	BRZ	148.0p	26,901mb	.	1	1	.	.	.	2	8	.	.	.
200-	-6	10.	pretorian	BRZ	137.0p	25,060mb	9	20	9	14	14	13	22	14	9	15	31
200-	+29	11.	IzeX	CFL	123.0p	20,448mb	.	8	6	.	9	.	11	.	28	7	.
200-	+2	12.	ls	AMNMP3	105.5p	23,556mb	10	17	10	28	15	23	15	23	14	13	20
200-	-4	13.	jess	420	99.0p	20,350mb	.	12	14	21	8	21	14	18	15	12	.
200-	+19	14.	lb	IND	86.0p	20,611mb	.	.	.	1	.	.	3	.	.	.	2
200-	+7	15.	ikegami	Unknown	73.0p	11,396mb	.	.	.	4	.	.	.	.	3	.	9
200-	-6	16.	kalle02	CFL	66.5p	18,201mb	15	21	13	40	18	12	13	27	35	24	24
200-		17.	txx	Unknown	64.5p	8,324mb	4	.	.	.	10	.	.	.	.	.	.
200-	-12	18.	unbel	CFL	64.0p	20,151mb	11	22	17	20	17	15	25	22	32	11	33
200-		19.	gotti	GFZ	59.5p	10,554mb	.	15	.	12	16	10	30	.	.	.	.
200-		20.	bios	DECIBEL	56.0p	10,156mb	12	14	46	13	25	31	55	.	.	40	44
200-	+11	21.	fewips	IND	55.5p	8,859mb	.	.	.	.	.	7	.	13	6	.	.
200-		22.	J-man	Unknown	54.5p	8,465mb	.	.	.	2	.	.	.	10	.	.	40
200-	+16	23.	Theil	Unknown	50.5p	8,406mb	.	.	.	7	.	6	.	.	.	.	.
200-	+1	24.	Bono	GFS	46.0p	9,390mb	.	9	.	.	.	.	.	.	.	.	5
200-		25.	r0mAz	DECIBEL	45.0p	11,316mb	21	11	16	56	44	37	16	21	.	32	.
200-		26.	voven	BRZ	44.5p	13,145mb	16	19	15	16	20	35	23	26	34	.	.
200-	-4	27.	DdK	GFS	42.5p	9,034mb	.	.	.	.	.	.	.	2	.	.	7
200-		28.	Chipie	Unknown	42.0p	7,363mb	.	.	.	60	.	.	4	.	10	.	.
200-	+23	29.	InvisblE	GFS	40.5p	8,040mb	.	.	.	.	40	8	.	61	7	.	32
200-	+5	30.	fuze	420	34.0p	14,425mb	13	25	19	35	19	26	39	29	27	16	48
200-	-15	31.	luckyluke	EQMP3	32.0p	14,972mb	14	26	24	17	23	18	27	24	23	19	50
200-	-3	32.	faz	DNSJ	29.0p	11,618mb	.	.	.	.	.	.	32	48	.	10	3
200-	-16	33.	jdigital	AODMP3	28.0p	6,478mb	.	.	.	.	13	.	18	16	.	.	.
200-		34.	bl44t	GFS	25.5p	3,609mb	.	.	.	.	.	.	.	.	4	.	.
200-		35.	WHiTEHEAT	Unknown	24.0p	2,435mb	.	.	.	9	.	.	.	.	.	.	.
200-	+22	36.	Nomadic	WTF	22.5p	4,987mb	.	.	.	.	.	.	.	11	16	.	38
200-		37.	soc	Unknown	22.5p	3,492mb	.	.	.	.	.	.	.	6	.	.	.
200-	-20	38.	Mickske	IND	21.0p	4,669mb	.	.	.	31	.	16	.	.	12	.	.
200-	+18	39.	resistans	PR	20.5p	9,932mb	.	.	.	22	.	17	19	.	18	14	.
200-	-9	40.	dyzma	GFS	20.0p	15,694mb	.	.	.	.	.	.	.	.	50	.	1
200-		41.	defiler	Unknown	20.0p	4,525mb	.	13	.	.	28	.	.	.	.	.	36
200-	-16	42.	Lambda1	Unknown	20.0p	3,022mb	.	.	.	.	11	.	.	.	.	.	.
200-	-9	43.	nomar	Unknown	17.0p	6,055mb	.	.	.	.	.	.	.	.	.	.	4
200-		44.	yale	Unknown	15.0p	1,740mb	.	.	.	.	.	.	.	.	11	.	.
200-		45.	ads	Unknown	13.0p	4,442mb	.	.	.	.	.	.	.	.	.	.	8
200-		46.	messiahh	GFS	12.5p	3,852mb	.	16	.	.	.	.	26	.	.	.	.
200-	-2	47.	mucka	Unknown	11.0p	3,845mb	.	.	.	.	.	.	.	.	.	.	10
200-		48.	gavin	AMNMP3	10.5p	11,178mb	19	24	20	32	31	28	29	.	24	18	.
200-	-22	49.	Voodoo	CFL	10.0p	8,617mb	17	32	26	41	30	32	37	31	40	22	.
200-	-20	50.	lucky	EPTMP3	10.0p	4,477mb	.	.	.	19	.	.	.	17	.	.	28
200-		51.	orphan	Unknown	10.0p	3,524mb	.	.	.	.	.	.	.	.	.	.	11
200-	-33	52.	modzel	AODMP3	9.0p	6,404mb	.	.	.	18	.	19	.	28	.	.	25
200-		53.	atrox	GFS	9.0p	3,975mb	.	.	.	.	.	.	21	15	.	.	.
200-		54.	joreno	AODMP3	9.0p	3,330mb	.	.	.	.	.	.	.	.	.	.	12
200-		55.	ensign2	CFL	8.5p	11,396mb	18	34	25	29	26	24	24	30	22	20	.
200-	-15	56.	boot	WTF	7.5p	6,627mb	.	.	18	.	.	.	28	.	21	.	21
200-		57.	Trolden	Unknown	6.0p	2,925mb	.	.	.	.	.	.	.	.	.	.	15
200-		58.	g0nEAwAY	Unknown	6.0p	2,397mb	.	.	.	.	.	.	17	.	.	.	.
200-	-35	59.	pro	DECIBEL	5.5p	9,273mb	20	.	27	27	37	.	20	20	.	.	27
200-		60.	tauron	AMNMP3	4.0p	7,844mb	.	31	32	39	.	27	45	35	31	17	42
200-	-8	61.	nbk	EPTMP3	4.0p	4,374mb	.	.	.	23	.	.	.	42	.	.	17
200-		62.	nox	DECIBEL	3.0p	6,174mb	23	.	30	25	43	34	52	19	33	.	.
200-		63.	way2late	Unknown	3.0p	2,767mb	.	.	.	.	.	.	.	.	.	.	18
200-	-26	64.	Andain	Unknown	1.5p	3,839mb	.	.	.	24	.	20	.	.	25	.	.
200-		65.	lasermaker	DNSJ	1.5p	1,423mb	.	.	.	46	.	.	.	.	20	.	.

Figure 8. wkup stats from *The Marshall Mussolini Show* in 2003. Source: "wkup," *The Marshall Mussolini Show* (tmms_issue_054-2003_48.nfo), December 2003, DeFacto2.

site; the points would be 20 × 3, which would be 60 points. The points are then being gathered from the sites, and allocated into the weekend score for that user."[35]

The introduction to the first issue of *The Marshall Mussolini Show* exhibits the typical scene traits of boasting, as loudly as possible, about secrecy, scarcity, elitism, and its own organizational setup. As the compilers write, "it is a pleasure to have you as our elite audience! By now, you understand why I call you an elite audience! [...] Some people have access, some do not. If you have access, we are glad to have you. If you do not have access, you wouldn't see this magazine anyway. [... P]eople who are not supposed to read this magazine will never have a chance to see this."[36] Of course, the irony of this statement will not be lost here.

The other common Scene traits that come through in these courier charts, though, and the reason that I have here expanded upon them, is an extremely high level of analytical organization, coupled with a bathetic plunge into puerility and crudity of language. Consider the group standings analysis that was a weekly feature of these charts shown in Figure 9. These feature intricate point calculations for the group's overall score, including percentage breakdowns for each group member that show whether they have pulled their weight this week. However, each element of group analysis also carries a usually somewhat immature analysis section. Here we can see that EQMP3 ("jokingly" phoneticized with leetspeak to "eekuu Σmpeekolome" or "ee," "kuu," "em," "pee," and then, for some unknown reason, "kolome") are referred to as "the tall gay finns," exhibiting levels of casual homophobia that are reminiscent of 1990s children's playgrounds and that we saw in Chapter Three's analysis of Scene humor.

---

35 "RULES OF KETCHUP," *Ketchup* (ketchup_issue_19-2003.nfo), April 2003, DeFacto2.

36 "news," *The Marshall Mussolini Show* (tmms_issue_001-2002_47.nfo), November 2002, DeFacto2.

```
200- /* Group standings */
200-
200- Spot Group                                                    Points     Mbytes Percent
200- ------------------------------------------------------------------------------------
200-   1. EQMP3 (eekuu Σmpeekolome)                               215.5p  207,555mb
200- ------------------------------------------------------------------------------------
200-        1. M LC TS RSN MD DOT BB                              130.0p  129,401mb   60.3%
200-        2. TR AKS T                                            54.0p   44,539mb   25.1%
200-        4. ACX                                                 10.5p   12,125mb    4.9%
200-        5. NB B1                                               21.0p   21,490mb    9.7%
200- ------------------------------------------------------------------------------------
200-        2. IzeX                                               346.5p   50,365mb   28.5%
200-        4. drkev                                              316.5p   48,282mb   26.0%
200-        6. fewips                                             257.5p   42,802mb   21.2%
200-       10. kurgan                                             182.0p   22,602mb   15.0%
200-       17. luckyluke                                          110.0p   25,074mb    9.1%
200-       55. vixxen                                               2.5p    8,052mb    0.2%
200-           xnick                                                0.0p    9,665mb    0.0%
200-           cece                                                 0.0p    5,673mb    0.0%
200-           crash                                                0.0p    2,302mb    0.0%
200-           samsara                                              0.0p      603mb    0.0%
200- ------------------------------------------------------------------------------------
200-
200- What a week from the tall gay finns!
200- Finishing #1 this week after some nice trading from
200- Izex(#2) and gynaecologist Kev(#4).With backup tradin
200- from fewips(#6) and Kurgan who did one of his
200- better weeks lately ending at #10.
200-
200- MIA: Luckyluke and the daltoon brothers.
200-
```

Figure 9. Group analysis from *The Marshall Mussolini Show.* Source: "Group Standings," *The Marshall Mussolini Show* (tmms_issue_071-2004_13.nfo), March 2004, DeFacto2.

At the same time, the sophistication and organization of the chart system are evident in the way that the archive presents it. The courier obtains the chart in question by issuing a command on one of the sites that are ranked by the chart. This is clear from the 200 responses that precede each line and the command seen at the top of such files ("site tmms tmms_issue_071-2004_13.nfo").[37] It is clear, from the files in the DeFacto2 archive, that this chart was accessed by using a custom script assigned to a site, in this case "tmms-lister by spirhor version 200211191400." In this respect, the chart makers are correct to assert that their system is elite and hard to access. The only way to obtain this chart, which nonetheless took a substantial amount of work and

37 "Group Standings," *The Marshall Mussolini Show* (tmms_issue_071-2004_13.nfo), March 2004, DeFacto2.

organization to create every week, is to be on one of the sites. On the other hand, the DeFacto2 archive has now made this work generally available, presumably against the wishes of the chart's creators. The chart had stated that "if anybody with access talks, pastes, what the fuck ever in any way shape or form to distribute this text in any form beyond which we are already distributing it, they will have access removed, and their group may suffer a similar fate."[38]

Given the scoring system's intricacies, it is also highly likely that *The Marshall Mussolini Show* charts were created automatically by parsing the site's wkup commands. However, this is not universally the case. Courier Weektop Scorecards issue 72 was a total disaster, a case of organizational failure. Here, of the European Top Couriers, the authors write: "!!!THERE IS NONE, DUE TO LACK OF WKUPS / THERE WEREN'T EVEN 50 TRADERS TO SCORE / SEND WKUPS TO: weektops@cws.couriers.org!!!."[39] Further, in the "Sites Received" section, the authors extend "big thanks to prozax this week, he was the ONLY person to send in wkups."[40] The fact that the records from *The Marshall Mussolini Show* came from a few years later indicates a substantial escalation in technical proficiency concerning score integration in courier charts and, perhaps, the mass adoption of glftpd, a specific File Transfer Protocol Daemon. In 1999 the charts relied on individuals on the sites emailing in wkup scores. By 2002 to 2004 it seems that the charts were much better integrated with sites' own systems.

From release groups, through to courier groups, through courier charts, and rankings of sites, what is revealed is a portrait of *organization*. The Scene is anarchic in many senses. However, it is also intricately structured and organized. Like every good game, it has strict rules. But how should we relate this type of organization to notions of organized crime?

---

38 "news."

39 "European Top Couriers," *Courier Weektop Scorecard* (CWS-72.txt), October 2, 1999, DeFacto2.

40 "Sites Received," *Courier Weektop Scorecard* (CWS-72.txt), October 2, 1999, DeFacto2.

THE ORGANIZATION OF ORGANIZED CRIME

It may seem surprising that the Warez Scene has a strict internal system of rules and regulations. Considering that the entire structure is a clear violation of national and international copyright law, it seems ridiculous to expect that this criminal subculture would itself be subject to inviolable codes of conduct. Yet many criminal networks, such as the Japanese yakuza, have their own internal codes and laws, which is a distinguishing feature of organized crime.[41] It is just that such codes and laws are not the codes and laws of the state. In the case of the Scene, it is these internal laws that are themselves the very component that make the Scene an organized crime network. How should we understand the Scene — a dangerous and illegal, alternative reality game — in relation to notions of organized crime?

Since the 1920s there has been scholarly debate that contests the notion of organized crime two primary axes. As Paoli Letizia frames it, the poles of this movement are between, first, "a set of stable organizations illegal per se or whose members systematically engage in crime" and second, "a set of serious criminal activities, particularly the provision of illegal goods and services, mostly carried out for monetary gain."[42] In the broader public consciousness, organizations, such as the Sicilian mafia, fit the former of these definitions, while elsewhere in countries without such well-known criminal gangs, it is the activities themselves that are the organized component. As Paoli and Tom Vander Beken posit, "the evolution of the organized crime debate worldwide over the past one hundred years can be synthesized in a shift from 'What' to 'Who' and a reverting tide from 'Who' to 'What,' with an increasing merger of the two."[43]

---

41 Jake Adelstein, "Global Vice: The Expanding Territory of the Yakuza," *Journal of International Affairs* 66, no. 1 (2012): 156–57.

42 Letizia Paoli, "Introduction," in *The Oxford Handbook of Organized Crime*, ed. Letizia Paoli (Oxford: Oxford University Press, 2014), 2.

43 Letizia Paoli and Tom Vander Beken, "Organized Crime: A Contested Concept," in *The Oxford Handbook of Organized Crime*, ed. Paoli, 14.

The Warez Scene sits in a strange relation to these notions of and debates about organized crime. When referring to activities, the loose term "organized crime" usually denotes serious and violent undertakings with a monetary component attached. However, the Warez Scene is potentially none of these things. There is no physical or violent component involved. As noted elsewhere in this book, the Scene tends to spurn all direct monetary involvement, although it costs money to build topsites, maintain the high-speed link architecture, meet the electricity costs, and so on. How serious one deems its activities presumably correlates to the extent to which the piracy of multimedia artifacts directly affects one's income and livelihood. The conflation of "organized" and "serious" crime remains one of the core weaknesses of this terminology.

In a similar vein, if one takes the "who" framing of organized crime, the Scene is also oddly placed. As I note in the chapter on aesthetic subcultures, the Scene grew alongside the legal DemoScene groups of the 1980s.[44] These Demo groups are legitimate organizations with a genuine artistic purpose as recognized, even, in some countries' registers of significant cultural activities. However, many Warez Scene groups exist solely to perpetuate the spread of pirate artifacts. In other words, these groups are sometimes split between legitimate demo divisions and illegal ISO divisions (ISO refers to the file format for CD-ROMs specified in the standards document ISO 9660. It traditionally means "computer games distributed on CD-ROMs"). It then becomes complicated to know whether membership of such groups should be classed as illegal.

44 Markku Reunanen, Patryk Wasiak, and Daniel Botz, "Crack Intros: Piracy, Creativity and Communication," *International Journal of Communication* 9 (2015): 798–817.

Nonetheless, whether one wishes to use the terms of illegal enterprises and networks,[45] criminal groups[46] or mafias,[47] organized crimes,[48] profit-driven crime,[49] criminal entrepreneurship,[50] or the organization of serious crimes for gain,[51] the Scene remains organized in many ways.[52] It is also possible, of course, that existing terminologies are insufficient to classify the way that globally dispersed cyber-networks of criminality emerge. As Kim-Kwang Raymond Choo and Peter Grabosky note, "[c]ontact made in IRC chatrooms between people who have never met each other (and may never meet each other) in physical space can evolve into hacker groups, piracy or 'warez' groups."[53]

The primary ways in which the organized characteristics of the Scene present themselves are through Scene standards, nukes, NukeNets, dupes, and other quality-control mechanisms. It is to these sophisticated mechanisms of permission, quality-control, and rules that the remainder of this section is devoted.

---

45 Carlo Morselli and Tom Vander Beken, "Opportunistic Structures of Organized Crime," in *The Oxford Handbook of Organized Crime,* ed. Paoli, 288–302.

46 Carlo Morselli, Mathilde Turcotte, and Valentina Tenti, "The Mobility of Criminal Groups," *Global Crime* 12, no. 3 (2011): 165–88.

47 Federico Varese, "Introduction," in *Organized Crime: Critical Concepts in Criminology,* ed. Federico Varese (London: Routledge, 2010), 1–35.

48 Derek B. Cornish and Roland V. Clarke, "Analyzing Organized Crimes," in *Rational Choice and Criminal Behaviour: Recent Research and Future Challenges,* eds. Alex R. Piquero and Stephen G. Tibbetts (New York: Routledge, 2002), 41–64.

49 R.T. Naylor, "Towards a General Theory of Profit-Driven Crimes," *The British Journal of Criminology* 43, no. 1 (2003): 81–101.

50 Peter Gottschalk, *Entrepreneurship and Organized Crime: Entrepreneurs in Illegal Business* (Cheltenham: Edward Elgar, 2009).

51 Adam Edwards and Michael Levi, "Researching the Organization of Serious Crimes," *Criminology & Criminal Justice* 8, no. 4 (2008): 363–88; Michael Levi, "Organized Crime," in *The Oxford Handbook of Criminology,* ed. Mike Maguire, Rodney Morgan, and Robert Reiner, 3rd edn. (New York: Oxford University Press, 2002).

52 This taxonomy of terms is derived from Paoli and Beken, "Organized Crime," 25.

53 Kim-Kwang Raymond Choo and Peter Grabosky, "Cybercrime," in *The Oxford Handbook of Organized Crime,* ed. Paoli, 484.

SCENE STANDARDS: INTERNAL LEGAL DOCUMENTS

Scene standards are sets of rules for releases that have been agreed by a consortium of release groups. These rules are then implemented locally by topsites as the grounds for valid releases or otherwise, although a site technically could overrule the Scene-wide standards for a release. Releases found to violate these rules are deemed nukes and are systemically marked as such throughout the topsite network. In order to understand the structure and mechanisms of these rules, I will analyze the "Official.FLAC.Standard.Rules v3.0" document that forms the current ruleset for the Free Lossless Audio Codec (FLAC) Scene.[54] In the interest of sparing the reader from endless "Ibid" footnotes, I will note that it is from this document that most of this section derives. I will also examine the controversy surrounding this ruleset and the disputes that played out over the consensus of its introduction. The development of these standards, including metadata standards, turns out to have import for understanding the development of digital media commodities. For instance, several commentators have argued that there is a reciprocal feedback loop between the standards of the pirate Scene and the improvement of the sold artifacts with which they compete.[55] It is also crucial, as Maria Eriksson has framed it, to understand that "piracy standardization efforts are central to the ways in

54 The only other scholars to examine Scene release rules in any detail are Maria Eriksson, "A Different Kind of Story: Tracing the Histories and Cultural Marks of Pirate Copied Film," *Tecnoscienza: Italian Journal of Science & Technology Studies* 7, no. 1 (2016): 87–108; Virginia Crisp, "Release Groups & The Scene: Re-Intermediation and Competitive Gatekeepers Online," *Cinéma & Cie* 17, no. 29 (Fall 2017): 67–79; and Alf Rehn, "Electronic Potlatch: A Study on New Technologies and Primitive Economic Behaviors" (PhD diss., Royal Institute of Technology, Stockholm, 2001).

55 Christopher Charles, "Psyculture in Bristol: Careers, Projects, and Strategies in Digital Music-Making" (PhD diss., University of Bristol, 2019), 138; Basilisk, "The Beginner's Guide to Ektoplazm," *Ektoplazm*, July 12, 2012, https://ektoplazm.com/blog/a-beginners-guide-to-ektoplazm. See also Jeremy Wade Morris, *Selling Digital Music, Formatting Culture* (Berkeley: University of California Press, 2015), 70–71.

which digital pirate copies are brought forth as cultural artifacts; they do not only help to adjust these object's production methods, but also assist in organizing their future lives by serving as a background for quality assessment."[56] That is to say that pirate standards are a crucial marker of Scene distinction and quality for releases, founded on a quasi-democratic, quasi-legalistic framework of rules, that feed back into mainstream culture.

The music standard under discussion, FLAC, provides a means of dramatically reducing the file size of music productions but without sacrificing any of the original file in the compression process. A FLAC file is smaller than its raw-audio equivalent, that is, PCM WAV, but the original raw audio is the same when decompressed. This differs from formats such as MP3 that work by altering the underlying audio stream, removing parts of the playback that are inaudible to human hearing.[57] When an MP3 file is decompressed, the audio stream revealed is different from the original source. Information has been lost. This type of compression is referred to as "lossy." By contrast, the FLAC format is lossless—the decompressed audio stream is identical to the input document. This lossless compression means that FLAC files maintain the exact same level of audio quality as the original, whereas formats such as MP3, that technically only remove sound information that is inaudible, have lower overall sonic fidelity at lower bitrates.

This FLAC rules document has been signed by the groups 2Eleven, 86D, ATMO, BCC, BriBerY, c05, CMC, CUSTODES, dh, dL, EMP, FATHEAD, FiH, FrB, FWYH, GRAVEWISH, HBFD, JLM, k4, LiTF, LoKET, MAHOU, Mrflac, mwnd, NBFLAC, PERFECT, psyCZ, SCF, SCORN, SMASH, SPL, TiLLMYDEATH, VOLDiES, WRE, and YARD, representing a broad church of acceptance for the principles contained therein. The rules set out in this document went into force on June 16,

56 Eriksson, "A Different Kind of Story," 103.

57 For more, see Jonathan Sterne, *MP3: The Meaning of a Format* (Durham: Duke University Press, 2012).

2016.[58] One of the most glaring elements of the FLAC ruleset is the quasi-legalistic tone of the document. The document begins, for instance, with a set of definitions and notes on interpretation, stating that "MUST=obligatory (release not allowed if rule not followed)," "SHOULD=suggested (release allowed if not followed)," and "CAN+MAY=optional (release allowed if not followed)." In legal documents, such definitional preambles usually follow the section known as recitals.

In legal documents, recitals are highly formulaic and widespread, appearing in approximately 85 percent of contracts.[59] As Marcel Fontaine and Filip De Ly describe them, "[a] large number of contracts, particularly those dealing with international trade, begin with so-called 'recitals.' The parties to such contracts use recitals to set out a series of statements that they regard as useful before approaching the body of the contract. Often, the parties introduce themselves and state their respective qualifications. They describe the purposes of their contract and the circumstances that have brought about their collaboration. The history of their negotiations is sometimes given. Recitals record a wide variety of statements and acknowledgements."[60] The FLAC rules exhibit all attributes of formal legal recitals, although not in the conventional ordering. This even goes down to the level of the history of negotiations, which in this document takes the form of a changelog:

> CHANGELOG:
> 2011-10-03 first version (v1.0)
> 2011-10-10 rule 1.10 with NOTE added to forbid single file+cue unless source is single track with index.
> 2011-10-10 rule 3.5.1 added (explanation for TYPE tag).
> 2011-10-10 rule 3.8.1 added (explanation for ARTIST and TITLE tags).

58 2Eleven et al., "Official.FLAC.Standard.Rules v3.0 (nfo_2016_FLAC.nfo)," Scenerules.org, June 15, 2016, scenerules.org.

59 Marcel Fontaine and Filip De Ly, *Drafting International Contracts: An Analysis of Contract Clauses* (Ardsley: Transnational Publishers, 2006), 60.

60 Ibid., 59.

2011-10-10 rule 5.1 adjusted
2011-10-10 rule 5.5 adjusted
2011-10-10 rule 5.5.1 added
2012-05-15 GENERAL section 1.0 splitted.
2012-05-15 rule 1.3 adjusted
2012-05-15 rule 1.4 adjusted and NOTES removed.
2012-05-15 DUPES section created 2.0

The recitals here have an impact on the interpretation of the rules, just as they do in conventional contract law. While "[t]he classical theory of contracts says nothing whatever about recitals," it is nonetheless the case that, in the recitals, "one reaches the threshold of the contract. There has been a meeting of minds and it is in the very document, which records their agreement, that the parties feel the need to describe some of the circumstances surrounding that agreement. It would be paradoxical if recitals were to be without any legal implications when such implications are recognized in certain aspects of the pre-contractual negotiations."[61] The postscript of the signatories to the FLAC ruleset also constitute a form of recital and document the mutual assent to the terms of all parties and the binding nature of the rules document.

The recitals of the FLAC ruleset also contain a preamble statement that clarifies the purpose of the document. The document's drafters note that "[a]fter 4 years of enjoying the FLAC scene and with ruleset wording misinterpretations, it is time to revise and add/update some rules." In other words, it is precisely the ambiguity of former Scene rule documents that has led to the evolution of these statements to quasi-legal, semi-contractual forms. This statement forms a declaration of objective for the parties agreeing. The document has been drafted to provide comprehensive clarity over what is and is not allowed within the FLAC Scene. Importantly, the recitals portion of the rules document does not indicate the spirit in which the signatories

61 Ibid., 60.

have agreed.[62] This is significant because all parties should enter freely into the agreement in legal, contractual terms. In fact, it is not clear that all groups who have signed the Scene rules had an equal say in their drafting. The history of Scene groups shows various levels of domination by specific central figures, which may lead to a situation in which, with apologies to George Orwell, *all groups are equal, but some groups are more equal than others.*

Furthermore, while this document is drafted in a style that suggests consensus, with signatory groups agreeing on the terms set out as though they agreed to a contract between the parties, the reality is that the document is more akin to a piece of criminal legislation. Thus, any new FLAC group that enters the Scene would not necessarily be expected to sign this document as they would were its function contractual. Instead, they will be subject to its rules, as though it were national legislation, enforced both Scene-wide and at the local site level. In this way, the parties that co-signed the document are probably better viewed as lawmakers (appointed based on reputation and track record), with nukers as the judiciary branch who interpret the law and enact punishment, with topsites as the delegated court spaces in which the judgements take place. Of course, there are challenges with such a legal analogy. The Scene is also subject to real lawmaking and its enforcement in the external world. These internal rules are by-laws and codes of conduct. Nonetheless, given the fact that the Scene space is a separate "world" in some ways to the outside universe, there is some merit in laying aside temporarily the objections to this analogy.

Further, this document proved to be highly controversial. In response to its release, unknown parties pred a release called "INVALID_OFFICIAL_FLAC_STANDARD_RULES_V3.0-SCENENOTICE"[63] that set out why they felt the current new

62 Ibid., 67.

63 The quoted material henceforth refers to the document, "Invalid Official FLAC Standard Rules V3.0 (INVALID_OFFICIAL_FLAC_STANDARD_RULES_V3.0-SCENENOTICE.nfo)," January 9, 2017.

ruleset to be illegitimate. Using a bold, and impolite, "netiquette" (i.e., net etiquette) form of all-caps, the notice begins by stating that the current FLAC Scene regime is a "DICTATORSHIP" that has "A RULESET CREATED BY PEOPLE THAT AREN'T EVEN LEADING FORCES IN THE FLAC SECTION." More specifically, the countermanding document alleged: "1. Rules get created by groups that are supplying a section since years and responsible for the content you all benefit from"; and "2. Our common understanding of a legit rule set is that a so-called 'COUNCiL' gets formed out by leaders of the most active groups in a section to control the quality and create the standards for future releases"; but in this case, neither of these features applied. The dissenting document claims that "[g]roups were forced to follow them and signed them without the chance to change them." Clearly, quasi-judicial consensus lawmaking was not followed in this instance, although with the extensive signatory list, it is hard to tell whether this dispute is simply the work of one begrudging party or whether there is truly deeper division sown here.

The rules themselves for this audio format can be broken down into a taxonomy of categories, with rules pertaining to

- general standards,
- media sources,
- duplication,
- encoding standards,
- name formatting,
- metadata standards,
- bootlegs,
- evidential documentation,

The general standards rules contain a set of specifics that pertain to the structure of the release. For instance, the rules state that every release "MUST contain an SFV, NFO, and JPG proof." The Simple File Verification (SFV) file contains checksums of all other files in the release. It allows topsite zipscripts to verify that the release contents have been accurately transferred onto their disks. The NFO file, as covered elsewhere in this book, contains iNFOrmation about the release including source, tracklist, reviews, and so on. Examples of source information that must be included are "[c]odec (DTS-HD Master Audio, Dolby TrueHD, LPCM)," the "[b]itrate (640kbps, 768kbps, 1536kbps...)," and the "[n]umber of channels (Stereo, 5.1, 7.1)," although the precise data vary by source type. The NFO file may also contain notes or errata on the release itself. For instance, it is noted that if "the tracklist has changes, for example, due to pressing errors, it is encouraged to correct and explain them in the .nfo." Finally, the JPG proof file, to which I will turn shortly, shows evidence of the release's original sourcing.

The general rules also provide some guidance for the conditions under which analog media rips can be considered bad. Concerning vinyl rips for example, the FLAC rules state that valid reasons to deem a rip "bad quality" include: "[t]he tracks are distorted and constantly clipping" or "[t]he tracks contain a constant hiss which was avoidable." Some of the factors that lead to bad-rip, nuke-status are subjective. For instance, "[l]ow sound, mono rips (from stereo sources) and other factors easily heard by the human ear" will subjectively depend on the quality of the judger's hearing. Nonetheless, these rules ensure that releases fulfill the criterion of being near-identical with the original media and being of a standard that can be played back as a substitute for that original.

The general rules further provide some assurance of intersystem operability. For instance, the requirement that "[t]he maximum directory and filename length is 128 characters" is designed to ensure that releases will be transferable between filesystems, some of which impose hard limits as to the length of filenames and directories. Given that many end-users operate on Microsoft Windows systems while topsites operate on Unix-derivative OSes and that both of these operating systems have support for multiple different filesystem formats, the approach is to work to the most reasonable, lowest common denominator. This is also clear in the directive that "filenames MUST only contain valid characters: a-z A-Z 0-9 _ . - ()," which is not technically true of all filesystems, although conforming to these standards is helpful for system interopability. This does pose some challenges for the Scene. For example, many musical artists take advantage of unique glyphs in order to style their names differently. For instance, ŦĦ€ ØĐĐŇ€ŞŞ, Prince's "love symbol," "BANNΞRS," or even just "Röyksopp" are unacceptable characters for FLAC Scene filenames. This in turn can pose problems for site-indexing functionalities that rely on people knowing the idiosyncratic transcriptions that encoders have used to replace the underlying text.

The "Invalid Official FLAC Standard Rules" also details various workings of different formats, again designed most closely to preserve the original source medium. The FLAC Scene stipulates music may be extracted from "BLURAY, CD, DVD(A), HDDVD and VINYL" as valid sources, excluding cassettes, reel to reel recordings, and, it seems, born-digital releases. This latter element is curious. Much music, released only as digital downloads, is available behind paywalls. In this iteration at least, FLAC Scene rules do not allow for such releases. This could be an effort to save space on topsites rather than reaching for the comprehensiveness that such an approach would take. Within these forms, it is stated that "[a]ll physical mediums (including mixed CD(s) / e.g. DJ-Mixes) MUST be ripped as separate tracks according to the TOC (Table Of Contents) on the medium."

The physical, media element is clearly of huge importance to the FLAC Scene and the rules make it clear that rippers must prove they own the original form. For this reason, the rules insist that "[r]eleases MUST always contain a proof CAMERA picture in JPEG format." In fact, it is stated that "[p]roof camera pictures MUST contain both, medium(s) and cover together" and that "[i]f there is no cover, a booklet or promo sheet or anything valid MUST be included to prove that the ripper has the release." The group must also prove that they have not stolen the release from another group. They do this by including a piece of paper in the photograph of the original medium with the group name written on it according to the rule, "[t]he proof picture MUST include a small piece of paper over the medium(s) and/

or the cover with GROUP name." Demonstrating the physical provenance here is all part of the inter-group competition, showing that the groups have a hard-copy supply chain in place.

What is most interesting about the insistence on physical media and the proof that the ripper has the artifact in question is that crediting and claiming ownership over the rip appears more important than simply releasing music. While there are additional security risks that come with uploading tracks to topsites from commercial digital music stores — in particular, individually watermarked audio streams — it seems more likely that the obsession with the physical media is more about the status of elite suppliers. On the day of a digital release, anyone can pay to download an album and then upload it. Sceners are not interested in this model because it would then be easy to gain Scene access simply by buying digital media and uploading it. Instead, they are interested in elite supply routes that can obtain music releases before they hit the shops, pre-oday material (that is, before the release date). Having the latest Lady Gaga album three weeks before its released is the aim of the FLAC Scene, it would seem; it is not to develop a comprehensive archive of all music ever, including digital-format releases.

Indeed, the second part of the Scene's dissenting document expressed outrage that web releases were forbidden in the new ruleset. While acknowledging that there was a problem with users "hacking google.play" to obtain web rips, the counterforce asserted that this "is no excuse to forbid all WEB content." The dissident(s) also noted that higher bitrates (e.g., "24 Bit/96 kHz") were possible in web formats, and that in many cases, there would be "NO DIFFERENCE to the retail product. There is just no physical medium anymore!" In other words, the focus in the FLAC Scene on physical media sources is by no means a shared concern of all members.

The inclusion of proof image files is also an interesting move in terms of risk-benefit balance. Images can reveal identifiable information about the poster both in the contents of the image itself and the EXIF (Exchangeable Image File Format) metadata. As the rules note, users should take "[s]ecurity precautions." For instance, it is specified that "EXIF metadata should be removed from JPEG files! Uniquely identifying information such as the camera serial number and GPS coordinates can pose a security threat if not removed, so this is very ESSENTIAL!" At the same time, the astute reader will nonetheless recognize that this is only a "should" condition despite the end warning that is it "ESSENTIAL." It is also noted that "[i]f the medium/cover/booklet contains anything that may expose your identity, then that part of image can be blurred or blackened."

This rule should, I believe, cause some alarm among Sceners. While the entire enterprise is a balance of risks and of conducting clearly illegal activities while taking precautions and hoping not to be caught, the rules expressly acknowledge that there is scope to introduce identifiable information into the proof image. In the quest to ensure that rippers prove that they possess the original medium from which the rip came, there is a substantially increased risk of being identified. Indeed, if the FLAC Scene were entirely serious about security, this rule would not exist, allowing, as it does, for image modification "to hide anything that might expose [the] ripper." As above, it is clear this proof rule is present to ensure that the Scene's focus lies in obtaining prerelease albums and in having an elite supply chain.

Such a focus is also evident in the section of the FLAC rules on advance and promo releases. These releases demonstrate that suppliers are truly on the inside of the music industry, as advance and promo releases refer not just to having the material ahead of launch but instead having a copy that was specifically mailed out to special contacts before the release date. As the rules put it, "[a]n ADVANCE or PROMO is not available at retail and is usually labelled with some variation of the words Advance and/or Promotional. Having a release before its retail date does not automatically make it an ADVANCE." The differential value placed on advance and promo releases is demonstrated compared to having pre-retail access. The latter can be obtained by persuading a shop clerk at a record store to allow access to material before it is released. In some cases, it will be employees of music shops who are the suppliers. However, these individuals are unlikely to have access to advance and promo releases.

That said, it is not straightforwardly the case that advance and promo releases are accorded higher worth than pre-retail releases. For one thing, some of these releases are watermarked with voiceovers and other features primarily designed precisely to stop the kind of prerelease leaking in which the FLAC Scene specializes. Hence, the Scene rules tell us, "ADVANCE and PROMO releases with voice overs, silence, or cuts on tracks are not allowed." Further, as I will discuss more below, in the section on dupechecking, the rules state that "ADVANCE and PROMO releases can always be duped by any retail release even if the tracks on both releases are identical." That is to say that the final release version of a record can always be released alongside an advance or promo, regardless of whether the sonic qualities of the record are identical. This demonstrates a differential value placed on advance and promo releases. It is not that these titles are unilaterally viewed as superior to their retail counterparts; rather they are seen as a different category with a unique set of constraints in acquisition and checking involved. For one thing, given the ban on voiceovers, periods of silence, and so forth, it is clear that the ripper must actually listen to the material before it is released. Although this can be done in parallel to other activities, such as encoding, tagging, uploading, disseminating, and then pre-ing, it nonetheless adds an hour or so of work for each album-length release. Given the often time-critical nature of Scene releases, this is far from a trivial matter.

Other standards, such as encoding parameters, are present in the rules for different reasons. As noted earlier, in Susan Leigh Star's appraisal, in addition to the fact that infrastructures function on the grounds of standardization, there are unique Scene characteristics and rationales for standardization. The encoding section of the ruleset, for instance, specifies that "[a] release MUST be encoded using FLAC 1.3.1" and that "[a] release MUST be encoded using the --compression-level-8 option." The reasons for this rule are diverse. First, by specifying the same encoding parameters across releases, the rules ensure that release groups do not inflate the size of releases for courier racing purposes (that is, to give themselves more file credit). As lower compression settings yield larger files, and level eight is the highest level of FLAC compression, there could be a temptation for the ripper to inflate the release size to capitalize on the 1-to-3 ratio of upload to download afforded by most sites. While the ratio does not apply to all accounts, and many rippers will have exempt leech accounts, larger files change the dynamic of racing for the couriers and use more of the topsite's hard disk space.

Second, though, this level of compression and the use of a unified, standard version of FLAC change the speed qualities of a race to release. By creating smaller files, the files that are more heavily compressed are quicker to upload and spread to all of the group's topsite pre areas. On the other hand, compressing files at level eight requires slightly more CPU capacity and takes longer. Compared to the upload bottleneck, it is not likely that the additional CPU load will result in any substantial delay for a group. When a release comes down to seconds, anything that changes the time dynamics can be significant. Third and finally, some settings in the FLAC encoder can alter the lossless nature of the compression. One of these is replay gain, which attempts to normalize the perceived loudness of audio tracks. If this option is applied, FLAC's decompression routine will produce a different output to the original input source. Hence, the rules state that "[a] release MUST NOT be encoded using --replay-gain or any kind of option that changes the audio source quality."

The largest part of the FLAC Scene rules is dedicated to the naming conventions for releases. This ranges from insistences; the tag "FLAC" "MUST be in uppercase in the release name and always before -YEAR and -GROUP tags" to a list of valid "TYPE" tags, that include "Advance, Promo, Retail, Bonus, Mag, Split, OST, Digipak, Audiobook, Bootleg, Demo, Sampler, Whitelabel, Reissue, Remastered. <country> (eg: JP_Retail, US_Reissue), Ltd, Limited, Limited_Edition, Ltd_Edition, Tour_Edition, Deluxe_Edition, Special_Edition, Digipa(c)k, Digipa(c)k_Edition, Clean, Explicit, Expanded_Edition, Collectors_Edition, Boxset." This culminates in a naming format that includes much pertinent artist and album information within the directory structure itself, with a minimum of "Artist-Title-SOURCE-FLAC-YEAR-GROUP" and a maximum of "Artist-Title-(CATALOGUE)-LANG-ADDITIONAL-TYPE-SOURCE-FLAC-YEAR-GROUP." An example of a final release name is "VA-Masterpiece_Created_By_Andrew_Weatherall-3CD-FLAC-2012-DeVOiD."

As ugly as it is, the naming standard is sculpted to interact with the trading clients of couriers. Formatting release names in this way makes it easy to parse the year of publishing, the group who released it, the source, and other items. This is pertinent because different sites will have different rules for what is allowed. For instance, some sites may have a maximum limit of two CDs within a release. Hence, the above "3CD" can be parsed and algorithmically determined that the release should not be transferred to sites that prohibit it. Likewise, sites may specify that only releases from the current year or the year before are allowed. Encoding the year in the release name allows for easy parsing and site selection. That this automatic parsing is a crucial component is clear from the insistence in the rules on the ordering of information, allowing for a predictable sequence; for instance, "CATALOGUE and TYPE are optional tags (except for rule 4.10). When they are used, they MUST be placed in the correct order." There are similar restrictions and prescriptions for filenames that, again, allow for easy parsing.

The penultimate section of the rules that I will discuss pertain to metadata within the FLAC files. These take the form of Vorbis comment tags, a metadata container standard that is common to many different types of media and that contains a set of field codes. Unlike their correlate ID3 tags in the MP3 format, Vorbis metadata fields are free-text, so consensus is required to decide, de facto, on which tags to use. The FLAC rules specify that the "TRACKNUMBER, ARTIST, TITLE, ALBUM, GENRE, and DATE (format: YYYY)" fields must be present. Of note here is the genre tag. For the same reasons as above, it seems that some topsites have genre restrictions. Embedding this information within the files allows sitebots to announce the genre and for trading clients then to understand the valid target site set for the release. This is clear because the genre tag is specified as containing, compulsorily, text from a limited subset: "A Cappella, Acid, Acid Jazz, Acid Punk, Acoustic, AlternRock," and so on.

The FLAC format also allows for the embedding of picture data. The FLAC Scene rules state that "[t]he FLAC picture block (METADATA_BLOCK_PICTURE) MUST be empty," meaning that embedding album art within the file itself is prohibited. While it is not clear what the precise rationale is for this, it could be because allowing the embedding of arbitrary-length base64 encoded binary objects within the file can substantially inflate the FLAC file size, thereby changing the dynamics of a race. As players do not universally support this block, it may also be seen as redundant when rule 9.5 of the FLAC Scene's "Invalid Official FLAC Standard Rules" specifies that releases must include images as separate files regardless.

This discussion has covered, for the most part, the high-level outlines of the FLAC Scene. Every sub-Scene has a similar set of principles that govern releases. For instance, in one of its clauses, the oday Scene has a detailed specification document that neatly embodies the link between the rules or principles and the topsite Scene on the ground: "[t]hese rules and guidelines are intended for release-groups in the first place, and sites secondary. We hope that in time many sites will take over the majority of these rules."[64] (Confusingly, "oday" refers not only to meaning on or before the day of release of a piece of software, but also to a class of smaller applications, such as office system utilities.)

Importantly, there is one area that I have not examined in this section that has used the FLAC Scene as a case study for Scene rules: duping, dupes, and dupechecking. It is to these important elements of Scene practice that we now turn.

---

64 ACME et al., "oday Scene Release Rules (nfo_2010.1_0DAY.nfo)," *Scenerules.org*, January 12, 2010, scenerules.org.

DUPES AND DUPECHECKING

Perhaps the most notable and, for those outside the Scene, curious, aspect of the rules pertains to dupes and dupechecking. These refer to the idea that only one release group may put out a version of a specific pirate artifact. Duplicates, in other words, are not allowed. It is certainly somewhat surprising that a culture that works on the very basis of illegally duplicating software, games, movies, music, pornography, and other media forms should have rules stipulating that one group may not duplicate the work of another. However, this contradiction in terms does not pose a problem for Sceners who value novelty above almost anything else. As the oday ruleset says, "[s]tealing cracks/keygens from P2P, WEB, or other scene groups is clearly not allowed!"[65] A culture that specializes in stealing the work of others — despite all the problems with that term in the digital space — has a set of stringent rules about not stealing the work of others.

To return to the FLAC Scene rules document analyzed in the last part of this chapter, the section on dupes is extensive. In the FLAC Scene, the most important rule is that "[a] release MUST not be identical to a previous release, except ADVANCE/PROMO releases (Rule 7.2)."[66] There are, clearly, ambiguities around what constitutes identical to a previous release, and the rules are clear in specifying this. "A release is not identical to a previous release," the rules state, "if: 1 The previous version has a different mastering; 2 The previous version has a different tracklist; 3 The previous version has a different version of a track."[67]

An important note here is that the duplication rules for the FLAC Scene are much more lenient than those found on private, audiophile, Bittorrent music trackers. The ruleset for the enormously popular What.CD tracker is available and publicly archived on the web, and it makes for interesting comparative

65 Ibid.
66 2Eleven et al., "Official.FLAC.Standard.Rules v3.0 (nfo_2016_FLAC.nfo)."
67 Ibid.

reading.[68] In the What.CD rules, duplicates are determined by the precise audio characteristics of each edition, and they are not merely based on the tracklist. In the What.CD model, there are several key factors that determine whether a version of an album should be considered a duplicate — media Table of Contents (TOC); track peak level; track pre-gap; and CRC values.

In the What.CD rules, the CD TOC plays an important role. "The Table of Contents (TOC of the extracted CD)," as they put it, "lists the tracks present on the CD, the various lengths of each track, and the order of the tracks. The TOC also lists the exact data sector values for the boundaries of each track. Differences in the TOC between two album versions typically, although not always, denote separate album editions." On What.CD, this TOC was combined with the track peak levels: "[t]he peak level value for each track (1–100% for EAC [Exact Audio Copy] and 0.001–1.000 for XLD [X Lossless Decoder]) indicates the loudness of the track. A value of 100% for an EAC-ripped track corresponds to the maximum loudness for that track. Different album editions tend to have substantial differences in the peak level values for corresponding tracks, resulting from distinct album mastering/remastering processes for the two editions."

Two other factors combine to yield distinct albums in the What.CD model. The first of these is track pre-gap lengths. "The pre-gap lengths," the What.CD rules explain,

> describe the amount of time separating two adjacent tracks. These periods of time typically consist of silence. This can be a good source of information for distinguishing album editions. However, because EAC and XLD both offer a number of choices with respect to gap detection the values can vary wildly (between either EAC and XLD or even between different versions of the same program) and still denote the same edition. For example, EAC offers three gap detection methods. On some CDs, using any one of the three methods will give you identical pre-gap length values. Yet on other CDs,

68 "Rules," What.CD, n.d., http://rescene.wikidot.com/what-cd-rules.

gap detection Method A will give the most accurate results when compared to B or C. Pre-gap lengths have no effect on the audio data and are not as important in determining album edition as the two previous benchmarks.

The above factors are all seen alongside the CRC (Cyclic Redundancy Check) value of the track rips. "The CRC value," the rules say, "is a representation of the data contained in an audio file. Each track for a properly-ripped album will contain a Test CRC value and a Copy CRC value. If the Test and Copy values match, you are assured that the data transfer from CD to hard drive was performed as faithfully and as accurately as possible. If there is a mismatch between the Test and Copy CRC values, you can be equally sure that there is some error with your rip for that particular track." In addition, the CRC value may differ between different versions of the same album.

What.CD allowed multiple formats of audio file (e.g., AAC, MP3, and FLAC) and rips within these categories were of varying standards. Varying standards ranged from the mechanics of FLAC files to FLAC files with a log, documenting the rip and its provenance. Using the software "Exact Audio Copy," for instance, with a 100% log score and a .cue file allowed the end download precisely to reproduce the original CD data layout. Due to these varying standards, dupes in this tracker were a complex matter, as demonstrated in Figure 10.

The system of duplicates and format trumping on the audiophile private tracker system of What.CD is much more inclusive and comprehensive than the system used in the FLAC Scene. That is not to say that there is not a hierarchy of releases and duplicates within the Scene. For instance, there are rules about the source media and what can dupe what: "BLURAY cannot dupe any other source, except HDDVD. HDDVD cannot dupe any other source, except BLURAY. CD cannot dupe any other source, except BLURAY and HDDVD. DVD cannot dupe any other source. VINYL cannot dupe any other source." Vinyl and DVD releases, at the bottom of the list, cannot be duplicates of any other format. If a vinyl version of a CD is available and the

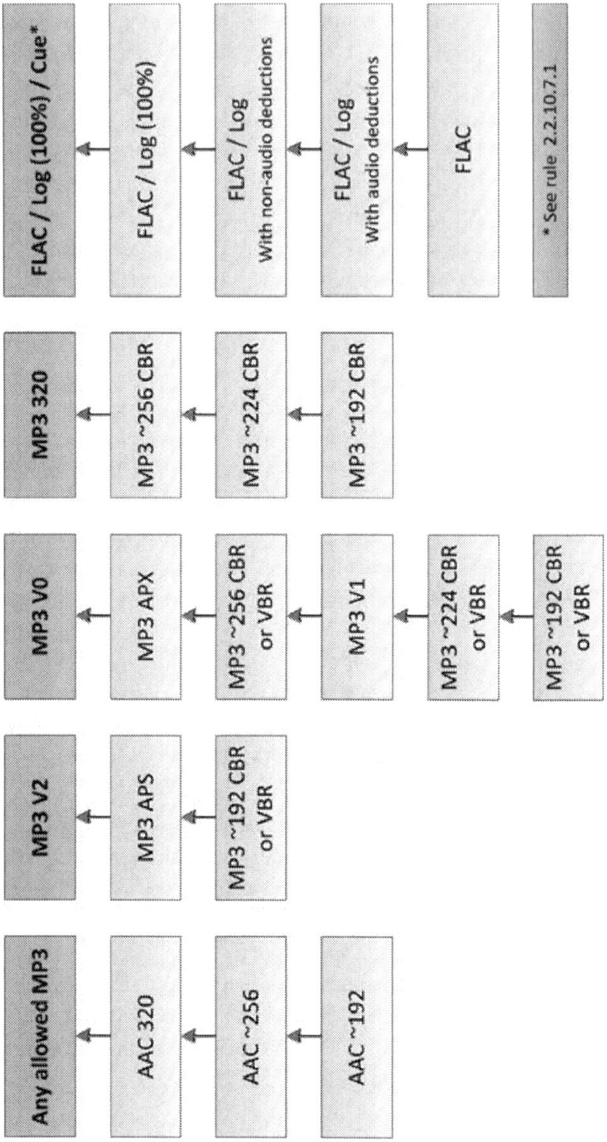

Figure 10. The What.CD Dupe/“Trump” Chart.

CD has already been released in the FLAC Scene, then the vinyl version cannot be ripped and released. Any group who did so would incur a nuke and subsequent penalty.

This is to note that What.CD aimed for comprehensiveness while the FLAC Scene aims at functional uniqueness and privileged the unique rip. What.CD encouraged posting multiple editions that, at times, had inaudible differences, such as minor changes in the data layout on the CD due to manufacturing processes. It also allowed different sources to co-exist in any order. That is, on What.CD users could upload a vinyl version with the same tracklist as an existing CD and not be penalized. The FLAC Scene, by contrast, stipulates that a "release MUST not be a collection of discs that have already all been individually released. For example, releasing a 2CD that combines a CD and EP after they have both been indivually [*sic*] released is not allowed."

Further, the checking process required to confirm uniqueness in the FLAC Scene is complicated. Rule 2.5 states that a "release MUST not have all its tracks included in one previous release. Examples: a CDS [CD single] cannot be released after a CDM [CD maxi-single] that includes all the tracks on the CDS. An album cannot be released after a boxset that includes all the tracks from that same album. A CDM or CDEP [CD extended play] cannot be released after a release has been reissued with all tracks." In other words, a release group must check, at the file level, that the tracks in question have not appeared on other releases. That said, the rules on fresh mastering that constitute a new release can make this tricky to ascertain. I argue that the FLAC Scene should not be viewed as a quest for total inclusivity. On the contrary, the rules are designed to make it hard to find new releases, to introduce an element of scarcity into the proceedings, and to increase the Scene's competitiveness. This fits with the other characteristics of racing and speed obsession in this space, making it a difficult alternative reality game. This "emphasis on only releasing new titles," argues Virginia Crisp, "inevitably skews the titles that circulate online" in the Scene.[69]

69 Crisp, "Release Groups & The Scene," 75.

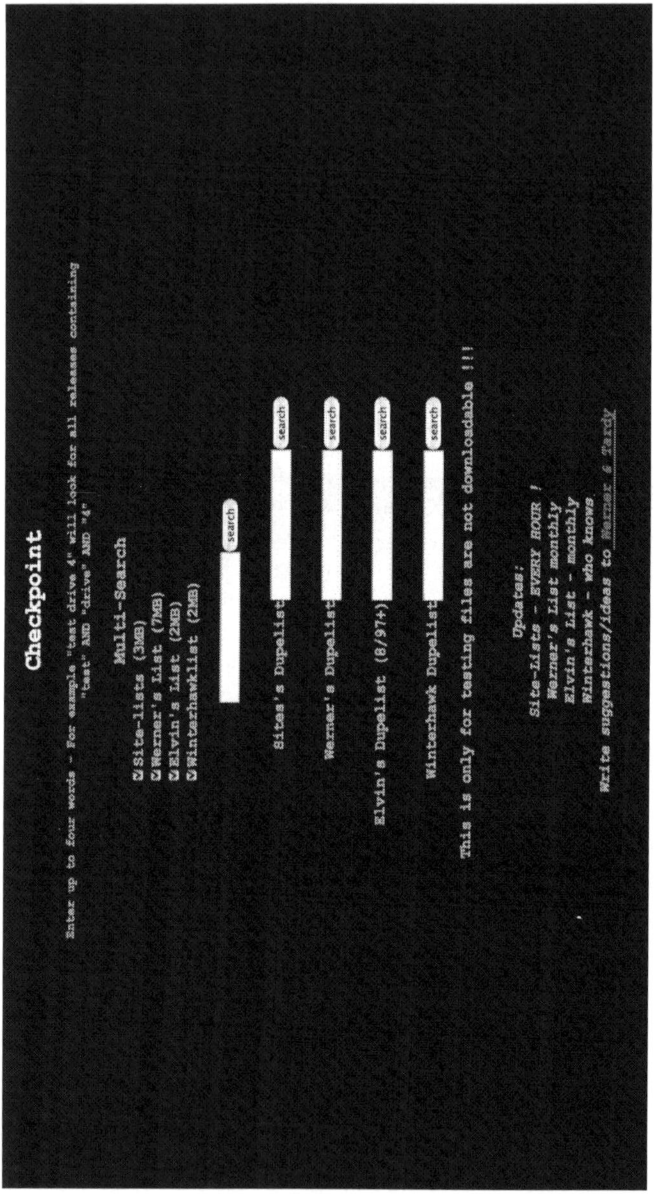
Checkpoint
Enter up to four words - For example "test drive 4" will look for all releases containing
"test" AND "drive" AND "4"
Multi-Search
Site-lists (3MB)
Werner's List (7MB)
Elvin's List (2MB)
Winterhawklist (2MB)
search
Sites's Dupelist
search
Werner's Dupelist
search
Elvin's Dupelist (8/97+)
search
Winterhawk Dupelist
search
This is only for testing files are not downloadable !!!
Updates;
Site-Lists - EVERY HOUR !
Werner's List monthly
Elvin's List - monthly
Winterhawk - who knows
Write suggestions/ideas to Werner & Tardy

Figure 11. Checkpoint in 1997.

In order to determine whether a release is allowed, a ripper and group require access to a dupechecker. A dupechecker is a database of existing releases, often containing the file list and other information about the releases. Given that the Scene has been operative for several decades, comprehensive dupecheckers are large databases. Some dupecheckers—also known as pre-dbs—are public. At the moment, there are several public pre-dbs, of which perhaps the most prominent is srrDB. These sites do not host any warez themselves. Instead, they host metadata about releases. srrDB, for instance, notes in its footer that "srrDB is an historical record of the [W]arez [S]cene. We do not offer illegal downloads nor links to these works. All metadata gets added by our awesome users. Photographs or pictures can be part of these historical records, deemed fair use (news reporting and research) and are only a part of the complete work, but copyrights are owned by their respective creators or right holders."

The public srrDB contains 6,142,334 releases and has stored copies of 6,131,900 NFOs alongside these releases, as well as stored proof JPG files and other metadata. Searches of this very large database tend to take up to four seconds to execute, although this time increases in proportion to the complexity of the query. As this database allows searching of files contained within the releases as per the FLAC Scene rules, it can be used to determine whether a title is a dupe or not.

Dupecheckers must be linked to the Scene in some way or another. While releases are spread far and wide, the critical point is that they must harvest their data from topsites in some fashion. This may be at a remove; for instance, users on topsites may run a script that pulls down the NFO and associated metadata and then automatically uploads it onto a metadata-only dump site. Nonetheless, regardless of whether the dupecheck is fed directly by sites or by third-party aggregation, this link to the Scene obviously makes such databases a target of interest for law enforcement.

This link to the Scene dates to historic dupecheck systems. One of the earliest of these, *Checkpoint,* was created by Werner & Tardy, a single individual who went by the nickname werner_t and who was a member of The Council Music Group (CMG). Checkpoint combined several existing Scene databases to underpin its system. These included dupelists from topsites themselves and lists compiled by the users Werner, Elvin, and Winterhawk. In 1997 the database sizes ranged from 2MB to 7MB but are undoubtedly much larger in the present day, given that metadata and images are usually now stored in dupecheckers. The note that the "Site-Lists" are updated "EVERY HOUR," shown in Figure 11's screenshot of Checkpoint from 1997, indicates that the update mechanism is drawing on sites themselves.

Riskily, Checkpoint and other dupecheckers sat and still sit on publicly accessible domain names. In its public acknowledgments, consider that a CMG NFO from 1999 listed "WWW.DUPECHECK.COM" and "WWW.MP3CHECK.COM." The Internet Archive's stored copies of these pages yield to the user a selection process where they can choose to connect to a European or American source for the dupechecking, again indicating that there is some link to a topsite behind the scenes. For instance, in the *NetMonkey* weekly courier report of the site dupe command that is embedded in glftpd, when lester notes that "most anyone in the [S]cene can go through and site dupe and if they are around long enough they will recognize dupes without even having to search real hard."[70]

glftpd has a built-in dupechecker that indexes all material uploaded and that allows users to search it. As the manual states, this command "[s]earches the dupe database (ftp-data/logs/dupelog) for a match. Searching a big database can take quite some time so please be patient. Do NOT include wildcards! This will only search for directories!"[71] Notably, these

70 lester, "Deep Thoughts," *Netmonkey Weekly Report* (nwr17.txt), August 16, 1998, DeFacto2.

71 greyline, "glftpd-LNX-2.04_1.0.1e-glFTPD TLS README (2+deb7u3_x86_docs/README.TLS.txt)," *mewbies.com,* 2014, http://mewbies.com/glftpd-LNX-2.04_1.0.1e-2+deb7u3_x86_docs/README.TLS.txt.

latter limitations are significant and would not help with the need for file-level searches. It is also the case that not every site will have every release. A local search will only yield a subset of Scene releases. It is for this reason that third-party aggregating dupecheckers are created. Some courier and release charts even list the publicly accessible dupechecker as the source for their work. For instance, the *Front Line Release Report* notes that "the only source i use to create these stats is da well known dupecheck system (www.dupecheck.com). this duper is one of the most accepted in da scene, so i think its the best way to calculate the stats."[72] The decentralization of the Warez Scene and the lack of any official dupechecker poses real problems for participants. In another example, the *Unbiased DOX Report* points out, in its July 2005 issue, in a comment on Caterpillar_Construction_Tycoon_NoCD_Crack-TNT, that "there could be a prior NoCD by INDUCT, as one is listed in a dupechecker. However, it could be a fake dir, since only 1 out of 4 dupecheckers showed it. And it is not on any sites anywhere; we thusly ignore it!."[73] That is to say that even the weekly reporting systems suffer from a lack of reliable dupechecking.

Dupecheckers, therefore, could prove themselves to be fertile ground for law enforcement efforts. Given that the construction of a dupechecker is not itself illegal, as a mere documentary effort toward not infringing copyright, it seems possible that law enforcement agents could volunteer to establish a dupechecker and then to snoop on individuals who participate. This appears to be the case for werner_t's dupecheck. On May 2, 2004, a user claiming to be werner_t posted to the ISO news forum, a thread that reads as follows:

> i have not shown my face on here for quite some time (and never with my true nick).

---

72 dustie, "some little notes," *Front Line Scene Release Report* (frontline_week_010.txt), July 7, 1999, DeFacto2.

73 Lamer, "TNT," *The Unbiased DOX Report* (DR200510.TXT), July 11, 2005, DeFacto2.

Figure 12. The ASCII Art Logo of the Nuke Council by mR novo8.

> but over the past 9+ years i have ran the [S]cene dupecheck (#dupecheck on efnet and linknet as well as the old public dupe checker @ [URL].
>
> I was contacted about 6 months ago regarding the bnc.us domain and the activities of dupeXXX bots on the irc networks. I have cooporated with the authorities in question, and ok'd advanced logging of the irc channels.
>
> i dont want to alarm too many [S]ceners, as there is only so much info that may be obtained from your hostname/ip address once connected to the irc servers.

> as it stands i was the sole operator of the dupecheck database, and quite honestly i never really understood why the [S]cene trusted me so much.
>
> anyways, its been a great 10+ years.
>
> peace
>
> werner[74]

Although the impact of this admission remains unclear, it appears to indicate that law enforcement efforts actively log dupecheck activities, knowing, as they do, that this is one of the major weaknesses in decentralized Scene infrastructure.

Nukes and Nukers

The release rule standards, coupled with dupecheck procedures, make for an environment of quality control. It is a space with strict determinations on what is allowed, which is of course ironic given the illicit nature of the environment and its very raison d'être. Yet how is this enforced? In this wild west of a world, how can participants, who have already shown themselves to be lawbreakers in broader society, be compelled to behave according to codes of conduct and rulesets?

The answer is a system known as nuking. To nuke a release means to mark it as bad. Nukes are enforced at the site level. File Transfer Protocol Daemons (FTPDs), such as glftpd, contain a built-in site nuke command that staff can use to mark a release. Nukes also come with multipliers. That is, when a release is marked as nuked 1×, the user who uploaded the release will lose the credit they gained, but they will break even. If a nuke comes with a higher multiplier, the user will lose more than they gained from the upload. At the site level, a nuke of 3×, for in-

74 werner, "FLT Busts," *Theisonews,* May 2, 2004, https://www.theisonews.com/forums/index.php/topic,117995.msg1559546.html?#msg1559546.

stance, would mean that the uploading user would lose three times the credit of their upload size.

There are various reasons for nukes, some of which pertain to rules on individual sites, while others are Scene-wide nukes. On individual sites, reasons for nuking can be the preferences of site administrators. For instance, if a site specifies that only particular genres of music are allowed to be uploaded, then a local nuke can be applied to the release to penalize the courier or release group who uploaded a contraband item. A severe violation of the rules (e.g., uploading child pornography, revealing the site name to others, leaking details of the site, behaving in an insecure way, and autotrading) can also result in the user losing their site account. At times, other site operators will also be notified of these serious infractions, which result in a SceneBan. That said, it is difficult truly to enforce a Scene-wide ban. As users are identified only by pseudonyms and handles and can adjust their ident, nicknames, and even hostnames at will, it is tough to correlate one user with another. That said, to build one's standing from zero, having been banned would be a tall order indeed. Other nukes are Scene-wide. For instance, a nuke for reasons of duplication will apply on all sites, unless the release is marked as internal. Likewise, non-working cracks, bad vinyl rips, poor video quality, and so on are all problems about the release, rather than pertaining to individual site rules. In these cases, the nuke is usually announced in a pre-channel and duplicated down to the site level.

The need for Scene-wide coordination of nuking has led to the emergence of so-called NukeNets. Using names such as "Nukleotide," "Nuclear," "SheepNet," "ZoNeNET," and "LocalNET," these networks are trusted to nuke releases simultaneously across a number of sites when Scene-wide nukes come into effect. As you might expect, these networks compete to be the best and fastest at ensuring accurate, timely nukes.

First formulated in 2008, NukeNet conduct is determined by and set out in the Nuke Council Rules.[75] This document states that "The Nuke Council is a coalition of nuke networks working together to ensure nukers bias, nukewars and many other problems that plague the nuke scene become a thing of the past. It is our goal to create a universally accepted and proper nuking environment that adheres to basic rules agreed upon by all who sign this document." Among other things, this document specifies a precise format for issuing nukes to ensure a standardized log of record. For instance, the document states that duplicates should use the format "dupe.GRP.YYYY-MM-DD (do not use sameday)" while, say, out-of-sync errors in video files are to be tagged with "out.of.sync (correct timestamps must be used see sec 1.3)." Perhaps most importantly, the general rules of the Nuke Council set out the conduct of nukers and NukeNets. For instance, the document specifies that a nuker "may NOT nuke with personal opinions/comments" and "may NOT nuke with profanity in the reason." Reiterating this first point, it is stipulated that "[a]ll nukes MUST be valid, nuking with a bias is strictly forbidden." The main reason for these rulesets is the presence of so-called nukewars.

According to the Nuke Council rules, Nukewars are the cases where a release "has been nuked or unnuked 4 or more times." Such a nukewar typically happens when nukers disagree or the evidence for a nuke is contentious. For instance, the rule that a nuker "may NOT nuke mp3's for being re-encoded without substantial proof" is prone to subjective interpretation. What counts as substantial? Who judges? In short, just as Scene rulesets acted as laws, the nuke rules act as principles of allegation, prosecution, trial, and conviction. They set out the terms on which the enforcement principles will be applied and provide basic standards of fairness in the application of penalties. Nukewars also sometimes occur when nukers are unable

75 Most of this section comes from SheepNet et al., "Nuke Council Rules (nfo_2008_NC.nfo)," *Scenerules.org,* November 8, 2008, scenerules.org. Unmarked citations should be considered to reference this document.

precisely to identify the timing of a release. The result is confusion over which release is a duplicate. The precedent for when releases are pred in the same second as one another is that both releases will be allowed, showing how truly competitive these situations are.[76]

As might be expected with the formation of different NukeNets and groups, a set of competitive practices has emerged among these rival factions. As a result, there are prohibitions against stealing the work of an enemy network. We can see this in the Nuke Council document, which stipulates that "[s]tealing nukes/unnukes is STRICTLY FORBIDDEN, if discussed on a network it may not get nuked on a different network unless nuker (or the one who gave notice of the nuke) gives permission, this also applies to NUKE-REQ's that are echoed to only one network." Groups of nukers compete to show themselves as the best arbiters of quality and work to become known for finding the most flawed releases. If a nuke group or net finds a valid nuke reason, it is forbidden for other NukeNets to appropriate this reasoning and propagate it through their systems. Of course, individual site nukers may take the reason and duplicate it, but automatic nuking by other networks is prohibited, thereby introducing a competitive element into nukes. NukeNets also hold themselves to a high standard and work to ensure that bad moderators are quickly removed: "[b]ad nukers (multiple time offenders) will be added to the council ban database, which will permenantly [*sic*] ban the user from all council member networks."

Nukes are a controversial topic. Several Scene magazines have discussed them over the years. Of particular significance is lester's article in the *NetMonkey Weekly Report* #17, where he decides to write about nukes because "in the past week I have experienced quite a few, how shall I put it, complete fucking morons trying to nuke? (I think that covers it)."[77] For lester, the position of nuker is to be considered separate from other roles.

---

76 See "UNNUKE fine_pred.same.second.so.both.rls.are.fine/ZoNeNET" in a pre-db such as srrDb.

77 lester, "Deep Thoughts."

It requires people who are free of external, competing interests: "[y]ou want," he writes, "unbiased, experienced, and levelheaded people to nuke for you."[78] He goes on to claim that this explicitly excludes couriers because they have a motivation in nuking releases that other traders have transferred: "[s]o right off the bat you have to say no traders get nuke, why does someone being #1 qualify them to nuke properly? It doesn't, most of them just mirror another sites [*sic*] nukes anyways. And why do traders want nuke so bad anyways? Because it can enhance their trading position. Yes traders are that pathetic and competitive:)."[79]

The issue of bias is not easy to exclude, as Lester concedes: "[s]o you want someone with knowledge, but without bias. This is virtually impossible, because the average Joe who isn't in any group or has ANY feeling on any particular group, isn't going to know jack shit about what to nuke."[80] lester's solution to the issue of bias is itself, however, slightly problematic. He suggests a list of people who can be trusted and have experience but can act dispassionately. The challenge is that the list includes lester himself: "there's some options, you find people who have been nuking for a long time, obvious choices are Winterhawk/Jess/Myself, and anyone who has been around that has done this kind of thing long enough where they know wtf is going on."[81] lester claims that these people are as unbiased as is possible, given their group memberships, but he does not comment on the fact that he has immodestly recommended himself: "[n]ow, even these people are in groups, and have their own preferences to who wins, but in my experience they are fair and do not nuke to let their guys win or not nuke something because that group upped it, etc. etc. …"[82]

There are two other complaints about NukeNets. As with any top-down imposition of rules and authority in the Scene, the first is that the nuking standards set by the Nuke Council

78 Ibid.
79 Ibid.
80 Ibid.
81 Ibid.
82 Ibid.

are "just some master control program by networks not doing any real release work for the [S]cene."[83] This is the flip side of lester's complaint. Namely, if siteops employ dedicated nukers, who are not part of any group or recognized as longstanding members of the Scene, they will not be respected in their role as nuker. The fundamental issue here is one of authority to nuke and to enforce the rules. Just as judges in broader society must derive their authority from a combination of legal expertise and an appointment process linked to, but independent of, other branches of government, the system of nuking requires respect and authority for it to work.[84]

The second complaint pertains to site security. To enact Scene-wide nukes, it seems that NukeNets have accounts on many sites. While it is clear that in some site systems, local nukers copy information from NukeNet echo or announce IRC channels to the local site's nuke database; in other cases, the NukeNets themselves have accounts on the sites. The dissenter(s) who authored the critique of the official FLAC Scene rules document, for instance, decry the creation of centralized rings and databases of sites: "[t]he worst thing is that those individuals created decent siterings and a database with all [S]cene sites listed."[85] Likewise, this commentator adds, "[i]f one big ring is infiltrated and busted, a whole part of the [S]cene is shut down! GREAT! AGAIN GET A BRAIN! Or imagine this database(s) get leaked!?"[86]

While this grousing document does not specifically mention NukeNets, some of the measures it mentions pertain to securing sites and sharing information about bad users. It

83 "Invalid Official FLAC Standard Rules V3.0 (INVALID_OFFICIAL_FLAC_STANDARD_RULES_V3.0-SCENENOTICE.nfo)."

84 For more on the intricacies and recent development of juridical selection in the context of the UK, for instance, see Erin Delaney, "Searching for Constitutional Meaning in Institutional Design: The Debate Over Judicial Appointments in the United Kingdom," *International Journal of Constitutional Law* 14, no. 3 (2016): 752–68.

85 "Invalid Official FLAC Standard Rules V3.0 (INVALID_OFFICIAL_FLAC_STANDARD_RULES_V3.0-SCENENOTICE.nfo)."

86 Ibid.

thus seems clear that there is a NukeNet-like component here: "[t]o hide their missing operating system skills and understanding of Linux, programming languages and everything you need to secure a server probably they even invented an IP-banning system that forcing couriers and groups to drop all sites that are rented/colocation or with setups not common for their understanding."[87] In other words, NukeNets and other common security systems that have slots on multiple sites, in this allegation, pose a security threat.

The author certainly has a point. Any centralization within the Scene carries with it additional risk. NukeNets that hold accounts on a range of sites present themselves as targets for law enforcement action, leading to the discovery of a whole subset of topsites. On the other hand, this constitutes a trade-off against convenience as it does with all matters of security. As lester puts it, "what is a poor siteop who doesn't want to spend his time nuking everything to do?"[88]

LOCAL SITE RULES

All rules in the Scene and nukes are eventually enforced and enacted at the site level. The *ReScene* archive provides topsite rule NFOs that sample the types of laws and enforcement prevalent in the Scene.[89] The number of available topsite rulesets is far fewer than other types of Scene artifacts, but those that do exist in the archive document the rules of the sites ANZ, HS ("HyperSpace Unit"), and a suspected Hungarian site, whose name I do not know.

All sites have one basic rule: "[n]ever talk about this site."[90] There is also a set of privacy rules that are common to all rulesets: "[d]o Not give any info about Axx/Chan," and "[d]o not talk about IRC chans." In other words, as in the Chuck

87 Ibid.
88 lester, "Deep Thoughts."
89 "Topsite Rules," *ReScene,* 2020, http://rescene.wikidot.com/topsite-rules#toc4.
90 The below material all draws on the topside rule documents found at ibid.

Palahniuk novel and film *Fight Club* (1996, 1999), the number one rule of all sites pertains to security and the need to keep a low profile. That this is the case hardly needs to be said. Nonetheless, it is reiterated throughout the Scene. Some sites have additional security requirements that go beyond the basics. For example, on HS, if one does not "use BNC @ chan" — that is, use a bouncer to connect to the channel — one will be deleted from the site. On some sites, there are also rules that prohibit trading to FXP boards: "[d]o not trade to FXP boards" on penalty of "DELUSER." This is a security principle. By instructing the site to conduct a site-to-site transfer to a hacked box, anyone investigating the FXP board Scene and its hacked pubstros (covered in the previous chapter on FXP Boards) could find themselves in possession of a topsite IP, enabling them to track it down. This principle, generally enshrined among Sceners, is meant to protect the topsite Scene from the dangerous, hacking activities of FXP boards.

There is also a set of meta-rules that pertain to the circumstances of arbitration. Users learn that "THE STAFF CAN DELETE YOUR ACCOUNT AT ANY TIME" and that, on pain of "DELUSER," one should "NOT COMPLAIN ABOUT NUKES." One should also not "ask for leech or credits" or "beg for credits, money, or weed." One should never "ASK FOR EXTRA LOGINS." These rule-setting elements yield, in a sense, the meta-judicial qualification of site membership. They provide the rules that pertain to disputing the rules. These statements map the terrain of understanding the rules' enforcement and what it means — in a social contract — to be a site member. Arguing with the law, this rule says, is futile and grounds for termination of that contract. In this same category of meta-law is the penalty of deletion if one receives "15 NUKES a week." A set of minor infractions amount, in their totality, as equivalent to one serious, deletable offense. In such a rule, it is not clear whether Scene nukes (which are beyond the ability of racers to determine) versus local site nukes (which are violations of the rules) count differently. Nonetheless, "[g]eneral stupidity," it is noted, "will not be tolerated."

Sites also specify the rules of conduct for racing. For instance, one must "[b]e on chan, at least while racing," at the risk of a 5GB penalty. One must also not delete any files after a race is "HALFWAY" complete, on at least some sites. Different sites have different policies on many matters of racing. For example, on some sites, "DUAL UPLOAD in same dir is allowed," whereas it is not clear that this was the case on other sites. There are also different pre-time limits. Some sites stipulate, for instance, that there is a "[m]ax [of] 5 minutes after PRE" for any newly transferred release. Others have a blanket statement that "PRETIME [is] 20MINS IN ALL ENGLISH SECTIONS." These rules on racing and timing enforce the parameters of competition. Sites do not want to be in a situation where users upload material that is several hours old. Therefore, they only allow material released within a specific, very narrow time limit. That this is determined in minutes gives a flavor of the speed and level of competition here involved. Users are further told that they must "COMPLETE UPLOADS WITHIN 3 HOURS OF STARTING," ensuring that races do not drag out over extremely long periods. It is also often specified that "LEECH IS NOT FOR TRADING." User accounts that are not using a ratio — and thus have unlimited credits effectively — are not to be used to build credits on other sites.

Other parameters of competition are also apparent in the site rules. Users must, for example, "UPLOAD SFV, NFO AND SAMPLE FIRST." This changes the dynamics of a race. The individual who creates the race or release folder and begins the transfer must, under these parameters, upload three minor, small files first. The SFV, as noted elsewhere, contains the checksums of the files in the release. It allows the site's zipscripts to anticipate the files that will be received and verify their integrity when uploaded. The NFO file contains information about the release. The sample is, literally, a sample of the video, which demonstrates the quality of the encoding and the nature of the movie. These three files are small. They are not likely to result in any significant credit gains. However, due to the nature of FTP and FXP, uploading a file contains several commands that take time to issue to both servers. In a server-to-server FXP, both servers must then open a channel between them by involving Transport Layer Security (TLS) negotiation, which adds seconds to the clock. There are significant disadvantages to being the person who initiates a race. In addition to the "mkdir" command (which creates the directory), the first three files transferred are not likely to help the user build credit. Therefore, these principles, while potentially necessary, add a curious, strategic angle to couriering and racing. In an MP3 release, where there may only be an SFV, an NFO, and one small MP3 file, a courier who starts the race may get no credits for the upload if they have to transfer the SFV and the NFO first. Waiting until someone else has created the directory and the SFV, and then transferring the content file just as the initial racer begins the NFO, is likely to be a winning strategy. To pull this off requires a combination of guesswork and cunning. Such a strategy requires traders to develop their clients in such a way to help with this goal. For instance, a client may only join a race once someone else has started, unless the release is approaching the pretime limit. Such a client could, at the 2:50-mark, begin a race itself if nobody else has started it. This gives just a taste of the tricky dynamics of racing.

There are also requirements of users concerning inactivity and pruning. For example, the rule that one must "NOT BE INACTIVE FOR MORE THAN FOUR WEEKS" is a deletable offense on one site. Others have even stricter limits. For instance, on ANZ, "[u]ser[s] without an excuse is [*sic*] idle longer than 7 days" are deleted. These enforce Scene activities as a crucial part of a user's working week. Such rules send a clear message: if you are not willing to make a firm commitment to the Scene, logging in every week, participating in site channels, trading weekly, then you are not welcome on the site.

This inactivity also has a second component: low activity. On ANZ, the "[t]op 10 Trader[s] are Save[d] for the next Month." Those in the top ten monthup (the highest scoring uploaders in any monthly period) retain their accounts. Anyone who falls outside of this group is offered a stark choice: "the other -150gig at the end of [m]onth or delpurge you [d]ecide." That is, any trader who is not in the top ten must decide whether to lose 150GB of credits on the site or to be permanently and irrevocably deleted. If a clearer indication of enforced competition were needed, it would be hard to find. The message here is: participate and compete or lose your slot. It is unclear what would happen to users who do not have 150GB to lose. While glftpd and other daemons do have support for negative credits, it is likely that such a stance would not be tolerated for any lengthy period by siteops.

New users also face a brutal challenge in being added to sites such as HS. This site specifies that "[t]rial is 7GB first week," or the new user will be deleted. Further, trialers are "NOT allowed to fill REQUEST" (that is, they may not upload releases that others have requested). Filling a request would, usually, be an easy way for a user with an archive to complete their trial period. Some releases will total 7GB, and a trial user with access to an archive site could meet the criteria simply by uploading this one, asked-for release. By forbidding trialers from filling requests, the site rules here ensure that traders who join will participate on a sustainable basis in the future. It is made impossible to fluke the trial by filling requests. Not every site has rules about the trials of new couriers or users. Those that do ensure that users who join fulfill the elite requirements that the site expects, making it clear that users will need to continue participating if they wish to retain their slots.

There are also media-specific rules that take the form of section demands. These often pertain directly to the content of the media, as opposed to the meta-standards of Scene or site rules. For instance, in the "XXX" sections of the sites, it is often stipulated that various forms of (sometimes illegal) pornography are not allowed: "[n]o Gay, Children, Animals etc." This is important for the degree of criminality of sites, although it is interesting that this rule problematically juxtaposes two illegal categories against a wholly legal form in many countries (i.e., "gay"). Siteops may be willing to break copyright law to pursue their illicit hobby, but facilitating the distribution of videos of child sexual abuse, one would hope the vast majority of people would agree, is an entirely different level of wrongdoing. Frequently, as noted above, the section rules do also specify characteristics of the release. For instance, one site specifies that the "MAX SIZE IS 1 DVD OR 4 CDS"; on another site, HS, the "[m]ax release size is 5 CDs, 1 DVD unless approved." In addition, particular release sources can be allowed or disallowed, which is another important reason for storing this information in the release or directory name. For example, on HS it is stated that "NO CABLE, SBD, TV, DVB, FM, DAB" releases are allowed in the MP3 section.

There are also often approval processes for releases characterized as internals. These releases seem to occur when a group puts out a release version that would otherwise be a duplicate. Potential reasons for this behavior include

- creating a higher-quality encode, even when the original release did not break any rules;
- re-releasing something subsequently popular that went unnoticed at the time of its release;
- putting out a release that likely has a broad audience when the original release was quite some time ago.

This can be of merit when a group's encodings are highly respected, for instance, or when a media form has a particularly lengthy afterlife. An example of this is iNCiTE's internal release of the James Bond film, *GoldenEye* (1995). In the NFO for this release, they state that "[t]his speaks for itself. Enjoy the entire collection of the legendary 007 James Bond series. We'd like to give credit to QiX" — the Warez group who originally released the first Scene version of the film — "for encoding the whole set a few years ago but feel that it's time for a new release."[91] Such releases, when not released by affiliates onto the site itself, usually require approval (i.e., couriers may not transfer internal releases). Approval may be granted in the case of culturally sig-

91 iNCiTE, "007 GoldenEye 1995 iNTERNAL DVDRip XviD (incite-goldeneye-xvid.nfo)," March 23, 2005, srrDB.

nificant releases or when a work comes to prominence long after its initial release (Moby's 1999 album, *Play,* for instance, climbed the charts years after its first appearance).

Site section rules often have language rules. Although I cannot tell for sure, it seems that ANZ is most likely a German site. Many of its sections specify that "[o]nly German Releases" or "germ/engl" languages are allowed. One of the other sites to whose rules file I have access is clearly Hungarian, stipulating in several sections that "ONLY ENGLISH/HUNGARIAN" releases are permissible. In this way, we can see segmentations of the Scene into geographical release clusters. While English-language releases generally seem to transcend the geographic locations of sites — just as, due to colonial legacies, the language itself does likewise — there are micro-Scenes based within each country, releasing content in particular languages.[92]

There are two final areas of sites whose existence we can infer from the available rules files: speed test areas and requests. The speed test area is, presumably, important for couriers who wish to test the routing from various shells and sites. If one is to win a high-speed transfer race, it is essential to know which sites will yield the fastest transfer to another via FXP or what the routing is like from one's own shell. However, in order not to clutter the site, any files in the speed test area that are not deleted will incur a nuke penalty, potentially costing the courier credits. "DELETE YOUR SPEEDTEST FILES WHEN FINISHED," thunders one ruleset.

The final area that we can understand through reference to site rules is the request system, which allows users to ask for specific releases that are not already on the site. While I have touched above on the rules around trialers filling requests, additional rules show how this section works. First, requesters must use the formal request system. One must "USE SITE COMMANDS FOR REQUESTS" and not post, say, requests into IRC channels. This is not a problem in some sites as only

92 For more on multiple sub-Scenes, see Crisp, "Release Groups & The Scene," 70–71.

certain classes of users have permission to make requests: "[r]equests only by STAFF." At the same time, this rule sits oddly in tension with others. For instance, the same site that stipulates that only staff can make requests also specifies that user must "[n]ever ever fill an own request" on the penalty of "DELUSER." It seems odd that a staff member on a site might be deleted for filling their own request. In the interests of keeping the site tidy, requests must be placed in the directory of the request: "UPLOAD RELEASE DIRECTORY WITHIN REQ- DIRECTORY." Likewise, to keep the site clean, on some sites, "[r]equests are removed if not filled 7 days after request." This ensures that there is not an accumulation of requests that remain unfilled. Finally, one must mark requests as complete so that others do not waste their time searching for something that is no longer required: "MARK REQUEST AS FILLED WHEN COMPLETE WITH SITE REQFILLED." This yields an ordered system of requests that sit within the same highly regulated framework as other Scene parameters.

Numbering the rules for future reference is a notable marker of the Scene's quasi-judicial process. Sometimes split into subsections that issue period-delimited sub-rules, these rules are meant to be referenced and are set in stone with hierarchically addressable content (for example: "as per rule 2, subsection 4…"). By studying these enactments of Scene rules, we can understand their actual enforcement. I have argued, throughout this chapter, that the Scene has developed a set of shared operational principles that are enacted as de facto standards, stemming from de jure pronouncements that have community consensus. In this way, the Scene goes through cycles of internal legalistic development, based on shared understandings between participants, that shape how the alternative reality game is played. As I showed with the dissent with the FLAC rules, occasionally this consensus principle breaks down. However, over time, with this alternation between pronouncement, consensus, dissension, adoption, nuke-implementation, and legal-esque framework, a system emerges that "just works." It is a strong demonstration of anarchic principles resulting in organized chaos. As we will now see in the following chapter, as with most organized societies, the Scene also has its own spaces of artistic practice, as though work (trading) and play (art) must go together within the game space.

FIVE

Aesthetics

"Art's made by artists, but artists are enabled by a scene."

— David Mitchell, *Utopia Avenue*[1]

ANTAGONISTIC REMIXES

As I pointed out in the introduction to this book, if one is to understand the motivations of Warez Sceners in playing their dangerous game, it is first necessary to grasp the histories and cultures from which they emerged. Specifically, the Warez Scene must be understood within the academic purview of the study of "subcultures." In his landmark and genre-defining study of subcultures, Dick Hebdige wrote of the style of underground groups as denoting "form as the status and meaning of revolt, the idea of style as a form of Refusal, the elevation of crime into art."[2] While, for Hebdige, "the 'crimes' are only broken codes," in the case of the Warez Scene, this is certainly not the case; there is a genuine set of crimes being committed, albeit in ways that I contend constitute an aesthetic act. I argue that, like Hebdige, we should pay attention to the "expressive forms and rituals of those subordinate groups — the teddy boys and mods and rock-

1 David Mitchell, *Utopia Avenue* (London: Sceptre, 2020), 449.

2 Dick Hebdige, *Subculture: The Meaning of Style* (London: Routledge, 2002), 2.

ers, the skinheads and the punks—who are alternately dismissed, denounced and canonized; treated at different times as threats to public order and as harmless buffoons."[3] This view, originating in the Centre for Contemporary Cultural Studies at the University of Birmingham in the 1970s, has been contested. It is also one that prioritizes the aesthetic or style as a mode of resistance in and of itself. I do not go this far and continually note that the actual illegality of the Warez Scene is core to its identity and to any perceived resistance. That said, this does not preclude an ongoing understanding of the Warez Scene as a subcultural phenomenon in which style plays a key role.[4]

In the case of the Scene, this analysis of style in the alternative reality game equates to understanding two differing artistic or aesthetic cultural roots. An important part of the Scene I have hitherto only touched upon is its intersection with two unique digital art communities: the DemoScene and the ASCII art space. It is due to the shared genealogy with the former of these two activities that the Scene is called "the Scene." In this chapter I turn to the background contexts of the DemoScene and chart a history of ASCII art in a lineage of concrete poetry and information aesthetics.

Many of the traditional accounts of the Warez Scene and its root in Bulletin Board System (BBS) cultures focus on the liberatory power of digital copying. Pirates are viewed misguidedly as operating within an economic system in which they view themselves as "helping others" to get something for nothing. This ethos may be true for the development of later peer-to-peer (P2P) networks, for example Napster, as Douglas Thomas suggests and the sharing therein.[5] However, it has been one of my fundamental arguments that this view is mistaken with respect to the Warez Scene.

3 Ibid.

4 Ibid.

5 Douglas Thomas, "Innovation, Piracy and the Ethos of New Media," in *The New Media Book*, ed. Dan Harries (London: British Film Institute Publishing, 2004), 82–91.

To return to the argument in Chapters One and Two, the Scene values originality and the importance of being the first to release the "liberated" copy: they see their creations as original, pirate material. There is a fundamental valorization of speed but also of the creation of a "new original." Releases embody craft and skill, functionality and beauty. The supply routes of a group imply elitism and scarce access. As I noted, because the Warez Scene is directly descended from computer-artistic cultures where programming skill, musical ability, and visual flare were key elements of its practice, the Warez Scene should be understood primarily as an aesthetic subculture.

In the first two chapters, I suggested that we might consider the Scene's activities as a form of remix culture. How does thinking in terms of remix help us to conceptualize the activities of the Scene, though? Across many spheres of endeavor, creative practitioners have made arguments for the reworking and reuse of other, often in-copyright works. As T.S. Eliot put it: "[i]mmature poets imitate; mature poets steal; bad poets deface what they take, and good poets make it into something better, or at least something different."[6] By this characterization, in a strange and perhaps even sick utilitarian inversion of which Eliot would surely disapprove, we might consider Sceners to be good poets who improve the end-user experience by removing the annoyances of Digital Rights Management (DRM) and other copy protections.

Nonetheless, this debate about creative reuse runs right up to the current era. For instance, Jonathan Lethem, a well-known contemporary novelist, has written several pieces calling for a reevaluation of artistic reuse. "Lethem," writes Joseph Brooker, "questions the way that copyright goes as unquestioned as the law of gravity."[7] Building on work by Lawrence Lessig and others, Lethem suggests, as have many others, that artistic practice is continually building on other ideas and silently or not so silently

6 T.S. Eliot, *The Sacred Wood: Essays on Poetry and Criticism* (New York: Alfred A. Knopf, 1921), 114.

7 Joseph Brooker, *Jonathan Lethem and the Galaxy of Writing* (London: Bloomsbury Academic, 2020), 16.

appropriating previous work.[8] Indeed, one might even suggest that there is no such thing as true originality and that all works are, in some way, derivative. For example, David Shield's collage work, *Reality Hunger: A Manifesto* (2010), weaves together many other published writing pieces into a new, tapestry form.[9]

Various sampling music cultures have also been embroiled in legal battles over what is "fair" in the reuse of other work. These have ranged from the reuse of melody lines from traditional music that are nonetheless held under corporate copyright (e.g., Men At Work's 1980 hit, "Down Under") through to disputes over original song authorship (e.g., Procol Harum's 1967 "A Whiter Shade of Pale").[10] Perhaps the most well-known disputes have been in hip hop music. In 1991 the first lawsuit on sampling was decided in court, Grand Upright Music Ltd. v. Warner Brothers Records. While previous cases dealt with sampling and reuse, all other instances had been settled outside of court. In this case, though, Judge Kevin Thomas Duffy ruled that Biz Markie's "Alone Again," a composition from that same year that sampled Gilbert O'Sullivan's 1972 "Alone Again (Naturally)," violated copyright. Further, the judge advocated for the criminal prosecution of the individuals involved, noting that

> "[t]hou shalt not steal" has been an admonition followed since the dawn of civilization. Unfortunately, in the modern world of business this admonition is not always followed. Indeed, the defendants in this action for copyright infringe-

8 Lawrence Lessig, *Free Culture: The Nature and Future of Creativity* (New York: Penguin Books, 2004); Lawrence Lessig, *Remix: Making Art and Commerce Thrive in the Hybrid Economy* (New York: Penguin Books, 2008).

9 David Shields, *Reality Hunger: A Manifesto* (London: Hamish Hamilton, 2011).

10 Joel Gibson, "Kookaburra Sits on a Small Fortune: Ruling on Down Under Royalties," *The Sydney Morning Herald,* July 6, 2010, https://www.smh.com.au/entertainment/music/kookaburra-sits-on-a-small-fortune-ruling-on-down-under-royalties-20100706-zy5l.html; "Organist Wins Procol Harum Battle," *BBC News,* December 20, 2006, http://news.bbc.co.uk/1/hi/entertainment/6196413.stm.

> ment would have this court believe that stealing is rampant in the music business and, for that reason, their conduct here should be excused. The conduct of the defendants herein, however, violates not only the Seventh Commandment, but also the copyright laws of this country.[11]

Notably, the lawyers in Biz Markie's case did not argue for any fair-use principle, although it is doubtful whether this would have been any more successful. Other types of reuse, though, have been found fair. For instance, in 1994 the Supreme Court of the United States heard Campbell v. Acuff-Rose Music, Inc. This case turned on whether the sampled guitar from Roy Orbison's 1964 "Oh, Pretty Woman," alongside lyrics that distinctly parody Orbison's own, should be considered a copyright violation.[12] Because the nature of the reuse here was for parody, the court upheld the right to reuse. In this instance, the lyrics' interaction with the musical elements contributed to the sense of parody and let the samplers off the hook.

To understand when and where sampling is legally permissible, one must look at the social context within which the piece is produced and received. Judgments are contextual. There are also, in some accounts, different typologies of sampling and reuse that come with different legal connotations. For instance, Amanda Sewell produces a taxonomy or typology of sampling that includes structural, surface, and lyric reproductions. Under these high-level headings, she gives percussion-only, intact, non-percussion, and aggregate for "structural"; constituent, emphatic, and momentary, for "surface"; and singular and recurring for "lyric." In the period that Sewell studies, there was a marked drop in surface samples. In contrast, lyric samples in-

11 Siva Vaidhyanathan, *Copyrights and Copywrongs: The Rise of Intellectual Property and How It Threatens Creativity* (New York: New York University Press, 2003), 142.

12 Joanna Teresa Demers, *Steal This Music: How Intellectual Property Law Affects Musical Creativity* (Athens: University of Georgia Press, 2006), 54–59.

creased; hence the effect that legal rulings have on sampling and reuse is not a direct inhibition.[13]

What does this all mean for the analogy of the Scene? The outputs from the Scene are not really going to cut any mustard for fair use. It is not as though these works "sample" an original and create a new work through tapestry. It is, instead, more as though they take the original and graft their own smaller sample underneath it. To continue the musical analogy, this is akin to the edit culture of contemporary electronic dance music, in which often famous works are taken and have relatively minor additions made to them. This form of remix is an inversion of a rework, in which instead of massively altering the original track, a more subtle approach to overlay and modification comes to the fore.

Such an inversion is also prevalent in mainstream remix work. An excellent example of this is the Jason Nevins remix of Run-DMC's "It's Like That" in 1997. A sleeper hit that sold five million copies, the remix far outperformed the original single. However, Nevins was paid only $5,000 or so for the remix, despite this astonishing commercial performance. The main reason often cited is that many critics felt that the Nevins remix only added minor details to the track—and details that did not necessarily improve it. For instance, Freaky Trigger, which publishes popular musical criticism on every number-one single in the UK, wrote of the Nevins remix that

> Jason Nevins, encountering this bomb-blast of a record, decides it would be improved by a crunching, unflinching house beat. He is wrong. This remix is, admittedly, loud and effective, almost as brutal in its unrelenting way as the original. But it's far less accomplished and interesting. Its inane additions—the sped-up "Run DMC and Jam Master Jay!"

13 Amanda Sewell, "How Copyright Affected the Musical Style and Critical Reception of Sample-Based Hip-Hop," *Journal of Popular Music Studies* 26, nos. 2–3 (2014): 295–320.

> squeaks, for instance—just disrupt the relentless, overlapping forward motion of the original MCs.[14]

Indeed, the artist credit for the remix version was "Run-DMC vs. Jason Nevins." Tom Ewing notes that "[r]arely was a 'versus' more earned."[15] In other words, this is a remix context that is billed as confrontational, one in which the remixer is pitted as an opponent against the original and adds his or her own stylistic elements, which may not be significant but that nonetheless transform the original. This now sounds much closer to the media piracy practices of the Warez Scene. Indeed, the analogy here is to an adversarial relationship of transformative modification, in which the original looms larger than the changes, but in which there is, despite this, an element of skill and craft in the antagonistic edits. Further, such edits are often not welcomed by the original producers. In seeking credit for these antagonistic changes, the Scene begins to emerge as an aesthetic subculture.

Nonetheless, while I here argue for an understanding of the Scene as an aesthetic subculture, it differs from other such subcultures in some distinct ways. Consider, for instance, Sarah Thornton's influential study of club and rave cultures. Her work probes the disco and dance music scenes, examining how a quasi-economic exchange of "cool" works as though it were itself a currency. Designating such club cultures as "taste cultures," Thornton notes that "[c]lub crowds generally congregate on the basis of their shared taste in music, their consumption of common media and, most importantly, their preference for people with tastes similar to their own. Taking part in club cultures builds, in turn, further affinities, socializing participants into a knowledge of (and frequently a belief in) the likes and dislikes, meanings and values of the culture."[16] To a limited ex-

14 Tom Ewing, "Run-DMC vs Jason Nevins—'It's Like That,'" *FreakyTrigger*, May 4, 2014, http://freakytrigger.co.uk/popular/2014/05/run-dmc-vs-jason-nevins-its-like-that/.

15 Ibid.

16 Sarah Thornton, *Club Cultures: Music, Media and Subcultural Capital* (Cambridge: Polity Press, 1995), 15.

tent, such an analysis can be carried across to the Warez Scene. There are certainly parallels in how club cultures manifest a "veiled elitism and separatism," in which the "majority of clubbers" define themselves against a "mainstream" culture, which itself relies on a non-mainstream culture for its definition.[17] Yet the fact that the activity of Sceners is illegal and that they must congregate behind avatars of anonymity renders the binding of these groups very different, although commentators such as J.P. Williams have already examined how subcultures can develop across time and space on the internet.[18] It is also clear that a shared love of media type is not really key to the identity of Sceners. Sceners are not film or music lovers, for instance, or, at least, they do not usually define themselves by such identities. Instead, the mainstream against which they pitch themselves oscillates between the poles of mainstream computer users, who are not elite enough to participate in the Scene; mainstream media purchasers, who do not have the access needed to avoid paying for software, movies, music, and so forth; and even lower levels of software piracy, which are deemed simply inferior to the Scene.

As a closing note before turning to the DemoScene, it is worth pointing out that the terminology of subcultures has been hotly contested. In recent years, the competing field of post-subcultural studies has emerged. Subcultural studies demarcate style itself as a resistive element, a way in which subcultures distinguish themselves from other groupings including the mainstream. The field of post-subcultural studies emerged to contest the "romanticism" of the Centre for Contemporary Cultural Studies (CCCS) at the University of Birmingham, where subcultural studies emerged. This was a view in which "radical potential" lay "in largely symbolic challenges" to a hegem-

17 Ibid., 17.

18 J. Patrick Williams, "Authentic Identities: Straightedge Subculture, Music, and the Internet," *Journal of Contemporary Ethnography* 35, no. 2 (2006): 173–200.

onic norm.[19] A post-subcultural inflection is one in which "the potential for style itself to resist appears largely lost, with any 'intrinsically' subversive quality to subcultures exposed as an illusion."[20] Indeed, some post-subcultural approaches have even adopted the label "scene" to describe their field of endeavor.[21] Others have been critical of this direct substitution of the term "scene" for "subculture," believing that it has substantially muddied the waters: "its use has been very ambiguous, or perhaps more accurately, downright confusing."[22]

While it is problematic to think that "scene" could be a straightforward drop-in substitute term for subculture—the latter of which, in the heyday of subcultural analysis, was predominantly concerned with examining class—the term is the self-selected, grouping word used by the pirates. Hence, the term "scene" registers a loose affiliation that lacks the precision of class-based subculture dominant in the CCCS ideology. There are also many strands to post-subcultural theory, some of which attempt entirely to jettison the CCCS approach to subcultural theory and discard them as useless while still analyzing subcultures themselves. Other attempts seek to further abandon the notion of subculture as a useful paradigm within which to think.

This work adopts the former of these approaches. I treat the Scene as a distinct subcultural entity with codes of practice and aesthetic frames of existence (i.e., style). Although I treat the stylistic and aesthetic practices as significant and even key elements of practice within this domain, I do not claim that on their own these represent the elements of resistance. Instead, the legal transgression allows us to understand the Warez Scene as a space of misguided resistance in its antagonistic remix edits. The aesthetic forms and practices are key to understanding

19 David Muggleton and Rupert Weinzierl, *The Post-Subcultures Reader* (New York: Berg, 2003), 4–5.

20 Ibid.

21 Will Straw, "Systems of Articulation, Logics of Change: Communities and Scenes in Popular Music," *Cultural Studies* 5, no. 3 (1991): 368–88.

22 David Hesmondhalgh, "Subcultures, Scenes or Tribes? None of the Above," *Journal of Youth Studies* 8, no. 1 (2007): 28–29.

the Scene's demarcation as a subcultural space, which I persist in calling an aesthetic subculture, but they are not themselves the transgressive enablers. Indeed, it is the complicated legality of the artwork components of the Scene that are most curious here, with both above-board, legitimate DemoScenes and ASCII art communities coming to distinct prominence. Nonetheless, in the "art of the crack," where there is demonstrable skilled ability among sceners in removing copy protection routines, these legal and illicit functions combine to yield a subcultural form of resistance that sits at the Scene's heart.

THE DEMOSCENE

The Warez Scene is integrally linked to the computer art practices and histories of a space called the DemoScene. As Antti Silvast and Markku Reunanen describe it,

> [t]he demoscene is a technically oriented community that emerged in Europe in the 1980s. Concurrently with the growing popularity of the home computer, the members of the demoscene wanted to distance themselves from the common uses of computers such as productivity or gaming. Instead of utility or entertainment, their interest lay in creative experimentation [...]. They formed an international community, eventually called "the demoscene" or just "the [S]cene," once it became aware of its existence. The main artifacts of the demoscene are demos that showcase the programming and artistic skills of their creators. Simply put, a demo is a computer program that displays a series of real-time visual effects combined with a soundtrack.[23]

23 Antti Silvast and Markku Reunanen, "Multiple Users, Diverse Users: Appropriation of Personal Computers by Demoscene Hackers," in *Hacking Europe: From Computer Cultures to Demoscenes*, ed. Gerard Alberts (New York: Springer, 2014), 151.

Much like the Warez Scene, in essence the DemoScene is a male-dominated space for showcasing programming, graphics, and music-making skills. The demos are relatively short, but they often involve a file-size limit. That is to say that part of the skill is working under severe, programming constraints. There are also different competition categories, for example, at Finland's annual DemoScene party, "Assembly," that often correspond to the hardware on which the demo must run. For instance, there are Amiga categories, PC categories, and so on. The National Inventory of Living Heritage in Finland, which adheres to UNESCO's Convention for the Safeguarding of the Intangible Cultural Heritage, has the DemoScene as one of its protected "objects."[24]

The DemoScene collides with the Warez Scene because, early in its history, software cracking was not illegal. Indeed, as Ben Garrett puts it, "[w]hen nfos were first popularised in the 1990s there was no issue with regards to the Feds reading the files. Not for profit software piracy was not a criminal act during this period. It was the signing of the World Intellectual Property Organization Copyright Treaty in December 1996 by 89 WTO member countries that started the change. It gave software the same protection as other copyrighted literary works and it criminalised the act of bypassing copy protection and rights management."[25]

In this early phase of legality, software crackers sought credit for their work and wished to showcase their skill for their antagonistic remixes. To do so, they often coded brief and not-so-brief demonstrations of their skill, demos, that would play either at the start of a game or within the key generator.[26] In

24 Leena Marsio, "Demoscene, Musical Saw Playing and Horsemanship of the Roma — 12 New Elements Inscribed on the National Inventory of Living Heritage," *Museovirasto,* September 4, 2020, https://www.museovirasto.fi/en/articles/demoskene-sahansoitto-ja-romanien-hevostaidot-elavan-perinnon-kansalliseen-luetteloon-12-uutta-kohdetta.

25 Roman, "Q&A with DeFacto2: The NFO File," January 22, 2013, 4, DeFacto2, https://defacto2.net/file/detail/ac2b81.

26 The best summary to date of the intersections of the Warez Scene and the Demoscene is in Markku Reunanen, Patryk Wasiak, and Daniel Botz, "Crack Intros: Piracy, Creativity and Communication," *International Journal of Communication* 9 (2015): 798–817.

this way, crackers were able to highlight their skill in the crack itself and in the competition to bundle the best demo with their work. As Silvast and Reunanen put it, "the game cracking scene [...] was the forerunner of the demo scene."[27] Garrett also reiterates this interrelation of the Warez Scene and the artistic DemoScene, noting that it was the former that provided the germination space for the latter: "[t]he art-scene never merged into the warez-scene, rather in the very early 1990s much of the art scene spawned from the warez-scene. The split came about from artists who had mostly worked for 'elite' bulletin board systems but either outgrew the warez-scene or just wanted more creative freedom."[28] This is also linked to cultures of attribution and merit that are core both to cracking and to the subsequent DemoScene, that is, "including your name in the crack and being seen as 'good'" are two sides of the same coin.[29] Nonetheless, as Reunanen et al. argue, "[t]he visual style of Amiga cracktros had a major impact on the aesthetics of future cracking scenes such as those of the IBM PC and game consoles. Communicating the act of cracking remained the main purpose, and the visual form of the crack intro served as an advertisement within the scene."[30]

To comprehend the skill involved in demo coding, one must know a little about comparative file sizes and graphical programming practices. Many contemporary computer games feature state-of-the-art graphics. However, these games often have enormous accompanying file sizes. For instance, *Doom Eternal,* the latest in the Doom first-person shooter series, released in 2020, required 50 gigabytes of space (approximately 50,000,000 kilobytes). The 64k category of the DemoScene gives programmers 64 kilobytes total as an upper bound for what they can submit. In other words, DemoScene programmers in the 64k category have 781,250 times less space to work with than did the programmers of *Doom Eternal* (64 vs 50,000,000). For one

27 Silvast and Reunanen, "Multiple Users, Diverse Users," 157.
28 Roman, "Q&A with DeFacto2: The NFO File," 5.
29 Silvast and Reunanen, "Multiple Users, Diverse Users," 157.
30 Reunanen, Wasiak, and Botz, "Crack Intros," 808.

more comparison, the original version of *Doom*, written in 1993, took 2.39 megabytes of space (2,930 kilobytes).[31] In other words, DemoScene programmers are still working with forty-five-times less space than was afforded to programmers creating a three-dimensional graphic game in 1993.

DemoScene programmers must work fractally, coding procedural generation of images, rather than bundling enormous texture files and so forth. Of course, since 1993, the application programming interfaces that are available to programmers have drastically increased in quality. That is, programmers today can take advantage of the DirectX and OpenGL ecosystems, which handle much of the interaction with low-level hardware, thereby providing an easier way to render high-quality graphical outputs. The contemporary iterations of *Doom* are also able to use these infrastructures, yet they would not, nonetheless, fit on a floppy disk.

An example of the types of output that the DemoScene creates can be seen in iq, puryx, and mentor's demo, *elevated*. While additional software was provided by kusma, skrebbel, and blueberry, to get the executable file size down, this production weighed in at a mere 4 kilobytes; that is, sixteen-times smaller than a 64k demo and 12,500,000 times smaller than *Doom Eternal*. *elevated* presents a procedurally generated flight over a mountain range, covered in snow-topped peaks, shown in Figures 13 and 14. As the authors describe it, with all original phrasing preserved, "this a (too) low density flat mesh displaced with a procedural vertex shader. there arent any texturemaps for texturing, instead texturing (and shading) is defferred and computed procedurally in a full screen quad. this means there is zero overdraw for the quite expensive material at the cost of a single geometry pass. then another second full screen quad computes the motion blur. camera movements are computed by a shader too and not in the cpu, as only the gpu knows the procedural

31 Klint Finley, "The Average Webpage Is Now the Size of the Original Doom," *Wired*, April 23, 2016, https://www.wired.com/2016/04/average-webpage-now-size-original-doom/.

Figures 13 &14. screenshots of *elevated*. Copyright, the authors. Used by permission of Iñigo Quilez.

definition of the landscape."[32] As this highly technical description indicates, *elevated* is a complicated mathematical proposition implemented by skilled practitioners. One of its lead authors, iq, Iñigo Quilez, has a formidable background, having worked for Pixar (for instance, creating, painting, shading, and coding the forest's grass, moss, bushes, tree canopies and weeds in the 2012 film, *Brave*) and for Facebook's virtual reality outfit, Oculus. It is also notable that the trick here is to offload much of the processing onto powerful graphical processing hardware (GPU). "[S]ize optimizations," write the authors, "forced us to ask you for a pretty decent graphics card."[33]

elevated combines sophisticated lighting effects, camera motion and motion blur, shadows, and lens flare effects, all while flying over lakes and snowy mountains. Admittedly, for our comparison to games such as *Doom,* in *elevated,* the user does not interact with the mountain scape. Instead, the demo plots its own route over the hills and valleys. The demo also has a cinematic, musical soundtrack built-in with sound-to-light visualization. A virtual synthesizer inside the application, written by puryx, plays the score.

In short, elevated creates a three-dimensional world and flies through it. Of course, it possesses nowhere near the sophistication and complexity of the three-dimensional engines that sit behind third-person shooter games such as *Doom Eternal.* However, the sheer ambition and skill of implementing this world in such a small volume of code and resource space are staggering. Most jobbing programmers would struggle to design something of this quality even with no constraints. To operate within such confines is nothing short of remarkable. It demonstrates just the sort of elite skills and abilities, that few possess, that are treasured by the DemoScene and also by the Warez Scene.

Understanding the ethnography of the DemoScene and the etymology of its terminology can help us place the Warez Scene within a broader, hobbyist, computing phase. However, it can

32 TBC and rgba, "elevated (elevated.nfo)," 2009, pouet.net.

33 Ibid.

also help think through various behavioral traits that emerge therein. Key to this notion is the idea of community and performance. As John Irwin writes, "the word 'scene' reflects an emergent urban psychological orientation—that of a person as 'actor,' self-consciously presenting him- or herself in front of audiences."[34] Performance in the DemoScene and in the Warez Scene consists of playing back one's skillful and artistic computer creations in front of others. However, it is as much about the hacker ethos as it is about the artifacts themselves.

The mentality of tinkering or working things out by experiment, as a "psychological orientation," is core to this presentation of hacking that one sees in the DemoScene.[35] The terminology of "hacker" here refers not to someone who breaks into computer systems (as it did in the previous chapter on FXP Boards) but to someone who is willing to hack things apart in order to understand them and, ideally, to (re)build them. Indeed, Gabriella Coleman charts instances of outrage at media presentations of hacking as an illegal activity. For instance, when Kevin Mitnick was described as a hacker in the media for his computer and wire fraud, a free-software activist retorted, with an interesting inflection for the discussion in this book, that "Kevin is not a hacker. He is a cracker."[36] While the term hacker was used among hobbyist software developers and those who worked within the DemoScene, the term cracker was introduced in the mid-1980s to attempt to counter the negative associations of the term that began to appear in the media at that time. As Coleman notes, "[a]ccording to *The Hacker Jargon File,* crackers are those who hack for devious, malicious, or illegal ends, while hackers are simply technology enthusiasts. Although some hackers make the distinction between crackers and hackers, others also question the division."[37] This is because,

---

34 John Irwin, *Scenes* (Thousand Oaks: SAGE Publications, 1977), 23.

35 For more on this, see Gabriella Coleman, *Coding Freedom: The Ethics and Aesthetics of Hacking* (Princeton: Princeton University Press, 2012).

36 Ibid., 16.

37 Ibid.

to quote the individual whom Coleman cites, "[v]ery often the same techniques that are used in hacking 2 [the more illegal kind] are an important part of hacking 1."[38]

No doubt, as readers will have noticed, the terminology of a "crack" in the Warez Scene pertains to this particular ethos of coding for illegality. Software cracking was, at least for a time, referred to as "breaking" in the 1980s. As Morton Kevelson puts it, "for those unfamiliar with this term, 'breaking' a program refers to the process whereby the true hacker disassembles a copy-protected program and removes the original protective code," an etymology that he compares to the "activity burglars perform in the still of night."[39] Nonetheless, as the term "cracker" arose to describe nefarious hacking activities, despite the fact it has never caught on in the popular press, it became applied to the Warez Scene and the artifacts that it produces.

The skillsets of coders in the DemoScene and crackers in the Warez Scene overlap with one another. Consider, for instance, that *elevated* achieves its extreme compactness because much of it is written in assembly language. This allows for precision control of memory and avoids the bloat that is introduced by high-level language compilers as they attempt to optimize code automatically. Although, it should be noted that in most cases, high-level language compilers produce better assembly code than a human would or could. Nonetheless, familiarity with low-level assembly language and memory architectures is also crucial to the activities of crackers in the Warez Scene. Being an extremely skilled software engineer is core both to crackers in the Warez Scene and coders in the DemoScene.

It is also worth noting that the skillsets are nonetheless different. The mathematics of geometry and two-dimensional and three-dimensional graphics inherent in creating demos are different low-level programming expertise to those possessed by warez crackers. Instead, what is desired from DemoSceners in the crossover to the Warez Scene is an appreciation of credit

38 Ibid.
39 Morton Kevelson, "Isepic," *Ahoy!*, October 1985, 72.

and the hacking skill that can go into making the coolest demo, alongside the pirated software. That said, the usual claimed history—that the DemoScene branched out into a purely legal spinoff of the Warez Scene—is contested. As Markku Reunanen notes, "the actual story might be more complicated" because "many groups continued the legal and illegal activities in parallel, cracking games and making legal demos at the same time."[40]

It is also true that DemoSceners need to specialize along several different axes; it is not all about programming skills. Just as the Scene itself has individuals who fulfill various roles (e.g., siteops, nukers, couriers, suppliers, encoders, and crackers), the DemoScene requires artists and musicians alongside coders. It is a mistake to believe that the DemoScene is all about programming skill, although this remains a core attribute. Musicians and artists are appraised by different criteria to their programming counterparts but are nonetheless held in high regard within this space. It is also true that there is no hard and fast distinction between coders and these other groups. The coders must embed the graphics and music within a compressed context and ensure synchronization of playback with the rest of the demo. In short, the lines between these disciplinary areas are not fixed, and there is a team dynamic at play.

The same can be said, in many ways, of release groups in the Warez Scene. While certainly individual skill and ability are core assets and there is some disdain between classes of users (i.e., it is universally accepted that there is more skill to cracking software than to being a Scene courier), the Scene is composed of pirate groups. Although the ability of individuals is vital, release groups, courier groups, NukeNets, dupechecks, and topsites all require individuals to work in concert with one another. It is the nature of piracy that pirates do not work in isolation, even while individual pirates may gain notoriety and fame.

In its intersection with the legitimate DemoScene, the Warez Scene finds its artistic and stylistic home. A minimalist aesthetic

40 Markku Reunanen, "Computer Demos—What Makes Them Tick?" (Master's Thesis, Aalto University, 2010), 23.

aiming for maximum impact, the DemoScene showcases extreme programming skills combined with aesthetic flare. We should not, however, lose sight of how odd the DemoScene seems to those outside it. Why would one choose, as a hobby, to make small, self-contained, computer graphics demonstrations? Similar questions, though, can be asked of the Warez Scene. Why would one choose, for fun, to spend hours every day moving material from one high-speed remote server to another, attempting to do so more quickly than one's rivals? The answer, as ever, is the gamified nature of prestige accumulation within an economy-like environment that makes this hard. Given that recognition and flare are key to individuals' standings in the Scene, the DemoScene's artistic side, the showcasing spectacle, must not be overlooked. However, there is an exciting point to be made about the Warez Scene's aesthetic practices and style in terms of subcultural analysis. In traditional subcultural analysis, the codes of style are themselves the violation, the act of defiance and resistance. In other words, it is the aesthetic act that is the violation.

Within the context of the Warez Scene, there are two ways in which demos function as aesthetic illegality that contravene society's normative standards. First, demos were often part of cracks and key generators (i.e., keygens). That is, demos were often not bundled as standalone applications that sat apart from the pirated software themselves but were themselves part of the distribution. Users saw the demo when they opened the keygen—the illegal artifact that allowed for circumvention of copyright protection. In this case, the illegality or transgression did not come from the style of the keygen but from the fact that it was the skeleton key to the illegally copied software. At the same time, keygens and cracks were aesthetically styled through demos. That is, they exuded a "geek cool" that cannot be overlooked. These pirate artifacts come with a style of their own.

There is a second stylistic-illicit crossover point in the art of the crack, to which I have already alluded. Cracks themselves are an artform that possess a particular style. Admittedly, the audience who can appreciate the elegance, or otherwise, of a crack is small. It is more likely that most users will simply appreciate whether a crack works or not. A small cadre of individuals will appreciate elegance and beauty in a crack. It is this toward which crackers strive. Exact parallels are not necessarily found in other areas of the Scene (i.e., music and movie piracy), as there is no skilled equivalent to cracking; although access to an elite supply chain may carry similar prestige connotations and confer admiration upon an individual. Within the subculture of the Scene, the aesthetics of a crack will carry prestige and reputational benefit. Again, the illegality of the artifact makes it counter-hegemonic and disruptive, not so much the fact of its internal aesthetic composition. In the antagonistic remixes of the Scene, these elements combine to create an aesthetic environment predicated on extreme programming skill. In the formation of the legal DemoScene, the Warez Scene created its legitimate cousin. However, to this day, demo-esque aesthetics remain core to the makeup of the Scene and, in some ways, signify its transgressive nature.

NFO FILES AND ASCII ART

Throughout this book I have documented the structures of the Warez Scene using NFO files. In reading a surfaced archive of documents for iNFOrmation, I have been able to piece together the practices, histories, and even humor of this subcultural space. NFO files yield insight into topsites, releases, courier groups, and scene busts, as I discuss later. Although these files are informative, a crucial element overlooked in much of the secondary literature[41] is that there is also an aesthetic to NFO files and their text-based artworks.[42] This is to say that while NFOs

41 Perhaps the exception is Maria Eriksson, "A Different Kind of Story: Tracing the Histories and Cultural Marks of Pirate Copied Film," *Tecnoscienza: Italian Journal of Science & Technology Studies* 7, no. 1 (2016): 87–108.

42 David Décary-Hétu, Carlo Morselli, and Stéphane Leman-Langlois, "Welcome to the Scene: A Study of Social Organization and Recognition among Warez Hackers," *Journal of Research in Crime and Delinquency* 49, no. 3 (2012): 368.

are information communication tools, groups also encode visual-textual artwork inside these NFO files, even though they are "plain" text.[43] This form of plain-text decoration is called ASCII (American Standard Code for Information Interchange) art. It uses textual character codes to create a visual effect. ASCII is an underlying standard that converts a binary, numerical representati]on into universal character representations, in the same way as children might devise a simple code in which A=1, B=2 etc.[44]

Ironically, given that NFO files advertise activities, the format's extension was first introduced by a group called "The Humble Guys" (THG) in 1990.[45] The standardization of the file extension unified the disparate cultures of "phile" distribution that had developed throughout the BBS Scene histories and spelled out alliances, feuds, and credits.[46] As with demo groups, these NFO/ASCII Art groups competed to be the best in the business and to develop notoriety for their creations. As Garrett puts it, these groups "earned their reputation at being one of the best groups by creating art for the best pirate boards of the time."[47] In parallel to other elements of Scene practice, there is a level of craft and skill involved in the work of creating the ASCII Art of NFO files, which was, itself, descended from mid-twentieth-century

---

43 Although, of course, as Dennis Tenen reminds us, the term "plain text" hides a plethora of dangerous assumptions. Dennis Tenen, *Plain Text: The Poetics of Computation* (Stanford: Stanford University Press, 2017).

44 Portions of this chapter were also speculatively ventured in Martin Paul Eve, *The Digital Humanities and Literary Studies* (Oxford: Oxford University Press, 2022).

45 Ben Garrett, "Online Software Piracy of the Last Millennium," April 27, 2004, 6, DeFacto2, http://www.defacto2.net/file/download/a53981.

46 For instance, see Knight Lightening and Taran King, "Phrack Pro-Phile 3: Featuring: User Groups and Clubs," *Phrack Magazine*, June 10, 1986, http://phrack.org/issues/6/2.html.

47 Garrett, "Online Software Piracy of the Last Millennium," 6.

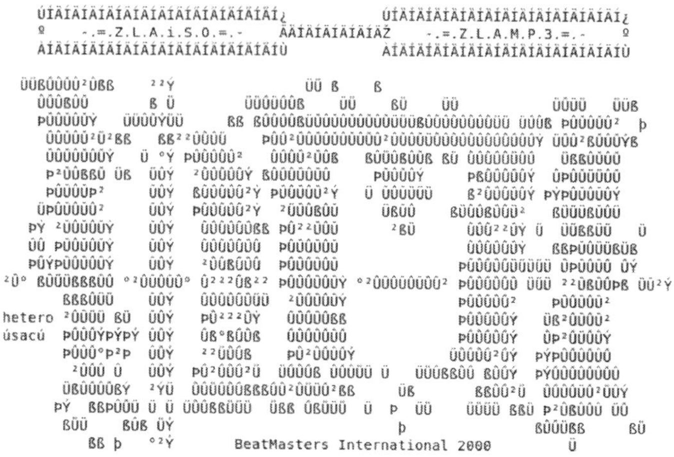

Figure 15. BeatMasters International (BMI) NFO from the year 2000 with ASCII art by hetero/sac.

typewriter art.[48] As one report put it, NFO files have become the de facto "press releases for piracy groups."[49]

NFO files have changed form over time. As Garrett charts, evolutions in the form of NFOs have taken place "both in the information they conveyed and aesthetic layout," with the changes being spurred through "competition or from a needs basis."[50] In Garrett's historical account, one of the general directions of movement was the redaction of identifying information from the files. "One early change," as he writes, "was groups or crackers that listed their BBS phone numbers so they could increase their membership of long-distance callers. They believed this could increase users and would improve the catchment and

48 Alexis C. Madrigal, "The Lost Ancestors of ASCII Art," *The Atlantic*, January 30, 2014, https://www.theatlantic.com/technology/archive/2014/01/the-lost-ancestors-of-ascii-art/283445/.

49 Brian Prince, "Tracking the Crackers — A Look at Software Piracy," *EWEEK*, November 14, 2008, https://www.eweek.com/security/tracking-the-crackers-a-look-at-software-piracy.

50 Roman, "Q&A with DeFacto2: The NFO File," 3.

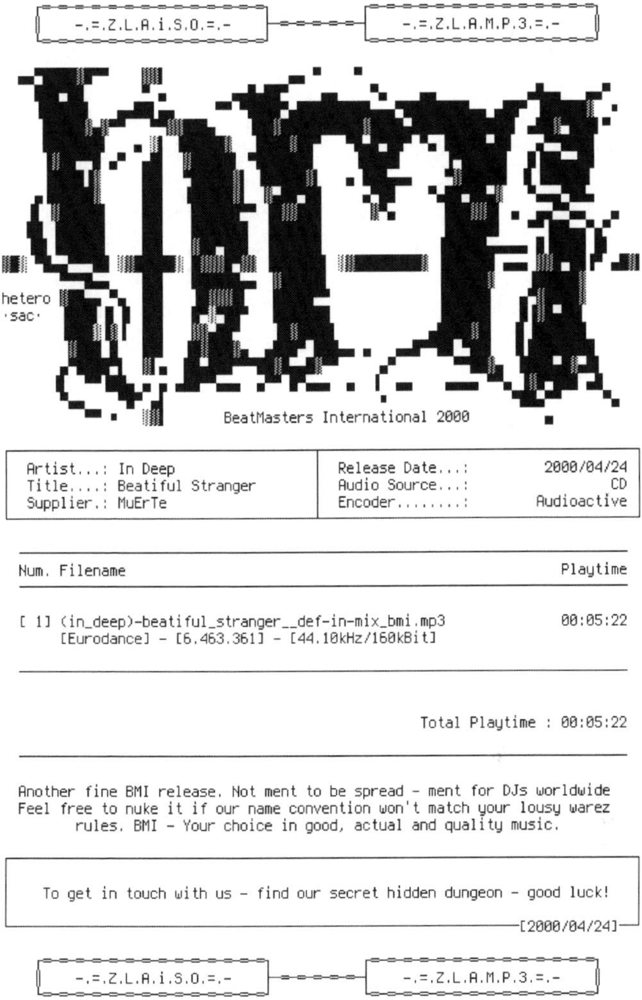

```
-.=.Z.L.A.i.S.O.=.-          -.=.Z.L.A.M.P.3.=.-

hetero
·sac·
                BeatMasters International 2000

Artist...: In Deep                 Release Date...:      2000/04/24
Title....: Beatiful Stranger       Audio Source...:              CD
Supplier.: MuErTe                  Encoder........:     Audioactive

Num. Filename                                              Playtime

[ 1] (in_deep)-beatiful_stranger__def-in-mix_bmi.mp3       00:05:22
     [Eurodance] - [6.463.361] - [44.10kHz/160kBit]

                                     Total Playtime : 00:05:22

Another fine BMI release. Not ment to be spread - ment for DJs worldwide
Feel free to nuke it if our name convention won't match your lousy warez
      rules. BMI - Your choice in good, actual and quality music.

  To get in touch with us - find our secret hidden dungeon - good luck!
                                                        [2000/04/24]

-.=.Z.L.A.i.S.O.=.-          -.=.Z.L.A.M.P.3.=.-
```

Figure 16. the same BMI NFO file transformed into its intended viewing format. ASCII art by hetero/sac.

variety of uploads to the bulletin boards. As in the early BBS days there were no true cross-continental groups, let alone an international [S]cene on the PC." Alongside this editorial function, however, early NFOs also served a verification role. "Later groups," he writes, "added membership lists and official bulletin board affiliations into their NFOs to stop people from claiming false association with a group."[51] As criminalization of Warez activities grew in the 1990s, the NFOs became increasingly cagey. Once "the act of bypassing copy protection became a criminal offence, the more revealing pieces of information had gone from the NFOs."[52] Nonetheless, Garrett claims, "even with this self-imposed security censorship, NFO files still were great tools of propaganda for rival groups."[53] For this reason, the artistic sentiment and styling of NFO files remained.

When viewed in a standard text viewer, NFO files can appear very messy. For example, Figure 15 shows one of these files from around the year 2000. As is clear, the file is composed of several accented characters not used in the English language. These include "Ü," "Ý," "Þ" and many others.

What may not be immediately clear here is that if one switches the font to an appropriate monospaced terminal style, these characters are transformed into blocks, as shown in Figure 16.

While the possibly deliberate spelling errors in this document, or "ment," might dissuade some of the literary merits of such artifacts, the significant point here is very different. Indeed, following the work of Bronać Ferran, I believe that these digital documents can best be located within a broad history of visual and spatial concrete poetry that exhibits both constructivist and de(con)structivist tendencies.[54]

51 Ibid.

52 Ibid.

53 Ibid.

54 This section is entirely indebted to Ferran's doctoral thesis, "Hansjörg Mayer's Typoetic Intervention in Concrete Poetry and Experimental Literature of the 1960s," which I am supervising. All credit for anything here should be attributed to her while any errors are mine alone.

The history of concrete poetry—a form of writing in which the visual elements play a key, poetic role—is difficult to explain concisely. The terms of engagement are contested, and the debate's terrain is international, spanning West Germany to Brazil from the 1950s onwards.[55] Concrete poetic form has a complex relationship to literary modernism and particularly the work of Ezra Pound, from whose work the *noigandres* journal and loosely affiliated group, the authors of the "Pilot Plan for Concrete Poetry," took their name.[56] Key properties of concrete poetry include a focus on typography, spatial layout, positioning as poetic quality, and some idea of movement and kinesis, a "critical evolution of forms" as the Pilot Plan has it.

Core to much concrete poetry are ideas of economy and sparsity, an aesthetic that discards the superfluous in breakdown. Hansjörg Mayer's 1965 *oil,* for instance, resolutely sticks to its deconstructing, minimalist use of three letters, repetitiously placed within its invisible grid. At the same time, though, there is a concurrent, constructivist countertendency of overloading at work. This often takes the form of repetition and over-printing, in which typographical elements are overlaid atop one another in the printing process.

55 Some of the better-known background sources that have handled this include Mary Ellen Solt, *Concrete Poetry: A World View* (Bloomington: Indiana University Press, 1970); Stephen Bann, *Concrete Poetry: An International Anthology* (London: London Magazine, 1967); Stephen Bann, ed., *The Tradition of Constructivism* (London: Thames and Hudson, 1974); Johanna Drucker, *The Visible Word, Experimental Typography and Modern Art, 1909–1923* (Chicago: University of Chicago Press, 1997); Johanna Drucker, *Figuring the Word: Essays on Books, Writing, and Visual Poetics* (New York: Granary Books, 1998); Johanna Drucker, *Graphesis: Visual Forms of Knowledge Production* (Cambridge: Harvard University Press, 2014); Marjorie Perloff, *The Poetics of Indeterminancy: Rimbaud to Cage* (Princeton: Princeton University Press, 1981); Marjorie Perloff, *Radical Artifice: Writing Poetry in the Age of Media* (Chicago: University of Chicago Press, 1991); and Marjorie Perloff, *Unoriginal Genius: Poetry by Other Means in the New Century* (Chicago: University of Chicago Press, 2010).

56 Augusto de Campos, Decio Pignatari, and Harold de Campos, "Pilot Plan for Concrete Poetry," in *Concrete Poetry,* ed. Solt, 71–72.

Such a model for poetry thereby yields a double temporality, one in which the building and the breakdown are simultaneously present. Ideas of construction and destruction are prompted into temporal translation on the page of the concrete poem. Even the final logical endpoint of overloaded construction (e.g., overprinting to the extent that the page is black once more) leads to a form of destruction. When translated into temporal terms by a reader, this dialectical formulation is how the concrete poem includes a notion of motion within its otherwise static environment.

The NFO file shown above possesses some of the qualities of this temporal movement across the multiple display forms in which it can be accessed. Indeed, as well as possessing the spatial framing layout seen in much concrete poetry that prompts the dialectic, where alphanumerical, typographical elements are laid out in a particular form on the page for aesthetic effect, these digital artifacts are versioned and mutable in their display. The reader can access the form in its textual or graphical modes, demonstrating the principle of kinesis attributed to much concrete poetry but in a very different way. For while Mayer and others were interested in typographical control (e.g., the sustained use of the Futura typeface that Ferran notes was perceived to be a highly neutral font), the movement of NFOs comes from reader control over display technologies. The text moves from its constructivist phase, where ASCII characters are visible in their alphanumeric forms, into a breakdown of those characters into solid blocks as the correct monospacing font is applied. In this movement, there is at once a distinct loss of detail — we no longer know what the underlying linguistic or symbolic representation of the character might be, even though it has not changed in its fundamental digital representation — and a further construction as the image form of the document becomes visible.

In many ways, this is the type of metaphorical slippage that Dennis Tenen has charted in his book on plain text.[57] It is

57 Tenen, *Plain Text*, 23–54.

a model in which the digital-metaphorical form presented to the end user is only tangentially associated with the physicality and materiality of the operation. The example that Tenen gives is the delete operation on a computer system. One might assume that pressing delete within one's operating system would lead to the removal of the relevant file's contents from the hard drive. However, this is not actually the case. In many contemporary computer file systems, files are stored in at least two and sometimes three separate locations. The first, the metadata inode, contains a pointer to the second storage location called the indirect block. The second storage location, the indirect block, contains two numbers that point to two further locations on the disk: a start block and an end block for the file in question. In some file systems, the inode directly contains the information from the indirect block, hence there are sometimes two stages and sometimes three. The file is then actually written on disk to the space between these location numbers. This is to say, there is a pointer on the disk that directs the operating system to the actual physical sectors on the storage device where the file's contents lie. When one deletes a file, the file contents itself are not usually removed from the disk. Instead, the inode is unlinked. That is, the metadata for the file is removed, but the actual contents remain on the storage and the space where the file is stored is made available for the storage of other files. This means that in specific circumstances, it is possible but difficult to recover deleted files. Over time, the file's location will be overwritten with new file data, linked to different inodes. Files will also be distributed between inodes at different on-disk locations for different fragments of their data.

The metaphor of deletion, often signified by a skeuomorphic trashcan in the iconography of computer operating systems, rarely performs an analogous "trashing" of the underlying data. Instead, it is more akin to saying that one will empty one's bookshelf by crossing out the books one does not want from a list of books, only to remove the books later when one has a new book to add. Certainly, such metaphorical slippage is helpful to an end-user. But few users are aware of the implications masked by such metaphorical terminology. One's files remain on the disk, even after you have deleted them.

The NFO is subject to an analogous metaphorical representation between its layers where different font overlays transform typographic blocks into visual versions of the underlying characters. Because the format takes advantage of unique, typographic features that rely on the selection of particular fonts and highly specific domain-knowledge requirements, elements of the process of metaphorization become more visible as we shift between the graphic and typo-graphic modes. Once one knows that certain accented characters in the Unicode format are misrepresented as solid blocks when one switches the font to a monospaced terminal layout, the perspectival and metaphorical trickery of the mediating layers are rendered transparent. Of course, for some readers, this will remain opaque; they might not understand why the file can appear in two different forms, and the metaphor will continue to function. This is not to say that metaphor does not function even when we know it is metaphor. It is just that a critical ability to appraise metaphor depends on recognition of substitutability.

Further, there is a history of computational colonialism at work in this double-layered process that can be read out the NFO files. The characters that translate into ASCII art blocks when used in an appropriate font are all drawn from the non-English alphabet. Just as search engines have premised their models on the cultural assumption of the transcendental, white subject, and the history of computing has worked to erase women from its record, here we see a geographic and linguistic bias to which the final chapter of this work will return.[58] The acutely accented "u" ("ú"), for instance, is a glyph used in Czech, Faroese, Portuguese, Spanish, and Vietnamese, among others. It does not

58 Safiya Umoja Noble, *Algorithms of Oppression: How Search Engines Reinforce Racism* (New York: New York University Press, 2018); Mar Hicks, *Programmed Inequality: How Britain Discarded Women Technologists and Lost Its Edge in Computing* (Cambridge: MIT Press, 2018).

occur in English. For this reason, this character appears in the Latin-1 Supplement of the Unicode specification.

This translation of certain non-English characters to blocks is just part of how a longer, computational, linguistic colonialism has emerged in contemporary writing. Another instance of this can be seen in the response to the Unicode implementation of the Ho language. In 2007, K. David Harrison and Gregory Anderson noted in a letter to the Unicode consortium that

> [t]he current Unicode proposal (authored by Michael Everson, dated 1999-01-29) is incomplete in its current form and notably requires consultation and fact-checking with the user community. While it is crucial that the Ho orthography be included in Unicode, this can only be done in close consultation with Ho scholars at every step of the process. As a practical and ethical matter, we urge the Unicode consortium to accept only proposals that emerge from or are formulated in close consultation with native speaker communities. To do otherwise is to espouse a kind of linguistic colonialism that will only widen the digital divide.[59]

Indeed, one of the basic premises seen in the Unicode specification is that English-language, Latinate characters are the first to appear in the table, while other linguistic systems are often relegated to much higher assignations. Sometimes, as Sharjeel Imam points out, these other languages are spread across many different blocks rather than in the more concentrated forms of the Latin alphabet.[60] "Internationalization" here means a spread outwards from a "centered" English to other "peripheral" cultures, demonstrating a strong Anglocentrism. As Don Osborn writes, for example, "[a]part from Arabic, the development of the use of African languages in computing and the internet has

59 K. David Harrison and Gregory Anderson, "Review of Proposal for Encoding Warang Chiti (Ho Orthography) in Unicode," *Unicode.org*, April 22, 2007.

60 @imaams, *Twitter*, November 24, 2017, https://twitter.com/_imaams/status/934109280285765632.

been relatively slow for a number of linguistic, educational, policy and technical reasons" while "a particular problem for a number of languages written with modified letters or diacritic characters — or entire alphabets — beyond the basic Latin alphabet (the 26 letters used in English) or the ASCII character set (that alphabet plus basic symbols) has been the way in which computer systems and software handle these."[61] As "an industrial standard controlled by the industry," in Domenico Fiormonte's words, we should be skeptical around "claims about the neutrality or impartiality of" Unicode, a schema that has pretenses towards universal character representation.[62]

The doubled nature of the layering here at once both highlights and masks this history. Those from countries using Latinate alphabets who open the text file while using a font that supports the extended set will encounter characters from Cyrillic alphabets, as just one example, and may be perplexed about why their screen is full of unfamiliar accented characters. After all, the artwork is not clear, as the above image shows, without the correct font being used. In this instance, a savvier user will understand that the problem lies in the intermediating font's lack of support for the extended character set.

To explain this a little further: the font's depiction of the underlying ASCII character is contingent upon an economy of choice. For each character displayed, the font must provide a corresponding glyph that the operating system can render. That is, the designer must craft an "a," a "b," a "c," but also a "ú." Given that there are thousands upon thousands of characters that each need a glyph, often, font designers may restrict themselves to a subset of the complete Unicode specification, selecting only the glyphs that they feel will be commonly used. They may then substitute all other glyphs with a different display character,

61 Don Osborn, *African Languages in a Digital Age: Challenges and Opportunities for Indigenous Language Computing* (Cape Town: HSRC Press, 2010), 59–60.

62 Domenico Fiormonte, "Towards a Cultural Critique of the Digital Humanities," *Historical Social Research / Historische Sozialforschung* 37, no. 3 (2012): 64.

such as a solid block (or different types of block, such as 50% grayscale). As the first contiguous block of the Unicode specification, Latinate alphabets are far more rarely blocked out. The priority is placed upon these characters while the disregard for glyphs that are specific to non-Anglophone cultures continues.

In another sense, though, this intermediation of font design masks this relegation. If a user goes straight into the "correct" font, they will be unaware that below the surface of the smooth blocks lurks this economy of choice in font design. Indeed, it will be utterly opaque that the character is anything other than the design block as which it appears. In other words, the exploitation of marginalized font glyphs that are apparent in the crafting of NFO files is at once one that hides and highlights colonial histories of computing culture, even when this is not apparent to those working within the subcultures that produce such artifacts.

There is also another level of intermediation here that can act to mask these historical systems. This is because often designers of NFO files are working with software that assists them in their designs. A designer would rarely craft an NFO file entirely by hand. Instead, pieces of software will attempt to match a set of undefined or unspecified, non-Latinate font glyphs to the pixel shades within an image. Under this creation model, there is a greater obfuscation of the underlying histories because even the designer is unlikely to be aware that the shadings that they are producing result from undefined glyphs within the font set.

Notably, the NFO, as its abbreviated name implies, is not a poem. However, it is an artifact that contains a textual, aesthetic (i.e., "literary") component as a core part of its existence. Instead, it is primarily the vessel for the dissemination of information about material that is being circulated in contravention of civil copyright law and perhaps even criminal copyright conspiracy laws. Thus, as Jacques Rancière wrote, the "ideal effect" of a work that entwines art and politics, or, I would argue, information, "is always the object of a negotiation between opposites, between the readability of the message that threatens to destroy the sensible form of art and the radical uncanniness that threatens to destroy all political meaning."[63] The NFO is a documentary object, often poorly written with crude slurs made on other groups — "lousy warez rules" is about as mild as it will get. At the same time, the artifacts have an aesthetic quality due to the ASCII art frames. These are enmeshed within a complex play of symbolic and material capital that Alan Liu has framed as "cool."[64]

Understanding how the laws of cool play out within this space requires a little more background social context. Certainly, James F. English has traced how the cultural prestige of prize culture works among the big literary prizewinning novels of our day.[65] Likewise, Ted Underwood has examined the phenomena that lead to literary status and prestige over a long period.[66] Yet what is in it for "hetero 'sac,'" the originator of this NFO file's design? (The individual here is "hetero" while "sac," "superior art creations," is the group.) Indeed, this work will not be entered into any high-brow poetry or design competitions, and it would not win anyway if it were. Nevertheless, the author has taken considerable time and effort to craft the logo, understand how it will appear across multiple systems, and produce the template within which the release group can insert its documenting information. Why? It seems most likely that "hetero 'sac'" will have some kind of topsite access as a reward for designing the NFO.

However, this simple answer — a material reward — is also wrong or overly simple. Those who hold such slots often have them across multiple sites and almost all releases end up on all sites within a few second of release, that is, the exclusivity of affiliation to groups is a matter of minutes or seconds difference in whether a site has access to such material. Hence, although

63 Jacques Rancière, *The Politics of Aesthetics: The Distribution of the Sensible*, ed. and trans. Gabriel Rockhill (London: Bloomsbury Academic, 2018), 59.

64 Alan Liu, *The Laws of Cool: Knowledge Work and the Culture of Information* (Chicago: University of Chicago Press, 2004).

65 James F. English, *The Economy of Prestige: Prizes, Awards, and the Circulation of Cultural Value* (Cambridge: Harvard University Press, 2005).

66 Ted Underwood, *Distant Horizons: Digital Evidence and Literary Change* (Chicago: University of Chicago Press, 2019), 68–110.

the terminology of subcultures is hotly contested, it strikes me that there is a prestige economy of a subculture at work here that does not translate back into determinate and precisely commensurable, material reward.[67] That is to say that the levels of prestige of design work and the groups for whom a designer works will determine the quality of the sites to which they are given access. This quality has not anything to do with access to pirated material. It is, instead, more about the "cool" of the site; boasting rights of access and eliteness of status here are seen as far more important than actually downloading the material that is released.

Overall, then, it seems only fitting to conclude that the artistic subculture of ASCII art falls into the same types of competitive, quasi-economic alternative reality game-playing that pervades the other structures of the Scene. It is not true to separate the artistic practices from other core practices. The Scene, while an alternative reality game, is also an aesthetic subculture.

THE FEEDBACK LOOPS OF DIGITAL RIGHTS MANAGEMENT

The craft, skill, and aesthetics of piracy also feedback into mainstream cultural production. Indeed, it was never a tenable division to believe that mainstream producers simply made material that pirates then copied. Writers such as China Miéville, for instance, have long noted how new, cultural artifacts can be generated as a result of "piracy,"[68] although one has to query whether, if one has permission or the author's blessing, such practices remain "piratical." As Adrian Johns has pointed out,

67 For a few of the key texts in this area, see Hebdige, *Subculture*; Thornton, *Club Cultures*; Muggleton and Weinzierl, *The Post-Subcultures Reader*; and Geoff Stahl, "Tastefully Renovating Subcultural Theory: Making Space for a New Model," in *The Post-Subcultures Reader*, ed. David Muggleton and Rupert Weinzierl (New York: Berg, 2003), 27–40.

68 Charlotte Higgins, "China Miéville: Writers Should Welcome a Future Where Readers Remix Our Books," *The Guardian*, August 21, 2012, http://www.theguardian.com/books/2012/aug/21/china-mieville-novels-books-anti-piracy.

when the term "pirate" was first banded around to denote illicit copying, during the early book trade, the interplay between copy and original was extensive and bidirectional.[69]

We see the same in innovative copyright protection measures that modify gameplay in contemporary computer games.[70] That is to say that the Scene's cracking activities have altered the aesthetics of computer games themselves. Early games in the 1990s from Sierra On-Line and Lucasfilm Games, for example, required a user to input phrases from a physical manual shipped with the game in order to prove that they possessed the material correlate — another example of introducing a pure, rivalrous scarcity into the digital space.[71] A failure to identify oneself as a legitimate user altered the gameplay itself in games as far back as 1988's *Zak McKracken and the Alien Mindbenders*. In this title, if the user entered the serial key incorrectly five times, they were moved to a pirate jail, where they received a severe admonishment for stealing the title.[72] Despite debates over the efficacy of such DRM technologies, more imaginative interplay loops between piracy and content have emerged.[73]

Take, for instance, the example of *The Sims 4*, a game in which the player works to build a simulated environment within which their characters can thrive. In regular gameplay, one's characters are afforded the basic decency of having their genitals pixelated out when using the bathroom and other activities in a state of undress. In pirated editions of the game, however, the pixelation spreads gradually to engulf the whole screen, thereby

69 Adrian Johns, *Piracy: The Intellectual Property Wars from Gutenberg to Gates* (Chicago: University of Chicago Press, 2011).

70 The definitive study on this concept is Andrew V. Moshirnia, "Giant Pink Scorpions: Fighting Piracy with Novel Digital Rights Management Technology," *DePaul Journal of Art, Technology & Intellectual Property Law* 23, no. 1 (2012): 1–67.

71 Marcella Favale et al., "Human Aspects in Digital Rights Management: The Perspective of Content Developers," *SSRN Electronic Journal* (2016): 4.

72 James Newman, *Videogames* (London: Routledge, 2013), 146.

73 Peter Holm, "Piracy on the Simulated Seas: The Computer Games Industry's Non-Legal Approaches to Fighting Illegal Downloads of Games," *Information & Communications Technology Law* 23, no. 1 (2014): 61–76.

rendering the game unplayable.[74] In other words, the anti-pirate mechanism fills the screen with a giant pixelated genital organ, presenting a phallic rejoinder to the illegitimate user.

Other games have opted for more subtle approaches that nonetheless prevent the player from progressing. *Serious Sam 3: BFE* developer, Croteam, embedded an unkillable Adult Arachnid "boss" character in the game when a pirated edition is detected. This enemy chases the player indefinitely throughout the game.[75] While this may sound like a nightmare scenario, resourceful modders actually went so far as to develop an add-on that would deliberately spawn these "DRM scorpions" throughout the game as a challenge to players.[76] This is a strange instance where legitimate customers have felt left out from participating in the elements of the artform that are directed solely at pirating users.[77] The list goes on. *Grand Theft Auto IV* features cars that accelerate beyond the pirating user's control. In *Command & Conquer: Red Alert 2* the illegitimate player's base would self-destruct after a short period of time. In *Settlers 3*, pirates can only produce pigs, not iron. Croteam's *The Talos Principle* featured elevators that would become stuck halfway to their destination if one has pirated the game.[78] Bohemia Interactive's "FADE" or "DEGRADE" DRM protection is specifically designed gradually to destroy the experience of pirates as games progress.[79]

---

74 Timothy J. Seppala, "'The Sims 4' Turns into a Pixelated Mess If You Pirate It," *Engadget*, September 5, 2014, https://www.engadget.com/2014-09-05-sims-4-pirate-pixelation.html.

75 J.C. Fletcher, "The Painful Sting of Serious Sam 3's Anti-Piracy Protection," *Engadget*, December 7, 2011, https://www.engadget.com/2011-12-07-the-painful-sting-of-serious-sam-3s-anti-piracy-protection.html.

76 Ryason55, "DRM Scorpions," May 11, 2014, https://steamcommunity.com/sharedfiles/filedetails/?id=259074771&searchtext=.

77 For more on modding cultures, see Tanja Sihvonen, *Players Unleashed! Modding The Sims and the Culture of Gaming* (Amsterdam: Amsterdam University Press, 2011).

78 "The Best In-Game Piracy Punishments," *PC Gamer*, September 14, 2017, https://www.pcgamer.com/the-best-in-game-piracy-punishments/.

79 Nathan Grayson, "Interview: Bohemia Interactive's CEO on Fighting Piracy, Creative DRM," *PC Gamer*, November 17, 2011, https://www.pcgamer.

To end this catalog of creative, video-game responses to piracy, I would like to draw attention to perhaps the most meta example of which I am aware, that of 2012's *Game Dev Tycoon,* produced by Greenheart Games. To be clear, this game is exactly as it sounds: it is a simulation of running a video-game development studio. The aim for the player is to develop and bring to market a set of video games. In pirated versions of the game, the user is repeatedly warned that "it seems that while many players play our new game, they steal it by downloading a cracked version rather than buying it legally. If players don't buy the games they like, we will sooner or later go bankrupt." The player of the pirated edition would then gradually find that over time, they would lose money in the game, until they eventually did indeed go bankrupt.[80]

It is not clear whether such creative DRM responses to piracy have the desired didactic effect upon players. After all, proper cracked versions of video games nearly always emerge eventually as versions in which even these humorous DRM elements have been removed. In the end, developers are always playing catch-up against the pirates and can hope only to delay, rather than to avoid, the illegal distribution of their games. However, I contend that two key points emerge from these instances of gameplay-modifying DRM systems:

1. that piracy has had an active effect on the art form of these works, feeding into them and contributing aesthetic elements to their development that would not exist otherwise; and

2. that certain executable, media forms, such as games and other software applications, are particularly susceptible to this

com/interview-bohemia-interactives-ceo-on-fighting-piracy-creative-drm/.

80 Patrick Klug, "What Happens When Pirates Play a Game Development Simulator and Then Go Bankrupt Because of Piracy?" *Greenheart Games,* April 29, 2013, https://www.greenheartgames.com/2013/04/29/what-happens-when-pirates-play-a-game-development-simulator-and-then-go-bankrupt-because-of-piracy/.

type of activity in a way that other art forms, such as music, are not.

On this second point, it is the self-executing nature of games and software that makes these creative DRM responses tenable. It may be the case that this is not generalizable to a broader media ecology. Understanding this difference requires a brief foray into an explanation of file types. Some computer files are executable. They contain sequential instructions that the computer understands and can process. Other types of files contain data that another program can read, such as musical or pictorial data. The effect of processing each of these file types is very different.

In the case of games and software, one of the mechanisms that can be used is for the program to verify its checksum. A checksum is a mechanism for verifying the contents of a file. Checksums are produced by one-way hashing algorithms that essentially take an input message and digest that message. In each case, the process is irreversible. A checksum will be replicable for the same input and should feature a low number of collisions — cases where different inputs produce the same output. However, it is impossible to reconstruct the input if one has only the digest output. For instance, the SHA1 (Secure Hash Algorithm 1) program produces the output "a94a8fe5ccb19ba61c-4c0873d391e987982fbbd3" for the input "test." This output digest does not contain the data "test," and so it is not reversible except by guessing and by the fact that this is a very well-known, short input message. For the present discussion, it is only important to know that this hashing process is possible not only on strings of text, as I have demonstrated here, but also upon whole files. A file can be fed into a hashing algorithm to produce an output message that is unique for that file but that will remain the same every time the process is run. Even small changes to the file will result in a completely different hash.

This is useful and relevant because such algorithms can ascertain whether a file has been modified. "Crackers" in the piracy scene work to break the digital protection measures in software and games so that they may illegally distribute the files.

They do this by altering the software's logic within the distributed executable binary. In so doing, however, crackers change the checksum of the executable file. Hence, the simplest way of detecting an unwanted modification to an executable file (e.g., in cases where copy protection has been removed) is to see whether the checksum is the same as expected. If it is not, then it is likely that the user is playing a pirated version of the game in question.

This is the type of logic that leads to these in-game situations. The software checks itself to see whether it has been modified and, if so, alters the game states to achieve the desired effects. Such checks are often missed during the first round of cracking because they do not behave like generic, copyright protection systems that might simply block the program from starting. That is, crackers who wish to pirate a game are on the lookout for logic within software code that shuts down execution entirely, the most common kind of DRM. They will also be searching for messages that indicate that a piece of code is designed to prevent piracy. In the case of logic such as that in *Grand Theft Auto IV*, however, the anti-piracy detection system is cunningly tied to an in-game alteration to automotive physics, which is not the expected usual outcome of DRM technologies.

Executable software can verify whether it has been modified; however, there is no guarantee that pirates will not, in turn, modify the logic that causes these creative responses. The situation is very different in non-executable media, such as movies, music, and pictures. These file formats contain data interpreted by separate executable software, such as a movie player. The movie player reads the data from the movie file, which contains a frame-by-frame description of how to illuminate each pixel on a screen to produce the illusion of film, and then displays it. The movie file itself cannot perform branching logical instructions, as did the software, and it is instead reliant on third-party software to display its contents.

This has far-reaching consequences for piracy's creative loop. For while we have seen a limited number of examples of software that has been influenced by the knowledge of piracy, there are few instances where films and music have had such reciprocating loops of practice (System of a Down's 2002 album, *Steal This Album!*, might be one of the few counter-examples in using its title to refer to piracy). There are no DRMed films, for instance, where the antagonist becomes suddenly unstoppable or where a different, less satisfying ending is presented to those who have not paid for the movie, beyond deliberate, bad, Scene releases by the studios themselves. This is because non-software artifacts such as music files rely on DRM implementation elsewhere as a generic feature. That is to say that films and music certainly are frequently protected by DRM and other technological protection measures. This usually works by the software being provided with a specific license key for decryption once it has shown that it will adequately implement the requested DRM system. In most circumstances, this means that unauthorized players will be unable to decrypt the media content and, therefore, unable to copy it. However, these media depend on the developers of this viewing software, which must handle all movies and not just a specific list of movies. Hence, there is little creative freedom in the aesthetic DRM responses for music and movies, as opposed to software and games.

This is not to say that piracy has no aesthetic consequences for illegally copied film and music. As Virginia Crisp drew to my attention, there are pirate covers created for these artifacts. There are also instances of professional studios adopting a "pirate aesthetic" as part of their own marketing efforts, recuperating piracy in the service of official sales. For example, Sony sent out *The Girl with the Dragon Tattoo* (2012) "in its box as a blank home-burned DVD with the title carelessly hand-written in a black permanent marker."[81] This gave the impression that the media was, itself, a pirated form and that people had received a "rip-off" edition. Finally, enthusiasts can create remixes and

81 Florence Waters, "Film Buyers Fooled by Sony's 'The Girl with the Dragon Tattoo' DVD Joke," *The Telegraph,* March 21, 2012, https://www.telegraph.co.uk/culture/film/film-news/9158437/Film-buyers-fooled-by-Sonys-The-Girl-with-the-Dragon-Tattoo-DVD-joke.html.

fan edits that come with their own aesthetic. These edits are facilitated by access to materials that have the DRM protections removed. That is to say, piracy may facilitate such more legitimate creative endeavors.

This is to make a more limited case for how the economic logic of piracy conditions aesthetic responses. It is certainly the more exciting argument to believe that underground networks of piracy could have positive feedback loops that change mainstream production. This is true in some cases, notably in the space of self-executing software. Most digital artforms do not respond aesthetically to piracy in quite such innovative and creative ways. Whether for technical reasons or simply because they were unaware, most works do not contain witty ripostes to DRM circumvention. Thus, we should take care not to overstate the case of these outsider examples, no matter how amusing they may be.

DISRUPTING AESTHETIC FORMS

A key question for those interested in the Scene is, what motivates Sceners to participate in this alternative reality game? As this book has argued all along, it varies hugely, and there is no single motivating factor. However, I would argue that prestige and status are key elements that Sceners seek, over and above pirate artifacts. From the observations of this chapter on Scene aesthetics, we might posit that kudos and "cool" are also vital.

This insight yields some interesting observations. If participants are active because there is a certain level of kudos and cool associated with being "in the Scene," then there is a potential avenue by which law enforcement can disrupt the Scene that has not previously been explored. If the Scene were to be made boring or uncool, interest would dry up. There are many ways that law enforcement might approach this, some of which have dubious ethical status. For instance, infiltrating the DemoScene or ASCII art communities is a possibility. However, this would involve infiltrating a legitimate internet subculture on the off chance a connection can be found to the Warez Scene that can be exploited.

The fact of the matter remains, though, that topsites are FTP sites. They are fundamentally dull and, in many ways, uncool. Giving them a veneer of sheen and aesthetic cool is what lures people to these sites, coupled with their secrecy, exclusivity, and powerful hardware. Making the Scene boring is a route that seems to have gone relatively unexplored—perhaps because it is impossible—but could be a viable law enforcement tactic as subcultural theory seems to suggest.

Of course, the type of cool that applies to geek underground subcultures is hardly the same kind of cool that applies in society more generally. The word "geek" is a pejorative term that originally referred to "a carnival performer, often billed as a wild man whose act usually includes biting the head off a live chicken or snake."[82] In contemporary technological usage, the counterpoint to the term "geek" is the more pejorative "nerd." Certainly, these terms both sit within a sphere of a sort of masculinity. Their conversion to prevalent slang is best framed on "the continuum of masculine improprieties," even though Sceners are and can be female, as I have noted elsewhere.[83] While the etymology of "nerd" is unknown, though the word first appeared in a Dr. Seuss book in 1950,[84] the distinction between these two terms is famously debated in Douglas Coupland's *Microserfs* (1995), where there is an extended discussion on "[w]hat, exactly, is the difference between a nerd and a geek?" In Coupland's novel, the difference is subtle and instinctual. The reply is that "geek implies hireability, whereas nerd doesn't necessarily mean your skills are 100 percent sellable. Geek implies wealth."[85] While "geeks were usually losers in high school who didn't have

82 Mike Sugarbaker, "What Is a Geek?" *Gazebo (The Journal of Geek Culture)*, 1998, http://www.gibberish.com/gazebo/articles/geek3.html.
83 Lori Kendall, "Nerd Nation: Images of Nerds in US Popular Culture," *International Journal of Cultural Studies* 2, no. 2 (1999): 264.
84 Geisel Theodor Seuss, *If I Ran the Zoo* (New York: Random House for Young Readers, 1950), 47.
85 Douglas Coupland, *Microserfs* (London: Flamingo, 1995), 174.

a life," the novel goes on, "not having a life [then] became a status symbol."[86] Although it is not just the accumulation of wealth that has led to this, through figures such as Sheldon Cooper in the TV series, *The Big Bang Theory,* the "transition from geek-as-sideshow-freak to geek-as-intelligent-expert has moved the term from one of insult to one of endearment."[87]

This use of the term "wealth" is curious in Coupland's description. It is true that, within the context of Coupland's novel, geek knowledge went on to lead to highly paid Silicon Valley jobs. For Warez Sceners, wealth is access to pre-release software rather than directly material in terms of money. It is nonetheless from their investment in geeky activities that this access and wealth arises. The wealth of the Warez Scener is, in fact, though, more akin to fanatics' or comic book completists' spirit of collecting.

Consider, for example, that in the comic-book-collecting subculture, prestige and status are "based on the ability to acquire canonical texts, as determined by either plot or creator significance. By possessing these comics, the reader substantiates his or her participation in fandom."[88] Knowledge of the plot, characters, narrative, and style of these artifacts does, of course, play a role. However, the actual significance for the geek collector lies in possession of the object, not in the actual use of the comic book. The same is true of Warez Sceners. The terabytes upon terabytes of material that sit on the hard drives of topsites must go mostly unused. There are more media on these servers than it would be possible to consume in a lifetime. End-use is not the goal. Instead, it is the accumulation that here plays the role, as though these objects, which are scarce by their difficulty to obtain, were themselves a currency. Sites with the largest archives, along with the best internet links and affiliates, are the most highly valued. Individuals who can hoard the most will

---

86 Ibid.

87 J.A. McArthur, "Digital Subculture: A Geek Meaning of Style," *Journal of Communication Inquiry* 33, no. 1 (January 2009): 61.

88 Jeffrey A. Brown, "Comic Book Fandom and Cultural Capital," *The Journal of Popular Culture* 30, no. 4 (Spring 1997): 26.

likewise gain respect because they are able to fill requests on sites. In short, there is a fanbase-like hoarding phenomenon at work in the game of the Scene that is akin to the collecting instincts seen in other geek communities (e.g., comics, vinyl, and so on). Certainly, one of the motivations of Sceners is to collect these artifacts even if not to use them.

Within this collecting mentality, the destruction of historic, pirate archives, when this happens, for instance through law enforcement action, has a twofold function. First, it makes it harder to acquire historical material. The fact that duplicate releases are not allowed means that if substantial portions of the Scene's historic output become inaccessible, Sceners cannot obtain the material via another route. At the same time, this increases the value of access to the back catalog. The scarcity of back catalog releases increases the prestige of access to them. The fewer people have access, the more elite it is to get hold of such material on request. In other words, until the point of total eradication, shutdowns of historic, Scene-archive topsites increase the stakes in the game of prestige played out inside the Warez Scene through an economy of scarcity. Indeed, it may be the case, paradoxically, that shutting down archive topsites could motivate Sceners into further participation, seeking out ever-scarcer, ever-more elite forms of access. This, again, shows how the scarcity of the Scene has an economic character.

It is true that, for some categories of individuals, the use-value of the Scene's outputs do play a role beyond the general collector impulse that I have just documented. For example, fans of specific musical subgenres (e.g., drum 'n' bass or death metal) or film styles (e.g., science fiction or horror) will find few richer sources than the Scene for high-quality rips of this material; however, it is questionable whether the Scene provides better longstanding back-access to this material when compared with private torrent trackers, as I have already discussed. Indeed, it is often the case that material that is extremely hard to acquire in real life, such as rare vinyl records, will find themselves ripped within the Scene context. This means that there may be a limited subset of Scene users who participate to gain actual access to media content that they would not otherwise possess. The extent to which these niche, subgenre fan bases exist within the Scene is not widely known, but it is a topic that would merit further investigation in future interview work.

This also supposes that there are two levels of collection and taste-determination within the Warez Scene. In conventional collecting circles, "a collection's quality is overdetermined by knowledge and taste and, therefore is subject to field-specific forms of valuation," as Benjamin Woo puts it.[89] In the Warez Scene, at the "meta-collecting" level — where it does not matter what one is collecting, so long as it is a Scene release — the ability to "to claim status among [...] fellow geeks" is determined by access to scarce warez and not by any particular principles of taste and style.[90] By contrast, another level of collecting, such as artifact and genre-based collecting, carries with it the same principles of style and taste that one would see in external geek cultures. Moreover, this latter group may attract symbolic currency (e.g,. prestige, respect) in groups outside the Scene because of their internal access. The punk-rock lover who manages to acquire access to works that others cannot, via the Scene, will garner exterior respect in a different community because of that access. Hence, geek collecting mentalities in the Scene have both interior and exterior projects of cultural capital accumulation. The former are media agnostic, while the latter fit within existing descriptive paradigms of taste and subcultural behavior.

Another definition of geek focuses more keenly on the obsessive nature of interest. For instance, McCain et al. proffer the distinction that "[n]erds were considered to be socially awkward and overly intellectual, whereas geeks were prone to obsessive interest in marginalized or obscure hobbies such as the *Dungeons and Dragons* game, comic books, and personal computing."[91] This description seems accurate, except that one

89 Benjamin Woo, "Alpha Nerds: Cultural Intermediaries in a Subcultural Scene," *European Journal of Cultural Studies* 15, no. 5 (2012): 662.

90 Ibid.

91 Jessica McCain, Brittany Gentile, and W. Keith Campbell, "A Psychological Exploration of Engagement in Geek Culture," *PLOS ONE* 10, no. 11 (2015): 2.

of these media is not like the others. While *Dungeons and Dragons* and comic books are single-subject activities, being into "personal computing" is a very different interest as the computer itself can present many different scenarios. For instance, being interested in "personal computing," at least now, could mean that a user enjoys making music, creating visual artworks, playing games, programming, building computers, chatting online, or participating in the Warez Scene. Of course, this technical distinction hardly matters given the bullying concepts within which the term was developed and used. Notably, an interest in computers could be lumped in these same categories.

Nonetheless, the geeks of the Scene find that their social identities are greatly sculpted by operating within this milieu. As J.P. Williams posits, "[f]or individuals who do not participate in face-to-face scenes, however, the internet is more than a medium; it is a social space through which personal and social identities are constructed, given meaning, and shared through the ritual of computer-mediated interaction."[92] This means that, for many Warez Sceners, their primary life identity is sculpted by a partially asynchronous online subculture.

The asynchronicity of the Scene is both a defining feature and an element that the Scene tries to eliminate. While the Scene is an international network that spans the globe, it is also split into geographical regions, mitigating the effects of timescales. For instance, as noted, there are separate courier charts for EU, US, and Asian regions, implying that racing between these regions is less common and comes with speed challenges of internet routing (it is usually much slower to transfer a file from an Asian region to an EU region than it would be to transfer a file within those borders). In addition, this division into time zones means that individuals will mostly be online at the same time within their geographic bubbles and so will have space for social interaction.

The actual time spent online by Sceners varies hugely. A Wired article that interviewed a Scene member noted that

92 Williams, "Authentic Identities," 195.

"Clickety used to spend 12 hours a day online."[93] Topsite rules for couriers specify that a certain quota must be met every month, as noted above in the section on geek humor. In turn, this ensures that users must spend a certain proportion of time online to meet this demand and keep their slot on the site. As a side effect, these quotas force users to be online at similar times, thus ensuring more of a synchronous community experience. Of course, there are still periods of users being "AFK," or away from keyboard. However, many site rules are designed to minimize this and ensure that end-users congregate for the synchronicity of social encounters. Internet Relay Chat (IRC) bouncers are another element that provides for a synchronous encounter, even within an asynchronous environment. By leaving an avatar present at all times on IRC, users avoid the need to reinvite themselves into many different site channels with passwords and on-site invite commands and give the appearance of presence at all times, affirming synchronicity once more.

While many forms of geek culture eventually worked to reclaim the label and to self-appropriate the term, the Warez Scene faces additional challenges that licit subcultures do not. Mainstream geek culture has tended to focus, for example, on "science-fiction and fantasy, comic books, roleplaying games, costuming, etc." and "[t]hese interests tended to share common themes, such as larger-than-life fantasy worlds (e.g., Tolkein's Middle Earth), characters with extraordinary abilities (e.g., Superman), the use of magic or highly advanced technologies (e.g., futuristic technologies in *Star Trek*), and elements from history (e.g., renaissance fairs) or foreign cultures (e.g., Japanese cartoons, or anime)."[94] Importantly, the visible performance or demonstration of a "knowledge of or devotion to these interests became a form of social currency between self-proclaimed

93 David McCandless, "Warez Wars," *Wired*, April 1, 1997, https://www.wired.com/1997/04/ff-warez/.

94 McCain, Gentile, and Campbell, "A Psychological Exploration of Engagement in Geek Culture," 2.

geeks" that culminated in the now enormously popular Comic-Con events.[95]

Comic-Con, with its famed, outlandish cosplay, gives geeks "a gathering space where attendees can attend panels, buy merchandise, and wear costumes to show their devotion to a particular show or comic book character."[96] It also clearly yields a way for once-employed science fiction actors to receive an ongoing revenue stream, as fans will queue for hours and pay handsomely to have their photograph taken with their heroes. Furthermore, recent studies have shown that mainstream geek culture is "a lucrative target for advertisers as well as being high-spenders with the power to make or break billion-pound brands."[97] Using the UK's currency, the British Pound, this work showed that geeks "number a seven million strong audience for ad agencies and estimates that the 'geek pound' is worth a staggering £8.2b [USD 10.58b] a year." Finally, this survey, conducted by Sci-Fi channel service reveals that geeks are not anti-social loners. Instead, it "shows that geeks these days have discovered a social life — with 52% more likely than the average person to have had four holidays in the last 12 months and 125% more likely to visit pubs, clubs, and bars. And nearly 40% of them believe their special interests make them attractive to the opposite sex."[98]

This mainstream geek culture, and Comic-Con in particular, provides an apt counterpoint for the Warez Scene. While Comic-Con yields a public outlet venue in which geeks can perform with pride, the illegality of the Warez Scene forces members into secrecy to avoid detection. This is not to say that there is not pride among Warez Sceners. Clearly, leaking information to public documentary websites, such as *TorrentFreak,* is a key way in which Sceners can show off their creds and insider knowledge without a great deal of risk. This breaking of interiority

95 Ibid.

96 Ibid., 2.

97 Timothy Lithgow, "Sci-Fi Unveils the 'Geek Pound,'" *MediaWeek,* June 27, 2005, https://www.campaignlive.co.uk/article/sci-fi-unveils-geek-pound/510998.

98 Ibid.

is frowned upon by members of the Scene, while clearly there is a lure to do so in order to bask briefly in the reflected glory of providing the inside story to someone without access. This comes with some risk to the Scene member in question as they will have to reveal some elements of their identity to a journalist or blogger — who could, indeed, be a member of law enforcement — although it is relatively trivial to send anonymous emails with tips.

It is also, clearly, the case that the Warez Scene cannot be monetized in the same way as other geek scenes. While Comic-Con and other events provide commercial loci, points at which social interaction melds with trade, the Warez Scene does not work in this way. For one, face-to-face meetings would entail far too much physical risk for participants, and only long-established, quasi-legitimate DemoScene groups such as Fairlight can even risk this (see the section on Fairlight in Chapter Six). While there is research that suggests that other geek subcultures may meet in the real world and that approaches to their study must examine the overlap between online and offline experience, this seems less likely in the context of the Warez Scene.[99] For a second point, it is unclear what conceivable merchandise could be provided around this type of activity. Other forms of "geek scene" have their own media, which results in substantial product placement. For instance, George Lucas made an extremely savvy move in retaining the merchandising rights for the Star Wars franchise. It is hard to imagine what commodities might circle the topsite Scene. Models of one's favorite server? USB keys with classic releases and demos on them? A "build your own topsite" stall or a top trumps game? Competitive, live, courier racing? In short, the illegality and the inherently non-commercial nature of the Warez Scene render it a different space for the types of in-person, highly commodified circulation that one sees among other geek scenes.

---

99 Thomas J. Holt, "Subcultural Evolution? Examining the Influence of On- and Off-Line Experiences on Deviant Subcultures," *Deviant Behavior* 28, no. 2 (2007): 172.

There are indeed other improbable types of geek culture meet-ups. Consider the rise of large-scale gaming parties, in which competitors bring their computers to a shared locale to game against one another. The biggest of these can number thousands of participants. One could also point again to the DemoScene, where digital artists come together in person to show off their creations, to socialize, and so forth. There are also CTF Hacking meetings. These are "Capture the Flag" games for computer crackers that involve breaking in, as a team, to a remote server. These hacker events provide a safe space for computer security experts to demonstrate their acumen, within a legal environment, under fun, competitive conditions.

This is all to say that while Scene cultures may appear too esoteric to merit in-person social events, there are possible ways that individuals from these spaces would like to meet. The illegality of the Scene is most likely the impinging factor that holds them back. To conclude, the Scene seems to function as do other aesthetic, geek subcultures. This comes with one significant conclusion. I have argued throughout this book that prestige and reputation are the currencies that power the game of the Warez Scene. Recent psychological studies of geek subculture offer some confirmation of this: "[o]ur findings suggest that geek media is especially attractive to narcissists, independent of demographic variables."[100] It is the need to show off that comes through most strongly in the Warez Scene, and this is why it is so prominently linked to the aesthetic cultures of the DemoScene and the ASCII art scene. It is this pride that will often come before a fall. The need to perform one's elite status in public is where many Sceners meet their end, accidentally showing off in front of law enforcement.

100 McCain, Gentile, and Campbell, "A Psychological Exploration of Engagement in Geek Culture," 33.

```
 .______.___  _____  ____
 |   ___/:  _|  \    \_/   /
 |___   \|  :  |   \___ ___/
 |      /|     |   /  _   \
 |__:__/ |     |  /__/ \___\
    :        |___|
```

Takedowns

One of the defining features of the Warez Scene is that the game is illegal, although many participants do not consider this most of the time. While the "motivations of warez traders may vary" and "pure profit is not the sole or even dominant consideration for many," there is, as Gregory Urbas writes, "a widely-shared conception of warez groups, both by themselves and more generally within the online community, as not really engaged in criminal exploits at all, but rather operating on the fringes of officialdom or the corporate world by pirating expensive software and making it freely—or at least inexpensively—available to others."[1] Unfortunately, this belief is misplaced as the many law-enforcement raids of pirate groups have shown.

In this chapter, I detail the major raids conducted against the Scene since the millennium. Specifically, I turn to Operation Cyber Strike and associated early raids, Operation Buccaneer,

1 Gregor Urbas, "Cross-National Investigation and Prosecution of Intellectual Property Crimes: The Example of 'Operation Buccaneer'," *Crime, Law and Social Change* 46, nos. 4–5 (December 2006): 209. See also Sameer Hinduja, "Neutralization Theory and Online Software Piracy: An Empirical Analysis," *Ethics and Information Technology* 9, no. 3 (2007): 187–204; Aron M. Levin, Mary Conway Dato-on, and Kenneth Rhee, "Money for Nothing and Hits for Free: The Ethics of Downloading Music from Peer-to-Peer Web Sites," *Journal of Marketing Theory and Practice* 12, no. 1 (2004): 48–60.

Operation Fastlink, Operation Site Down, and the most recent bust, the SPARKS raid of 2020. These raids seem to follow a recurrent pattern. The enforcement action triggers a temporary shutdown of much of the Scene, followed by a period of recuperation before it all starts up again. Thus far, every time there has been a raid, the Scene has recovered and recommenced operations almost precisely as before, albeit each time with more stringent security precautions. Often conducted by covert agents, the raids offer another point at which the Scene surfaces into mainstream culture.[2] Indeed, while it is possible, as I have done, to piece together the Scene from leaks of its own documents on the web, there are relatively few points at which official accounts independently even verify the existence of this subculture. The closest we will get to an official, non-self-published account of the workings of the Scene is when an official US Department of Justice press release is issued. The issue might state, as this one from 2004 has for instance, that "groups exist solely [...] to be the first to place a newly pirated work onto the Internet — often before the work is legitimately available to the public" via "'elite' sites."[3] It is in this way that law-enforcement raids form an important documentary source and archival context in which to read the Warez Scene.

OPERATION CYBER STRIKE (1997), OPERATION FASTLANE (2001), AND OPERATION BUCCANEER (2002)

Operation Buccaneer was the designation given by the US Customs Service to its raids of the Warez Scene, beginning in October 2000. Buccaneer is usually charted as the first raid against the Scene, but it was actually preceded by Operation Cyber Strike six years earlier, which targeted the Bulletin Board Sys-

2 J.D. Lasica, *Darknet: Hollywood's War against the Digital Generation* (Hoboken: Wiley, 2005), 47–48.

3 "Justice Department Announces International Piracy Sweep," *US Department of Justice*, April 22, 2004, https://www.justice.gov/archive/opa/pr/2004/April/04_crm_263.htm.

tems (BBS) precursors to File transfer Protocol (FTP) topsites and on which very little information is available.[4] That said, a 1997 interview with "The Punisher" claims that Operation Cyber Strike hit some of Razor 1911's "most prestigious boards" at the time.[5] A similar but brief interview with The Crazy Little Punk indicated that even at this early stage, it was impossible to avoid raids: "if the feds are going to watch us, they'll get into our channel secretly and not let us know it. Invite only isn't going to keep them out."[6]

The primary target of the much more ambitious later Operation Buccaneer was the group DrinkOrDie. The US Customs Service referred to this group as "the oldest and most well known" piracy outfit, a claim of dubious merit that many people have called into question.[7] Other groups hit by the raid included RiSC, Razor 1911, RiSCISO, Request To Send (RTS), ShadowRealm (SRM), WomenLoveWarez (WLW), and POPZ.[8] A full list of individuals implicated as a result of these raids is shown in Table 2.

---

4 "FBI Hunts Software Pirates," *CNET,* January 28, 1997, https://www.cnet.com/news/fbi-hunts-software-pirates/; "Operation Cyber Strike," *Bankers Online,* March 1, 1997, https://www.bankersonline.com/articles/103656; Jonathan R. Basamanowicz, "Release Groups & Digital Copyright Piracy" (Master's Thesis, Simon Fraser University, 2011), 16; "Cyber Strike: FBI Agents Confiscated Computers And...," *Chicago Tribune,* https://www.chicagotribune.com/news/ct-xpm-1997-01-29-9701300206-story.html.

5 Anemia, "Interview with The Punisher (interview with the punisher - anemia1.png)," January 29, 1997, DeFacto2.

6 Saint Tok, "Interview with The Crazy Little Punk," *DeFacto2* (df2-02.txt), February 1997, DeFacto2.

7 Farhad Manjoo, "Were DrinkOrDie Raids Overkill?" *Wired,* December 13, 2001, https://www.wired.com/2001/12/were-drinkordie-raids-overkill/.

8 Paul J. McNultey, "Warez Leader Sentenced to 46 Months," *US Department of Justice,* May 17, 2002, https://www.justice.gov/archive/criminal/cybercrime/press-releases/2002/sankusSent.htm.

Name	Scene Handle	Charge	Alleged Activities	Groups
David Anderson				DrinkOrDie
Alex Bell	Mr 2940	Conspiracy to defraud		DrinkOrDie
Richard Berry	Flood	Conspiracy	Hardware supplier	DrinkOrDie, POPZ
Anthony Buchanan	spaceace	Criminal copyright infringement		
Andrew Clardy	Doodad	Criminal copyright infringement Aiding and abetting		DrinkOrDie, POPZ
Myron Cole	t3rminal	Criminal copyright infringement		DrinkOrDie
James Cudney	BeCre8tive			DrinkOrDie
Ian Dimmock		Copyright act violations		
Steven Dowd	Tim	Conspiracy to defraud		DrinkOrDie
Andrew Eardley		Conspiracy to defraud		
Derek Eiser	Psychod	Criminal copyright infringement		DrinkOrDie
Barry Erickson	Radsl	Conspiracy	Supplier	DrinkOrDie, RiSCISO, POPZ
Hew Raymond Griffiths	Bandido			DrinkOrDie, Razor1911

Name	Scene Handle	Charge	Alleged Activities	Groups
David A. Grimes	Chevelle	Conspiracy	Supplier and topsite administrator	DrinkOrDie, RiSC, RTS
Robert Gross	targetpractice	Criminal copyright infringement		DrinkOrDie
Nathan Hunt	Azide	Conspiracy	Supplier	CORPS, DrinkOrDie
Armvid Karstad	ievil		IRCD administrator	DrinkOrDie, Razor1911
Kent Kartadinata	Tenkuken	Conspiracy	DrinkOrDie mail server operator	DrinkOrDie
Michael Kelly	Erupt	Conspiracy	IRC bot operator	AMNESiA, CORE, DrinkOrDie, RiSC
Stacey Nawara	Avec	Conspiracy	Courier	DrinkOrDie, Razor1911, RTS
Mike Nguyen	Hackrat	Conspiracy	Site administrator of The Ratz Hole	Razor1911, RiSC
Dennis Osdashko		Copyright act violations		

Name	Scene Handle	Charge	Alleged Activities	Groups
Kirk Patrick	thesaint		Site adminis-trator of GodCom-plex	DrinkOrDie
Sabuj Pattan-ayek	Buj	Conspiracy	Cracker	CORPS, DrinkOrDie, RTS
Shane Pitman			Conspir-acy	Razor1911
John Riffe	blue/ blueadept	Criminal copy-right infringe-ment		
David Russo	Ange		Software tester	DrinkOrDie
John Jr. Sankus	eriFlleH	Conspira-cy	Co-leader of Drink-OrDie	DrinkOrDie, Harm
Mark Shu-maker	markalso			
Christopher Tresco	BigRar	Conspiracy	Topsite adminis-trator	DrinkOrDie, RiSC
Mark Vent		Conspiracy to defraud		

Table 2: Individuals arrested and charged in the raids of December 2001.[9]

9 Paul Craig, *Software Piracy Exposed* (Rockland: Syngress, 2005), 196–97; Eric Goldman, "Warez Trading and Criminal Copyright Infringement," SSRN *Electronic Journal* (2004), 28; Urbas, "Cross-National Investigation and Prosecution of Intellectual Property Crimes," 212–14; "Pair Convicted of Internet Piracy," *BBC News,* March 16, 2005, http://news.bbc.co.uk/1/hi/technology/4336401.stm; Rosie Cowan, "Jail for Net Pirates Who Saw Themselves as Robin Hoods," *The Guardian,* May 7, 2005, http://www.

The Buccaneer raids provide a compelling account of how news spreads within Scene announcement files. For instance, the initial NFO that went around the MP3 scene at the time listed a far more extensive list, totaling thirty-two screen names, than the eventual set of those indicted:

> BUSTED: HiTech666 (ex-PWZ/ex-FTS/ex-Razor 1911/Myth/Deviance/RTS, Montreal, Canada), jozef (RogueWarriorz, Canada), Elisa (EGO, RogueWarriorz), Bierkrug (RogueWarriorz), Lord Hacker (RogueWarriorz), Axxess (RogueWarriorz), Waldorf (RogueWarriorz), Demonfurby (RogueWarriorz), Dr Infothief (RogueWarriorz), doodad (pop), tenkuken (dod), eRUPT (author of ruptbot, dod, Miami), doc-x (dod council, Miami), heckler (TiL), zielin, sui (tfl/wlw), hackrat (wlw/razor/dod, California), shark (wlw/razor/dod; RatzHole siteop, Australia), thraxis (not busted; but raided — 700 cds and computer; risc, pgc, dod, Queensland, Australia), maverick (from skidrow, not from omega; dod council), sony, bandido (razor, dod council, risc council), erifleh (dod council, Philadelphia), bigrar (christopher tresco 23 y/o, dod council, risc, ex-MnM, ex-PSF (Proper Stuff), Boston), avec (former fts, rts, rise, former DOD council, razor), buj (cracker; dod council, former rts senior, razor, former corpgods leader, ex-PGC, Durham North Carolina), forcekill (dod, turku Finland), radsl (dod, popz founder, Oregon), chevelle (Dallas), billyjoe (Austin), ievil (dod, razor, an ircop, had retired already, Arnvid Karstad), superiso (inferno; got raided), ^stealth (Oregon), BaLLz (CSR)[10]

---

theguardian.com/technology/2005/may/07/crime.uknews; Sam Dibley, "Former Leader of Razor 1911, the Oldest Game Software Piracy Ring on the Internet, Sentenced," *US Department of Justice,* June 6, 2003, https://www.justice.gov/archive/criminal/cybercrime/press-releases/2003/pitmanSent.htm.

10 "Operation Buccaneer (operation_buccaneer.txt)," 2000, mp3scene.info.

While some of these turned out to be correct — hackrat, erifleh, ievil, Erupt, avec, etc. — there are many individuals here named who do not appear on the indictment list. Whether this was simply because there was insufficient evidence to charge them remains unclear. What is obvious though is that these initial news reports within the Scene should be understood within the framework of rumor.

Rumor is both a type of message with an uncertain truth value and a dissemination process for that material.[11] However, the internet has radically changed the nature of gossip and rumor.[12] At least one key feature of rumor dissemination in the virtual space is the rapidity of its spread, compared to conventional networks, and the apparent network effects of sourcing in which it appears that the rumor has merely circulated without an authoritative source.[13] Like their cousins in the legitimate world news space, Scene news announcements mutate rapidly as new facts become known on the ground: "RELOAD THE PAGE, CONSTANTLY UPATED! [*sic*]," one of the Buccaneer news updates reads.[14]

When we view Scene-wide announcements of busts, we also need to consider that initial reports are not only inaccurate but function as a type of rumor machine that can make or break a Scener's reputation as well. For instance, the Operation Buccaneer Scene notice says that "BadGirl was accused of narqing on a site in Germany. They got her purged from most sites and deleted from Checkpoint. She use to be in TR, a MP3 release group."[15] These news releases in the Scene can quickly become

11 Martin Sökefeld, "Rumours and Politics on the Northern Frontier: The British, Pakhtun Wali and Yaghestan," *Modern Asian Studies* 36, no. 2 (2002): 300.

12 Gordon W. Allport and L.J. Postman, *The Psychology of Rumor* (New York: Holt, Rinehart and Winston, 1947); Ralph L. Rosnow and Gary A. Fine, *Rumor and Gossip: The Social Psychology of Hearsay* (Amsterdam: Elsevier, 1976).

13 For instance, see Glen A. Perice, "Rumors and Politics in Haiti," *Anthropological Quarterly* 70, no. 1 (January 1997): 8.

14 "SceneBusts10 (scenebusts10.htm)," 2000, paraZite.

15 "Operation Buccaneer (operation_buccaneer.txt)."

powerful tools by which enemies are denounced. In these types of online spaces, "[o]ur reputation is an essential component to our freedom, for without the good opinion of our community, our freedom can become empty."[16] These types of doxxing NFOs that reveal information about an individual for public shaming are weapons for the erosion of reputation.[17] Even the suggestion that people have been caught can lead to negative reputational inference in the Scene, with a cracker named MoRf remarking that "[o]nly peasants get caught."[18]

This issue of reputation and rumor concerning busts is important in order to understand the Scene as a community. In Francis Fukuyama's not uncontentious analysis, "[t]rust is the expectation that arises within a community of regular, honest, and cooperative behavior, based on commonly shared norms, on the part of other members of that community" and "[s]ocial capital is a capability that arises from the prevalence of trust in a society or in certain parts of it."[19] Given the importance to Sceners of social capital and feeling that other members of the Scene can be trusted not to cooperate with law enforcement operations, being named in an NFO file as having been busted, or having cooperated, would have serious consequences of ostracization. For instance, it is claimed that Shark, apparently a siteop of "The Ratz Hole," "was a police officer in Sydney, Australia." This would presumably cause alarm. However, the NFO goes on, "[h]e wasn't an informant though, but rather a target of the busts"—that is, he was a police officer who was also a Scener and not involved in the investigations. It is unclear what effect this type of rumor would have on the individual's reputation, but it would undoubtedly lead to disquiet. At the same time, Sceners do not believe notices with an uncritical acceptance. As

---

16 Daniel J. Solove, *The Future of Reputation: Gossip, Rumor, and Privacy on the Internet* (New Haven: Yale University Press, 2007), 30.

17 Ibid.

18 Manjoo, "Were DrinkOrDie Raids Overkill?"

19 Francis Fukuyama, *Trust: The Social Virtues and the Creation of Prosperity* (New York: Free Press, 1995), 26.

the Buccaneer notice puts it: "ONLY write a message if you are 200% sure that it's true. we do NOT need any new rumours."[20]

We can also trace the way that news spreads between different outlets when there is a Scene bust. For instance, a different announcement source, #dodbusts on EFNET, claimed:

> BUSTED: heckler, zielin, wizy (risciso, til), sui (tfl/wlw), hackrat (wlw/razor/dod, California), shark (wlw/razor/dod; RatzHole siteop), thraxis (not busted; but raided—700 cds and computer; risc, pgc, dod, Queensland, Australia), maverick (from skidrow, not from omega; dod council), sony, bandido (razor, dod, risc council), erifleh (dod council, Philadelphia), bigrar (dod, risc, Boston), avec (former fts, rts, rise, former DOD council, razor), buj (dod, Durham North Carolina), forcekill (dod, turku Finland), radsl (dod, Oregon), chevelle (Dallas), billyjoe (Austin), ievil (razor, an ircop, had retired already), superiso (inferno; got raided), raftman (Norway)[21]

Although it is not possible to trace the direction in which this information flowed, the direct repetition of "thraxis (not busted; but raided—700 cds and computer; risc, pgc, dod, Queensland, Australia)" is a clue that many of these news sources are copying and pasting from each other, recycling the same rumor, albeit with different names in this particular update (wizy, for instance, who appears nowhere else). It is further worth noting that there are reputational advantages in being the person in the news cycle who can be the first to reveal accurate information. Given that most of the Scene works on a who-you-know basis, accurately identifying members of elite Scene groups can be used to the newscaster's advantage. That is, being the person who can correctly identify, say, that shark was busted and that they were a member of Razor1911 and siteop of The Ratz Hole is, in itself, a form of bragging that one knows the internal

20 "Operation Buccaneer (operation_buccaneer.txt)."
21 "SceneBusts10 (scenebusts10.htm)."

Scene structure and is acquainted with high-status individuals. Indeed, such reporting carries a false modesty, or humblebrag, within it, akin to saying that one "bumped into Mick the other day," when one means Mick Jagger. We can, therefore, discern a motive in these announcements for the naming of apparently high-ranking Sceners who were not actually busted; naming such individuals and revealing their details confers status on the person who does the naming.

It is also clear that these busts attempt to target key network figures; group leaders and co-leaders who are the nodes through which much of the Scene operates. Such individuals can be understood through the triplicate functions that they occupy. They are career Sceners, they are gatekeepers, and they hold particular dispositions towards the field and the mainstream.[22] This is to say that, with limited resources available with which to conduct law-enforcement operations, the involved organizations make targeted choices to focus on supposed central individuals. In a structure that appears to be networked, rhizomatic, and dispersed, the efficacy of this approach seems to be questionable. As can be seen through the history of Scene busts, every time that one head of the hydra is severed, another five appear to regrow: "RTSMP3 currently shutdown, but will return in the future."[23]

OPERATION FASTLINK (2004)

After the relative success of Buccaneer, the FBI, the US Department of Justice, the Computer Crimes and Intellectual Property Section (CCIPS) of the Criminal Division, and Interpol coordinated to launch a fresh series of raids in 2004.[24] The largest component of Operation Fastlink was Operation Higher Education,

22 Benjamin Woo, "Alpha Nerds: Cultural Intermediaries in a Subcultural Scene," *European Journal of Cultural Studies* 15, no. 5 (2012): 666.

23 "Operation Buccaneer (operation_buccaneer.txt)."

24 Lucas Logan, "The IPR GPR: The Emergence of a Global Prohibition Regime to Regulate Intellectual Property Infringement," in *Piracy: Leakages from Modernity,* ed. Martin Fredriksson and James Arvanitakis (Sacramento: Litwin Books, 2014), 144–45.

a series of synchronized raids on topsites based at universities "which resulted in more than 120 search warrants executed in the United States, Belgium, Denmark, France, Germany, Hungary, Israel, the Netherlands, Singapore, Spain, Sweden, and the United Kingdom; the confiscation of hundreds of computers and illegal online distribution hubs; and the removal of more than $50 million worth of illegally copied software, games, movies and music from illicit distribution channels."[25] These sites could benefit from the relatively high link speeds of university campuses, although such sites sometimes had seasonal shutdowns to avoid detection over the holiday periods. Operations Fastlink and Higher Education were designed to signal that running topsites on campuses was no longer a certain, safe activity. The primary target of Operation Fastlink was the prolific and highly respected release and cracking group, Fairlight, with subsidiary raids against members of Kalisto, Echelon, Class, and DEViANCE.

As with many cracking groups, Fairlight had its co-origins in the Commodore DemoScene, a computer art subculture that focuses on creating short video artworks within self-contained executables. The merging with the illegal warez subculture came when cracks of commercial software began integrating the demo visualizations of the DemoScene, covered in the preceding chapter. Nonetheless, Fairlight was a highly successful Scene group, and a brief digression into its history is merited. Founded in Malmö, Sweden, the group scaled new heights of speed for releases by using a train conductor as a courier to get the latest games from founder and supplier Tony Krvaric ("strider"), who worked in a computer shop, to the cracker Fredrik Kahl ("gollum"). This localization and speed of transfer meant that they could outpace their rivals with ease, beating other groups to the release by a substantial margin.[26] This focus on the speed

25 US Attorney's Office, "Florida Man Who Participated in Online Piracy Ring Is Sentenced," *FBI*, May 6, 2009, https://www.fbi.gov/newhaven/press-releases/2009/nh050609a.htm.

26 Daniel Goldberg, "'We Might Be Old, But We're Still the Elite,'" *Computer Sweden*, April 20, 2012, https://computersweden.idg.se/2.2683/1.444716/

of shipment and obtaining supply at pace can also be seen in internal group NFOs, such as Miracle, who created a list of US companies who would rapidly ship software and games and that could, therefore, be used as a supply route.[27] At this time, trading cracked software was not a crime in Sweden.

The demographic qualities of the individuals involved are also telling and, in at least one case, remarkable. Krvaric has since emigrated to the United States and is now the chairman of the San Diego Republican Party. There, his biography notes that while he was "[b]orn and raised in Sweden," he claims to have been "inspired by Ronald Reagan's optimism and unshakable belief in free enterprise, individual liberty and limited government."[28] The biography does not specify whether Richard Nixon similarly inspired Krvaric. While, of course, it is possible that Krvaric changed his politics over time, during the period it was alleged that he was involved in Fairlight, he apparently used the slogan "Kill a Commie for Your Mommie," according to several news sources, demonstrating a right-wing bent even in his teenage years.[29] Indeed, an early Fairlight demo called "Space Age" appears to show Krvac throwing a Nazi salute in front of an animated dancing Hitler according to news reporting.[30] Krvac's desire "to leave Swedish social democracy," as an article on him in *RawStory* alleges, challenges the assertion that the Warez

---

we-might-be-old-but-were-still-the-elite.

27 Miracle, "USA retail shipment speeds (USA shops and speed.txt)," n.d., DeFacto2.

28 "Chairman Tony Krvaric," *The Republican Party of San Diego County,* n.d., http://www.sandiegorepublicans.org/chairman-tony-krvaric.html.

29 Don Bauder, "Chairman of San Diego GOP Co-Founded International Piracy Ring, Says Online News Website | San Diego Reader," *San Diego Reader,* April 29, 2008, https://www.sandiegoreader.com/weblogs/financial-crime-politics/2008/apr/29/chairman-of-san-diego-gop-co-founded-international/.

30 Ryan Bradford, "Tony Krvaric Has Always Sucked," *AwkwardSD,* September 3, 2020, https://awkwardsd.substack.com/p/tony-krvaric-has-always-sucked; Amita Sharma and J.W. August, "Video Resurfaces Featuring Images of Hitler and Local GOP Party Chair Tony Krvaric," *KPBS,* August 21, 2020, https://www.kpbs.org/news/2020/aug/21/video-surfaces-images-hitler-and-tony-krvaric/.

Scene should be viewed as a socialistic or communistic enterprise.[31] Instead, the Scene is an environment of extreme speed and competition — an eminently capitalistic space — and one to which, it would seem, Krvac's political temperament is well suited. On the other hand, "gollum" — Fredrik Kahl — is now a Professor of Mathematics who has held positions at Lund University and Chalmers University in Sweden, reflecting the extreme level of skill and intelligence required in cracking software.

Although Fairlight started as a legal demoscene enterprise, it was definitively illegal by the time of its later PC ISO (i.e., games) Warez Scene operations. This led to Operation Fastlink. Like previous busts, initial rumors spread like wildfire through the Scene and contained some truth. For instance, an early report on the raids notes that "toxin" of Fairlight was busted.[32] This tallies with subsequent FBI press releases that identified toxin as Greg Hurley, a supplier for the group. However, the initial Scene bust report did not note that "ripvan," Nathan Carrera, was also successfully prosecuted and convicted of "serving as a site operator for at least one FTP warez site."[33] Indeed, the initial Scene reports, in the case of Fastlink, were, for once, understated. Although the notification states that one hundred people were targeted, this seems accurate because in the US alone, Operation Fastlink resulted in over sixty felony convictions for software piracy offenses.[34]

Some Scene members had thought that specific subgenres of release were safer than others. For instance, existing sources state that prosecutors were more interested in pursuing mainstream movie and game release groups than other content types.

---

31 Miriam Raftery, "San Diego GOP Chairman Co-Founded International Piracy Ring," *The Raw Story,* April 29, 2009.

32 "opfastlink.txt," 2002, http://144.217.177.36:1421/EBooks/paraZite/opfastlink.txt.

33 US Attorney's Office, "Florida Man Who Participated in Online Piracy Ring Is Sentenced."

34 "60th Felony Conviction Obtained in Software Piracy Crackdown 'Operation Fastlink,'" *US Department of Justice,* March 6, 2009, https://www.justice.gov/opa/pr/60th-felony-conviction-obtained-software-piracy-crackdown-operation-fastlink.

As Paul Craig writes, "FBI activity focuses on game and movie piracy, not because the FBI considers this to be the largest threat, but because that's where the money is."[35] He also notes the interview with "DOM" where this Scener says, "to date, no one has been sentenced for ripping adult media," showing a belief that the XXX genre of the Scene is safe, as might be other areas.[36] (This is possibly because law enforcement does not wish to be seen to be protecting the pornographic industry.) However, a retrospective analysis of the convictions from Fastlink tells a different story and one in which the MP3 division of the Scene became implicated.[37] Consider, for instance, that Derek A. Borchardt, Matthew B. Howard, Aaron O. Jones, and George S. Hayes were convicted of being members of "pre-release music groups," Apocalypse Crew (APC) and Chromance (CHR).[38] While Fastlink primarily targeted Fairlight's PC ISO activities, the consequences of the raids reached far into various media types.

OPERATION SITE DOWN (2005)

Unlike other raids that had worked to infiltrate release groups, Operation Site Down in 2005, along with its subset investigation, Operation Copycat, worked by establishing two sting topsites, LAD and CHUD, that were run by an FBI agent, using the handle "Griffen." Totaling 11 terabytes of data, these sites attracted prominent affiliate groups, such as CENTROPY, and co-siteops who were willing to help with scripting (the user "xooox,"

35 Craig, *Software Piracy Exposed,* 200.

36 Ibid., 178.

37 MP3 piracy is organized into different levels. Studies to date have focused on the DCC file exchange level rather than the higher-level Scene on which this book works. See Jon Cooper and Daniel M. Harrison, "The Social Organization of Audio Piracy on the Internet," *Media, Culture & Society* 23, no. 1 (2001): 71–89.

38 "Justice Department Announces Four Pleas in Internet Music Piracy Crackdown," *US Department of Justice,* February 28, 2006, https://www.justice.gov/archive/opa/pr/2006/February/06_crm_103.html.

David Fish) and users who brokered relationships ("dact") with release groups themselves.[39]

The studies of Operation Site Down and the affidavits of the FBI agent who operated the sting, Julia B. Jolie, are among the most informative legal documents about the Warez Scene. Of these documents, special commendation should go to Jonathan R. Basamanowicz's Master's thesis at Simon Fraser University, "Release Groups & Digital Copyright Piracy," which is both accurate and enlightening.[40] For instance, in his analysis, taking the arrests and prosecutions as a random sampling mechanism, Basamanowicz can show, of those convicted in this raid, the different demographic breakdowns for each type of individual. While the average age of Sceners was 27.4 years, siteops and group administrators trended above this age at around 29, while couriers and crackers tended to be much younger individuals. Testers and packagers are also substantially above the mean age range for Scene individuals at 40.5 years, but this is skewed by a limited sample of only two people and a standard deviation of 9.2 years.[41]

The sentence lengths for individuals of different group types are also telling. Release group administrators received the highest sentence lengths, at an average of 22 months, followed closely by suppliers at 18 months. Siteops, on average, received a sentence of 17.4 months, while testers of cracks received 15.5 months. Curiously, crackers themselves seemed not to receive criminal sentences in this analysis. Of the types of individuals who were imprisoned, couriers received the lowest sentence levels, at an average of 4.5 months.[42]

39 Richard Seeborg, "United States of America v. Chirayu Patel, Aka Nebula, Aka Nabwrk, Aka Aluben, Aka Notneb, Aka Aluben: Warrant for Arrest," June 28, 2005, 4.

40 Jonathan Basamanowicz and Martin Bouchard, "Overcoming the Warez Paradox: Online Piracy Groups and Situational Crime Prevention," *Policy & Internet* 3, no. 2 (January 31, 2011): 79–103.

41 Basamanowicz, "Release Groups & Digital Copyright Piracy," 37.

42 Ibid., 37.

The court documents and Basamanowicz's analysis are also fascinating for the defenses advanced for various criminal behaviors. The first is that often defendants pointed out that the piracy element was incidental to their behavior, which was addictive and compulsive. For instance, one defense read, "[m]y involvement in the warez scene had become such a routine in my life that it completely went out of control [...]. I enrolled in classes, but seldom did attend them, I stayed up until 5 or 6 in the morning day after day, constantly chatting online and seeing if there were new pirated works to spread around [...]. It was the illusion of power and fame that got to me I believe."[43] That the activity was piracy was, in some ways, not even relevant to the addictive behavior.[44] It is true that its illegality engenders the difficulty of participating in the Scene and that there is a high level of competition and danger; for many the behavior is akin to a high-stakes lifestyle. As I have noted throughout, crackers in particular are motivated by the difficulty of the challenge. As Bryan T. Black writes, "his participation in the warez scene was driven by the intellectual challenge presented by the codes and a sense of membership in a collection of like-minded computer-heads on the internet."[45] The alternative reality game of the Warez Scene — as a "crime behaviour system," as Décary-Hétu et al. term it — is a communal and social intellectual adrenaline sport.[46]

In other cases, defenses used evidence that group members had not been pulling their weight to downplay their significance. For instance, although pertaining to Operation Fastlink, "Christopher Eaves, a supplier for the group aPC, was threatened with banishment from the group because of his lack of

43 Ibid., 52.

44 For more on addiction and self-control, see Sameer Hinduja, *Music Piracy and Crime Theory* (New York: LFB Scholarly Pub., 2006), 43–78.

45 Basamanowicz, "Release Groups & Digital Copyright Piracy," 57.

46 David Décary-Hétu, Carlo Morselli, and Stéphane Leman-Langlois, "Welcome to the Scene: A Study of Social Organization and Recognition among Warez Hackers," *Journal of Research in Crime and Delinquency* 49, no. 3 (2012): 359–82.

contribution," a fact that he used at his trial to attempt to show his lack of influence/impact.[47] In other cases, though, the prosecution looked at the formal structure of the groups — such as the fact that they had quality assurance mechanisms in the role of a software tester — to show that there was a professional element to these outfits' work.[48] Indeed, as Basamanowicz puts it, "copyright infringement of this nature is inherently a crime of organized and purposive groups acting in concert."[49] Yet, as Basamanowicz continues, "despite this aptitude, no research has been conducted on the network structure of these illicit networks, and it is unknown if the courts considered such issues when assigning sentence."[50]

Basamanowicz's analysis is also interesting because he asks whether the idea of network centrality correlates to longer prison sentences. That is, in his analysis of Operation Site Down, Basamanowicz sought to work out whether it was in fact the best connected individuals in the raids who ended up with the harshest sentences. It turns out, though, that this not how things work. As Basamanowicz notes, "there are actors in the network who are highly central, and significant to the connectivity of the network, but were over-looked by the courts in terms of sentencing."[51] This makes sense when we adopt a role-based understanding of how the Scene works, and it highlights the weaknesses of the network approach. It is clear that couriers have a high level of network centrality, connected as they are to multiple sites and groups. However, while central in the network, their activities are not central to the activities of procuring the pirate release. They are also individuals who can easily be replaced, whereas crackers and suppliers are scarcer. Hence, while a network centrality analysis can clarify where individuals sit within the network and its activities, connectivity to one

47 Basamanowicz and Bouchard, "Overcoming the Warez Paradox," 10.
48 Ibid., 65.
49 Ibid.
50 Ibid.
51 Ibid., 73.

another within the Scene is not a benchmark of the relative importance — or the severity of the crime — of individuals.[52]

PRQ RAIDS (2010)

While most Scene raids and busts are high-profile events, undertaken by the FBI and other well funded, anti-crime initiatives in the US with grandiose names (e.g., "Operation Buccaneer," "Operation Fastlink"), several smaller busts have attracted less attention. These smaller raids, like their larger cousins, rarely result in long-term disruption. On the other hand, the low-level continuous threat of smaller-scale raids seeks to create a constant reminder of the danger of legal sanction. It is not clear to what degree this succeeds, given that individuals carry on their activities nonetheless. It is also the case, it seems, that not all raids go to plan.

In any case, an excellent example of the small-scale, ongoing-raid philosophy, but one that had an unclear outcome, can be seen in the European raids in 2010. By all accounts, this was meant to be a large raid. Police in fourteen countries swooped in on topsites and attempted to take them offline. Sites in Sweden (BAR, SC), The Netherlands, the Czech Republic (LOST), and Hungary went offline. As the piracy news website, TorrentFreak, noted, "[w]hile there were reports of individuals having been taken in for questioning yesterday, for an operation of this size those numbers seem unusually low."[53] It is also the case that *TorrentFreak* believes that "certain sites probably survived due to the techniques they employed to thwart this kind of an attack."[54] The official press release from the Swedish police noted that the "investigation has focused on both those who provide the network with films before they are released on the market, as well as on the servers on which a large number of films are uploaded

52 Ibid.

53 Andy Maxwell, "Inside Yesterday's European Warez Piracy Raids," *TorrentFreak*, September 8, 2010, https://torrentfreak.com/inside-yesterdays-european-warez-piracy-raids-100908/.

54 Ibid.

(so-called Top-sites), and its administrators. The effort in Sweden has mainly been directed at suspected 'top sites.'"[55]

It is possible to speculate which of these sites' security measures worked. The most likely is the system of bouncers. Perhaps the authorities raided a location believing it to be the site, but it was only in fact the bouncer. This would mean that, upon raiding the premises, they would find only a server that forwarded on connections and no pirated material itself. While previous convictions show that operating a bouncer is sufficient activity to merit jail time at least in the US, this is like finding the signpost to a secret cave rather than the cave. Of course, if a bouncer is seized, a site will likely go offline.

There are also some hypothetical defenses against topsite raids, although it is unclear if these are viable or have ever actually been implemented in practice. For example, in Neal Stephenson's novel *Cryptonomicon* (1999), the server "Tombstone" is protected inside a room with an electromagnetic coil wound around the doorframe. This means that any hard drive that "was actually carried through that doorway would be wiped clean."[56] This is a nice idea in theory. However, as a humorous, online, fan exchange shows, there are many flaws with its implementation in reality, not least of these was that any magnetic field powerful enough to degauss a hard drive would also be sufficiently powerful as to cause potential injury to anyone carrying a ferromagnetic object anywhere near the field.[57] That is, anyone entering the room would likely notice the magnetic field before they got anywhere near dismantling the server inside. Instead, the measures that yielded protection here are likely more prosaic.

55 Translated from the Swedish at Frederick Ingblad, "Tillslag Mot Fildelningsnätverk," *Åklagarmyndigheten,* September 8, 2010, https://web.archive.org/web/20100908084809/https://www.aklagare.se/Media/Nyheter/Tillslag-mot-fildelningsnatverk1/.

56 Neal Stephenson, *Cryptonomicon* (New York: Random House, 2012), 722.

57 SQB, "Could a Hard Drive Actually Have Been Erased as Described in 'Cryptonomicon'?" *Physics Stack Exchange,* May 1, 2014, https://physics.stackexchange.com/questions/110870/could-a-hard-drive-actually-have-been-erased-as-described-in-cryptonomicon.

It is also notable that these raids were targeted at the Internet Service Provider (ISP) level, with five officers visiting the hosting service, PRQ.[58] This host is known as a provider for controversial websites. It has previously provided hosting for The Pirate Bay, WikiLeaks, and even pedophilia "advocacy" groups. As such, the site has become known as a safe harbor for many types of controversial activities. It has also learned to defend them. For instance, as of 2008, the internet technology news site, *The Register,* declared that PRQ "has amassed considerable expertise in withstanding legal attacks from powerful corporate interests."[59] However, raids against PRQ resulted in the disclosure of email communications: "[t]hey were interested in who were using two IP addresses from 2009 and onwards. We have no records of our clients but we're handing over the e-mail addresses for those behind the IPs. However, it's rare that our clients have mail addresses that are traceable."[60]

The interesting twist in the raids against PRQ is that under usual circumstances, the raids would target the sites themselves. These are often hosted at universities, so any raid at the ISP level would be asking for a university's cooperation. In this case, the raid deliberately attempted to intercept Scene operations at an intermediary level. This can be tricky from a legal perspective as such providers are usually immune from prosecution for the content they host if they did not, themselves, produce it. This is what is called the "safe harbor" provision of the US's Digital Millennium Copyright Act (DMCA).

To understand the challenges of prosecuting at the ISP level, it is worth turning to the example of the intermediary level,

58 Quoted in Andy Maxwell, "Police in File-Sharing Raids across Europe, WikiLeaks Host Targeted," *TorrentFreak,* September 7, 2010, https://torrentfreak.com/police-in-file-sharing-raids-across-europe-wikileaks-host-targeted-100907/.

59 Dan Goodin, "Wikileaks Judge Gets Pirate Bay Treatment," *The Register,* February 21, 2008, https://www.theregister.com/2008/02/21/wikileaks_bulletproof_hosting/.

60 Maxwell, "Police in File-Sharing Raids across Europe."

Cloudflare, particularly in the legal context of the US.[61] In recent days, Cloudflare has come under fire for providing services to entities with illegal, or even just hateful, purposes. That Cloudflare did not make editorial decisions pertaining to its chosen customers was at one point vital to its definitional status under US law concerning free speech.[62] At least two cases in New York state have declared that a publisher is defined by the editorial selection of the material that it elects to publish.[63] By refusing to select, Cloudflare works around this. In turn, this has effects for DMCA and the legal status of organizations that publish content instead of those that disseminate it. This situation was remedied in part by the 1996 Communications Decency Act (CDA), which protected "any action voluntarily taken in good faith to restrict access to or availability of material that the provider or user considers to be obscene, lewd, lascivious, filthy, excessively violent, harassing, or otherwise objectionable, whether or not such material is constitutionally protected."[64] In this act, "[n]o provider or user of an interactive computer service shall be treated as the publisher or speaker of any information provided by another information content provider."[65] In other words, digital providers are free to screen the material they host according to their own internal standards, rather than simply those items that are constitutionally protected, and will not be treated as though they were a publisher, speaker, or endorser of that material.

61 This section is derived from my work in Martin Paul Eve, "Lessons from the Library: Extreme Minimalist Scaling at Pirate Ebook Platforms," *Digital Humanities Quarterly* (2022), forthcoming.

62 Jack M. Balkin, "Free Speech Is a Triangle," *Columbia Law Review* 118, no. 7 (2018): 2011–56.

63 Leisure, Cubby, Inc. v. CompuServe, Inc., No. 776 F Supp 135 (United States District Court, S.D. New York October 29, 1991); Stuart L. Ain, Stratton Oakmont, Inc. v. Prodigy Services Co., No. 23 Media L Rep 1794 (Supreme Court, Nassau County, New York May 24, 1995).

64 "47 U.S. Code § 230 — Protection for Private Blocking and Screening of Offensive Material," *LII / Legal Information Institute*, 1996, https://www.law.cornell.edu/uscode/text/47/230.

65 Ibid.

Until relatively recently, however, Cloudflare had operated in parallel with this US law and offered no additional level of screening of material. This changed when it decided to terminate service to *The Daily Stormer,* a far-right platform, and *8chan,* a noticeboard known for its lawless nature. Cloudflare introduced its own moderation system.[66] At this point, the protection of the earlier cases became invalid, but the provider was protected under CDA. What is clear is that there is no distinction between free speech and action when the act of publishing words is, in itself, the final act of illicit infringement. The Cloudflare example highlights some of the problems for law enforcement in tackling the Scene by intervening at the ISP level. While they may, indeed, garner information about topsite operations by raiding ISP headquarters and demanding that information be turned over, sites are likely to cease operation once this becomes known or to move their location. In other words, gathering information via uncooperative ISPs is likely not an effective strategy.

The mixed fortunes of this operation may be why these raids did not go on to yield high-profile legal proceedings. It is, in fact, difficult even to find press reports on the original raids.[67] While some Nordic sources report that charges were brought, it is nearly impossible to locate the court cases that were brought as a result of these raids.[68] It does not help that, at the same time as these raids, the famous torrent-sharing site, The Pirate Bay, also coincidentally went offline, giving the impression that this

66 Bharath Ganesh, "The Ungovernability of Digital Hate Culture," *Journal of International Affairs* 71, no. 2 (2018): 38; Alex Rosenblat, *Uberland: How Algorithms Are Rewriting the Rules of Work* (Berkeley: University of California Press, 2018), 167; Viveca S. Greene, "'Deplorable' Satire: Alt-Right Memes, White Genocide Tweets, and Redpilling Normies," *Studies in American Humor* 5, no. 1 (2019): 31–69; David Mytton, "Cloudflare, Free Speech and the Rule of Law," *David Mytton,* August 15, 2019, https://davidmytton.blog/cloudflare-free-speech-and-the-rule-of-law/.

67 "Swedish Police Raid File Sharing 'Scene,'" *The Local,* September 7, 2010, https://www.thelocal.se/20100907/28826.

68 Lars Akerhaug and Nicolai Heyerdahl, "Nordmann Siktet for Fildeling Etter Internasjonal Storaksjon," *Aftenposten,* September 7, 2010.

bust was targeted at a different segment of the piracy pyramid.[69] What was clear is that there was not a fifteen-year "gap" between Operation Site Down and the SPARKS raids. Instead, law enforcement was operative, albeit at a slower pace and lower level than the higher profile international busts.

THE SPARKS RAID (2020)

Things nonetheless did go somewhat quiet in terms of significant scene busts for nearly fifteen years. Then, in August 2020, amid the global, coronavirus pandemic, the Warez Scene was thrown into disarray by the unsealing of US indictments against core members of the release group SPARKS and "several linked affiliate groups including GECKOS, DRONES, ROVERS and SPRINTER." In particular, the documents revealed that in January 2020 an indictment and Grand Jury charges were filed against a 50-year-old British national living on the Isle of Wight. Alongside this was a 39-year-old Norwegian, whom it is alleged went by the handle "Artist" and who remains at large as of September 2020. Finally, for the initial indictments, a 36-year-old American (known, ironically, by the handle "Raid") was arrested in Kansas and pled not guilty to the charges.[70]

The Grand Jury indictment filed by or on behalf of the United States Attorney General, Geoffrey S. Berman, alleges a copyright infringement conspiracy in which "[f]rom at least in or around 2011, up to and including in or around January 2020 [...] the defendant, and others known and unknown, were members

69 Marc Chacksfield, "Police Arrest European File Sharers in Co-Ordinated Raids," *TechRadar*, September 7, 2010, https://www.techradar.com/news/internet/police-arrest-european-file-sharers-in-co-ordinated-raids-715004.

70 Andy Maxwell, "US Indictments and Raids of Piracy Group Members in 'The Scene' Throw Top-Tier Piracy World Into Chaos," *TorrentFreak*, August 26, 2020, https://torrentfreak.com/us-indictments-and-raids-of-piracy-group-members-in-the-scene-throw-top-tier-piracy-world-into-chaos-200826/; Andy Maxwell, "Alleged SPARKS Member 'Raid' Pleads Not Guilty to Piracy Charges," *TorrentFreak*, September 8, 2020, https://torrentfreak.com/alleged-sparks-member-raid-pleads-not-guilty-to-piracy-charges-200908/.

of a criminal conspiracy known as the 'Sparks Group.'"[71] While the indictment is light on actual details, it mentions the topsite Scene, alleging that the defendant worked to "compromise the copyright protections on the discs, reproduce and upload the copyrighted content to servers controlled by the Sparks Group."[72] The indictments against all defendants were nearly identical to one another.[73]

The impact of the SPARKS raid went well beyond these three individuals. The piracy news website, TorrentFreak, noted that the "USDOJ revealed that an operation was underway on three continents, with law enforcement partners in eighteen countries carrying out raids and seizures, declaring that around sixty servers had been taken down."[74] This included work in the Nordic countries but also in the Netherlands.[75] An internal "Scene notice" NFO was also spread around topsites and detailed what had happened. The figures here — which, as always, must be taken with a pinch of salt, as there is no such thing as an "official" Scene announcement — claim that twenty-nine sites were busted within fourteen countries. The claim in the Scene NFO was that the Linknet IRC network was compromised by a user

71 Geoffrey S. Berman, "United States of America v. George Bridi," August 1, 2020.

72 Ibid.

73 Geoffrey S. Berman, "United States of America v. Umar Ahmad a/k/a 'Artist,'" August 1, 2020; Geoffrey S. Berman, "United States of America v. Jonatan Correa a/k/a 'Raid,'" August 1, 2020; James Margolin and Nicholas Biase, "Acting US Attorney Announces Federal Charges And International Operation To Dismantle Online Piracy Group," *US Department of Justice,* August 26, 2020, https://www.justice.gov/usao-sdny/pr/acting-us-attorney-announces-federal-charges-and-international-operation-dismantle-0.

74 Andy Maxwell, "New 'Scene' Security Notice: 'SPARKS' Piracy Raids Busted Dozens of Sites," *TorrentFreak,* September 1, 2020, https://torrentfreak.com/new-scene-security-notice-sparks-piracy-raids-busted-dozens-of-sites-200901/.

75 Andy Maxwell, "SPARKS Piracy Busts: Facts, Rumors & Fear Point to Something Huge," *TorrentFreak,* August 27, 2020, https://torrentfreak.com/sparks-piracy-busts-facts-rumors-fear-point-to-something-huge-200827/.

in France, allowing federal agents to eavesdrop on communications that were not secured by additional blowfish encryption.[76]

The Scene-wide announcement NFO also indicated that these raids are not likely to deter longtime pirates. Rather than calling for any disbandment, the document instead provides a set of security tips for locking down sites and IRC networks. As the NFO puts it: "we will [be] back and we will thrive again!"[77] However, the SPARKS raid triggered a historic decline of Scene release outputs in the short term. As charted by *TorrentFreak* using the predb.org public pre database, on "Wednesday, August 19, there were 1,944 new releases" and just one week later, "a day after the first raids, this number was down to 168 releases."[78]

THE EFFICACY OF RAIDS AND LEGAL ENFORCEMENT

Perhaps the fundamental question that comes out of the enforcement actions that I have detailed in this chapter is, do raids and other legal means of disrupting Scene activities have any long-lasting, or even short-term, effects? Are raids and legal enforcement efficacious? This is the question to which David Décary-Hétu turns in his article in *Policy & Internet,* "Police Operations 3.0: On the Impact and Policy Implications of Police Operations on the Warez Scene."

Décary-Hétu rightly notes that the high-level Warez Scene is an attractive target for law enforcement as it is "a very (if not the most) important source of intellectual property illegally distributed online."[79] The Scene is an organized crime system that even, ironically, has its own internal rules against plagiarism and a

76 "Scene Busts and Mitigations (Scene_busts_And_Mitigations.png)," 2020, DeFacto2.

77 Ibid.

78 Ernesto Van der Sar, "Scene Bust Triggered Historic Drop in 'Pirate' Releases," *TorrentFreak*, September 4, 2020, https://torrentfreak.com/scene-bust-triggered-historic-drop-in-pirate-releases-200904/.

79 David Décary-Hétu, "Police Operations 3.0: On the Impact and Policy Implications of Police Operations on the Warez Scene," *Policy & Internet* 6, no. 3 (September 2014): 317.

mechanism that functions at least tangentially like copyright, which prohibits groups from claiming credit for each others' work.[80] At the time that Décary-Hétu was writing, it appeared that large-scale piracy bust operations were on the decrease. As he puts it, it seemed that "law enforcement agencies have moved away from large-scale police operations."[81] Décary-Hétu credits this to the "lack of impact" that these operations have had.[82] However, the SPARKS raid of 2020 puts paid to the claim that these larger-scale busts of the high-level piracy Scene are a thing of the past. Indeed, the sporadic appearance of a police presence may be all that is required to maintain the threat of action, which may function as a sufficient deterrent to those who would be deterred.

In his analysis of the decline of police operations, Décary-Hétu compares the Scene to organized drug networks, which share many characteristics (e.g., decentralization, many small actors, high levels of competition). Décary-Hétu points out that in the drug world, there are also similar enforcement problems, namely that actions tend to result only in short-lived reductions in criminal activities and that offenders tend rapidly to adjust to new mechanisms to avoid detection, as the security advice to siteops in the Scene notice about the SPARKS raids shows. On the other hand, the visibility of police operations has been shown to work as a deterrent in some cases.

It is also worth noting that it may be both easier and more difficult, in different ways, to deter people from the type of crime with which we are here dealing. A computer crime involves staying at home and rarely leaving the house. It does not come with the same level of risk and violence as drug dealing. On the one hand, it may be easier to deter people from the crime because there are few coercive threats that group leaders can use against Warez Scene members. Generally, these individuals are free to leave at any time, which is certainly not the case in

80 Ibid., 318.
81 Ibid., 321.
82 Ibid.

drug cartels, which have systems of enforced bondage that hold mules and others in servitude with an extreme threat of physical violence. In this sense, it should be easier to deter individuals from participating in the Scene. On the other hand, because the crime is so easy to commit in one sense — that it only involves sitting at one's desk, regardless of the skill involved — it may be harder to persuade people to leave because the risk is not apparent. That is, the crime appears safe, and so offenders will quickly return to the activity. Décary-Hétu's analysis shows that each of the above raids had, in the long term, little to no impact on the volume of material that was shared through the illicit practices of the Warez Scene.[83]

Scene raids are also challenging to enact from a legal perspective because they require international cooperation between law enforcement units, which may be hard to come by. This is particularly the case when offenders are based in jurisdictions that have, at best, only cordial relationships, such as those between Russia and the US. Conversely, in terms of quantitative output, raids do not impact on Scene activities, and Décary-Hétu posits an important aspect of social disruption. The Warez Scene, he notes, is a community of individuals that relies on trust. By injecting federal agents and others into this community, the raids disrupt the long-term trust that members can have in one another. It is also certainly the case that due to the high levels of interconnectivity and network spread of news, true members of the Warez Scene are almost always aware when there has been a major police raid or bust.[84]

While the majority of articles about legal sanctions against pirates are concerned with prosecutions of peer-to-peer (P2P) users, large-scale raids and busts against the topsite Scene have been ongoing for over two decades now.[85] For the most part, these busts are episodic and result in sudden, large-scale disrup-

83 Ibid., 327.

84 Ibid., 331.

85 Michael Bachmann, "Lesson Spurned? Reactions of Online Music Pirates to Legal Prosecutions by the RIAA," *International Journal of Cyber Criminology* 1, no. 2 (2007): 213–27.

tion that then follows a pattern of gradual return to normality in the Scene. In particular, the events that were Operation Buccaneer and Operation Fastlink resulted in massive, near-total, but temporary shutdowns of the Scene. Conversely, the smaller-scale arrests and searches, such as the PRQ raids in 2010, paint a more continuous story, one in which raids and investigations are ongoing all the time. Both types of investigation have benefits for law enforcement. If the aim is to deter the activity, then the breakthrough moments of Buccaneer and Fastlink highlighted law-enforcement operations and gave a jolt of fear to those who participate. By contrast, the narrative of smaller scale, but continuous, investigation is helpful to law enforcement for instilling a sense among perpetrators of being continuously watched and monitored. It also helps to damage trust among Scene members who may be more and more reticent to share personal details with each other, which can then disrupt operations.

It is important to note that while most Scene practices take place anonymously in and on private and encrypted IRC channels and servers, there seem always to be weak points that law enforcement officers can exploit. Consider the early days of Fairlight, where gollum received packages by train courier, but founder and supplier Tony Krvaric, strider, clearly knew his name and address. Things are very different now, but it remains the case that if there are copy protections on a disk, it may be necessary to ship the physical item from a supplier to a cracker or copy-protection specialist. While it is possible to use mail routing facilities and P.O. Boxes, for instance, to obfuscate the trail of physical media and postage, these also introduce delays that may cost a release group the race. Indeed, this demand for speed will, in the end, be the undoing of many individuals. To meet the tight turnaround times required in racing to beat copy protections, individuals are likely to take more significant risks concerning anonymity. Security is always a trade-off that must balance protection against convenience. When the balance tips too far in favor of the latter, law enforcement has an opportunity to intervene.

Sites also rely on donations of both finance and hardware, as testified by the role of "hardware supplier." Before 2009, any transfer of money would have been traceable by law enforcement agencies. However, the anonymity of cash at Western Union, for instance, can make this much harder than following the money on Paypal and other online service providers, which provide greater convenience at the expense of security. In 2009 with the release of Bitcoin, tracing financial transactions became a much more complex process. The anonymity of Bitcoin and other blockchain-based cryptocurrencies is certainly appealing for those in the Warez Scene. It allows the easy transfer of funds without the risk of getting caught. At the same time, though, Bitcoin is a problematic currency if used for any real-world purchases because it is so volatile.[86] Indeed, it is entirely possible that within a twenty-four-hour window, the cryptocurrency's value will have altered so dramatically as to make it impossible to carry out the intended purchase. There is also as likely a chance that the funds will have risen in value; it just cannot be known ahead of time. Intermediaries that can help to mitigate these problems will inevitably re-introduce the very aspects of regulatory oversight and identity verification whose absence made these currencies appealing to Sceners in the first place.[87] Nonetheless, Bitcoin poses substantial, new challenges for law enforcement officers who wish to use financial tracing as a mechanism to hunt down site operators.

In this chapter I have detailed the major busts against the Scene over the past two decades, up to the most recent raids on the SPARKS group in 2020. As I argued from the outset, studying formal, legal documents, such as court indictments and DOJ press releases, about the Scene can help cement our understanding of the practices therein, which are usually opaque and only verified by documents produced within the Scene itself. It is also

86 William J. Luther, "Bitcoin and the Future of Digital Payments," *The Independent Review* 20, no. 3 (Winter 2015/2016): 397–404.

87 Cameron Harwick, "Cryptocurrency and the Problem of Intermediation," *The Independent Review* 20, no. 4 (Spring 2016): 569–88.

interesting to note that most studies of the Scene focus on these raids in the discipline of digital criminology. Much research into the Scene has been conducted on this legalistic aspect, warping some of the historical understandings in favor of analyses of practices shadowed by industry discourses. It also means that studies of Scene prosecutions often conflate actions against this highest level of the piracy pyramid with action against P2P file sharers. As it has been the goal of this book to document, this is an extreme category error. The motivations, actions, and organization of the Warez Scene are in an entirely different space to those found lower down the piracy food chain. Yet, regardless of whether we reframe the Scene in terms of an alternative reality game, the reality is that the stakes in such a game are extremely high and have often resulted in prison sentences.

Conclusion

This book has detailed the operations, the artforms, the sociality, the technical infrastructures, and the legality of the underground, computer subculture known as the Warez Scene. Distinct from other levels of piracy, such as the popular, public Bittorrent communities, this highly organized and efficient digital, criminal underworld is characterized by its sophistication, logistical savvy, and relative lack of mainstream prominence. Emerging from the computer art DemoScene of the early 1990s, the Scene has shown itself to be resilient to legal attack, professional in its security and organization, and well resourced in its operation.

The Scene is a highly organized space specializing in the release of software, movies, music, pornography, and other media forms before the official release dates of these items for sale. Growing from the DemoScene in the 1990s and sharing a common core of skilled ability to disassemble and crack software, the Scene is a sophisticated operation that involves suppliers, crackers, groups, testers, leaders, sites, site operators, IRC networks, bot suppliers, FTPD coders, prebots, bouncers, ASCII artists, demo programmers, musicians, artists, couriers, autotraders, nukers, NukeNets, quotas, rules and standards, charts, codes of conduct, loyalties, betrayals, infiltrations, takedowns, court cases, public news commentary, private information channels, rumors, hacking and cracking, hardware supplies, humor, homophobia, racism, bragging, cheating, stealing, mystique, and drudgery. It is a mythical space in its secrecy yet one that continually must rear its head in public to receive the legitimation and adulation that its members desire. The Scene is an elaborate performance of elitism, played in private, yet one that requires a public stage on which to act out its status. While some Scene members undoubtedly do manage to keep their heads down and work forever in the shadows, the lure for others is always too great, a fact evidenced in how Scene releases end up on public torrent sites and in other venues outside of their own formal structures.

Core to the argument of this book has been the contention that the Warez Scene is less about piracy itself and access to the end artifacts of that process than it is about a high-stakes alternative reality game of elitism and competition. Despite allegations that pirates might be communists or socialists who believe in the free sharing of anything for anyone, the truth of the matter is that, structurally, the Scene is a highly competitive and economic space that thrives on scarcity. There are very few top slots on topsites, fought over by many competitors. The Scene has an elaborate ruleset for its game that is structurally enforced by the presence of NukeNets and local nukers, by release rule standards, and by an honor code and the notion of a lifelong SceneBan. Far from an equitable space in which all players are equal, the Scene more accurately resembles an extreme, laissez-faire, capitalist marketplace, in which intra-agent competition and inequality represent the core conditions.[1] While there is no over-arching authority that enforces these market circumstances as we might see in historical Ordoliberal economic regimes, the accrued authority of top Sceners make de facto pronouncements the core operational principles and, by default, set a series of rules in place.

1 For more on the role of inequality in contemporary capitalist economies, see William Davies, *The Limits of Neoliberalism: Authority, Sovereignty and the Logic of Competition* (Thousand Oaks: SAGE Publications, 2014).

The Warez Scene is nonetheless difficult to research. Other books, such as Paul Craig's *Software Piracy Exposed,* use a range of interview techniques, conscripting Sceners who were willing to speak and provide anecdotes on condition of anonymity. In this work, I have adopted a different approach. While it is possible to garner background information on the Scene and its operation from secondary academic sources, my approach has been to seek out original documentary artifacts from the Scene and to infer its operations from these archival objects. This is possible due to the DeFacto2 archive, among other sources, which hoards a wealth of NFO files, DemoScene executables, and other Scene documents.

However, the very existence of these artifacts points to a core contention of this book: the Warez Scene should also be considered an aesthetic subculture. A type of "geek community," topsites are styled and have their own advertorial NFO files — release groups, likewise. Hence, the entire Scene is structured on a delicate balance between showcasing one's activities and seeking to remain hidden. It is a world in which show-off egotists and narcissists seek constant validation through the circulation of credit and respect but also one in which the entire subculture must remain hidden for legal reasons. While Sceners prize reputation within the Scene, it is clearly not enough, and the fame of conducting covert interviews with piracy news sites, such as *TorrentFreak,* proves too tempting for many. It is thanks to these artifacts that document and advertise the efforts of the Scene that this book was possible. The subculture of the Warez Scene cannot bear to keep itself dull or quiet, and it is the presence of these aesthetic objects that leads to information leakage.

The aesthetic subculture of the players in the Warez Scene works similarly to many other geek communities, though with some key differences. While the DemoScene group, Fairlight, met in person legally once, most Sceners will never know one another's identities. There are some exceptions to this; on occasion, the supply of artifacts will require the transfer of physical media between parties within a release group, which leads to potential points of compromise. Again, it takes only one slip of identity and address for such information to become near-permanently incriminating for participants.

For this reason, most Sceners appear to do a good job of keeping their identities unknown, existing only under the aliases of their pseudonymous online personae. Nonetheless, for many Sceners, this underground culture is their main life identity. It is more than just a way to acquire content. As *TorrentFreak* put it: the Scene is "a stress headache that most pirates can do without," and it is not wholly clear why people would participate if the goal were simply to acquire pirate media.[2] While it is true that "many people aspire to become a 'member'" of the Scene to hope "to bathe in the collective mystery, kudos and notoriety," the volume of effort that is invested is not commensurate to the access that is gained or provided.[3] Instead, as this article continues, "if people really must obtain all the latest movies and TV shows for free, doing it quietly via torrent sites seems much, much less stressful than getting tightly involved in The Scene or anyone close to it. Indeed, The Scene seems more of a complex lifestyle choice than a hobby for many participants, but one that could implode at any second."[4] The Scene is not just a sideshow way to obtain content. It is an entire social structure, or an alternative reality game, that seems to become the dominant model of life activity for many participants. While it is easy to deride such geek or nerd cultures for the unusual form of social contact they represent — and the Scene is weirder than most with its level of illegality — it is a mistake to underestimate the sociality of this space.

In this respect, law enforcement often misunderstands the Scene. Although the law is correct, in one sense, in viewing it as a criminal cartel intent on multimedia piracy on a broader scale, even if not with a broader userbase, than any other operation,

---

2 Andy Maxwell, "The Scene: A Stress Headache That Most Pirates Can Do Without," *TorrentFreak*, September 6, 2020, https://torrentfreak.com/the-scene-a-stress-headache-that-most-pirates-can-do-without-200906/.

3 Ibid.

4 Ibid.

simply punishing Sceners as such has unilaterally failed to stem the flow of releases. Instead, legal efforts thus far have played a game of whack-a-mole with topsites and release groups, steadily infiltrating them only to cut off a single head before the whole thing starts up again. Certainly, this approach does act as a deterrent for some Scene members. Retirements do seem to be announced in the wake of busts. However, law enforcement efforts have generally been unsuccessful at stopping the Scene en masse. This is probably partially because less effort is invested in curbing the Warez Scene when it constitutes such a small slice of the general piracy pie, even if it makes up a core supply route for downstream activities. But the agencies tasked with shutting down the Scene are simply not as well resourced as they would need to be to stem the tide. The Scene is also, to mix metaphors, a keystone to the bridge of the entire pirate distribution network. Removing the Scene causes many other public elements to collapse, and anti-piracy efforts need to do what they can to stop the linchpin work of the Scene. Nonetheless, legal efforts remain more tightly focused on the mass-scale piracy in public, such as The Pirate Bay and its ilk. Given that these too have had limited success, it seems unlikely that mass-scale legal action against the Scene is likely to win soon.

Another indication of how the Scene is more than an outfit based on access to pirate material, and is more akin to a lifestyle subculture or all-engrossing, alternative reality game, is the development of specific language vocabularies and humor among participants. For example, the well-known phenomenon of l33tspeak or "leetspeak" sits in ambiguous tension among Sceners. While this language is used and members need a working knowledge of its linguistic codes, it is also true that leetspeak is deployed ironically in many cases. The insider linguistic codes that developed in these computer subcultures are also seen as somewhat regressively childish, which is unsurprising given that most Sceners appear to be on the cusp of middle age. Hence, uncritical blasts of leetspeak are not likely to gain much kudos, but a knowing irony pervades many of the Scene documents in the DeFacto2 archive.

Scene humor possesses an ironic quality but also relies on extreme levels of insider know-how. While the level of actual amusement such material can generate is debatable, this is not its purpose. Such humor functions as another demarcation of insider and outsider status. The role here is not to make people laugh but to allow Sceners to congratulate themselves on getting the joke, even if it is not funny. When "quotes of the week" feature either named or anonymized individuals, the Scener who can say that they "saw the original" or who can reveal to others the hidden identity in anonymized cases performs the possession of an esoteric knowledge, demonstrating further elitism. Part of playing the alternative reality game of the Scene lies in social networking.

However, the naming of individuals in quotes of the week for humorous purposes is the perfect example of risk-taking behavior in the Scene. Of course, a truly professionalized criminal network would hardly flaunt the identifiable, online nicknames in documents that, although private, inevitably find their way into unintended hands. Nevertheless, this desire to perform in semi-public is an instance of how the Scene functions as an aesthetic subculture, and not, despite its extensive security precautions, a purely criminal endeavor.

There is some debate as to whether the Scene will continue in all its forms. The MP3 and then FLAC Scenes that emerged to distribute music have in many ways been eclipsed by the success of Oink's Pink Palace, What.CD, and other current and private, Bittorrent trackers. Arguably, these torrent sites can achieve greater total coverage of all music media than was ever accomplished by the Scene. On the other hand, none of these systems have survived as long as the Warez Scene. Lasting just a few years in each case, these sites have also only gained near-comprehensive coverage by having a userbase that is permeable, if not open. In turn, this presents a far larger attack surface for law enforcement. In other words, compared to the security precautions of the Scene, private Bittorrent trackers are significantly less safe and a great deal more centralized while requiring broader access. All three features contribute to better coverage of the pirate media that these systems contain, but they also make it exponentially more likely that such sites will be shut down.

The Scene must strike a delicate balance between openness to meritocracy and working with known individuals who can be trusted. The more raids that are conducted upon the Scene, the more the upper hierarchies will close down to admit only those with a proven track record of safety. This leads to negative consequences from the Scene's perspective. Without fresh supply routes and new coding talent, the release supply chain quickly dries up. This is why it is interesting that there is a pecking order of release groups. While younger, less experienced, and less prestigious release groups often advertise a contact method in their NFO for new prospective members to get in touch, these are not present among the higher echelons. Instead, these groups tend to prefer to watch and wait. When new members of the Scene have proven themselves among the lower release groups, they may be invited to the more prestigious ranks. In other words, there is a process — almost akin to Artists and Repertoire (A&R) recruiting in the music industry — by which new members are audited and judged. This keeps the top tier of the Scene relatively safe from most busts, even while it exposes those further down the food chain.

One of the problems with breaking up the Scene is that there is no equivalent online social structure from which ex-members can get their adrenaline fix. Other communities that focus on hoarding and accumulating, or even just collecting, have also been destroyed in the wake of the internet. As we reach an era in which the world of, for example, crate digging for rare records has been outshone by the comprehensive databases of Discogs and other online retailers, it is ever harder for those with prestige addiction to find an outlet for their love of competition and scarcity.

As a final conclusion, the Warez Scene, which continues to this day, is a major, underground alternative reality game. A secret computer aesthetic subculture, it is a significant but overlooked player in the contemporary digital world. This book has hoped to shed some light on its practices and mechanisms.

Appendix: Topsites and Dumps in the shroo.ms nfo.sites Collection

This appendix lists the most that is known about a variety of topsites operating at the turn of the millennium using the most recent information that can be gathered about each site from the shroo.ms nfo.sites collection at DeFacto2. Location is inferred from statements such as "ehq" (presumed to mean "European headquarters") or more specific data where available. Hardware and software configurations are the last known listing. Unsourced fields in the table are drawn from the NFO referenced in the "sitename" field. For expediency, known affils ("affiliateds") are the last-listed set only in the most recently dated NFO available, unless a non-dated NFO contains more information. Occasionally this means that important affiliation changes are lost (e.g., The Bleach Box was previously an affil of the significant group, Razor 1911, in October 1996 but seems to have lost this status by December of that year or at least no longer advertises it. The same goes for The Boxer Rebellion and Terminal Velocity.).[1] Dates of information validity are listed in the refer-

1 BB, "The Bleach Box Topsite (BBX-bleach.box.1996.10.17.nfo)," October 17, 1996, DeFacto2, warez.scene.nfo.collection.v1.0.24351.shroo.ms.zip; TBR, "The Boxer Rebellion Topsite (TBR-the.boxer.rebellion.1997.12.09.nfo)," December 9, 1997, DeFacto2, warez.scene.nfo.collection.v1.0.24351.shroo.ms.zip; TV, "Terminal Velocity Topsite (TV-terminal.velocity.1998.12.27.

ence. Capitalization of affiliated groups is as written in the NFO. Affiliations do not distinguish between release groups, courier groups, or even individuals, but merely present the listing as shown in the NFO. Sites are ordered by the abbreviation given in the shroo.ms pack, hence some sites are under "T" where their name begins with "The" while others are not.

Sitename	Known Affils	Known Hardware/Software	Location	Siteops and Nukers/Notes
722[2]	PINNACLE, OXYGEN			LooZtrA, Khaotic, Zarkof, Astralo
Absolute Zero (Ao)[3]	Abrupt, Pentium Force Team, The Force Team, Sea Shell Commando			TheViking, Pandy, Pingu
Area One Four Four (A144)[4]	EcG, Demise, ACE, Paramount, RTA	"T3 10GB"	USA	BioVirus, BoB
Always Around Forever (AAF)[5]	United Warez, NATOSOFT, Impact, Citywarez, Boost, Legendaries	"T1 – 25 GiG"		Cyberjoy
Avatar (A)				

nfo)," December 27, 1998, DeFacto2, warez.scene.nfo.collection.v1.0.24351.shroo.ms.zip. For more on the longstanding significance of Razor 1911, see Patryk Wasiak, "Telephone Networks, BBSes, and the Emergence of the Transnational 'Warez Scene,'" History and Technology 35, no. 2 (2019): 189.

2 722, "722 Topsite (722-722.1998.06.12.nfo)," June 12, 1998, DeFacto2, warez.scene.nfo.collection.v1.0.24351.shroo.ms.zip.

3 Ao, "Absolute Zero Topsite (Ao-absolute.zero.XXXX.XX.01.nfo)," n.d., DeFacto2, warez.scene.nfo.collection.v1.0.24351.shroo.ms.zip.

4 A144, "Area One Four Four Topsite (A144-area.one.four.four.XXXX.XX.00.nfo)," n.d., DeFacto2, warez.scene.nfo.collection.v1.0.24351.shroo.ms.zip.

5 AAF, "Always Around Forever Topsite (AAF-always.around.forever.1998.07.18.nfo)," July 18, 1998, DeFacto2, warez.scene.nfo.collection.v1.0.24351.shroo.ms.zip.

Sitename	Known Affils	Known Hardware/Software	Location	Siteops and Nukers/Notes
The Abyss (ABY)[6]	HERiTAGE, DESYNC, AVALON, VOLiTiON		USA[7]	
AiR Force One (AF1)[8]	MYTH, Shock, FCN, ECL, UCF, TMG, CSWCN, TST		Europe[9]	
Angel Food (AF)[10]	ZONE, SiLENCE, XCRYPT, PriORITY, DEMON,LZ0, oDDiTY, PROPHECY, HTG, UCF, RBS	"9Gb" "2xt3" "(soon 155mbit)"	Poland	
The Ant Hill (AH)[11]	Fate, Masque, Rebels			

6 ABY, "The Abyss Topsite (ABY-abyss.1999.06.28.nfo)," June 28, 1999, DeFacto2, warez.scene.nfo.collection.v1.0.24351.shroo.ms.zip.

7 TDA, "The Digital Afterlife Topsite Ring (TDA-the.digital.afterlife.1997.01.20.nfo)," January 20, 1997, DeFacto2, warez.scene.nfo.collection.v1.0.24351.shroo.ms.zip.

8 AF1, "AiR Force One Topsite (AF1-air.force.one.2000.04.12.nfo)," April 12, 2000, DeFacto2, warez.scene.nfo.collection.v1.0.24351.shroo.ms.zip.

9 AF1, "AiR Force One Topsite (AF1-air.force.one.1998.02.12.nfo)," February 12, 1998, DeFacto2, warez.scene.nfo.collection.v1.0.24351.shroo.ms.zip.

10 AF, "Angel Food Topsite (AF-angel.food.2000.09.21.nfo)," September 21, 2000, DeFacto2, warez.scene.nfo.collection.v1.0.24351.shroo.ms.zip.

11 AH, "The Ant Hill Topsite (AH-the.anthill.1997.06.18.nfo)," June 18, 1997, DeFacto2, warez.scene.nfo.collection.v1.0.24351.shroo.ms.zip.

Sitename	Known Affils	Known Hardware/Software	Location	Siteops and Nukers/ Notes
Arrakis (AKS)[12]	myth, htg,int, dqf, tmg, fcn, amnesia, privcd, dvnvcd, dominion, divxcz, lfc, pdxn64, nme, cms, bpm, chr, ego	"4 bxs.eu"	Europe	
Agnos Land (AL)[13]				
Althea (ALT)[14]	KFK, IrN, KAC, MOTiV8	"80 GiGz" "OC3 Link"	USA	
Ambiquous (AMB)[15]	Renaissance, RiSE, GPF, Divine Canadian, RTN, GCRACK NA		Canada	
The Angry Moose (AM)[16]	CoRE, PtM,dSC, tfH, PiRASofT	"T1" "9 Gigs Online"		
Apocalypse (APC)[17]	AMNESiA, REBELS, DiViNE,TFT, MiSSiON		Europe	

12 AKS, "Arrakis Topsite (AKS-arrakis.2000.06.01.nfo)," June 1, 2000, DeFacto2, warez.scene.nfo.collection.v1.0.24351.shroo.ms.zip.

13 AL, "Agnos Land Topsite (AL-agnos.land.1998.09.06.nfo)," September 6, 1998, DeFacto2, warez.scene.nfo.collection.v1.0.24351.shroo.ms.zip.

14 ALT, "Althea Topsite (ALT-althea.1999.09.22.nfo)," September 22, 1999, DeFacto2, warez.scene.nfo.collection.v1.0.24351.shroo.ms.zip.

15 AMB, "Ambiquous Topsite (AMB-ambiquous.1998.02.18.nfo)," February 18, 1998, DeFacto2, warez.scene.nfo.collection.v1.0.24351.shroo.ms.zip.

16 AM, "The Angry Moose Topsite (AM-the.angry.moose.1997.08.06.nfo)," August 6, 1997, DeFacto2, warez.scene.nfo.collection.v1.0.24351.shroo.ms.zip.

17 APC, "Apocalypse Topsite (APC-apocalypse.1999.12.10.nfo)," December 10, 1999, DeFacto2, warez.scene.nfo.collection.v1.0.24351.shroo.ms.zip.

Sitename	Known Affils	Known Hardware/Software	Location	Siteops and Nukers/ Notes
Alpha Storage Place (ASP)[18]	AMNESiA, X-FoRcE, ONYX		USA[19]	
Atlantis (ATL)[20]	CORE, MYTH, PARADOX, oDDiTy, LIZZARD, ZENITH, LAXiTY, UCF, HERiTAGE, LaTeX, AOD, HSCONSOLE, LNDiSO, CNCiSO, RBSiSO, PDXCONSOLE	"100 MBIT"		
Atomic-X (ATX)[21]	KAC, ORIGIN, pHASE, VENGEANCE, RENEGADE, REVOLUTION		USA	
Alternate Void (AV)[22]	FCN, UCF2000, PHX, EcGiSO	"10 Mb/s" "20 Gigs"	Canada	

18 ASP, "Alpha Storage Place Topsite (ASP-alpha.storage.place.1998.08.27.nfo)," August 27, 1998, DeFacto2, warez.scene.nfo.collection.v1.0.24351.shroo.ms.zip.

19 ASP, "Alpha Storage Place Topsite (ASP-alpha.storage.place.1997.10.12.nfo)," October 12, 1997, DeFacto2, warez.scene.nfo.collection.v1.0.24351.shroo.ms.zip.

20 ATL, "Atlantis Topsite (ATL-atlantis.XXXX.XX.01.nfo)," n.d., DeFacto2, warez.scene.nfo.collection.v1.0.24351.shroo.ms.zip.

21 ATX, "Atomic-X Topsite (ATX-atomic.x.1999.05.05.nfo)," May 5, 1999, DeFacto2, warez.scene.nfo.collection.v1.0.24351.shroo.ms.zip.

22 AV, "Alternate Void Topsite (AV-alternate.void.1998.11.26.nfo)," November 26, 1998, DeFacto2, warez.scene.nfo.collection.v1.0.24351.shroo.ms.zip.

Sitename	Known Affils	Known Hardware/Software	Location	Siteops and Nukers/Notes
A Violent Fluid (AVF)[23]	TRPS, CRC, EXPRESS, MAGi, ZODIAC, nZPD, SSC	"12+ GiG" "MULTi-T1 connection [T1x5]"		
Avalon (AVL)[24]	IWA, DWA, GLOW, ISOWORLD, REALM, DISFUNCTION, ILLISIVE, DTD, MOI	"30GB"		
Another World (AW)[25]	ESPRiT, ECLiPSE, PINNACLE, ESPIRIT, FLUKE		Europe	
Alien Zone (AZ)[26]	HERITAGE, DUNE, FUSION	"t3+ speed" "50 GiG"	Europe	ActArUS, CybeRBoB, Cdogg
Back to Babylon (B2B)[27]	Robinhood, Rockdorce, SYNiCAL, Coalition, WLW, SWP, RTS, iNTENSiTY, DK, Weapon, PREVAiL, FFB, Pride, SCE			Atomik

23 AVF, "A Violent Fluid Topsite (AVF-a.violent.fluid.1997.11.18.nfo)," November 18, 1997, DeFacto2, warez.scene.nfo.collection.v1.0.24351.shroo.ms.zip.

24 AVL, "Avalon Topsite (AVL-avalon.XXXX.XX.00.nfo)," n.d., DeFacto2, warez.scene.nfo.collection.v1.0.24351.shroo.ms.zip.

25 AW, "Another World Topsite (AW-another.world.1999.07.02.nfo)," July 2, 1999, DeFacto2, warez.scene.nfo.collection.v1.0.24351.shroo.ms.zip.

26 AZ, "Alien Zone Topsite (AZ-alien.zone.1998.07.29.nfo)," July 29, 1998, DeFacto2, warez.scene.nfo.collection.v1.0.24351.shroo.ms.zip.

27 B2B, "Back to Babylon Topsite (B2B-back.to.babylon.1998.05.21.nfo)," May 21, 1998, DeFacto2, warez.scene.nfo.collection.v1.0.24351.shroo.ms.zip.

Sitename	Known Affils	Known Hardware/Software	Location	Siteops and Nukers/ Notes
Beyond All Reality (BAR)[28]	FLUKE, AMBiENCE, EMBRACE, EPS, LND, oDDiTy, AMNESiA, EliIApda, OriON, NLRiP, RTP, JADE, CAiNE	"100Mbit FD" "100 Gb"	The Netherlands	
Basilica (BAS)[29]	CORP, CST, DMSISO, RBSISO	"LINUX/ GLFTPD" "50+ GIGS"		
Brand Beer 2 (BB2)[30]	ENTiTY, DYNASTY, PARADiGM, UCF, DiMENSiON		Europe	
Busy Beavers (BB)[31]	ReZ, GWA, BLiZzARD	"34 MBit" "50 GB" "LiNUX" "gl-FTPd"		Hoopy, Stefan_, JG, AC-504, MeDlor, Twister, Cruller
The Bleach Box (BBX)[32]	RiSC, Scotch, FCN	"250 GB" bftpd[33]	USA	

28 BAR, "Beyond All Reality Topsite (BAR-beyond.all.reality.XXXX.XX.00.nfo)," n.d., DeFacto2, warez.scene.nfo.collection.v1.0.24351.shroo.ms.zip.

29 BAS, "Basilica Topsite (BAS-basilica.1999.04.22.nfo)," April 22, 1999, DeFacto2, warez.scene.nfo.collection.v1.0.24351.shroo.ms.zip.

30 BB2, "Brand Beer 2 Topsite (BB2-brand.beer.two.1998.07.02.nfo)," July 2, 1998, DeFacto2, warez.scene.nfo.collection.v1.0.24351.shroo.ms.zip.

31 BB, "Busy Beavers Topsite (BB-busy.beavers.1999.03.25.nfo)," March 25, 1999, DeFacto2, warez.scene.nfo.collection.v1.0.24351.shroo.ms.zip.

32 BB, "The Bleach Box Topsite (BBX-bleach.box.1996.12.19.nfo)," December 19, 1996, DeFacto2, warez.scene.nfo.collection.v1.0.24351.shroo.ms.zip.

33 lester, "Which Ftpd Is Right for You?," Netmonkey Weekly Report (Nwr36.Txt), February 22, 1999.

Sitename	Known Affils	Known Hardware/Software	Location	Siteops and Nukers/ Notes
Beat Diz (BZ)[34]	CROSSFIRE, CiA, Priority, FLUKE, LaTeX, CEREbRi		USA	
Black Forge (BF)[35]	ADDICTION, PHOENIX, GPF, TRPS, MAD	"30 GB" "Blazing Fast Cable"		
Black Lotus (BL)[36]		"Linux-2.0.30" "xftpd" "5 gigz" "T1 link-up speed"		Debber
The Blade (BLD)[37]	Nobliege, Esprit, Versus		Europe	
Blizzard (BLIZ)[38]	2000AD, RE-VOLT, DEVO-TiON		Europe[39]	
Byte Me (BM)[40]	2000AD, CRC, iTR, PDM, KALiSTO	"T3" "103GB+"	USA	

34 BDZ, "Beat Diz Topsite (BDZ-beatdiz.2000.11.20.nfo)," November 20, 2000, DeFacto2, warez.scene.nfo.collection.v1.0.24351.shroo.ms.zip.
35 BF, "Black Forge Topsite (BF-black.forge.1998.05.01.nfo)," May 1, 1998, DeFacto2, warez.scene.nfo.collection.v1.0.24351.shroo.ms.zip.
36 BL, "Black Lotus Topsite (BL-black.lotus.1997.06.12.nfo)," June 12, 1997, DeFacto2, warez.scene.nfo.collection.v1.0.24351.shroo.ms.zip.
37 BLD, "The Blade Topsite (BLD-the.blade.1998.03.23.nfo)," March 23, 1998, DeFacto2, warez.scene.nfo.collection.v1.0.24351.shroo.ms.zip.
38 BLIZ, "Blizzard Topsite (BLIZ-blizzard.1997.12.06.nfo)," December 6, 1997, DeFacto2, warez.scene.nfo.collection.v1.0.24351.shroo.ms.zip.
39 BLIZ, "Blizzard Topsite (BLIZ-blizzard.1997.06.02.nfo)," June 2, 1997, DeFacto2, warez.scene.nfo.collection.v1.0.24351.shroo.ms.zip.
40 BM, "Byte Me Topsite (BM-byte.me.1999.04.15.nfo)," April 15, 1999, DeFacto2, warez.scene.nfo.collection.v1.0.24351.shroo.ms.zip.

Sitename	Known Affils	Known Hardware/Software	Location	Siteops and Nukers/ Notes
Blood Pit (BP)[41]	Havoc97, Tft, Goe	"T1" "8Gb" "3 Online CD:s" "Offline Requesting"		Zilch, Aardvack
Bits Per Second (BPS)[42]				
Babylon Trading Post (BTS)[43]	CRC, SYNICAL, EWA, W1W, KYLIN, ILL, LG, SWP	"Dual T1 Speed" "18 Gigs Online"	USA	Vortech, ShagNasty, JeSsTeR, A1odor Hardware providers: N.O.S., Fitz, RooK, ANON
The Beggar's Tomb (BT)[44]	NATOsoft, zerawleets	"t1" "13+gb"		hammer, fo_twenny
The Bull (BULL)[45]				

41 BP, "Blood Pit Topsite (BP-blood.pit.1997.04.04.nfo)," April 4, 1997, DeFacto2, warez.scene.nfo.collection.v1.0.24351.shroo.ms.zip.

42 BPS, "Bits Per Second Topsite (BPS-bits.per.second.2000.07.03.nfo)," July 3, 2000, DeFacto2, warez.scene.nfo.collection.v1.0.24351.shroo.ms.zip.

43 BTP, "Babylon Trading Post Topsite (BTP-babylon.trading.post.XXXX.XX.02.nfo)," n.d., DeFacto2, warez.scene.nfo.collection.v1.0.24351.shroo.ms.zip.

44 BT, "The Beggar's Tomb Topsite (BT-the.beggars.tomb.1998.07.02.nfo)," July 2, 1998, DeFacto2, warez.scene.nfo.collection.v1.0.24351.shroo.ms.zip.

45 BULL, "The Bull Topsite (BULL-the.bull.1997.05.19.nfo)," May 19, 1997, DeFacto2, warez.scene.nfo.collection.v1.0.24351.shroo.ms.zip.

Sitename	Known Affils	Known Hardware/Software	Location	Siteops and Nukers/Notes
Camelot (CAM)[46]	TBS, Digital Factory, HARLEM COURIER, COUNCIL, BLIZZARD COURIER, BACKLASH		Germany[47]	
Crawling Chaos (CC)[48]				YtsEJam
Core Dump (CD)[49]	RefLUX, MENTALiTY, SOdOM	"dUAL T1 SiTE"		Thrill Kill, The White Tyger, iNGe, Bob226, dr ice Operation Buccaneer bust and raid info claims that "Core Dump" was a "fed site"[50]
Channel One (CH1)[51]				

46 CAM, "Camelot Topsite (CAM-camelot.1999.08.29.nfo)," August 29, 1999, DeFacto2, warez.scene.nfo.collection.v1.0.24351.shroo.ms.zip.

47 CAM, "Camelot Topsite (CAM-camelot.XXXX.XX.02.nfo)," n.d., DeFacto2, warez.scene.nfo.collection.v1.0.24351.shroo.ms.zip.

48 CC, "Crawling Chaos Topsite (CC-crawling.chaos.1998.04.06.nfo)," April 6, 1998, DeFacto2, warez.scene.nfo.collection.v1.0.24351.shroo.ms.zip.

49 CD, "Core Dump Topsite (CD-core.dump.1998.08.25.nfo)," August 25, 1998, DeFacto2, warez.scene.nfo.collection.v1.0.24351.shroo.ms.zip.

50 "SceneBusts10 (scenebusts10.htm)," 2000, paraZite.

51 CH1, "Channel One Topsite (CH1-channel.one.1998.09.05.nfo)," September 5, 1998, DeFacto2, warez.scene.nfo.collection.v1.0.24351.shroo.ms.zip.

Sitename	Known Affils	Known Hardware/Software	Location	Siteops and Nukers/ Notes
Cold Hell (CH)[52]	UCF, MnMiSO, RiSCiSO, WLW, RTS, X-Force, Divine	"Two T2 Systems for a total of 70 gigs" "20 gig for releases" "50 gigs for ISO's"	USA	Devestator, Coldblood, Symptom, AlphaKiller, Swank, Mason, Allanon, SirCyRo, Girdog, One-30
Cove Land (CL)	DGT	"100/155ATM" "9.1GB SCSI" "PII 450"	Europe	Anonz, Br4t, [insane]
Cemetery Gates (CMG)[53]	RiSE, MCG Courier, Thunder	"T1" "8Gb"[54]		
Covert Operation (CO)[55]	Razor 1911, Legends Never Die, TRSI, CRUX, Darkmoon Traders			
Claws of Death (COD)[56]	X-FoRCE, TRPS, Thunder, 2000AD		USA[57]	

52 CH, "Cold Hell Topsite (CH-cold.hell.1998.08.31.nfo)," August 31, 1998, DeFacto2, warez.scene.nfo.collection.v1.0.24351.shroo.ms.zip.

53 CMG, "Cemetery Gates Topsite (CMG-cemetary.gates.1998.09.21.nfo)," September 21, 1998, DeFacto2, warez.scene.nfo.collection.v1.0.24351.shroo.ms.zip.

54 CMG, "Cemetery Gates Topsite (CMG-cemetary.gates.1998.02.22.nfo)," February 22, 1998, DeFacto2, warez.scene.nfo.collection.v1.0.24351.shroo.ms.zip.

55 CO, "Covert Operation Topsite (CO-covert.operations.1998.08.25.nfo)," August 25, 1998, DeFacto2, warez.scene.nfo.collection.v1.0.24351.shroo.ms.zip.

56 COD, "Claws of Death Topsite (COD-claws.of.death.1998.11.02.nfo)," November 2, 1998, DeFacto2, warez.scene.nfo.collection.v1.0.24351.shroo.ms.zip.

57 COD, "Claws of Death Topsite (COD-claws.of.death.1998.09.18.nfo)," September 18, 1998, DeFacto2, warez.scene.nfo.collection.v1.0.24351.shroo.ms.zip.

Sitename	Known Affils	Known Hardware/Software	Location	Siteops and Nukers/Notes
Cong (CONG)[58]	MIRAGE Courier, Millennium		USA	
The Complex (CPX)[59]	rAZOR-1911			MegaPlex, bLACKENED
Castle Rock County (CRC)[60]	RiSC, PWA		Europe	
Cash Vault (CV)[61]	UDM, RfX, DkS, PDN, hTz, Factor, RiSE, QTM, TheVoid	"T1+"		
Dark Ambitions (DA)[62]	ML, gNA, aBRUPT	"bLAZING cABLE"	Canada	DV

58 CONG, "Cong Topsite (CONG-cong.1997.09.21.nfo)," September 21, 1997, DeFacto2, warez.scene.nfo.collection.v1.0.24351.shroo.ms.zip.

59 CPX, "The Complex Topsite (CPX-the.complex.1997.01.03.nfo)," January 3, 1997, DeFacto2, warez.scene.nfo.collection.v1.0.24351.shroo.ms.zip.

60 CRC, "Castle Rock County Topsite (CRC-castle.rock.county.1997.04.03.nfo)," April 3, 1997, DeFacto2, warez.scene.nfo.collection.v1.0.24351.shroo.ms.zip.

61 CV, "Cash Vault Topsite (CV-cash.vault.1998.08.25.nfo)," April 3, 1997, DeFacto2, warez.scene.nfo.collection.v1.0.24351.shroo.ms.zip.

62 DA, "Dark Ambitions Topsite (DA-dark.ambitions.XXXX.XX.00.nfo)," n.d., DeFacto2, warez.scene.nfo.collection.v1.0.24351.shroo.ms.zip.

Sitename	Known Affils	Known Hardware/Software	Location	Siteops and Nukers/ Notes
Divide by Zero (DBZ)[63]	Legends Never Die, United Cracking Force, Origin, Digital Factory, DarkSide Inc, 2000ad, German Warez Alliance, EViLiSO, FCNiSO, KALiSTO, iCOiSO, SHOCKiSO	"Two T-3 Systems" "Full Year Round Site" "186 GB+" "420GB ARCHIVED"	Eastern US Coast[64]	
Digital Corruption (DC)[65]	Renaissance, PWA, UCF			Ico, SirMagik, Vorteqz, Iceb, Aboul, biggy
Digital Crossroads (DC)[66]		"a t1" "6 gigs of oday online" "33 gigs of Appz/GameZ/CracZ offline"		FlameSpin, Eagle
Dream Castle (DC)[67]	ESPRiT, CRYSTAL, GWA, hV, TPC, TRSi, DeMoN		Europe	

63 DBZ, "Divide By Zero Topsite (DBZ-divide.by.zero.2000.01.21.nfo)," January 21, 2000, DeFacto2, warez.scene.nfo.collection.v1.0.24351.shroo.ms.zip.

64 DBZ, "Divide By Zero Topsite (DBZ-divide.by.zero.XXXX.XX.01.nfo)," n.d., DeFacto2, warez.scene.nfo.collection.v1.0.24351.shroo.ms.zip.

65 DC, "Digital Corruption Topsite (DC-digital.corruption.1998.03.18.nfo)," March 18, 1998, DeFacto2, warez.scene.nfo.collection.v1.0.24351.shroo.ms.zip.

66 DC, "Digital Crossroads Topsite (DC-digital.crossroads.1998.09.02.nfo)," September 2, 1998, DeFacto2, warez.scene.nfo.collection.v1.0.24351.shroo.ms.zip.

67 DC, "Dream Castle Topsite (DC-dream.castle.1999.03.29.nfo)," March 29, 1999, DeFacto2, warez.scene.nfo.collection.v1.0.24351.shroo.ms.zip.

Sitename	Known Affils	Known Hardware/Software	Location	Siteops and Nukers/ Notes
Daedalus (D)[68]	THD, DVN, PRM, iNSPiRE	"DS-3" "7Gigs"	USA	
Dark Data (DD)[69]	HoW	"T1" "25gb"		Shorty, Ryche
Deadeloth (DDT)[70]	ESPRIT			
DaFat of the Land (DF)[71]	DIVINE, FCN, MANIFEST COURIER, REBELS, REQUEST TO SEND	"Powered by 34mbit T3 Ethernet" "24 gigs"	East US	
DaFat of the Land 2 (DF2)[72]	DIVINE, FCN, MANIFEST DESTINY COURIER, REBELS, REQUEST TO SEND, RENEGADE, REVOLUTION		East US	

68 D, "Daedalus Topsite (D-daedalus.1998.01.05.nfo)," January 5, 1998, DeFacto2, warez.scene.nfo.collection.v1.0.24351.shroo.ms.zip.
69 DD, "Dark Data Topsite (DD-dark.data.1998.11.02.nfo)," November 2, 1998, DeFacto2, warez.scene.nfo.collection.v1.0.24351.shroo.ms.zip.
70 DDT, "Deadeloth Topsite (DDT-deadeloth.1997.11.17.nfo)," November 17, 1997, DeFacto2, warez.scene.nfo.collection.v1.0.24351.shroo.ms.zip.
71 DF, "DaFat of the Land Topsite (DF-da.fat.1998.09.16.nfo)," September 16, 1998, DeFacto2, warez.scene.nfo.collection.v1.0.24351.shroo.ms.zip.
72 DF2, "DaFat of the Land 2 Topsite (DF2-da.fat.two.1998.10.14.nfo)," October 14, 1998, DeFacto2, warez.scene.nfo.collection.v1.0.24351.shroo.ms.zip.

Sitename	Known Affils	Known Hardware/Software	Location	Siteops and Nukers/ Notes
DaFat of the Land 3 (DF3)[73]	DARKSTAR, DiMENSiON, ECLiPSE, MANiFEST DESTINY, PREMIERE, RENEGADE COURIER, REVOLUTION COURIER			
DagoBah System (DGB)[74]				
Distorted Illusions (DI)[75]	Pulsar, Motiv8, Sphinks, Rts, Ulysse, Magma	"17 mbit" "210+ gigs"		Poohy, Cleanup, Gramons
Digital Information Playground (DIP)[76]	CuRRuPTioN, aBRuPT, PCW, eSTeeM	"10mb Kable" "GIGS: 16"	USA	DiPSTiK, ELF_BOY, NJVAMPIRE, PHARO, MUFFINMAN, |BOBO|, SOULBENDR, JOOBIE, TOMCAT, DeeZ-NuTZ, RoWBie
Disaster (DIS)[77]	REBELS '97		Norway	Mr. Spoof, Crypto

73 DF3, "DaFat of the Land 3 Topsite (DF3-da.fat.three.1999.06.05.nfo)," June 5, 1999, DeFacto2, warez.scene.nfo.collection.v1.0.24351.shroo.ms.zip.

74 DGB, "DagoBah System Topsite (DGB-dagobah.1998.11.19.nfo)," November 19, 1998, DeFacto2, warez.scene.nfo.collection.v1.0.24351.shroo.ms.zip.

75 DI, "Distorted Illusions Topsite (DI-distorted.illusions.XXXX.XX.01.nfo)," n.d., DeFacto2, warez.scene.nfo.collection.v1.0.24351.shroo.ms.zip.

76 DIP, "Digital Information Playground Topsite (DIP-digital.information.playground.1998.02.28.nfo)," February 28, 1998, DeFacto2, warez.scene.nfo.collection.v1.0.24351.shroo.ms.zip.

77 DIS, "Disaster Topsite (DIS-disaster.1997.02.13.nfo)," February 13, 1997, DeFacto2, warez.scene.nfo.collection.v1.0.24351.shroo.ms.zip.

Sitename	Known Affils	Known Hardware/Software	Location	Siteops and Nukers/ Notes
Digital Kingdom (DK)[78]	BSC, DPN, BLC, DSN, XPT, ABT, CiFE, Request-VCD	"ATM DS3 45Mbit" "52 GiG + 14CD-ROM"		LiNuXBuG, Madd-Doc[79]
Dark Land (DL)[80]	TFA, ORIGIN, DiViNE, FALLEN, lSD, KALiSTO		United Kingdom	aXEN, Opel, sacX, Blas, poo, Judge, Slick, Raidman
DreamLand (DL)[81]	CRYSTAL, RAZOR1911, PHOENIX		USA	
Delerium (DLM)[82]	CLASS, RiSCiSO, SIEGE Courier	"50 Gig Online Running dFTPD"		
Darklands (DLS)[83]	BLiZZARD, LEGENDS NEVER DiE, VERSUS, EQUALITY, RAZOR 1911, PROPHECY		The Netherlands	

78 DK, "Digital Kingdom Topsite (DK-digital.kingdom.1999.11.17.nfo)," November 17, 1999, DeFacto2, warez.scene.nfo.collection.v1.0.24351.shroo.ms.zip.

79 DK, "Digital Kingdom Topsite (DK-digital.kingdom.1999.08.25.nfo)," August 25, 1999, DeFacto2, warez.scene.nfo.collection.v1.0.24351.shroo.ms.zip.

80 DL, "Dark Land Topsite (DL-dark.land.1999.01.13.nfo)," January 13, 1999, DeFacto2, warez.scene.nfo.collection.v1.0.24351.shroo.ms.zip.

81 DL, "DreamLand Topsite (DL-dream.land.1999.04.27.nfo)," April 27, 1999, DeFacto2, warez.scene.nfo.collection.v1.0.24351.shroo.ms.zip.

82 DLM, "Delerium Topsite (DLM-delirium.1998.05.20.nfo)," May 20, 1998, DeFacto2, warez.scene.nfo.collection.v1.0.24351.shroo.ms.zip.

83 DLS, "Darklands Topsite (DLS-darklands.2000.03.26.nfo)," March 26, 2000, DeFacto2, warez.scene.nfo.collection.v1.0.24351.shroo.ms.zip.

Sitename	Known Affils	Known Hardware/Software	Location	Siteops and Nukers/ Notes
Dream Machine (DM)[84]				Dream, Dark Thunder, MDios, MarkGoh
Damn Nation (DN)[85]	LTC, RC, TENUREMMI			sativa, morse
Digital Overload (DO)[86]				
Department of Pure Ecstacy (DOPE)[87]	TRPS COURIER, AOD, CORP COURIER		Europe	pozest, phromo, houdis, freakshow
D.-.P.A.R.T.-M.E.N.T (DPT-d)[88]	PWA, CNC, GWA, BLZ, AMOK, NBD	"XX MBiTZ" "22 GiGZ"		d-fens, peter, krusher, thejudge, twister, bvcyp, sol, fiDo
The Duplex (DPX)[89]	MOTiV8, SYN, SENATE, TDA			MoLdy, WKNiGHT, DAV321, Beck, UsurpeR, Doc-X

84 DM, "Dream Machine Topsite (DM-dream.machine.1997.10.14.nfo)," October 14, 1997, DeFacto2, warez.scene.nfo.collection.v1.0.24351.shroo.ms.zip.

85 DN, "Damn Nation Topsite (DN-damn.nation.1998.08.25.nfo)," August 25, 1998, DeFacto2, warez.scene.nfo.collection.v1.0.24351.shroo.ms.zip.

86 DO, "Digital Overload Topsite (DO-digital.overload.1998.04.19.nfo)," April 19, 1998, DeFacto2, warez.scene.nfo.collection.v1.0.24351.shroo.ms.zip.

87 DOPE, "Department of Pure Ecstacy Topsite (DOPE-department.of.pure.ecstacy.1999.03.31.nfo)," March 31, 1999, DeFacto2, warez.scene.nfo.collection.v1.0.24351.shroo.ms.zip.

88 DPT-d, "D.-.P.A.R.T.M.E.N.T Topsite (DPT-d.partment.1999.03.12.nfo)," March 12, 1999, DeFacto2, warez.scene.nfo.collection.v1.0.24351.shroo.ms.zip.

89 DPX, "The Duplex Topsite (DPX-duplex.1997.04.01.nfo)," April 1, 1997, DeFacto2, warez.scene.nfo.collection.v1.0.24351.shroo.ms.zip.

Sitename	Known Affils	Known Hardware/Software	Location	Siteops and Nukers/ Notes
Dropzone (DPZ)[90]	PARADOX, BLIZZARD, oDDiTy, DiSTiNCT, iNTUTiLS, ECN, PRiORiTY, SPHiNKS, PGC, ATM, DS, POW	"10mbit" "100gigs online"	Poland	
Dismal Surrection (DST)[91]	LND, MFD, PDM, UCF		West Coast USA	
The Dark Side (DS)[92]	FUTURE, KAC, TRPS, cX, HERiTAGE, XPC		USA	WarezWulf, Swan, |Napalm|, Birocratu, BoNzo
Ditto (DTO)[93]	jAG, EcG, iNTRiGUE98	"10gb+" "cable speed"		xVeNoMx
Diamond Valley (DV)[94]	RTS COURiER, Rebels, Weapon, TRPS	"72MBit Frac OC3"		
Dixieland (DXL)[95]	ZerawLeetZ, Drink or Die	"a fat T3 pipe"		Please beware that site NFO is deeply racially offensive.
Danger Zone (DZ)[96]	MUTH, SCOTCH, TFTiSO, TFT		Sweden	

90 DPZ, "Dropzone Topsite (DPZ-dropzone.2000.09.25.nfo)," September 25, 2000, DeFacto2, warez.scene.nfo.collection.v1.0.24351.shroo.ms.zip.

91 DST, "Dismal Surrection Topsite (DST-dismal.surrection.1999.07.27.nfo)," July 27, 1999, DeFacto2, warez.scene.nfo.collection.v1.0.24351.shroo.ms.zip.

92 DS, "The Dark Side Topsite (DS-the.dark.side.1998.08.19.nfo)," August 19, 1998, DeFacto2, warez.scene.nfo.collection.v1.0.24351.shroo.ms.zip.

93 DTO, "Ditto Topsite (DTO-ditto.1998.10.01.nfo)," October 1, 1998, DeFacto2, warez.scene.nfo.collection.v1.0.24351.shroo.ms.zip.

94 DV, "Diamond Valley Topsite (DV-diamond.valley.1998.07.27.nfo)," July 27, 1998, DeFacto2, warez.scene.nfo.collection.v1.0.24351.shroo.ms.zip.

95 DXL, "Dixieland Topsite (DXL-dixieland.1999.02.22.nfo)," February 22, 1999, DeFacto2, warez.scene.nfo.collection.v1.0.24351.shroo.ms.zip.

96 DZ, "Danger Zone Topsite (DZ-danger.zone.XXXX.XX.00.nfo)," n.d., DeFacto2, warez.scene.nfo.collection.v1.0.24351.shroo.ms.zip.

Sitename	Known Affils	Known Hardware/Software	Location	Siteops and Nukers/ Notes
The Dragonz Lair (DZL)[97]	Orb, Gmgrp, Appgrp, AVALON		USA	
East 999 (E999)[98]	EWC, GRC, RTN, MCG, MNT			MrQuija,RootDown
Echo Base (EB)[99]	PiNNACLE, 2000AD, TNO, HARLEM, EviL, EPC, RADiANCE, OXYGEN, PARADOX		Europe	
Eternal Chaos (EC)[100]	SHOCK, ECLIPSE, MSN	"100 GB"		
The Evil Drome (ED)[101]	DOD, TRPS, TRG, REFLUX, RADIUM	"OC3" "30Gigz" "Linux/GLftpD"	USA	_AsH_, |Croaker| VantMas
Evil Echo (EE)[102]	PHOENiX, DiViNE, CRYSTAL, PWA			

97 DZL, "The Dragonz Lair Topsite (DZL-the.dragonz.lair.1998.02.05.nfo)," February 5, 1998, DeFacto2, warez.scene.nfo.collection.v1.0.24351.shroo.ms.zip.

98 E999, "East 999 Topsite (E999-east.999.1997.05.03.nfo)," May 3, 1997, DeFacto2, warez.scene.nfo.collection.v1.0.24351.shroo.ms.zip.

99 EB, "Echo Base Topsite (EB-echo.base.1999.03.11.nfo)," March 11, 1999, DeFacto2, warez.scene.nfo.collection.v1.0.24351.shroo.ms.zip.

100 EC, "Eternal Chaos Topsite (EC-eternal.chaos.1999.05.19.nfo)," May 19, 1999, DeFacto2, warez.scene.nfo.collection.v1.0.24351.shroo.ms.zip.

101 ED, "The Evil Drome Topsite (ED-evil.drome.1998.07.26.nfo)," July 26, 1998, DeFacto2, warez.scene.nfo.collection.v1.0.24351.shroo.ms.zip.

102 EE, "Evil Echo Topsite (EE-evil.echo.1999.06.18.nfo)," June 18, 1999, DeFacto2, warez.scene.nfo.collection.v1.0.24351.shroo.ms.zip.

Sitename	Known Affils	Known Hardware/Software	Location	Siteops and Nukers/ Notes
The Emporium (EMP)[103]				
Endurance (END)[104]	Divine, F4CG, Century, Legacy		USA	
The Endz of the Earth (EOE)[105]	PhoeniX, Heritage			
Essence of Earth (EOE)[106]	DiViNE, MFD, SOLiTUDE, NLRiP, THD, PRiVCD, HZD			
Edge of Sanity (EOS)[107]	2000AD, Esprit, DeC, Spawn, bEYOND TiME		Norway	
Escape Reality (ER)[108]	HRS, RTN, The Reviewers Guild, Sea Shell Commando, Global Alliance of Superior Pirating		USA	

103 EMP, "The Emporium Topsite (EMP-the.emporium.1997.05.28.nfo)," May 28, 1997, DeFacto2, warez.scene.nfo.collection.v1.0.24351.shroo.ms.zip.
104 END, "Endurance Topsite (END-endurance.1998.03.01.nfo)," March 1, 1998, DeFacto2, warez.scene.nfo.collection.v1.0.24351.shroo.ms.zip.
105 EOE, "The Ends of the Earth Topsite (EOE-endz.of.the.earth.1997.09.19.nfo)," September 19, 1997, DeFacto2, warez.scene.nfo.collection.v1.0.24351.shroo.ms.zip.
106 EOE, "Essence of Earth Topsite (EOE-essence.of.earth.2000.09.26.nfo)," September 26, 2000, DeFacto2, warez.scene.nfo.collection.v1.0.24351.shroo.ms.zip.
107 EOS, "Edge of Sanity Topsite (EOS-edge.of.sanity.1997.11.01.nfo)," November 1, 1997, DeFacto2, warez.scene.nfo.collection.v1.0.24351.shroo.ms.zip.
108 ER, "Escape Reality Topsite (ER-escape.reality.1997.08.25.nfo)," August 25, 1997, DeFacto2, warez.scene.nfo.collection.v1.0.24351.shroo.ms.zip.

Sitename	Known Affils	Known Hardware/Software	Location	Siteops and Nukers/ Notes
Etirnity (ET)[109]	DEVOTiON, MORTALITY			
Evasion (EVN)[110]	ultim8	"T-3" "34 gig"	Europe	FuJY, Exodus
Foundation Two (F2)[111]	REBELS, DEVOTiON			
The Fat Babe Two (FB2)[112]	Coalition97, RTP	"10Gig" "10MBPS"		
Flashback (FB)[113]	THUNDER COURIER, SILENT CHAOS, LEGENDARY			
Fatal Error (FE)[114]	OVERKiLL, MORTALiTY			Bouncer operator (Richard Berry) busted in Operation Buccaneer
Fire Fox (FF)[115]	DEVOTiON, PFT, CORPORATION, CLASS		Europe	
Flash (F)[116]	LND, LNDiSO, TNO	"60+ Gigabytes"		SelfHi5, Hodd, Spin, Jono, Cedric

109 ET, "Etirnity Topsite (ET-etirnity.1996.08.10.nfo)," August 10, 1996, DeFacto2, warez.scene.nfo.collection.v1.0.24351.shroo.ms.zip.

110 EVN, "Evasion Topsite (EVN-evasion.1998.10.26.nfo)," October 26, 1998, DeFacto2, warez.scene.nfo.collection.v1.0.24351.shroo.ms.zip.

111 F2, "Foundation Two Topsite (F2-foundation.two.1997.04.26.nfo)," April 26, 1997, DeFacto2, warez.scene.nfo.collection.v1.0.24351.shroo.ms.zip.

112 FB2, "The Fat Babe Two Topsite (FB2-the.fat.babe.two.1997.07.12.nfo)," July 12, 1997, DeFacto2, warez.scene.nfo.collection.v1.0.24351.shroo.ms.zip.

113 FB, "Flashback Topsite (FB-flashbak.1998.08.25.nfo)," August 25, 1998, DeFacto2, warez.scene.nfo.collection.v1.0.24351.shroo.ms.zip.

114 FE, "Fatal Error Topsite (FE-fatal.error.1997.03.02.nfo)," March 2, 1997, DeFacto2, warez.scene.nfo.collection.v1.0.24351.shroo.ms.zip.

115 FF, "Fire Fox Topsite (FF-fire.fox.1999.06.28.nfo)," June 28, 1999, DeFacto2, warez.scene.nfo.collection.v1.0.24351.shroo.ms.zip.

116 F, "Flash Topsite (F-flash.1999.04.18.nfo)," April 18, 1999, DeFacto2, warez.scene.nfo.collection.v1.0.24351.shroo.ms.zip.

Sitename	Known Affils	Known Hardware/Software	Location	Siteops and Nukers/ Notes
FalseHood (FH)[117]	RAZOR 1911, RiSC, GRS			Gollie, Morbid[118]
Foo.Keen (FK)[119]	Flt, kal, ech, tcs, mnc, vnm, flix, trfc, obus, jgt, shk, twc, adx, harem[120]	"1gbit" "3tb"		
Frag Land (FL)[121]	Weapon, SPRiT, MiRACLE, PGC, TBS, KAC, UCF		Europe	
Fungus Land (FL)[122]	MFD, DK, ATN	"T3" "22GB"	USA	
Fortress of Solitude (FOS)[123]	RiSC, Drink or Die, RAZOR 1911, UCF, BLH, TRG		Europe	
Floating Point (FP)[124]	Swat, Motiv8, DsC, FcN, GDW			BiG_PeRM, Argonautz

117 FH, "FalseHood Topsite (FH-false.hood.1998.08.27.nfo)," August 27, 1998, DeFacto2, warez.scene.nfo.collection.v1.0.24351.shroo.ms.zip.

118 FH, "FalseHood Topsite (FH-false.hood.1998.02.26.nfo)," February 26, 1998, DeFacto2, warez.scene.nfo.collection.v1.0.24351.shroo.ms.zip.

119 FK, "Foo.Keen Topsite (FK-foo.keen.XXXX.XX.01.nfo)," n.d., DeFacto2, warez.scene.nfo.collection.v1.0.24351.shroo.ms.zip.

120 FK, "Foo.Keen Topsite (FK-foo.keen.1999.09.07.nfo)," September 7, 1999, DeFacto2, warez.scene.nfo.collection.v1.0.24351.shroo.ms.zip.

121 FL, "Frag Land Topsite (FL-frag.land.1998.05.15.nfo)," May 15, 1998, DeFacto2, warez.scene.nfo.collection.v1.0.24351.shroo.ms.zip.

122 FL, "Fungus Land Topsite (FL-fungus.land.1998.08.12.nfo)," August 12, 1998, DeFacto2, warez.scene.nfo.collection.v1.0.24351.shroo.ms.zip.

123 FOS, "Fortress of Solitude Topsite (FOS-fortress.of.solitude.1998.12.23.nfo)," December 23, 1998, DeFacto2, warez.scene.nfo.collection.v1.0.24351.shroo.ms.zip.

124 FP, "Floating Point Topsite (FP-floating.point.1997.06.08.nfo)," June 8, 1997, DeFacto2, warez.scene.nfo.collection.v1.0.24351.shroo.ms.zip.

Sitename	Known Affils	Known Hardware/Software	Location	Siteops and Nukers/ Notes
Fire Site (FS)[125]	Class, titan, ucf, mdf, devotion, harvest, oxygen, pentium force team		Europe	
Fuckin Stoned (FS)[126]	OVeRDRiVe, RTP, Rta, IMPaCT	"17 GiGS" "DuaL T1's"		Cracker
Fusion (FSN)[127]	AVN, CERTISO, RTN, DARKMOOR, FATAL, ROOTGEMS, HI-JACK, MERIDIAN		Europe	
Fucked Up Beyond All Recognition (FUBAR)[128]		"DualT1" "6 GiGS" "Plus 5 ONLiNE Cdz" "LiNUX" "XFTPD pimped"	USA[129]	
General Failure (GF)[130]	OVERKiLL			

125 FS, "Fire Site Topsite (FS-fire.site.2000.09.14.nfo)," September 14, 2000, DeFacto2, warez.scene.nfo.collection.v1.0.24351.shroo.ms.zip.

126 FS, "Fuckin Stoned Topsite (FS-fuckin.stoned.1997.10.30.nfo)," October 30, 1997, DeFacto2, warez.scene.nfo.collection.v1.0.24351.shroo.ms.zip.

127 FSN, "Fusion Topsite (FSN-fusion.XXXX.XX.00.nfo)," n.d., DeFacto2, warez.scene.nfo.collection.v1.0.24351.shroo.ms.zip.

128 FUBAR, "Fucked Up Beyond All Recognition Topsite (FUBAR-fucked.up.beyond.all.recognition.1997.01.20.nfo)," January 20, 1997, DeFacto2, warez.scene.nfo.collection.v1.0.24351.shroo.ms.zip.

129 TDA, "The Digital Afterlife Topsite Ring (TDA-the.digital.afterlife.1997.01.20.nfo)."

130 GF, "General Failure Topsite (GF-general.failure.1997.01.04.nfo)," January 4, 1997, DeFacto2, warez.scene.nfo.collection.v1.0.24351.shroo.ms.zip.

Sitename	Known Affils	Known Hardware/Software	Location	Siteops and Nukers/ Notes
Guru Heaven (GH)[131]	RPR, DEV, PNC, M8, RTS, OB			
Guru Meditation (GM)[132]	MiRAGE, DOD, AMNESiA			
Genesis (GNS)[133]	MnM, EtP, QuoruM	"10 Machines Running RedHat Linux v5.2" "190 GigS" "250 kbps Cable Modem Site / In & Out!" "GLFTPD"		BadThrax, ZipPer2
Green Skull (GS)[134]				Busted, Rare
Hemispheres Two (H2)[135]	Class, Dimension, Pentium Force Team, RiscISO, PiR8s Gone Crazy	"This site is powered by PiMPD" "T3 Speed" "26 Gb"[136]	USA	

131 GH, "Guru Heaven Topsite (GH-guru.heaven.1998.05.04.nfo)," May 4, 1998, DeFacto2, warez.scene.nfo.collection.v1.0.24351.shroo.ms.zip.
132 GM, "Guru Meditation Topsite (GM-guru.meditation.1997.03.07.nfo)," March 7, 1997, DeFacto2, warez.scene.nfo.collection.v1.0.24351.shroo.ms.zip.
133 GNS, "Genesis Topsite (GNS-genesis.1999.07.05.nfo)," July 5, 1999, DeFacto2, warez.scene.nfo.collection.v1.0.24351.shroo.ms.zip.
134 GS, "Green Skull Topsite (GS-green.skull.1997.05.25.nfo)," May 25, 1997, DeFacto2, warez.scene.nfo.collection.v1.0.24351.shroo.ms.zip.
135 H2, "Hemispheres Two Topsite (H2-hemispheres.two.1998.07.28.nfo)," July 28, 1998, DeFacto2, warez.scene.nfo.collection.v1.0.24351.shroo.ms.zip.
136 H2, "Hemispheres Two Topsite (H2-hemispheres.two.1998.05.27.nfo)," May 27, 1998, DeFacto2, warez.scene.nfo.collection.v1.0.24351.shroo.ms.zip.

Sitename	Known Affils	Known Hardware/Software	Location	Siteops and Nukers/Notes
Highway 2 Hell (H2H)[137]	FALLEN, PROPHECY, MUTH, RiSC, FCN, TFT, DVNiSO, TFTiSO		Europe	
Holocron (HCN)[138]	EViL, ATC	"T3" "20GB"		MerCurion, Slick, Ryche
Hades (H)[139]	PENTiUM FORCE TEAM, RiSE, GCRACK, THE REVIEWER'S GUiLD, DiMENSiON, CLASS	HADES FTPD[140]	Europe	
Hard Floor (HF)[141]	ORIGIN, DRINK OR DIE			
Hell Fire (HF)[142]	MOTiV8			
The Happy Hippo (HH)[143]	ECG, captiveX, HI-JACK	"T3" "12GiGS"		

137 H2H, "Highway 2 Hell Topsite (H2H-highway.2.hell.2000.08.27.nfo)," August 27, 2000, DeFacto2, warez.scene.nfo.collection.v1.0.24351.shroo.ms.zip.
138 HCN, "Holocron Topsite (HCN-holocron.XXXX.XX.00.nfo)," n.d., DeFacto2, warez.scene.nfo.collection.v1.0.24351.shroo.ms.zip.
139 H, "Hades Topsite (HDS-hades.1998.06.12.nfo)," June 12, 1998, DeFacto2, warez.scene.nfo.collection.v1.0.24351.shroo.ms.zip.
140 lester, "Which Ftpd Is Right for You?"
141 HF, "Hard Floor Topsite (HF-hard.floor.1999.09.20.nfo)," September 20, 1999, DeFacto2, warez.scene.nfo.collection.v1.0.24351.shroo.ms.zip.
142 HF, "Hell Fire Topsite (HF-hell.fire.1997.05.16.nfo)," May 16, 1997, DeFacto2, warez.scene.nfo.collection.v1.0.24351.shroo.ms.zip.
143 HH, "The Happy Hippo Topsite (HH-the.happy.hippo.1998.10.25.nfo)," October 25, 1998, DeFacto2, warez.scene.nfo.collection.v1.0.24351.shroo.ms.zip.

Sitename	Known Affils	Known Hardware/Software	Location	Siteops and Nukers/ Notes
Hades on Earth (HOE)[144]	DiMENSiON, CLASS, RiSE, PiNNACLE, DARKSTAR			
Hall of Illusions (HOL)[145]	RiSC, RAZOR 1911, X-FORCE, BliZZARD, RADiUM, Dsi, LAXiTY			
House of Music (HOM)[146]	CORE, TMG, DiSTINCT, INTENSION, CNC, DWP, EVIL, OxYGeN, ODDITY, DAMN, BLH, MIB, COREPDA, POEPDA, UCFPDA		Europe	
Hall of Warez (HOW)[147]	REFLUX, OUTBREAK, GEN-X, MOTIV8			
Hard Wired (HW)[148]	FTL, OVK, THD, OBT, AXD	"T3"[149]	Europe	

144 HOE, "Hades on Earth Topsite (HOE-hades.on.earth.1999.01.20.nfo)," January 20, 1999, DeFacto2, warez.scene.nfo.collection.v1.0.24351.shroo.ms.zip.

145 HOL, "Hall of Illusions Topsite (HOL-hall.of.illusions.1999.10.28.nfo)," October 28, 1999, DeFacto2, warez.scene.nfo.collection.v1.0.24351.shroo.ms.zip.

146 HOM, "House of Music Topsite (HOM-house.of.music.2000.10.05.nfo)," October 5, 2000, DeFacto2, warez.scene.nfo.collection.v1.0.24351.shroo.ms.zip.

147 HOW, "Hall of Warez Topsite (HOW-hall.of.warez.1997.05.24.nfo)," May 24, 1997, DeFacto2, warez.scene.nfo.collection.v1.0.24351.shroo.ms.zip.

148 HW, "Hard Wired Topsite (HW-hard.wired.1998.08.27.nfo)," August 27, 1998, DeFacto2, warez.scene.nfo.collection.v1.0.24351.shroo.ms.zip.

149 HW, "Hard Wired Topsite (HW-hard.wired.1997.03.27.nfo)," March 27, 1997, DeFacto2, warez.scene.nfo.collection.v1.0.24351.shroo.ms.zip.

Sitename	Known Affils	Known Hardware/Software	Location	Siteops and Nukers/ Notes
Identity Crisis (IC)[150]	SiEGE, Class, DEVOTiON, RADiUM, CORE, RAZOR			
The Imperium (IMP)[151]	AoD, VIGILANCE, WARRIOR, FATAL, GOH '99	"10GIG" "CABLE"[152]		GOD-EMPEROR
Infinity (INF)[153]	INFLiCTiON, LEGACY, RiSE, SEA SHELL COMMANDO, TRPS		USA	CnC, Cali, Hando
Internet Protocol (IP)[154]	LG, DW, DPN, WAR			
The Isle (ISLE)[155]	MNT, NvC, fCC, DSC, INJ, PGC, RNS, CDA, BDC, SST			[Trader]

150 IC, "Identity Crisis Topsite (IC-identity.crisis.1999.03.31.nfo)," March 31, 1999, DeFacto2, warez.scene.nfo.collection.v1.0.24351.shroo.ms.zip.

151 IMP, "The Imperium Topsite (IMP-imperium.1998.07.19.nfo)," July 19, 1998, DeFacto2, warez.scene.nfo.collection.v1.0.24351.shroo.ms.zip.

152 IMP, "The Imperium Topsite (IMP-imperium.XXXX.XX.01.nfo)," n.d., DeFacto2, warez.scene.nfo.collection.v1.0.24351.shroo.ms.zip.

153 INF, "Infinity Topsite (INF-infinity.1998.04.10.nfo)," April 10, 1998, DeFacto2, warez.scene.nfo.collection.v1.0.24351.shroo.ms.zip.

154 IP, "Internet Protocol Topsite (IP-internet.protocol.1999.10.05.nfo)," October 5, 1999, DeFacto2, warez.scene.nfo.collection.v1.0.24351.shroo.ms.zip.

155 ISLE, "The Isle Topsite (ISLE-the.isle.1997.06.10.nfo)," June 10, 1997, DeFacto2, warez.scene.nfo.collection.v1.0.24351.shroo.ms.zip.

Sitename	Known Affils	Known Hardware/Software	Location	Siteops and Nukers/ Notes
Insanity Storm (IST)[156]	DARKSiDE, MANiFEST DESTiNY, TOL, KYLiN, REVOLUTiON, SKELETON		"West US"[157]	
Intoxicated (IX)[158]	THE COUNCiL, GERMAN WAREZ ALLiANCE			
The Jungle (JNG)[159]	RADiUM, REBELS, WLW, WTA	"EQLFTPD" "Dual T-1" "8GB"		Manik Depressive, Druggy, Dizzy[160]
K2 (K2)[161]	RAZOR 1911, DRINK OR DIE, ABSOLUT			
Kane (K)[162]	ORiON, ANGELS ON DRUGS, LEGENDS NEVER DIE		Europe	

156 IST, "Insanity Storm Topsite (ISTORM-insanity.storm.1998.09.19.nfo)," September 19, 1998, DeFacto2, warez.scene.nfo.collection.v1.0.24351.shroo.ms.zip.
157 IST, "Insanity Storm Topsite (ISTORM-insanity.storm.1998.08.13.nfo)," August 13, 1998, DeFacto2, warez.scene.nfo.collection.v1.0.24351.shroo.ms.zip.
158 IX, "Intoxicated Topsite (IX-intoxicated.1999.12.26.nfo)," December 26, 1999, DeFacto2, warez.scene.nfo.collection.v1.0.24351.shroo.ms.zip.
159 JNG, "The Jungle Topsite (JNG-the.jungle.1998.08.18.nfo)," August 18, 1998, DeFacto2, warez.scene.nfo.collection.v1.0.24351.shroo.ms.zip.
160 JNG, "The Jungle Topsite (JNG-the.jungle.XXXX.XX.00.nfo)," n.d., DeFacto2, warez.scene.nfo.collection.v1.0.24351.shroo.ms.zip.
161 K2, "K2 Topsite (K2-k2.1998.03.21.nfo)," March 21, 1998, DeFacto2, warez.scene.nfo.collection.v1.0.24351.shroo.ms.zip.
162 K, "Kane Topsite (K-kane.XXXX.XX.01.nfo)," n.d., DeFacto2, warez.scene.nfo.collection.v1.0.24351.shroo.ms.zip.

Sitename	Known Affils	Known Hardware/Software	Location	Siteops and Nukers/ Notes
Kalles Kaviar (KK)[163]	ESPRiT, PHASE			
Krad (KRAD)[164]	ENDURANCE			
The Krib (KRIB)[165]		"T1" "50 GB"		
Krynn (KRYNN)[166]	Swat, FCN, Motiv8, LGD, Trps	"LINUX POWERED"	Europe	TheParain
Kashmir (KSH)[167]	Razor 1911, United Cracking Force, Legends Never Die		Europe	
Kinetics (KTS)[168]	Adrenalin, Addiction, TDA, Scandal	"4 Gigs" "Ethernet" "WarFTP"		
Lunatic Asylum (LA)[169]				
Lost in Space (LIS)[170]	Orbital			

163 KK, "Kalles Kaviar Topsite (KK-kalles.kaviar.1999.09.15.nfo)," September 15, 1999, DeFacto2, warez.scene.nfo.collection.v1.0.24351.shroo.ms.zip.
164 KRAD, "KRAD Topsite (KRAD-krad.1997.06.29.nfo)," September 15, 1999, DeFacto2, warez.scene.nfo.collection.v1.0.24351.shroo.ms.zip.
165 KRIB, "The Krib Topsite (KRIB-the.krib.1997.07.30.nfo)," July 30, 1997, DeFacto2, warez.scene.nfo.collection.v1.0.24351.shroo.ms.zip.
166 KRYNN, "Krynn Topsite (KRYNN-krynn.1997.11.25.nfo)," November 25, 1997, DeFacto2, warez.scene.nfo.collection.v1.0.24351.shroo.ms.zip.
167 KSH, "Kashmir Topsite (KSH-kashmir.1997.02.22.nfo)," February 22, 1997, DeFacto2, warez.scene.nfo.collection.v1.0.24351.shroo.ms.zip.
168 KTS, "Kinetics Topsite (KTS-kinetics.1997.01.15.nfo)," January 15, 1997, DeFacto2, warez.scene.nfo.collection.v1.0.24351.shroo.ms.zip.
169 LA, "Lunatic Asylum Topsite (LA-lunatic.asylum.1995.04.21.nfo)," April 21, 1995, DeFacto2, warez.scene.nfo.collection.v1.0.24351.shroo.ms.zip.
170 LIS, "Lost in Space Topsite (LIS-lost.in.space.1997.08.13.nfo)," August 13, 1998, DeFacto2, warez.scene.nfo.collection.v1.0.24351.shroo.ms.zip.

Sitename	Known Affils	Known Hardware/Software	Location	Siteops and Nukers/Notes
Low Lands (LL)[171]	MIB, dF, AMR, FFo			
Lost Shrine (LS)[172]	DMS, DNG, PRM	"Powered by Er33tD v 2.0" "T3 Speed" "32 GB"	Europe	
The Last Stand (LS)[173]				
Less Than Zero (LTZ)[174]	iNSOMNiA, PNC		USA	
The Lost World (LW)[175]	THUNDER			
Linux Unleashed (LXL)[176]	iNTUTiLS, digital.FACTORY, Digital District Couriers (ISO)	Presumed Linux	USA	
Lynx (LYNX)[177]	PREMIERE			

171 LL, "Low Lands Topsite (LL-low.lands.1999.09.08.nfo)," September 8, 1999, DeFacto2, warez.scene.nfo.collection.v1.0.24351.shroo.ms.zip.

172 LS, "Lost Shrine Topsite (LS-lost.shrine.1998.05.28.nfo)," May 28, 1998, DeFacto2, warez.scene.nfo.collection.v1.0.24351.shroo.ms.zip.

173 LS, "The Last Stand Topsite (LS-the.last.stand.1998.01.22.nfo)," January 22, 1998, DeFacto2, warez.scene.nfo.collection.v1.0.24351.shroo.ms.zip.

174 LTZ, "Less Than Zero Topsite (LTZ-less.than.zero.1997.11.02.nfo)," November 2, 1997, DeFacto2, warez.scene.nfo.collection.v1.0.24351.shroo.ms.zip.

175 LW, "The Lost World Topsite (LW-the.lost.world.1997.10.25.nfo)," October 25, 1997, DeFacto2, warez.scene.nfo.collection.v1.0.24351.shroo.ms.zip.

176 LXL, "Linux Unleashed Topsite (LXL-linux.unleashed.1999.06.29.nfo)," June 29, 1999, DeFacto2, warez.scene.nfo.collection.v1.0.24351.shroo.ms.zip.

177 LYNX, "Lynx Topsite (LYNX-lynx.1997.10.08.nfo)," October 8, 1997, DeFacto2, warez.scene.nfo.collection.v1.0.24351.shroo.ms.zip.

Sitename	Known Affils	Known Hardware/Software	Location	Siteops and Nukers/ Notes
Mutually Assured Destruction (MAD)[178]	TRPS, TiT-AINiUM, VLH		USA	WarezWulf, BoNzo, Swan, |Napaım|, Trillion
Menzoberranzan (MBZ)[179]	DEVOTiON, RAZOR 1911, DOD, iSOBELiX, PHEN-X, TEST		France[180]	Elves[181]
Murder Death Kill (MDK)[182]	FALLEN	"155 mbit" "13gb"	Europe	
Mercure (MERC)[183]	BS2000, CiFE, DOD, Esprit, LGD, TEST, TRG, UCF, KALiSTO, NBD, WackyISO, WeaPoN		France	PCFiL[184]

178 MAD, "Mutually Assured Destruction Topsite (MAD-mutually.assured.destruction.1999.01.29.nfo)," January 29, 1999, DeFacto2, warez.scene.nfo.collection.v1.0.24351.shroo.ms.zip.

179 MBZ, "Menzoberranzan Topsite (MBZ-menzoberranzan.1999.02.12.nfo)," February 12, 1999, DeFacto2, warez.scene.nfo.collection.v1.0.24351.shroo.ms.zip.

180 MBZ, "Menzoberranzan Topsite (MBZ-menzoberranzan.1999.01.03.nfo)," January 3, 1999, DeFacto2, warez.scene.nfo.collection.v1.0.24351.shroo.ms.zip.

181 MBZ, "Menzoberranzan Topsite (MBZ-menzoberranzan.XXXX.XX.00.nfo)," n.d., DeFacto2, warez.scene.nfo.collection.v1.0.24351.shroo.ms.zip.

182 MDK, "Murder Death Kill Topsite (MDK-murder.death.kill.XXXX.XX.00.nfo)," n.d., DeFacto2, warez.scene.nfo.collection.v1.0.24351.shroo.ms.zip.

183 MERC, "Mercure Topsite (MERC-mercure.1999.02.21.nfo)," February 21, 1999, DeFacto2, warez.scene.nfo.collection.v1.0.24351.shroo.ms.zip.

184 MERC, "Mercure Topsite (MERC-mercure.1998.01.16.nfo)," January 16, 1998, DeFacto2, warez.scene.nfo.collection.v1.0.24351.shroo.ms.zip.

Sitename	Known Affils	Known Hardware/Software	Location	Siteops and Nukers/ Notes
Magnetic Fields (MF)[185]	AMNESiA, DYNASTY, GLOBAL, REBELS, X-FORCE, 2000AD, MANiFEST, COUNCiL, XCRYPT	"100mbit"	Europe	
Manifest (MFT)[186]	DriNK OR DiE, APOCALYPSE		USA	
Midgaard (MG)[187]	LAXiTY, MFD, CLASS, DOD, EPTiSO, DEVi-ANCE, TFTiSO, VCD-EUROPE		Europe	
Madhaus (MH)[188]	HERITAGE	"35 GIGS"		Mad|Man
Made in Heaven (MIH)[189]	BLACK SQUADRON, FUSION, SKILL666, LUTIN	"52 GIGS" "DUAL T1"		
Monkey Island (MI)[190]				

185 MF, "Magnetic Fields Topsite (MF-magnetic.fields.2000.06.05.nfo)," June 5, 2000, DeFacto2, warez.scene.nfo.collection.v1.0.24351.shroo.ms.zip.

186 MFT, "Manifest Topsite (MFT-manifest.1997.10.21.nfo)," October 21, 1997, DeFacto2, warez.scene.nfo.collection.v1.0.24351.shroo.ms.zip.

187 MG, "Midgaard Topsite (MG-midgaard.2000.08.22.nfo)," August 22, 2000, DeFacto2, warez.scene.nfo.collection.v1.0.24351.shroo.ms.zip.

188 MH, "Madhaus Topsite (MH-madhaus.1997.09.22.nfo)," September 22, 1997, DeFacto2, warez.scene.nfo.collection.v1.0.24351.shroo.ms.zip.

189 MIH, "Made in Heaven Topsite (MIH-made.in.heaven.1999.05.21.nfo)," May 21, 1999, DeFacto2, warez.scene.nfo.collection.v1.0.24351.shroo.ms.zip.

190 MI, "Monkey Island Topsite (MI-monkey.island.1998.02.06.nfo)," February 6, 1998, DeFacto2, warez.scene.nfo.collection.v1.0.24351.shroo.ms.zip.

Sitename	Known Affils	Known Hardware/Software	Location	Siteops and Nukers/ Notes
Major Malfunction (MM)[191]	PWA, RTS, DEMON, DSI		Europe	
Mental Meltdown (MM)[192]				
Midnight Sun (MNS)[193]	DriNK OR DiE, THE FLAME ARROWS, REBELS, GLoW, DiViNE	"10MBits" "18 GiGz of Space"	Norway	
Mount Olympus (MO)[194]	LG, SWP, RFK, SiF, VLN, DL			DJ_Rican
Mos Eisley (MOS)[195]	EQUALiTY, RAZOR 1911, TFT, CORE	"EQLFTPD"	United Kingdom	
Mirage (MRG)[196]				
Mile Stone (MS)[197]	TFT, HYBRiD, SHOCK		Europe	

191 MM, "Major Malfunction Topsite (MM-major.malfunction.1999.07.29.nfo)," July 29, 1999, DeFacto2, warez.scene.nfo.collection.v1.0.24351.shroo.ms.zip.
192 MM, "Mental Meltdown Topsite (MM-mental.meltdown.1997.04.26.nfo)," April 26, 1997, DeFacto2, warez.scene.nfo.collection.v1.0.24351.shroo.ms.zip.
193 MNS, "Midnight Sun Topsite (MNS-midnight.sun.1999.01.23.nfo)," January 23, 1999, DeFacto2, warez.scene.nfo.collection.v1.0.24351.shroo.ms.zip.
194 MO, "Mount Olympus Topsite (MO-mount.olympus.1998.10.23.nfo)," October 23, 1998, DeFacto2, warez.scene.nfo.collection.v1.0.24351.shroo.ms.zip.
195 MOS, "Mos Eisley Topsite (MOS-mos.eisley.1998.03.25.nfo)," March 25, 1998, DeFacto2, warez.scene.nfo.collection.v1.0.24351.shroo.ms.zip.
196 MRG, "Mirage Topsite (MRG-mirage.1997.08.03.nfo)," August 3, 1997, DeFacto2, warez.scene.nfo.collection.v1.0.24351.shroo.ms.zip.
197 MS, "Mile Stone Topsite (MS-mile.stone.1997.07.04.nfo)," July 4, 1997, DeFacto2, warez.scene.nfo.collection.v1.0.24351.shroo.ms.zip.

Sitename	Known Affils	Known Hardware/Software	Location	Siteops and Nukers/Notes
Moonsine Vision (MSV)[198]	DEVOTiON, BliZZARD, PREMiERE			
Mist World (MW)[199]	RAZOR, RiSE, Dongle, MiLLENNiUM			
Maximum Power (MP)[200]	MiLLENNiUM			
Niobium (NBM)[201]	COUNCiL, ODDITY, CLASS, SHOCK, BACKLASH, BLiZZARD, OXYGEN			
Nocturne (NCT)[202]	DNG, MNM, RBS, SECT	"THE LATEST GLFTPD"		dajoint, odz, fjalar, fft, sitez
New Evil Incarnate (NEI)[203]	fATE	"71 Gigs"		Czar, Billy Bishop, Tornado

198 MSV, "Moonshine Vision Topsite (MSV-moonshine.vision.1998.08.26.nfo)," August 26, 1998, DeFacto2, warez.scene.nfo.collection.v1.0.24351.shroo.ms.zip.

199 MW, "Mist World Topsite (MW-mist.world.1998.06.04.nfo)," June 4, 1998, DeFacto2, warez.scene.nfo.collection.v1.0.24351.shroo.ms.zip.

200 MXP, "Maximum Power Topsite (MXP-maximum.power.1998.02.06.nfo)," February 6, 1998, DeFacto2, warez.scene.nfo.collection.v1.0.24351.shroo.ms.zip.

201 NBM, "Niobium Topsite (NBM-niobium.1999.02.14.nfo)," February 14, 1999, DeFacto2, warez.scene.nfo.collection.v1.0.24351.shroo.ms.zip.

202 NCT, "Nocturne Topsite (NCT-nocturne.1998.12.06.nfo)," December 6, 1998, DeFacto2, warez.scene.nfo.collection.v1.0.24351.shroo.ms.zip.

203 NEI, "New Evil Incarnate Topsite (NEI-new.evil.incarnate.1997.11.29.nfo)," November 29, 1997, DeFacto2, warez.scene.nfo.collection.v1.0.24351.shroo.ms.zip.

Sitename	Known Affils	Known Hardware/Software	Location	Siteops and Nukers/ Notes
Near Future 2000 (NF2K)[204]	TMG, DAMN,, VARiANCE, ARSENIC, PGC, HTG, SHOCK, ITN, AOD, COREPDA, RBSPDA, UCFPDA	"155Mb" "100Gb"	Europe	
Near Future (NF)[205]	OGN, SHOCK, PROS, PHS, WPN, DSI	"glftpd" "T3" "36 Go"[206]	Europe	
Neon Genesis (NGS)[207]	FBW, INTISO, KLN, SKL, AVN, RVL, BNW, GOH98, SCE, UCL, DED, NXS, NOVA, HIJACK	"ADSL" "27GIGS"		
Nihil (NHL)[208]	MOTiV8, SODOM, Hyrid		USA	
Narkos (NKS)[209]		"13 Mbits link" "Running FTP4ALL"		Cxxxxxx, hxxX, Jxx, Flxxxx, Sxxxx, Bxxxxx, Jxxxxxx

204NF2K, "Near Future 2000 Topsite (NF2K-near.future.2000.10.12.nfo)," October 12, 2000, DeFacto2, warez.scene.nfo.collection.v1.0.24351.shroo.ms.zip.

205NF, "Near Future Topsite (NF-near.future.1999.11.08.nfo)," November 8, 1999, DeFacto2, warez.scene.nfo.collection.v1.0.24351.shroo.ms.zip.

206NF, "Near Future Topsite (NF-near.future.1999.08.26.nfo)," August 26, 1999, DeFacto2, warez.scene.nfo.collection.v1.0.24351.shroo.ms.zip.

207NGS, "Neon Genesis Topsite (NGS-neon.genesis.XXXX.XX.00.nfo)," n.d., DeFacto2, warez.scene.nfo.collection.v1.0.24351.shroo.ms.zip.

208NHL, "Nihil Topsite (NHL-nihil.1997.03.02.nfo)," March 2, 1997, DeFacto2, warez.scene.nfo.collection.v1.0.24351.shroo.ms.zip.

209NKS, "Narkos Topsite (NKS-narkos.XXXX.XX.00.nfo)," n.d., DeFacto2, warez.scene.nfo.collection.v1.0.24351.shroo.ms.zip.

Sitename	Known Affils	Known Hardware/Software	Location	Siteops and Nukers/ Notes
Nemesis (NMS)[210]	PWA, RAZOR, TwiLiGHT, AMBiTiON, TRPS		United Kingdom	MindFink, Reznor, Slamdunk, Sminded, Akasha, d-unknown, Gal, Garoto, Mgd
Nos (NOS)[211]	SiEGE, ViCE, DNG, PARADOX		Europe	
Noptarus (NPT)[212]	Origin, Harlem		Canada	
Nuclear Dust (NUD)[213]	TFA, SLT, DiViNE, SHOCK, HazarD, CROSSFiRE, TMG	"T1 Speed" "12gb" "0-days only"	Czech Republic[214]	
Nexus (NXS)[215]	calibreX	"T3"		Zhrodague, utopian
Orbit Five (O5)[216]	NWO, Energy, UCF			
Omerta (OM)[217]	PHOENiX, KNO, FCN, TiCiN, RTSiSO		USA	

210 NMS, "Nemesis Topsite (NMS-nemesis.1998.09.08.nfo)," September 8, 1998, DeFacto2, warez.scene.nfo.collection.v1.0.24351.shroo.ms.zip.
211 NOS, "Nos Topsite (NOS-nos.1998.05.17.nfo)," May 17, 1998, DeFacto2, warez.scene.nfo.collection.v1.0.24351.shroo.ms.zip.
212 NPT, "Noptarus Topsite (NPT-noptarus.1999.02.03.nfo)," February 3, 1999, DeFacto2, warez.scene.nfo.collection.v1.0.24351.shroo.ms.zip.
213 NUD, "Nuclear Dust Topsite (NUD-nuclear.dust.2000.08.22.nfo)," August 22, 2000, DeFacto2, warez.scene.nfo.collection.v1.0.24351.shroo.ms.zip.
214 NUD, "Nuclear Dust Topsite (NUD-nuclear.dust.XXXX.XX.01.nfo)," n.d., DeFacto2, warez.scene.nfo.collection.v1.0.24351.shroo.ms.zip.
215 NXS, "Nexus Topsite (NXS-nexus.1998.05.07.nfo)," May 7, 1998, DeFacto2, warez.scene.nfo.collection.v1.0.24351.shroo.ms.zip.
216 O5, "Orbit Five Topsite (O5-orbit.five.1997.02.14.nfo)," February 14, 1997, DeFacto2, warez.scene.nfo.collection.v1.0.24351.shroo.ms.zip.
217 OM, "Omerta Topsite (OM-omerta.1999.12.31.nfo)," December 31, 1999, DeFacto2, warez.scene.nfo.collection.v1.0.24351.shroo.ms.zip.

Sitename	Known Affils	Known Hardware/Software	Location	Siteops and Nukers/ Notes
Operation Mindcrime (OM)[218]	iCT, CRC, XPC, Tha Mafia, ODV			Nite
Origin (ON)[219]	Energe, Dongle, Thunder Courier		USA	
Outskirts of Nowhere (OON)[220]	RBSiSO, MnMiSO, CaLiSO, DoWNLiNK, WLW	"T3" "336GB"		
Obscure Transmissions (OT)[221]	ZeroHour, eXcess, Microsux, eXpose, MiRAGE		USA	
Origin Underground (OU)[222]	Real Time Pirats, Sea Shell Comando, Associated Software Pirates, Naturraly Insane Couriers, Explosion, Demon	"10Mbit" "8 gig online"[223]		

218 OM, "Operation Mindcrime Topsite (OM-operation.mindcrime.1997.12.29.nfo)," December 29, 1997, DeFacto2, warez.scene.nfo.collection.v1.0.24351.shroo.ms.zip.

219 ON, "Origin Topsite (ON-origin.1997.12.04.nfo)," December 4, 1997, DeFacto2, warez.scene.nfo.collection.v1.0.24351.shroo.ms.zip.

220 OON, "Outskirts of Nowhere Topsite (OON-outskirts.of.nowhere.1998.12.15.nfo)," December 15, 1998, DeFacto2, warez.scene.nfo.collection.v1.0.24351.shroo.ms.zip.

221 OT, "Obscure Transmissions Topsite (OT-obscure.transmissions.1997.12.07.nfo)," December 7, 1997, DeFacto2, warez.scene.nfo.collection.v1.0.24351.shroo.ms.zip.

222 OU, "Origin Underground Topsite (OU-origin.underground.1998.01.13.nfo)," January 13, 1998, DeFacto2, warez.scene.nfo.collection.v1.0.24351.shroo.ms.zip.

223 OU, "Origin Underground Topsite (OU-origin.underground.1997.10.25.nfo)," October 25, 1997, DeFacto2, warez.scene.nfo.collection.v1.0.24351.shroo.ms.zip.

Sitename	Known Affils	Known Hardware/Software	Location	Siteops and Nukers/ Notes
Oxide (OX)[224]	Pentium, INjustice, Coalition97	"T?" "8GiGs"	USA	purning, PCX
Pier One Imports (P1)[225]	RVG, GNX, DMN, DEM, PCW	"T-3" "3 Gigs Online"		Rsvp2riP, code_zero, toxic2
Pandora's Box (PBOX)[226]	HERiTAGE, RAZOR 1911, dIGITAL.fACTORY, DTN	"10 mBiT" "18 gB"[227]	Europe	
Point Break (PB)[228]				
Pirates' Cove (PC)[229]	Reflux, Empure, Nemesis	"T3" "34 Gigs"		Comwood, Elmo, Nightsky
Plastik Dreams (PD)[230]	Dangerous, Premiere, Future, Pimps!, Insanity		USA	dA bALHEd, Stilgar
Playboys Dream (PD)[231]	RiSE, REBELS, MiSSION		Europe	TGC, XLOAD, SIRBUBU, ALEX[232]

224 OX, "Oxide Topsite (OX-oxide.1997.07.15.nfo)," July 15, 1997, DeFacto2, warez.scene.nfo.collection.v1.0.24351.shroo.ms.zip.

225 P1, "Pier One Imports Topsite (P1-pier.one.imports.1996.10.29.nfo)," October 29, 1996, DeFacto2, warez.scene.nfo.collection.v1.0.24351.shroo.ms.zip.

226 PBOX, "Pandora's Box Topsite (PBOX-pandoras.box.2000.07.23.nfo)," July 23, 2000, DeFacto2, warez.scene.nfo.collection.v1.0.24351.shroo.ms.zip.

227 PBOX, "Pandora's Box Topsite (PBOX-pandoras.box.1999.02.15.nfo)," February 15, 1999, DeFacto2, warez.scene.nfo.collection.v1.0.24351.shroo.ms.zip.

228 PB, "Point Break Topsite (PB-point.break.1998.12.12.nfo)," December 12, 1998, DeFacto2, warez.scene.nfo.collection.v1.0.24351.shroo.ms.zip.

229 PC, "Pirate's Cove Topsite (PC-pirates.cove.1997.03.02.nfo)," March 2, 1997, DeFacto2, warez.scene.nfo.collection.v1.0.24351.shroo.ms.zip.

230 PD, "Plastik Dreams Topsite (PD-plastik.dreams.1996.11.12.nfo)," November 12, 1996, DeFacto2, warez.scene.nfo.collection.v1.0.24351.shroo.ms.zip.

231 PD, "Playboys Dreams Topsite (PD-playboys.dream.1999.10.21.nfo)," October 21, 1999, DeFacto2, warez.scene.nfo.collection.v1.0.24351.shroo.ms.zip.

232 PD, "Playboys Dreams Topsite (PD-playboys.dream.1998.10.25.nfo)," October 25, 1998, DeFacto2, warez.scene.nfo.collection.v1.0.24351.shroo.ms.zip.

Sitename	Known Affils	Known Hardware/Software	Location	Siteops and Nukers/ Notes
Psychadelic Dreams (PD)[233]				
Paradox (PDX)[234]	MOD, FND, DWA, LFLISO, XCRYPT, REFLEX	"T1" "12+ GB"	Canada	djNghe, Jenlien, Subhuman[235]
Project Genocide (PG)[236]	demon, Warp98, TNO	"T3"	United Kingdom	]morph[, oleole, turrican, kaos[237]
Pirates' Hideout (PH)[238]	High Society, DiSTiNCT, Reideen, TSZ, Backlash, Divine, Electrocution, Stream		Europe	
Paradise Lost (PL)[239]	Future, Inspire			
Pirate Lair (PL)[240]	ILT, DWA, dP, BIOS		USA	DosE

233 PD, "Psychadelic Dreams Topsite (PD-psychadelic.dreams.1997.09.30.nfo)," September 30, 1997, DeFacto2, warez.scene.nfo.collection.v1.0.24351.shroo.ms.zip.

234 PDX, "Paradox Topsite (PDX-paradox.1999.02.26.nfo)," February 26, 1999, DeFacto2, warez.scene.nfo.collection.v1.0.24351.shroo.ms.zip.

235 PDX, "Paradox Topsite (PDX-paradox.1999.01.20.nfo)," January 20, 1999, DeFacto2, warez.scene.nfo.collection.v1.0.24351.shroo.ms.zip.

236 PG, "Project Genocide Topsite (PG-project.genocide.1998.08.21.nfo)," August 21, 1998, DeFacto2, warez.scene.nfo.collection.v1.0.24351.shroo.ms.zip.

237 PG, "Project Genocide Topsite (PG-project.genocide.1998.07.07.nfo)," July 7, 1998, DeFacto2, warez.scene.nfo.collection.v1.0.24351.shroo.ms.zip.

238 PH, "Pirates' Hideout Topsite (PH-pirates.hideout.XXXX.XX.00.nfo)," n.d., DeFacto2, warez.scene.nfo.collection.v1.0.24351.shroo.ms.zip.

239 PL, "Paradise Lost Topsite (PL-paradise.lost.1997.11.25.nfo)," November 25, 1997, DeFacto2, warez.scene.nfo.collection.v1.0.24351.shroo.ms.zip.

240 PL, "Pirate Lair Topsite (PL-pirate.lair.1999.08.03.nfo)," August 3, 1999, DeFacto2, warez.scene.nfo.collection.v1.0.24351.shroo.ms.zip.

Sitename	Known Affils	Known Hardware/Software	Location	Siteops and Nukers/ Notes
Primary Link (PL)[241]	RAPiER, SODOM, CLASS		Europe	
Prime Mover (PM)[242]	BLiZZARD, SiEGE, RefluX, RVL		USA	Maurauder, Cybrdeath, Novo, [NtDude], Factory, CptVorpal, Diablo[243]
Pelos Portal (PP)[244]	ESPRIT, EXPLOSION, INFECTED		Europe	
Piper's Pit (PP)[245]	CIFE, AODiSO, MAD, Silentchaos, Integrity	"Blazing Fast Cable Modem" "Lots of Gigs Online"		Piper, Fourth, Coba, NINE
Pussy Power (PP)[246]				
Phoenix Rising (PR)[247]	Carnage, PARADOX, CiFE, RTSiSO, LND, Warp, ViCE, BMI		United Kingdom	

241 PL, "Primary Link Topsite (PL-primary.link.1997.03.02.nfo)," March 2, 1997, DeFacto2, warez.scene.nfo.collection.v1.0.24351.shroo.ms.zip.

242 PM, "Prime Mover Topsite (PM-prime.mover.1998.08.13.nfo)," August 13, 1998, DeFacto2, warez.scene.nfo.collection.v1.0.24351.shroo.ms.zip.

243 PM, "Prime Mover Topsite (PM-prime.mover.1998.05.10.nfo)," May 10, 1998, DeFacto2, warez.scene.nfo.collection.v1.0.24351.shroo.ms.zip.

244 PP, "Pelos Portal Topsite (PP-pelos.portal.1998.04.22.nfo)," April 22, 1998, DeFacto2, warez.scene.nfo.collection.v1.0.24351.shroo.ms.zip.

245 PP, "Piper's Pit Topsite (PP-pipers.pit.1999.10.21.nfo)," October 21, 1999, DeFacto2, warez.scene.nfo.collection.v1.0.24351.shroo.ms.zip.

246 PP, "Pussy Power Topsite (PP-pussy.power.XXXX.XX.00.nfo)," n.d., DeFacto2, warez.scene.nfo.collection.v1.0.24351.shroo.ms.zip.

247 PR, "Phoenix Rising Topsite (PR-phoenix.rising.1999.10.12.nfo)," October 12, 1999, DeFacto2, warez.scene.nfo.collection.v1.0.24351.shroo.ms.zip.

Sitename	Known Affils	Known Hardware/Software	Location	Siteops and Nukers/ Notes
Parasite (PS)[248]	PREMiERE, GCRACK, DiViNE, MiRACLE		Europe	
Progressive (PS)[249]				
Possible Reality (PR)[250]	ITN, BLH, MiV, PDX, OMG, WLWMP3, MOD, CHR, NBD, NmE, STAR, reboot, CNCISO, GWL, VSN, GME2000, VIRA			
Prosperity (PST)[251]	THUNDER, PINNACLE, BLIZZARD			
Pzykotik Thoughts (PT)[252]				

248 PS, "Parasite Topsite (PS-parasite.1998.03.11.nfo)," March 11, 1998, DeFacto2, warez.scene.nfo.collection.v1.0.24351.shroo.ms.zip.
249 PS, "Progressive Topsite (PS-progressive.1997.03.11.nfo)," March 11, 1997, DeFacto2, warez.scene.nfo.collection.v1.0.24351.shroo.ms.zip.
250 PSR, "Possible Reality Topsite (PSR-possible.reality.XXXX.XX.00.nfo)," n.d., DeFacto2, warez.scene.nfo.collection.v1.0.24351.shroo.ms.zip.
251 PST, "Prosperity Topsite (PST-prosperity.1999.07.25.nfo)," July 25, 1997, DeFacto2, warez.scene.nfo.collection.v1.0.24351.shroo.ms.zip.
252 PT, "Pzykotik Thoughts Topsite (PT-pzykotik.thoughts.1997.05.19.nfo)," May 19, 1997, DeFacto2, warez.scene.nfo.collection.v1.0.24351.shroo.ms.zip.

Sitename	Known Affils	Known Hardware/Software	Location	Siteops and Nukers/Notes
Pre Whore House (PWH)[253]	NANGELS ON DRUGS, DiViNE, DRiNK OR DiE, PARADOX, DiGiTAL FACTORY, HERiTAGE, PHROZEN CREW, iNTENSiON, ZONE		Europe	
Quadcon (QC)[254]	RiSCiSO, Ranaissance, SHOCK, CoNCePT, RNG, GPF	"2 Separate T1 Systems" "43gb Main/ISO" "7gb Release"	USA	Katman, GaL, BanDiDo, Koyote, Poo, CorrupT
Quantum Reality (QR)[255]	RiSE, CELEBRE			
Restricted Area (RA)[256]	AMBiSO, CERTiSO, iSOBELiX, DTD, MNMiSO, VCDEUROPE	"3xT3" "54GIGS"	Czech Republic	Suvivant, KloWn__, Toaster, Bill, KIDSSHoW, Mackaque
Rebellion Authority (RAY)[257]	ESPRiT, BLiZZARD, PFT		Europe	

253 PWH, "Pre Whore House Topsite (PWH-pre.whore.house.2000.09.01.nfo)," September 1, 2000, DeFacto2, warez.scene.nfo.collection.v1.0.24351.shroo.ms.zip.

254 QC, "QuadCon Topsite (QC-quadcon.1998.02.09.nfo)," February 9, 1998, DeFacto2, warez.scene.nfo.collection.v1.0.24351.shroo.ms.zip.

255 QR, "Quantum Reality Topsite (QR-quantum.reality.1998.05.23.nfo)," May 23, 1998, DeFacto2, warez.scene.nfo.collection.v1.0.24351.shroo.ms.zip.

256 RA, "Restricted Area Topsite (RA-restricted.area.1999.06.13.nfo)," June 13, 1999, DeFacto2, warez.scene.nfo.collection.v1.0.24351.shroo.ms.zip.

257 RAY, "Rebellion Authority Topsite (RAY-rebellion.authority.1999.03.18.nfo)," March 18, 1999, DeFacto2, warez.scene.nfo.collection.v1.0.24351.shroo.ms.zip.

Sitename	Known Affils	Known Hardware/Software	Location	Siteops and Nukers/ Notes
The Rebellion (RBL)[258]				
Random Chaos (RC)[259]	O13, Motiv8, ORC, Corruption, Legendary, PCW		USA	
The Relic (RELIC)[260]	X-FORCE, ILLICIT		USA	DaliX, daLoner, Stinger, mandrake, mrsaint
Reality Flux (RFLUX)[261]	Phrozen Crew, Premiere	"linux powered" "t1"[262]	Canada	
Ratz Hole (RH)[263]	Razor 1911, Drink Or Die, Enterprise, We Love Warez, MOTiV8, TrPS		USA	Hackrat (Mike Nguyen)[264] shark[265]
Realms of Chaos (ROC)[266]	EQUALiTY, CORE, X-FoRCE, Dsi, DiViNE, FCN	"powered by EQLFTPD"		

258 RBL, "The Rebellion Topsite (RBL-the.rebellion.1997.02.19.nfo)," February 19, 1997, DeFacto2, warez.scene.nfo.collection.v1.0.24351.shroo.ms.zip.

259 RC, "Random Chaos Topsite (RC-random.chaos.1997.09.05.nfo)," September 5, 1997, DeFacto2, warez.scene.nfo.collection.v1.0.24351.shroo.ms.zip.

260 RELIC, "The Relic Topsite (RELIC-the.relic.1997.12.29.nfo)," December 29, 1997, DeFacto2, warez.scene.nfo.collection.v1.0.24351.shroo.ms.zip.

261 RFLUX, "Reality Flux Topsite (RFLUX-reality.flux.1998.07.03.nfo)," July 3, 1998, DeFacto2, warez.scene.nfo.collection.v1.0.24351.shroo.ms.zip.

262 RFLUX, "Reality Flux Topsite (RFLUX-reality.flux.1998.03.03.nfo)," March 3, 1998, DeFacto2, warez.scene.nfo.collection.v1.0.24351.shroo.ms.zip.

263 RH, "Ratz Hole Topsite (RH-ratzhole.1999.08.14.nfo)," August 14, 1999, DeFacto2, warez.scene.nfo.collection.v1.0.24351.shroo.ms.zip.

264 Paul Craig, Software Piracy Exposed (Rockland: Syngress, 2005), 197.

265 "Operation Buccaneer (operation_buccaneer.txt)," 2000, mp3scene.info.

266 ROC, "Realms of Chaos Topsite (ROC-realms.of.chaos.1998.11.23.nfo)," November 23, 1998, DeFacto2, warez.scene.nfo.collection.v1.0.24351.shroo.ms.zip.

Sitename	Known Affils	Known Hardware/Software	Location	Siteops and Nukers/ Notes
Relentless Pipeline (RP)[267]	PROPHECY, SHOCK	"10Mbit ConXtion" "15 Gigs Online" "glFtpD"	USA	_Hype_
RZ Soft (RZ)[268]		"10MB/s rFtpd" "21GB Online"		GL
Satan's Dome (SD)[269]	ESPRiT, MASSiVE, WARRiOR, RADiUM	"rFtpD" "15GiGz" "T3"[270]		D_S, Blas, nice
Sanitarium (SANI)[271]	SSC, MAD, Atomic-X	"31.2 GiGs"	USA[272]	Cdeth, GaL, Syn, CnC, Slashwolf
Secured Area (SA)[273]	OVK, AOD		Europe	JFM

267 RP, "Relentless Pipeline Topsite (RP-relentless.pipeline.1998.10.02.nfo)," October 2, 1998, DeFacto2, warez.scene.nfo.collection.v1.0.24351.shroo.ms.zip.

268 RZ, "RZ Soft Topsite (RZ-rzsoft.1997.12.22.nfo)," December 22, 1997, DeFacto2, warez.scene.nfo.collection.v1.0.24351.shroo.ms.zip.

269 SAD, "Satan's Dome Topsite (SAD-satans.dome.1998.08.30.nfo)," August 30, 1998, DeFacto2, warez.scene.nfo.collection.v1.0.24351.shroo.ms.zip.

270 SAD, "Satan's Dome Topsite (SAD-satans.dome.1998.07.29.nfo)," July 29, 1998, DeFacto2, warez.scene.nfo.collection.v1.0.24351.shroo.ms.zip.

271 SANI, "Sanitarium Topsite (SANI-sanitarium.1998.01.08.nfo)," January 8, 1998, DeFacto2, warez.scene.nfo.collection.v1.0.24351.shroo.ms.zip.

272 SANI, "Sanitarium Topsite (SANI-sanitarium.1997.06.13.nfo)," June 13, 1997, DeFacto2, warez.scene.nfo.collection.v1.0.24351.shroo.ms.zip.

273 SA, "Secured Area Topsite (SA-secured.area.1997.02.22.nfo)," February 22, 1997, DeFacto2, warez.scene.nfo.collection.v1.0.24351.shroo.ms.zip.

Sitename	Known Affils	Known Hardware/Software	Location	Siteops and Nukers/ Notes
San Bruno Club (SBC)[274]	PROPHECY, X-FORCE, CORPORATION, LAXiTY, ASiANPOWER	"50+ GigS" "Flaming DS-3"	USA[275]	SBC, dlThunder, warezone[276]
The Sandokan's Dome (SDK)[277]	AValoN, ORB, ZeroHouR, RoCkFoRcE, WTA, EsPRiT	"LiNuX 2.0.32" "P200" "64MB" [assumed RAM] "rFtpD v2.21B7" "10 Gigz" "10 Mbps"		BoLETo, DVST8, SANDOKAN, STRACAZZ
Solid Disruption (SD)[278]	LEGACY, WEAPON, F4CG		Europe	

274 SBC, "San Bruno Club Topsite (SBC-san.bruno.club.2000.02.26.nfo)," February 26, 2000, DeFacto2, warez.scene.nfo.collection.v1.0.24351.shroo.ms.zip.

275 SBC, "San Bruno Club Topsite (SBC-san.bruno.club.1999.12.27.nfo)," December 27, 1999, DeFacto2, warez.scene.nfo.collection.v1.0.24351.shroo.ms.zip.

276 There is some confusion in the archive, but I believe that San Bruno Club was previously known only as San Bruno, hence the merge here of NFOs for sites with different abbreviations. SB, "San Bruno Topsite (SB-san.bruno.1998.07.01.nfo)," July 1, 1998, DeFacto2, warez.scene.nfo.collection.v1.0.24351.shroo.ms.zip.

277 SDK, "The Sandokan's Dome Topsite (SDK-the.sandokans.dome.1998.02.25.nfo)," February 25, 1998, DeFacto2, warez.scene.nfo.collection.v1.0.24351.shroo.ms.zip.

278 SD, "Solid Disruption Topsite (SD-solid.disruption.1998.06.27.nfo)," June 27, 1998, DeFacto2, warez.scene.nfo.collection.v1.0.24351.shroo.ms.zip.

Sitename	Known Affils	Known Hardware/Software	Location	Siteops and Nukers/Notes
Surface Defect (SD)[279]	WARRIOR, ECG, ACE, CTW, Nexus	"T3" "18 gigs"		Hypocrisy, The_DoN, Culture Site rules: [S]ite [R]ules [01] Linfxp/Pftp/Scripting are banned [02] No Foreign/ISO Uploads [03] No Bookware/Freeware/Shareware [04] Beta's/Winbuilds okay [05] Alpha's are not allowed[280]
Savage Exile (SE)[281]	ILLICIT, FPS, OP CRITICAL ILLUSION	"TOO MUCH SPACE" "FAST SITE"		
Sonic Empire (SE)[282]	ZYLON, ESTEEM, ASSAULT, PGC			
Silicon Exchange (SEX)[283]	GCRACK, SCuM, TLT, RTN			

279 SD, "Surface Defect Topsite (SD-surface.defect.1998.09.25.nfo)," September 25, 1998, DeFacto2, warez.scene.nfo.collection.v1.0.24351.shroo.ms.zip.

280 SD, "Surface Defect Topsite (SD-surface.defect.1998.06.06.nfo)," June 6, 1998, DeFacto2, warez.scene.nfo.collection.v1.0.24351.shroo.ms.zip.

281 SE, "Savage Exile Topsite (SE-savage.exile.1997.10.25.nfo)," October 25, 1997, DeFacto2, warez.scene.nfo.collection.v1.0.24351.shroo.ms.zip.

282 SE, "Sonic Empire Topsite (SE-sonic.empire.1998.01.03.nfo)," January 3, 1998, DeFacto2, warez.scene.nfo.collection.v1.0.24351.shroo.ms.zip.

283 SEX, "Silicon Exchange Topsite (SEX-silicon.exchange.1999.05.24.nfo)," May 24, 1999, DeFacto2, warez.scene.nfo.collection.v1.0.24351.shroo.ms.zip.

Sitename	Known Affils	Known Hardware/Software	Location	Siteops and Nukers/ Notes
Springfield (SF)[284]	Kryptic, Heritage, Karma, GdW			Mr Burnz, maloo, stuph
Shadow Gate (SG)[285]	CertISO, High Voltage, Millenium, PHXiSO, RobinHood, Warez4Ever	"Blazing T3" "45 GBs"		
Shike (SHK)[286]				T3Mace, Mc
The Cellar (SLR)[287]	KAC, F4CG, Warpon, PWA, MiLLENiUM, ORiGiN		USA	Anthrax, Ruskin, MindFink, CoRRoS|oN, dev, MindFink, CoRRoS|oN, dARKsUN, Red_Obelisk, Akasha, Red_Obelisk, FaithMuse, Caster[288]
Sand Land (SL)[289]	PWA, CLASS, TFT, RC		Europe	
Socrates (SOC)[290]	REQUEST TO SEND	"13GIGS" "T3"		Chinese Eyes, NiNJA, Count Zero, Diztorted, Ordnance

284 SF, "Springfield Topsite (SF-springfield.1997.04.06.nfo)," April 6, 1997, DeFacto2, warez.scene.nfo.collection.v1.0.24351.shroo.ms.zip.
285 SG, "Shadow Gate Topsite (SG-shadow.gate.1999.04.21.nfo)," April 21, 1999, DeFacto2, warez.scene.nfo.collection.v1.0.24351.shroo.ms.zip.
286 SHK, "Shike Topsite (SHK-shike.1997.05.28.nfo)," May 28, 1997, DeFacto2, warez.scene.nfo.collection.v1.0.24351.shroo.ms.zip.
287 SLR, "The Cellar Topsite (SLR-the.cellar.1998.11.08.nfo)," November 8, 1998, DeFacto2, warez.scene.nfo.collection.v1.0.24351.shroo.ms.zip.
288 SLR, "The Cellar Topsite (SLR-the.cellar.1998.09.07.nfo)," September 7, 1998, DeFacto2, warez.scene.nfo.collection.v1.0.24351.shroo.ms.zip.
289 SL, "Sand Land Topsite (SL-sand.land.1997.10.29.nfo)," October 29, 1997, DeFacto2, warez.scene.nfo.collection.v1.0.24351.shroo.ms.zip.
290 SOC, "Socrates Topsite (SOC-socrates.1997.11.12.nfo)," November 12, 1997, DeFacto2, warez.scene.nfo.collection.v1.0.24351.shroo.ms.zip.

Sitename	Known Affils	Known Hardware/Software	Location	Siteops and Nukers/Notes
South of Heaven (SOH)[291]	Dark Star, Ambition Courier			
The Spade (SPADE)[292]	Deviance iSO, REBELS, ECG iSO, THE FLAME ARROWS iSO	"10MBits" "30 GiGz"	Norway	
Secret Paradise (SP)[293]				
Shattered Reality (SR)[294]	hv98, Control 98, Warez4Ever, HUNTERz, united warez, bi98, DWA, PrimeNemisis	"10mb CoNNeCTion" "18 GiGZ"		Warezguy, krumpet
Silly Symphonies (SS)[295]	MiLLENNiUM, Drink or Die, DARK SiDE		Finland	
Stairway to Heaven (STH)[296]	CLASS, PiRATES WiTH ATTiTUDES		Europe	cq, br, gi, he, fh[297]

291 SOH, "South of Heaven Topsite (SOH-south.of.heaven.1998.08.27.nfo)," August 27, 1998, DeFacto2, warez.scene.nfo.collection.v1.0.24351.shroo.ms.zip.

292 SPADE, "The Spade Topsite (SPADE-the.spade.1999.01.23.nfo)," January 23, 1999, DeFacto2, warez.scene.nfo.collection.v1.0.24351.shroo.ms.zip.

293 SP, "Secret Paradise Topsite (SP-secret.paradise.1998.08.30.nfo)," August 30, 1998, DeFacto2, warez.scene.nfo.collection.v1.0.24351.shroo.ms.zip.

294 SR, "Shattered Reality Topsite (SR-shattered.reality.1998.10.05.nfo)," October 5, 1998, DeFacto2, warez.scene.nfo.collection.v1.0.24351.shroo.ms.zip.

295 SS, "Silly Symphonies Topsite (SS-silly.symphonies.1998.05.13.nfo)," May 13, 1998, DeFacto2, warez.scene.nfo.collection.v1.0.24351.shroo.ms.zip.

296 STH, "Stairway to Heaven Topsite (STH-stairway.to.heaven.1999.08.27.nfo)," August 27, 1999, DeFacto2, warez.scene.nfo.collection.v1.0.24351.shroo.ms.zip.

297 STH, "Stairway to Heaven Topsite (STH-stairway.to.heaven.1997.02.16.nfo)," February 16, 1997, DeFacto2, warez.scene.nfo.collection.v1.0.24351.shroo.ms.zip.

Sitename	Known Affils	Known Hardware/Software	Location	Siteops and Nukers/ Notes
Sun (SUN)[298]	ExodusS, TMG			
Spice World (SW)[299]	DF, Harlem, LG		Europe	
Syn City (SYN)[300]	Razor 1911, MiLLENNiUM, Drink Or Die, XForce, RISC, AMN, Rapier, DEV, EMP, DIV, MNC, Fate	"T3" "Cisco4000" "100MB-TX" "15GB"[301]		Synapse, Doobie
Storm Zone (SZ)[302]	DWA, Rezent, DW, UW, BIOS, MIB, PULSAR	"54gb" "3mbit cable modem"		Stormeist, Gramonsm SoNiK, Spaten, BigLoo, Riptide
Talinc (TAL)[303]	AMBiSO, AMBiTiON, iCOiSO, FALLEN, PARADiGM, PiNNACLE, Dsi, SLT		Europe	
The Ancient Ruins (TAR)[304]	DW98, UFC2000, TBS, NIC, FATE			

298 SUN, "Sun Topsite (SUN-sun.1999.11.09.nfo)," November 9, 1999, DeFacto2, warez.scene.nfo.collection.v1.0.24351.shroo.ms.zip.
299 SW, "Spice World Topsite (SW-spice.world.1998.06.21.nfo)," June 21, 1998, DeFacto2, warez.scene.nfo.collection.v1.0.24351.shroo.ms.zip.
300 SYN, "Syn City Topsite (SYN-syncity.1998.08.27.nfo)," August 27, 1998, DeFacto2, warez.scene.nfo.collection.v1.0.24351.shroo.ms.zip.
301 SYN, "Syn City Topsite (SYN-syncity.1996.11.04.nfo)," November 4, 1996, DeFacto2, warez.scene.nfo.collection.v1.0.24351.shroo.ms.zip.
302 SZ, "Storm Zone Topsite (SZ-storm.zone.1999.09.17.nfo)," September 17, 1999, DeFacto2, warez.scene.nfo.collection.v1.0.24351.shroo.ms.zip.
303 TAL, "Talinc Topsite (TAL-talinc.1999.12.28.nfo)," December 28, 1999, DeFacto2, warez.scene.nfo.collection.v1.0.24351.shroo.ms.zip.
304 TAR, "The Ancient Ruins Topsite (TAR-the.ancient.ruins.1998.03.25.nfo)," March 25, 1998, DeFacto2, warez.scene.nfo.collection.v1.0.24351.shroo.ms.zip.

Sitename	Known Affils	Known Hardware/Software	Location	Siteops and Nukers/Notes
The Armageddon (TA)[305]	RBS, ATN, DMS, RSR, AMB	"T3-SPEED" "XX-GiGZ"		
The Black Box (TBB)[306]	AMBiSO, CERTiSO, PROPHECY, VCDUEUROPE			Survivant, KLoWn___, Flying-Toaster, hyd
Tera-Bit-Fit (TBF)[307]	AVALON	"8 GiGZ"	USA	THE AVALON MIRRORMEN
Turbulence (TBL)[308]	KIN, DMS, ZhR, hV, dWA, HT, FND, ODT			
The Bottomless Pit (TBP)[309]	Natosoft, SiEGE, Warp98	"T3" "23GIG"	USA	
The Boxer Rebellion (TBR)[310]	Drink or Die, RTS			

305 TA, "The Armageddon Topsite (TA-the.armageddon.1998.08.05.nfo)," August 5, 1998, DeFacto2, warez.scene.nfo.collection.v1.0.24351.shroo.ms.zip.
306 TBB, "The Black Box Topsite (TBB-the.black.box.1999.05.27.nfo)," May 27, 1999, DeFacto2, warez.scene.nfo.collection.v1.0.24351.shroo.ms.zip.
307 TBF, "Tera-Bit-Fit Topsite (TBF-tera.bit.fit.1999.01.15.nfo)," January 15, 1999, DeFacto2, warez.scene.nfo.collection.v1.0.24351.shroo.ms.zip.
308 TBL, "Turbulence Topsite (TBL-turbulence.1998.08.11.nfo)," August 11, 1998, DeFacto2, warez.scene.nfo.collection.v1.0.24351.shroo.ms.zip.
309 TBP, "The Bottomless Pit Topsite (TBP-the.bottomless.pit.1998.07.05.nfo)," July 5, 1998, DeFacto2, warez.scene.nfo.collection.v1.0.24351.shroo.ms.zip.
310 TBR, "The Boxer Rebellion Topsite (TBR-the.boxer.rebellion.1998.08.23.nfo)," August 23, 1998, DeFacto2, warez.scene.nfo.collection.v1.0.24351.shroo.ms.zip.

Sitename	Known Affils	Known Hardware/Software	Location	Siteops and Nukers/Notes
The Corner Deli (TCD)[311]	Thunder, Premiere, Global Crackers		USA	
The Center (TC)[312]	Backlash, GWA, Council		Germany	
Trash City (TC)[313]	SHOCK, FRONTiER, EXECUIVE, iNTENSITY, TFA		USA	Chrys, Dev, Gal, Rockz, Havok, CyberWar, AcidApple, X-Frog, Officedog[314]

311 TCD, "The Corner Deli Topsite (TCD-the.corner.deli.1998.01.31.nfo)," January 31, 1998, DeFacto2, warez.scene.nfo.collection.v1.0.24351.shroo.ms.zip.

312 TC, "The Center Topsite (TC-the.center.1997.10.24.nfo)," October 24, 1997, DeFacto2, warez.scene.nfo.collection.v1.0.24351.shroo.ms.zip.

313 TC, "Trash City Topsite (TC-trash.city.1998.03.02.nfo)," March 2, 1998, DeFacto2, warez.scene.nfo.collection.v1.0.24351.shroo.ms.zip.

314 TC, "Trash City Topsite (TC-trash.city.1998.01.23.nfo)," January 23, 1998, DeFacto2, warez.scene.nfo.collection.v1.0.24351.shroo.ms.zip.

Sitename	Known Affils	Known Hardware/Software	Location	Siteops and Nukers/ Notes
The Digital Afterlife (TDA)[315]		Sitering. FUBAR: USA, T3 NetherWorld: Europe, T1+ Da Crew, USA, T3 Kinetics, USA, T1 Gothom, USA, T1 Abyss, USA, T1 Bomb, 2xT1 Hall of Gnana, USA, T1 TGU, USA, T3	USA, Europe	Crimson, Renfro, Doc_X, phoxphyre, icu812, M-80, Deadchane, Phenomeno, Bigjilm, Grinder_, Demented, Dav312, WildWendy, cyphen, Net^king, Statics, observer
The Dragons Den (TDD)[316]	Millennium Courier, Eclipse Interactive		USA	Daphantm, Seven, Rare2[317]

315 TDA, "The Digital Afterlife Topsite Ring (TDA-the.digital.afterlife.1997.01.20.nfo)."
316 TDD, "The Dragons Den Topsite (TDD-the.dragons.den.1997.07.17.nfo)," July 17, 1997, DeFacto2, warez.scene.nfo.collection.v1.0.24351.shroo.ms.zip.
317 TDD, "The Dragons Den Topsite (TDD-the.dragons.den.1997.07.15.nfo)," July 15, 1997, DeFacto2, warez.scene.nfo.collection.v1.0.24351.shroo.ms.zip.

Sitename	Known Affils	Known Hardware/Software	Location	Siteops and Nukers/ Notes
The Dawg House (TDH)[318]	PHC, Dynamic, DST, HTG, EPI, Motiv8, FCC, FCN, TDA, Rapid		USA	SKYDEMON, SHMO
The Digital Harm (TDH)[319]	SSC, LIQUID, SHOCK, ADDICTION, NZPD, THIEVES, RISE, UCU			neotericE
The Desert Inn (TDI)[320]	LNDiSO, Rock-Force, FBW		USA	
The Dead Land (TDL)[321]	R.T.S., STONHENGE, DIVINE, SYNICLE		USA	
The Diamond Mind (TDM)[322]	SHOCK, AMNESIA, RAZOR	"granolaFTP"		MikDiamon, Slice-

318 TDH, "The Dawg House Topsite (TDH-the.dawg.house.1997.05.25.nfo)," May 25, 1997, DeFacto2, warez.scene.nfo.collection.v1.0.24351.shroo.ms.zip.
319 TDH, "The Digital Harm Topsite (TDH-the.digital.harm.1997.10.25.nfo)," October 25, 1997, DeFacto2, warez.scene.nfo.collection.v1.0.24351.shroo.ms.zip.
320 TDI, "The Desert Inn Topsite (TDI-the.desert.inn.1999.07.21.nfo)," July 21, 1999, DeFacto2, warez.scene.nfo.collection.v1.0.24351.shroo.ms.zip.
321 TDL, "The Dead Land Topsite (TDL-the.dead.lands.1998.05.25.nfo)," May 25, 1998, DeFacto2, warez.scene.nfo.collection.v1.0.24351.shroo.ms.zip.
322 TDM, "The Diamond Mine Topsite (TDM-the.diamond.mine.1997.01.10.nfo)," January 10, 1997, DeFacto2, warez.scene.nfo.collection.v1.0.24351.shroo.ms.zip.

Sitename	Known Affils	Known Hardware/Software	Location	Siteops and Nukers/ Notes
The Dawg Pound (TDP)[323]	CWS, FBW, Demise, RockForce, StyLe, SynicaL, AOD		USA[324]	^DaWg^, hoax, doors, explorer, himie009, kronder, vylent
The Devil's Pit (TDP)[325]	WaRP, GLoW, UCF, DEViOUS, TE, Future	"T3" "34GB"	USA	HSOBIC, ScabZ, necrosis, Xndo, Raskah
The Dark Site (TDS)[326]	RAPiD, GPF, Heritage		Canada	
The Dome (TD)[327]	PGC	"T3" "20 Gigabytes"	Canada	
The Drop Zone (TDZ)[328]	FPS, ILLICIT, IMPACT, COAL	"tEEtHREE"	USA	

323 TDP, "The Dawg Pound Topsite (TDP-the.dawg.pound.1998.05.02.nfo)," May 2, 1998, DeFacto2, warez.scene.nfo.collection.v1.0.24351.shroo.ms.zip.
324 TDP, "The Dawg Pound Topsite (TDP-the.dawg.pound.XXXX.XX.00.nfo)," n.d., DeFacto2, warez.scene.nfo.collection.v1.0.24351.shroo.ms.zip.
325 TDP, "The Devil's Pit Topsite (TDP-the.devils.pit.1999.01.07.nfo)," January 7, 1999, DeFacto2, warez.scene.nfo.collection.v1.0.24351.shroo.ms.zip.
326 TDS, "The Dark Site Topsite (TDS-the.dark.site.1997.06.29.nfo)," June 29, 1997, DeFacto2, warez.scene.nfo.collection.v1.0.24351.shroo.ms.zip.
327 TD, "The Dome Topsite (TD-the.dome.1998.08.31.nfo)," August 31, 1998, DeFacto2, warez.scene.nfo.collection.v1.0.24351.shroo.ms.zip.
328 TDZ, "The Drop Zone Topsite (TDZ-the.drop.zone.1997.11.03.nfo)," November 3, 1997, DeFacto2, warez.scene.nfo.collection.v1.0.24351.shroo.ms.zip.

Sitename	Known Affils	Known Hardware/Software	Location	Siteops and Nukers/Notes
The Third Total Eclipse (TE3)[329]	DSC, DF, HiD, LiVeEdgE			
The Electric Circus (TEC)[330]	AXiS, RoK, Rebels		Europe	Gromit, G-Bit, Druggy, Liquide
Trans Electronic Light (TEL)[331]	The Force Team			
The Temple (TEMP)[332]	CLASS, RELIANCE		USA	

329 TE3, "The Third Total Eclipse Topsite (TE3-total.eclipse.three.1999.07.09.nfo)," July 9, 1999, DeFacto2, warez.scene.nfo.collection.v1.0.24351.shroo.ms.zip.

330 TEC, "The Electric Circus Topsite (TEC-the.electric.circus.1998.08.27.nfo)," August 27, 1998, DeFacto2, warez.scene.nfo.collection.v1.0.24351.shroo.ms.zip.

331 TEL, "Trans Electric Light Topsite (TEL-trans.electronic.light.1997.07.16.nfo)," July 16, 1997, DeFacto2, warez.scene.nfo.collection.v1.0.24351.shroo.ms.zip.

332 TEMP, "The Temple Topsite (TEMP-the.temple.1997.09.21.nfo)," September 21, 1997, DeFacto2, warez.scene.nfo.collection.v1.0.24351.shroo.ms.zip.

Sitename	Known Affils	Known Hardware/Software	Location	Siteops and Nukers/ Notes
The Ether Net (TEN)[333]	ADDCTION [sic], MYTH, TRPS, IPA, 2000AD, ECLIPSE, CORE, RBSiSO, iNTUTiLS, XCRYPT, LAXiTY, WLW,	"174 GIG" "10MBIT"	USA	
The Enterprise (TE)[334]	INTENSITY, EXPLOSiON, TRPS		USA	
Total Eclipse (TE)[335]				Jacket, ^_TE_^, Arsenel, Kang6902, Vampire, C6, Endymiom, Leslie
The Fried Rabbit (TFR)[336]				
The Flash (TF)[337]	LND, RTS	"TEE THREE" "6.5 GIGS"	USA	

333 TEN, "The Ether Net Topsite (TEN-the.ether.net.XXXX.XX.00.nfo)," n.d., DeFacto2, warez.scene.nfo.collection.v1.0.24351.shroo.ms.zip.

334 TE, "The Enterprise Topsite (TE-the.enterprise.1998.05.13.nfo)," May 13, 1998, DeFacto2, warez.scene.nfo.collection.v1.0.24351.shroo.ms.zip.

335 TE, "Total Eclipse Topsite (TE-total.eclipse.1998.01.11.nfo)," January 11, 1998, DeFacto2, warez.scene.nfo.collection.v1.0.24351.shroo.ms.zip.

336 TFR, "The Fried Rabbit Topsite (TFR-the.fried.rabbit.1998.09.09.nfo)," September 9, 1998, DeFacto2, warez.scene.nfo.collection.v1.0.24351.shroo.ms.zip.

337 TF, "The Flash Topsite (TF-the.flash.1997.01.17.nfo)," January 17, 1997, DeFacto2, warez.scene.nfo.collection.v1.0.24351.shroo.ms.zip.

Sitename	Known Affils	Known Hardware/Software	Location	Siteops and Nukers/ Notes
The Gateway (TG)[338]	ENTiTY, REFLUX, PROPHECY	"20 GiGS" "100 mbit"	USA	X, Dee, Hazzy, Phiber, Dream, BasecW, Sting, Tinywulf, Gal[339]
The Haven (TH)[340]	EMPiRE, X-FORCE			
Tragic Kingdom (TK)[341]	NvC, X-Force	"T3" "12 Gigz"		Skydemon, SHmo, Icu812[342]
The Toilet (TLT)[343]	SWP, DARKSTAR, Tension, LG, MaD, fATE, WLW		USA	
The Mother Superior (TMS)[344]	ORiGIN, KAC, PREMiERE, DiMENSION		USA	

338 TG, "The Gateway Topsite (TG-the.gateway.1999.01.10.nfo)," January 10, 1999, DeFacto2, warez.scene.nfo.collection.v1.0.24351.shroo.ms.zip.

339 TG, "The Gateway Topsite (TG-the.gateway.XXXX.XX.00.nfo)," n.d., DeFacto2, warez.scene.nfo.collection.v1.0.24351.shroo.ms.zip.

340 TH, "The Haven Topsite (TH-the.haven.1998.08.30.nfo)," August 30, 1998, DeFacto2, warez.scene.nfo.collection.v1.0.24351.shroo.ms.zip.

341 TK, "Tragic Kingdom Topsite (TK-tragic.kingdom.1997.06.24.nfo)," June 24, 1997, DeFacto2, warez.scene.nfo.collection.v1.0.24351.shroo.ms.zip.

342 TK, "Tragic Kingdom Topsite (TK-tragic.kingdom.1997.06.06.nfo)," June 6, 1997, DeFacto2, warez.scene.nfo.collection.v1.0.24351.shroo.ms.zip.

343 TLT, "The Toilet Topsite (TLT-the.toilet.1998.12.13.nfo)," December 13, 1998, DeFacto2, warez.scene.nfo.collection.v1.0.24351.shroo.ms.zip.

344 TMS, "The Mother Superior Topsite (TMS-the.mother.superior.1999.02.13.nfo)," February 13, 1999, DeFacto2, warez.scene.nfo.collection.v1.0.24351.shroo.ms.zip.

Sitename	Known Affils	Known Hardware/Software	Location	Siteops and Nukers/ Notes
Terrible Mistake (TM)[345]	RPG, FUSION, WARP, DARKSTAR, PSYCHO		Russia	
The Matrix (TM)[346]	BLC, BSC, BNW, Natosoft, RockForce			
The Number of the Beast (TNB)[347]	TeKno Rage, PiraSofT, SToRM, MOTiV8, EsTeeM, File PRoPuLSiON SySTeMs	"19.5 GiGaByTeS" "266 BlaZing MhZ" "WAR-FTPd"	USA	LaZaRus
The New Forge (TNF)[348]	REVOLT, MOTiV8, TUR		USA	Eyes22, KoraK, riches, Goliath^
The Neverland (TNL)[349]	Natosoft, FBW, Warez Central, Reflex, Threat, MOD, Nytekill	"blazing t3" "22GB" "Linux 2.0.36" "Glftpd 1.18"[350]	West Coast USA	Papa, Eins, Dave/ Gniz, Blade

345 TM, "Terrible Mistake Topsite (TM-terrible.mistake.1999.02.13.nfo)," February 13, 1999, DeFacto2, warez.scene.nfo.collection.v1.0.24351.shroo.ms.zip.
346 TM, "The Matrix Topsite (TM-the.matrix.1999.09.25.nfo)," September 25, 1999, DeFacto2, warez.scene.nfo.collection.v1.0.24351.shroo.ms.zip.
347 TNB, "The Number of the Beast Topsite (TNB-the.number.of.the.beast.1997.10.21.nfo)," October 21, 1997, DeFacto2, warez.scene.nfo.collection.v1.0.24351.shroo.ms.zip.
348 TNF, "The New Forge Topsite (TNF-the.new.forge.1997.06.12.nfo)," June 12, 1997, DeFacto2, warez.scene.nfo.collection.v1.0.24351.shroo.ms.zip.
349 TNL, "The Neverland Topsite (TNL-the.neverland.1999.02.12.nfo)," February 12, 1999, DeFacto2, warez.scene.nfo.collection.v1.0.24351.shroo.ms.zip.
350 TNL, "The Neverland Topsite (TNL-the.never.land.1999.04.14.nfo)," April 14, 1999, DeFacto2, warez.scene.nfo.collection.v1.0.24351.shroo.ms.zip.

Sitename	Known Affils	Known Hardware/Software	Location	Siteops and Nukers/ Notes
The Nympho Temple (TNT)[351]	SiEGE, CLASS		USA	
The Orion Syndicate (TOS)[352]	SiEGE, CLASS, DEVOTiON, PGC, EviL			devestator, garoto, sj
Technology Overload (TO)[353]	SYNTHESiS, GLoW, TPC, TRPS, DiVINE	"10MBITS" "17 GiGS"	USA	techfuzz, CraZy-FiRE[354]
Temple of Torture (TOT)[355]	ESPRiT, CRYSTAL, GWA, RDC, 2000AD, CNC, DEMON, TPC		Europe	

351 TNT, "The Nympho Temple Topsite (TNT-the.nympho.temple.1997.07.12.nfo)," July 12, 1997, DeFacto2, warez.scene.nfo.collection.v1.0.24351.shroo.ms.zip.

352 TOS, "The Orion Syndicate Topsite (TOS-the.orion.syndicate.1999.03.29.nfo)," March 29, 1999, DeFacto2, warez.scene.nfo.collection.v1.0.24351.shroo.ms.zip.

353 TO, "Technology Overload Topsite (TO-technology.overload.1998.02.25.nfo)," February 25, 1998, DeFacto2, warez.scene.nfo.collection.v1.0.24351.shroo.ms.zip.

354 TO, "Technology Overload Topsite (TO-technology.overload.1998.02.10.nfo)," February 10, 1998, DeFacto2, warez.scene.nfo.collection.v1.0.24351.shroo.ms.zip.

355 TOT, "Temple of Torture Topsite (TOT-temple.of.torture.1999.04.24.nfo)," April 24, 1999, DeFacto2, warez.scene.nfo.collection.v1.0.24351.shroo.ms.zip.

Sitename	Known Affils	Known Hardware/Software	Location	Siteops and Nukers/ Notes
The Pharmacy (TPH)[356]		"T1+"		
The Prophecy (TP)[357]	MnM, CORE, DOD	"XFTP'd" "T3/DS3"[358]	USA	Sxxxxx, Kxxxx ,Exxxx[359]
The Pyramid (TP)[360]	MOONSHINE, LND, MYTH, SOLiTUDE, SCAR, dF, PROPHECY, GWA, HERITAGE, 2000AD, EPTiSO, DEViANCE, TFL, PARADOX, VCD-EUROPE	"OC48 Connection" "550GiG"	South Korea[361]	

356 TPH, "The Pharmacy Topsite (TPH-the.pharmacy.1998.07.27.nfo)," July 27, 1998, DeFacto2, warez.scene.nfo.collection.v1.0.24351.shroo.ms.zip.

357 TP, "The Prophecy Topsite (TP-the.prophecy.1998.03.11.nfo)," March 11, 1998, DeFacto2, warez.scene.nfo.collection.v1.0.24351.shroo.ms.zip.

358 TP, "The Prophecy Topsite (TP-the.prophecy.1997.08.01.nfo)," August 1, 1997, DeFacto2, warez.scene.nfo.collection.v1.0.24351.shroo.ms.zip.

359 TP, "The Prophecy Topsite (TP-the.prophecy.XXXX.XX.00.nfo)," n.d., DeFacto2, warez.scene.nfo.collection.v1.0.24351.shroo.ms.zip.

360 TP, "The Pyramid Topsite (TP-the.pyramid.2000.04.28.nfo)," April 28, 2000, DeFacto2, warez.scene.nfo.collection.v1.0.24351.shroo.ms.zip.

361 TP, "The Pyramid Topsite (TP-the.pyramid.1999.12.13.nfo)," December 13, 1999, DeFacto2, warez.scene.nfo.collection.v1.0.24351.shroo.ms.zip.

Sitename	Known Affils	Known Hard-ware/Software	Location	Siteops and Nukers/ Notes
The Raging Monkey (TRM)[362]		ftp4all[363]		
The Rising Sun (TRS)[364]	SiEGE, CLASS	"T3 SPEED" "10 GiGS" "RFTPD"	USA	Maloo, KRS-ONE[365]
The River (TR)[366]	MNM, RISE, THG		USA	
The Rock (TR)[367]	BLIZZARD, ORIGIN, PDA-ZONE, PWA, PREMIERE		USA	
The Sadistic Grand-daughter (TSG)[368]	Absolut, Esprit, Premiere, Prophecy, The Players Club		Europe	

362 TRM, "The Raging Monkey Topsite (TRM-the.raging.monkey.1997.09.18.nfo)," September 18, 1999, DeFacto2, warez.scene.nfo.collection.v1.0.24351.shroo.ms.zip.

363 lester, "Which Ftpd Is Right for You?"

364 TRS, "The Rising Sun Topsite (TRS-the.rising.sun.1998.01.18.nfo)," August 18, 1998, DeFacto2, warez.scene.nfo.collection.v1.0.24351.shroo.ms.zip.

365 TRM, "The Rising Sun Topsite (TRS-the.rising.sun.XXXX.XX.00.nfo)," n.d., DeFacto2, warez.scene.nfo.collection.v1.0.24351.shroo.ms.zip.

366 TR, "The River Topsite (TR-the.river.1997.05.29.nfo)," May 29, 1997, DeFacto2, warez.scene.nfo.collection.v1.0.24351.shroo.ms.zip.

367 TR, "The Rock Topsite (TR-the.rock.1999.03.13.nfo)," March 13, 1999, DeFacto2, warez.scene.nfo.collection.v1.0.24351.shroo.ms.zip.

368 TSG, "The Sadistic Granddaughter Topsite (TSG-the.sadistic.granddaughter.1999.04.20.nfo)," April 20, 1999, DeFacto2, warez.scene.nfo.collection.v1.0.24351.shroo.ms.zip.

Sitename	Known Affils	Known Hardware/Software	Location	Siteops and Nukers/Notes
The Site (TS)[369]	iNTUTiLS, oDDiTy, JGT, PGC, ViSION, DF		Sweden	
The Tombstone (TS)[370]	FCN, RTA, ECG		USA	hxxxx, Nxxxxxxxx, Cxxxxx, pxx, Sxxxxxxx, Ixxxxxx
The Toxic Dump (TTD)[371]	RAZOR NINETEEN ELEVEN, THE REVIEWERS GUILD, RTN			TOAST, MRMONSTER, NASH, HOZIRIS
Titty Twister (TT)[372]	MANiFEST, DYNASTY, COUNCiL, ECLiPSE, 2000AD, PiNNACLE, ORiGIN	"45 GiGz" "T3"[373]	Europe	
The Unknown Realm (TUR)[374]	Fluke, Mercury, VLN, Hi-Jack, Distortion			Tipz, Scumby, Garr

369 TS, "The Site Topsite (TS-the.site.XXXX.XX.00.nfo)," n.d., DeFacto2, warez.scene.nfo.collection.v1.0.24351.shroo.ms.zip.

370 TS, "The Tombstone Topsite (TS-the.tombstone.1998.12.24.nfo)," December 24, 1998, DeFacto2, warez.scene.nfo.collection.v1.0.24351.shroo.ms.zip.

371 TTD, "The Toxic Dump Topsite (TTD-the.toxic.dump.1998.02.04.nfo)," February 4, 1998, DeFacto2, warez.scene.nfo.collection.v1.0.24351.shroo.ms.zip.

372 TT, "Titty Twister Topsite (TT-titty.twister.1999.12.31.nfo)," December 31, 1999, DeFacto2, warez.scene.nfo.collection.v1.0.24351.shroo.ms.zip.

373 TT, "Titty Twister Topsite (TT-titty.twister.1999.03.19.nfo)," March 19, 1999, DeFacto2, warez.scene.nfo.collection.v1.0.24351.shroo.ms.zip.

374 TUR, "The Unknown Realm Topsite (TUR-the.unknown.realm.1998.09.16.nfo)," September 16, 1998, DeFacto2, warez.scene.nfo.collection.v1.0.24351.shroo.ms.zip.

Sitename	Known Affils	Known Hardware/Software	Location	Siteops and Nukers/ Notes
The Void (TVD)[375]				
The Vanishing Point (TVP)[376]				
Tar Valon (TV)[377]				
Terminal Velocity (TV)[378]	DIMENSION, FALLEN, ORIGIN, PENTIUM FORCE TEAM, RENEGADE, REVOLUTION	"T3" "50GB oday" "50GB iSO/ VCD"	USA	

375 TVD, "The Void Topsite (TVD-the.void.XXXX.XX.00.nfo)," n.d., DeFacto2, warez.scene.nfo.collection.v1.0.24351.shroo.ms.zip.

376 TVP, "The Vanishing Point Topsite (TVP-the.vanishing.point.1998.09.15.nfo)," September 15, 1998, DeFacto2, warez.scene.nfo.collection.v1.0.24351.shroo.ms.zip.

377 TV, "Tar Valon Topsite (TV-tar.valon.1998.09.28.nfo)," August 28, 1998, DeFacto2, warez.scene.nfo.collection.v1.0.24351.shroo.ms.zip.

378 TV, "Terminal Velocity Topsite (TV-terminal.velocity.1999.01.29.nfo)," January 29, 1999, DeFacto2, warez.scene.nfo.collection.v1.0.24351.shroo.ms.zip.

Sitename	Known Affils	Known Hardware/Software	Location	Siteops and Nukers/ Notes
The Wolves House (TWH)[379]	Equality, Shock, TRPS, Core, PRECiSE		The Netherlands[380]	Wolfje, Sony[381]
Twilight (TWI)[382]	F4CG, RBS, DVN, MFD, RTS, CiFE, DVNiSO, RBSiSO, PORNOLATION, DTD, DVNPSX, DVNVCD	"100Mbps connection"[383]	USA	
The Waste Land (TWL)[384]	REQUEST TO SEND, TRPS, UCF2000, WARRiOR, FATIGUED COURIERS NETWORK		Canada	SPEARFISH, DRUGGY, DiZZY, MARBiTOZ[385]

379 TWH, "The Wolves House Topsite (TWH-the.wolves.house.1999.12.30.nfo)," December 30, 1999, DeFacto2, warez.scene.nfo.collection.v1.0.24351.shroo.ms.zip.

380 TWH, "The Wolves House Topsite (TWH-the.wolves.house.1998.02.15.nfo)," February 15, 1998, DeFacto2, warez.scene.nfo.collection.v1.0.24351.shroo.ms.zip.

381 TWH, "The Wolves House Topsite (TWH-the.wolves.house.1997.03.21.nfo)," March 21, 1997, DeFacto2, warez.scene.nfo.collection.v1.0.24351.shroo.ms.zip.

382 TWI, "Twilight Topsite (TWI-twilight.1999.12.02.nfo)," December 2, 1999, DeFacto2, warez.scene.nfo.collection.v1.0.24351.shroo.ms.zip.

383 TWI, "Twilight Topsite (TWI-twilight.XXXX.XX.02.nfo)," n.d., DeFacto2, warez.scene.nfo.collection.v1.0.24351.shroo.ms.zip.

384 TWL, "The Waste Land Topsite (TWL-the.waste.land.1998.07.29.nfo)," July 29, 1998, DeFacto2, warez.scene.nfo.collection.v1.0.24351.shroo.ms.zip.

385 TWL, "The Waste Land Topsite (TWL-the.waste.land.1997.05.22.nfo)," May 22, 1997, DeFacto2, warez.scene.nfo.collection.v1.0.24351.shroo.ms.zip.

Sitename	Known Affils	Known Hardware/Software	Location	Siteops and Nukers/ Notes
Terra X (TX)[386]	AoD, CrC'98, KLN, UCL	"T-1+" "22Gb"	USA	Tys
Unhuman Creations (UC)[387]	SKL, LND, Motiv8, EPI			
United Centre (UC)[388]		"130 GB online"	United Kingdom (inferred from spelling of "Centre" in British English)	
Unconquered Dreams (UD)[389]		"3mbit ADSL" "30Gb Online"		DarkNinja[390]

386 TX, "Terra X Topsite (TX-terra.x.1998.02.14.nfo)," February 14, 1998, DeFacto2, warez.scene.nfo.collection.v1.0.24351.shroo.ms.zip.

387 UC, "Unhuman Creations Topsite (UC-unhuman.creations.1998.08.27.nfo)," August 27, 1998, DeFacto2, warez.scene.nfo.collection.v1.0.24351.shroo.ms.zip.

388 UC, "United Centre Topsite (UC-united.centre.1998.08.21.nfo)," August 21, 1998, DeFacto2, warez.scene.nfo.collection.v1.0.24351.shroo.ms.zip.

389 UD, "Unconquered Dreams Topsite (UD-unconquered.dreams.1999.01.28.nfo)," January 28, 1999, DeFacto2, warez.scene.nfo.collection.v1.0.24351.shroo.ms.zip.

390 UD, "Unconquered Dreams Topsite (UD-unconquered.dreams.XXXX.XX.01.nfo)," n.d., DeFacto2, warez.scene.nfo.collection.v1.0.24351.shroo.ms.zip.

Sitename	Known Affils	Known Hardware/Software	Location	Siteops and Nukers/Notes
Unleashed (ULS)[391]	CORE, CNC, TRSi, oDDity, GWA, MiB, ESPRiT, TRSiISO, COREpda, POEpda	"T3" "25+GB"	Europe	MeDlor, Sekmeth, AfterDark[392]
Universe (UNV)[393]	VIETSOUND, TRPS, F4CG, PHOENiX, SHOCK, MOTiV8		Europe	
Utwente (UT)[394]	ROYALGSM, ECLiPSE, CROSSFiRE, BliZZARD, LAXiTY, FALLEN, RiSE, DOMiNiON, RAZOR 1911, PARADOX, TFAiSO		The Netherlands (Based at the University of Twente, inferred from name)	
Under World (UW)[395]	OriGiN, iNTUTiLS, HARLEM, RBSiSO	"Scorching OC-12" "24 Gig"	USA	IsuGuy, IsuGal[396]

391 ULS, "Unleashed Topsite (ULS-unleashed.1999.09.14.nfo)," September 14, 1999, DeFacto2, warez.scene.nfo.collection.v1.0.24351.shroo.ms.zip.
392 ULS, "Unleashed Topsite (ULS-unleashed.1999.03.26.nfo)," March 26, 1999, DeFacto2, warez.scene.nfo.collection.v1.0.24351.shroo.ms.zip.
393 UNV, "Universe Topsite (UNV-universe.XXXX.XX.00.nfo)," n.d., DeFacto2, warez.scene.nfo.collection.v1.0.24351.shroo.ms.zip.
394 UT, "Utwente Topsite (UT-utwente.2001.07.17.nfo)," July 17, 2001, DeFacto2, warez.scene.nfo.collection.v1.0.24351.shroo.ms.zip.
395 UW, "Under World Topsite (UW-under.world.1999.05.06.nfo)," May 6, 1999, DeFacto2, warez.scene.nfo.collection.v1.0.24351.shroo.ms.zip.
396 UW, "Under World Topsite (UW-under.world.1999.02.15.nfo)," February 15, 1999, DeFacto2, warez.scene.nfo.collection.v1.0.24351.shroo.ms.zip.

Sitename	Known Affils	Known Hardware/Software	Location	Siteops and Nukers/ Notes
Vault Thirteen (V13)[397]				
Virtual Dimension Research Lake (VDR)[398]	CLS, DOD, DEV	"155Mbits"[399] "4 Gigabytes iDE - SCSi2"[400]	Europe[401]	Red Dragon's, JAMi-Li, Muss, Mrmorris Samuraion Sneeze
Vision Factory (VF)[402]	PDM, EQUALITY, CORE, RISCISO, PDMISO, MUD, DYNASTY, COUNCIL, GWA98, NBD, AMOK, DB	"70 GIG" "100Mbit"	Germany (implied: has German affils)	

397 V13, "Vault Thirteen Topsite (V13-vault.thirteen.1998.08.01.nfo)," August 1, 1998, DeFacto2, warez.scene.nfo.collection.v1.0.24351.shroo.ms.zip.

398 VDR, "Virtual Dimension Research Lake Topsite (VDR-vdr.lake.1998.04.02.nfo)," April 2, 1998, DeFacto2, warez.scene.nfo.collection.v1.0.24351.shroo.ms.zip.

399 VDR, "Virtual Dimension Research Lake Topsite (VDR-vdr.lake.1998.02.09.nfo)," February 9, 1998, DeFacto2, warez.scene.nfo.collection.v1.0.24351.shroo.ms.zip.

400 VDR, "Virtual Dimension Research Lake Topsite (VDR-vdr.lake.1997.06.06.nfo)," June 6, 1997, DeFacto2, warez.scene.nfo.collection.v1.0.24351.shroo.ms.zip.

401 VDR, "Virtual Dimension Research Lake Topsite (VDR-vdr.lake.1997.05.16.nfo)," May 16, 1997, DeFacto2, warez.scene.nfo.collection.v1.0.24351.shroo.ms.zip.

402 VF, "Vision Factory Topsite (VF-vision.factory.1999.03.18.nfo)," March 18, 1999, DeFacto2, warez.scene.nfo.collection.v1.0.24351.shroo.ms.zip.

Sitename	Known Affils	Known Hardware/Software	Location	Siteops and Nukers/ Notes
Violent Illusions (VI)[403]	Dongle, LiveEdge, LAXiTY, DF, GLoW, CWS	"Triple Dedicated T1" "35 GiG"	USA	sirebral, LHD, N3gative, Hack, PGN-Creed, duhme[404]
Vampyre's Lair (VL)[405]	PWA, Empire, SSC	"T3 SPEEDS" "21 – Gigs"	USA	Vampyre, Dwelar, KnickerZ, Midnight Avian
Valhalla (V)[406]	CLASS, SHOCK, EQUALITY, DYNASTY, CORE, INTENSION, HERITAGE, OXYGEN, FAIRLIGHT, RISEISO, EPTISO, RBSISO, SHKiSO, G.N.S., PNTiSO, PARADOX, HS	"200 gIG" "100 mBIT"	Europe	

403 VI, "Violent Illusions Topsite (VI-violent.illusions.1999.09.18.nfo)," September 18, 1999, DeFacto2, warez.scene.nfo.collection.v1.0.24351.shroo.ms.zip.

404 VI, "Violent Illusions Topsite (VI-violent.illusions.1999.06.11.nfo)," June 11, 1999, DeFacto2, warez.scene.nfo.collection.v1.0.24351.shroo.ms.zip.

405 VL, "Vampyre's Lair Topsite (VL-vampyres.lair.1997.10.21.nfo)," October 21, 1997, DeFacto2, warez.scene.nfo.collection.v1.0.24351.shroo.ms.zip.

406 V, "Valhalla Topsite (V-valhalla.2000.07.17.nfo)," July 17, 2000, DeFacto2, warez.scene.nfo.collection.v1.0.24351.shroo.ms.zip.

Sitename	Known Affils	Known Hardware/Software	Location	Siteops and Nukers/Notes
Warp Factor Ten (W10)[407]	EMPiRE, Pinnacle, TFT	"Er33tD"	Europe[408]	Beta, Bsphere, Icu812, Warp, Devan, Markgoh[409]
Wet Dreams (WD)[410]	REBELS, EQUALITY, DONGLE, PGC		Europe[411]	
Warez Free Zone (WFZ)[412]	MiB, iLT, M8, DDC	"T1 coNNEX-iON"		
White House (WH)[413]	EQUALITY, CORE, Siege, HiD	"COMPRESSED T-3 ONTO MCI BACKBONE"[414]	USA	

407 W10, "Warp Factor Ten Topsite (W10-warp.factor.ten.1997.11.07.nfo)," November 7, 1997, DeFacto2, warez.scene.nfo.collection.v1.0.24351.shroo.ms.zip.

408 W10, "Warp Factor Ten Topsite (W10-warp.factor.ten.XXXX.XX.00.nfo)," n.d., DeFacto2, warez.scene.nfo.collection.v1.0.24351.shroo.ms.zip.

409 W10, "Warp Factor Ten Topsite (W10-warp.factor.ten.1997.09.30.nfo)," September 30, 1997, DeFacto2, warez.scene.nfo.collection.v1.0.24351.shroo.ms.zip.

410 WD, "Wet Dreams Topsite (WD-wet.dreams.1999.05.27.nfo)," May 27, 1999, DeFacto2, warez.scene.nfo.collection.v1.0.24351.shroo.ms.zip.

411 WD, "Wet Dreams Topsite (WD-wet.dreams.1999.04.25.nfo)," April 25, 1999, DeFacto2, warez.scene.nfo.collection.v1.0.24351.shroo.ms.zip.

412 WFZ, "Warez Free Zone Topsite (WFZ-warez.free.zone.1999.07.10.nfo)," July 10, 1999, DeFacto2, warez.scene.nfo.collection.v1.0.24351.shroo.ms.zip.

413 WH, "White House Topsite (WH-white.house.1998.09.09.nfo)," September 9, 1998, DeFacto2, warez.scene.nfo.collection.v1.0.24351.shroo.ms.zip.

414 WH, "White House Topsite (WH-white.house.1998.03.15.nfo)," March 15, 1998, DeFacto2, warez.scene.nfo.collection.v1.0.24351.shroo.ms.zip.

Sitename	Known Affils	Known Hardware/Software	Location	Siteops and Nukers/Notes
Wonder Land (WL)[415]	SHINING, GWA, EXODUS, MiV	"20gIg" "34mbIt"	Estonia ("EEHQ")	
The Windmill (WND)[416]	Karma, Revolt, DoG, DsC, Dynamic		Europe	LoG, zz187
World of Chaos (WOC)[417]				
Wouldn't You Prefer A Good Game of Chess? (WOPR)[418]	KAC	"Cable"		
Warez Sector (WS)[419]	eXTReMe WaReZ CouRieRS, AOD, EWC, SHOCK, SWAT		East Coast USA ("eaST HQ")	

415 WL, "Wonder Land Topsite (WL-wonderland.XXXX.XX.00.nfo)," n.d., DeFacto2, warez.scene.nfo.collection.v1.0.24351.shroo.ms.zip.

416 WND, "The Windmill Topsite (WND-the.windmill.1997.06.19.nfo)," June 19, 1998, DeFacto2, warez.scene.nfo.collection.v1.0.24351.shroo.ms.zip.

417 WOC, "World of Chaos Topsite (WOC-world.of.chaos.1998.07.05.nfo)," July 5, 1998, DeFacto2, warez.scene.nfo.collection.v1.0.24351.shroo.ms.zip.

418 WOPR, "Wouldn't You Prefer A Good Game of Chess? Topsite (WOPR-wopr.1998.08.14.nfo)," August 14, 1998, DeFacto2, warez.scene.nfo.collection.v1.0.24351.shroo.ms.zip.

419 WS, "Warez Sector Topsite (WS-warez.sector.1997.04.17.nfo)," April 17, 1997, DeFacto2, warez.scene.nfo.collection.v1.0.24351.shroo.ms.zip.

Sitename	Known Affils	Known Hardware/Software	Location	Siteops and Nukers/ Notes
The World Trade Center (WTC)[420]	ENTiTY, MOTiV8, REUNiTED	"T3" "25+GiGz"	Europe	
Watch Tower (WT)[421]	Pirates Gone Crazy, Teenagers in Crime, 2000AD, Revolt, Real Time Pirates		USA	Txxxxxx Cxxxxxxx, Mxxxxxxx, Ixxxx, Vxxxxx xxxxx, Kxxxxxxx
Wild West (WW)[422]	AVALON Courier	"XFtpd" "2XT1" "18 Gig"		Darksch
X Filez (XF)[423]	AVN, DsC, INJ, MaD, Motiv8, NEC, O13, RTN, RTP, STORM, uCu	"T1" "12 Gigabytes"	USA[424]	Xfilez, MarkGoh
Xenosis (XNS)[425]	Class, MnM, RiSE, NOBLiEGE, DNG	"3xT3" "70 GiG"[426]	USA	KBM, Return Link, Xoen, Split242, Digitzz, Hodd, Moz, tdpriest, Daman

420 WTC, "World Trade Center Topsite (WTC-world.trade.center.1998.07.07.nfo)," July 7, 1998, DeFacto2, warez.scene.nfo.collection.v1.0.24351.shroo.ms.zip.

421 WT, "Watch Tower Topsite (WT-watch.tower.1998.03.02.nfo)," March 2, 1998, DeFacto2, warez.scene.nfo.collection.v1.0.24351.shroo.ms.zip.

422 WW, "Wild West Topsite (WW-wild.west.1998.09.04.nfo)," September 4, 1998, DeFacto2, warez.scene.nfo.collection.v1.0.24351.shroo.ms.zip.

423 XF, "X Filez Topsite (XF-x.filez.1997.08.15.nfo)," August 15, 1997, DeFacto2, warez.scene.nfo.collection.v1.0.24351.shroo.ms.zip.

424 XF, "X Filez Topsite (XF-x.filez.1997.07.25.nfo)," July 25, 1997, DeFacto2, warez.scene.nfo.collection.v1.0.24351.shroo.ms.zip.

425 XNS, "Xenosis Topsite (XNS-xenosis.1998.06.10.nfo)," June 10, 1998, DeFacto2, warez.scene.nfo.collection.v1.0.24351.shroo.ms.zip.

426 XNS, "Xenosis Topsite (XNS-xenosis.1998.05.18.nfo)," May 18, 1998, DeFacto2, warez.scene.nfo.collection.v1.0.24351.shroo.ms.zip.

Sitename	Known Affils	Known Hardware/Software	Location	Siteops and Nukers/ Notes
Xquizit (XQZ)[427]	Razor, X-Force, TRPS, UCF		USA	
X Zone (XZONE)[428]	WEAPON'98, Phoenix, Storm, Hazard	"2xT3" "4 gb & 20+ gb Soon" "Win-NT Server 4.0"[429]		Joker
Zeus (ZEUS)[430]	beatforge, cnc, gwa, nbl, ngit, ucf			
Zilla (ZLA)[431]	DOD, RZR, CST, ASP, TFA, SR, TFAiSO, PoRNoLATioN, DVNVCD, TFAMp3, BMI	"10MBiTS" "38 GiGS OF STORAGE"[432]	USA[433]	

427 XQZ, "Xquizit Topsite (XQZ-xquizit.1999.07.24.nfo)," July 24, 1999, DeFacto2, warez.scene.nfo.collection.v1.0.24351.shroo.ms.zip.

428 XZONE, "X Zone Topsite (XZONE-x.zone.1998.03.01.nfo)," March 1, 1998, DeFacto2, warez.scene.nfo.collection.v1.0.24351.shroo.ms.zip.

429 XZONE, "X Zone Topsite (XZONE-x.zone.XXXX.XX.00.nfo)," n.d., DeFacto2, warez.scene.nfo.collection.v1.0.24351.shroo.ms.zip.

430 ZEUS, "Zeus Topsite (ZEUS-zeus.1998.11.20.nfo)," November 20, 1998, DeFacto2, warez.scene.nfo.collection.v1.0.24351.shroo.ms.zip.

431 ZLA, "Zilla Topsite (ZLA-zilla.1999.06.30.nfo)," June 30, 1999, DeFacto2, warez.scene.nfo.collection.v1.0.24351.shroo.ms.zip.

432 ZLA, "Zilla Topsite (ZLA-zilla.1998.08.09.nfo)," August 9, 1998, DeFacto2, warez.scene.nfo.collection.v1.0.24351.shroo.ms.zip.

433 ZLA, "Zilla Topsite (ZLA-zilla.1999.02.17.nfo)," February 17, 1999, DeFacto2, warez.scene.nfo.collection.v1.0.24351.shroo.ms.zip.

Sitename	Known Affils	Known Hardware/Software	Location	Siteops and Nukers/ Notes
Z Land (ZL)[434]	Clockwerk, Illusion, BL98, Resource, DOG	"28 gigs" "3 MBit"		Zman

434 ZL, "Z Land Topsite (ZL-zland.1998.12.02.nfo)," December 2, 1998, DeFacto2, warez.scene.nfo.collection.v1.0.24351.shroo.ms.zip.

Bibliography

By necessity, the bibliography to this work must cite a number of unconventional works that are not covered by standard style manuals. In particular, I need to make reference to NFO files that contain ASCII art and other iNFOrmation about the Warez Scene. As noted more extensively in the introduction, one of the primary sources upon which I draw is the *DeFacto2* archive.

The format of some of these entries should be explained. For example, 722. "722 Topsite (722-722.1998.06.12.nfo)," June 12, 1998. DeFacto2, warez.scene.nfo.collection.v1.0.24351.shroo.ms.zip. refers to a group of individuals who run a topsite called "722," for which they created an advertorial NFO file about the site, called 722-722.1998.06.12.nfo, from 12 June 1998. The file itself can be found, in the archive, within the warez.scene.nfo.collection.v1.0.24351.shroo.ms.zip file.

Not all files in the *DeFacto2* archive are within zip packs. Some are directly accessible via the site itself. Given that the archive makes no guarantees as to the stability of its URL structure, I list the filenames of the artefacts in the knowledge that URLS would only degrade over time if they were included.

For more on the ethics of citing Scene magazines and crediting the original authors by their pseudonyms, please see the extensive discussion in the first chapter of this work.

"2b2t Photodiary: Inside Minecraft's Most Offensive Server." *PCGamesN*, October 17, 2016. https://www.pcgamesn.com/minecraft/2b2t-photodiary-inside-minecrafts-most-offensive-server.

"47 U.S. Code § 230 – Protection for Private Blocking and Screening of Offensive Material." *LII / Legal Information Institute*, 1996. https://www.law.cornell.edu/uscode/text/47/230.

"About." *psyBNC*. 2008. https://psybnc.org/about.html.

"A Day in the Life of a Warez Broker." *Phrack Magazine*, 1995. http://phrack.org/issues/47/20.html.

"Annual Death Toll from Piracy Rises." *ICC Commercial Crime Services*, 2004. https://www.icc-ccs.org/index.php/405-annual-death-toll-from-piracy-rises.

"Busted.allstarz.net.logs (Logs_Mandmore_4.txt)," n.d. DeFacto2, warez-scene-notices-2006-2010.

"Chairman Tony Krvaric." *The Republican Party of San Diego County*, n.d. Archived at https://web.archive.org/web/20160318222450/http://www.sandiegorepublicans.org/chairman-tony-krvaric.html.

"Cyber Strike: FBI Agents Confiscated Computers and…" *Chicago Tribune*, January 29, 1997. https://www.chicagotribune.com/news/ct-xpm-1997-01-29-9701300206-story.html.

"European Top Couriers." *Courier Weektop Scorecard* (CWS-72.txt), October 2, 1999. DeFacto2.

"FBI Hunts Software Pirates," *CNET*, January 28, 1997. https://www.cnet.com/news/fbi-hunts-software-pirates/.

"Glftpd: Security Vulnerabilities." *CVE Details*, November 16, 2020. https://www.cvedetails.com/vulnerability-list/vendor_id-346/Glftpd.html.

"Group Standings." *The Marshall Mussolini Show* (tmms_issue_071-2004_13.nfo), March 2004. DeFacto2.

"Group Standings." *The Marshall Mussolini Show* (tmms_issue_071-2004_13.nfo), March 2004. DeFacto2.

"Imperator's Base." *2b2t Wiki,* 2020. https://2b2t.miraheze.org/wiki/Imperator%27s_Base.

"International Scenes." *Phrack Magazine,* January 9, 1996. http://phrack.org/issues/65/15.html.

"Interview with raanu ('Interviewk')." *The Marshall Mussolini Show* (tmms_issue_082-2004_33.nfo), August 2004. DeFacto2.

"Invalid Official FLAC Standard Rules V3.0 (INVALID_OFFICIAL_FLAC_STANDARD_RULES_V3.0-SCENENOTICE.nfo)," January 9, 2017.

"iSSUE FiFTY EiGHT." *The Marshall Mussolini Show* (tmms_issue_124-2005_23.nfo), June 2005. DeFacto2.

"iSSUE FiFTY EiGHT." *The Marshall Mussolini Show* (tmms_issue_533-2013_14.nfo), 2013. DeFacto2.

"Justice Department Announces Four Pleas in Internet Music Piracy Crackdown." *US Department of Justice,* February 28, 2006. https://www.justice.gov/archive/opa/pr/2006/February/06_crm_103.html.

"Justice Department Announces International Piracy Sweep." *US Department of Justice,* April 22, 2004. https://www.justice.gov/archive/opa/pr/2004/April/04_crm_263.htm.

"LAMURGH QUOTES." *The Marshall Mussolini Show* (tmms_issue_082-2004_33.nfo), August 2004. DeFacto2.

"LAMURGH QUOTES." *The Marshall Mussolini Show* (tmms_issue_174-2006_22.nfo), June 2006. DeFacto2.

"LAMURGH QUOTES." *The Marshall Mussolini Show* (tmms_issue_190-2006_38.nfo), September 24, 2006. DeFacto2.

"LAMURGH QUOTES." *The Marshall Mussolini Show* (tmms_issue_394-2010_32.nfo), July 2010. DeFacto2.

"LAMURGH QUOTES." *The Marshall Mussolini Show* (tmms_issue_563-2013_44.nfo), November 2013. DeFacto2.

"Music File-Sharer 'Oink' Cleared of Fraud." *BBC News,* January 15, 2010. http://news.bbc.co.uk/1/hi/england/tees/8461879.stm.

"news." *The Marshall Mussolini Show* (tmms_issue_001-2002_47.nfo), November 2002. DeFacto2.

"Operation Cyber Strike." *Bankers Online,* March 1, 1997. https://www.bankersonline.com/articles/103656.

"Operation Buccaneer (operation_buccaneer.txt)," 2000. mp3scene.info.

"opfastlink.txt," 2002. http://144.217.177.36:1421/EBooks/paraZite/opfastlink.txt.

"Organist Wins Procol Harum Battle." *BBC News,* December 20, 2006. http://news.bbc.co.uk/1/hi/entertainment/6196413.stm.

"Pair Convicted of Internet Piracy." *BBC News,* March 16, 2005. http://news.bbc.co.uk/1/hi/technology/4336401.stm.

"Rank." *The Marshall Mussolini Show* (tmms_issue_054-2003_48.nfo), December 2003. DeFacto2.

"RELEASES OF THiS WEEK." *The Marshall Mussolini Show* (tmms_issue_171-2006_19.nfo), April 2006. DeFacto2.

"RELEASES OF THiS WEEK." *The Marshall Mussolini Show* (tmms_issue_293-2008_36.nfo), September 2008. DeFacto2.

"Rules." *What.CD,* n.d. http://rescene.wikidot.com/what-cd-rules.

"RULES OF KETCHUP." *Ketchup* (ketchup_issue_19-2003.nfo), April 2003. DeFacto2.

"Scene Busts and Mitigations (Scene_busts_And_Mitigations.png)," 2020. DeFacto2.

"SCENE QUOTES." *Ketchup* (ketchup_issue_19-2003.nfo), April 2003. DeFacto2.

"Scene.Ban.SCR.and.RiDERz.Leader.READNFO-iND (Scene.Ban.SCR.and.RiDERz.Leader.READNFO-iND.nfo)," n.d. DeFacto2, warez-scene-notices-2006-2010.

"SceneBusts10 (scenebusts10.htm)," 2000. paraZite.

"Scene.Notice.FiNaLe (finale.nfo)," n.d. DeFacto2, warez-scene-notices-2006-2010.

"Security.Warning.take.note.ppl-BwaRe (security.warning.take.note.ppl-bware.nfo)," n.d. DeFacto2, warez-scene-notices-2006-2010.

"Site.Info.Leaker.READ.NFO.Updated-iND (screamia.updated.nfo)," n.d. DeFacto2, warez-scene-notices-2006-2010.

"Site.Security.READNFO-acksyn (Site.Security.for.Users.Windows.XP.1.3-acksyn.nfo)," n.d. DeFacto2, warez-scene-notices-2006-2010.

"Sites Received." *Courier Weektop Scorecard* (CWS-72.txt), October 2, 1999. DeFacto2.

"stats." *The Marshall Mussolini Show* (tmms_issue_105-2005_04.nfo), January 2005. DeFacto2.

"Stats for CFL (CONTiNUOUS FLOW)." *The Marshall Mussolini Show* (tmms_issue_196-2006_44.nfo), October 2006. DeFacto2.

"Swedish Police Raid File Sharing 'Scene.'" *The Local,* September 7, 2010. https://www.thelocal.se/20100907/28826.

"The Best In-Game Piracy Punishments." *PC Gamer,* September 14, 2017. https://www.pcgamer.com/the-best-in-game-piracy-punishments/.

"The truth about depax (xdd22245.nfo)," n.d. DeFacto2.

"THEJudgeHolden." *2b2t Wiki,* 2020. https://2b2t.miraheze.org/wiki/THEJudgeHolden.

"Timeline." *2b2t Wiki,* 2020. https://2b2t.miraheze.org/wiki/Timeline.

"Topsite Rules." *Rescene,* 2020. http://rescene.wikidot.com/topsite-rules#toc4.

"wkup." *The Marshall Mussolini Show* (tmms_issue_054-2003_48.nfo), December 2003. DeFacto2.

[S]peedy. "What Was the Best Site of Alltime?" *Netmonkey Weekly Report* (nwr-19.txt), October 5, 1998. DeFacto2.

oompah. "Site list (sites.txt)," May 3, 2003.

2Eleven, 86D, Atmo, BCC, BriBerY, co5, CMC, et al. "Official.FLAC.Standard.Rules v3.0 (nfo_2016_FLAC.nfo)." *Scenerules.org,* June 15, 2016. scenerules.org.

722. "722 Topsite (722-722.1998.06.12.nfo)," June 12, 1998. DeFacto2, warez.scene.nfo.collection.v1.0.24351.shroo.ms.zip.

A0. "Absolute Zero Topsite (A0-absolute.zero.XXXX.XX.01.nfo)," n.d. DeFacto2, warez.scene.nfo.collection.v1.0.24351.shroo.ms.zip.

A144. "Area One Four Four Topsite (A144-area.one.four.four.XXXX.XX.00.nfo)," n.d. DeFacto2, warez.scene.nfo.collection.v1.0.24351.shroo.ms.zip.

AAF. "Always Around Forever Topsite (AAF-always.around.forever.1998.07.18.nfo)," July 18, 1998. DeFacto2, warez.scene.nfo.collection.v1.0.24351.shroo.ms.zip.

Abbate, Janet. *Inventing the Internet.* Cambridge: MIT Press, 2000.

ABY. "The Abyss Topsite (ABY-abyss.1999.06.28.nfo)," June 28, 1999. DeFacto2, warez.scene.nfo.collection.v1.0.24351.shroo.ms.zip.

ACME, AiR, ALiAS, ARN, BACKLASH, BEAN, BLiZZARD, et al. "0day Scene Release Rules (nfo_2010.1_0DAY.nfo)." *Scenerules.org,* January 12, 2010. scenerules.org.

Adelstein, Jake. "Global Vice: The Expanding Territory of the Yakuza." *Journal of International Affairs* 66, no. 1 (2012): 155–61.

AF. "Angel Food Topsite (AF-angel.food.2000.09.21.nfo)," September 21, 2000. DeFacto2, warez.scene.nfo.collection.v1.0.24351.shroo.ms.zip.

AF1. "AiR Force One Topsite (AF1-air.force.one.1998.02.12.nfo)," February 12, 1998. DeFacto2, warez.scene.nfo.collection.v1.0.24351.shroo.ms.zip.

———. "AiR Force One Topsite (AF1-air.force.one.2000.04.12.nfo)," April 12, 2000. DeFacto2, warez.scene.nfo.collection.v1.0.24351.shroo.ms.zip.

AH. "The Ant Hill Topsite (AH-the.anthill.1997.06.18.nfo)," June 18, 1997. DeFacto2, warez.scene.nfo.collection.v1.0.24351.shroo.ms.zip.

Ain, Stuart L. Stratton Oakmont, Inc. v. Prodigy Services Co., No. 23 Media L Rep 1794 (Supreme Court, Nassau County, New York May 24, 1995).

Akerhaug, Lars, and Nicolai Heyerdahl. "Nordmann Siktet for Fildeling Etter Internasjonal Storaksjon." *Aftenposten,*

September 7, 2010. https://www.aftenposten.no/norge/i/Jo2dP/nordmann-siktet-for-fildeling-etter-internasjonal-storaksjon.

AKS. "Arrakis Topsite (AKS-arrakis.2000.06.01.nfo)," June 1, 2000. DeFacto2, warez.scene.nfo.collection.v1.0.24351.shroo.ms.zip.

AL. "Agnos Land Topsite (AL-agnos.land.1998.09.06.nfo)," September 6, 1998. DeFacto2, warez.scene.nfo.collection.v1.0.24351.shroo.ms.zip.

Alexander, Peter J. "Peer-to-Peer File Sharing: The Case of the Music Recording Industry." *Review of Industrial Organization* 20, no. 2 (2002): 151–61. DOI: 10.1023/A:1013819218792.

Allport, Gordon W., and L.J. Postman. *The Psychology of Rumor.* New York: Holt, Rinehart and Winston, 1947.

ALT. "Althea Topsite (ALT-althea.1999.09.22.nfo)," September 22, 1999. DeFacto2, warez.scene.nfo.collection.v1.0.24351.shroo.ms.zip.

AM. "The Angry Moose Topsite (AM-the.angry.moose.1997.08.06.nfo)," August 6, 1997. DeFacto2, warez.scene.nfo.collection.v1.0.24351.shroo.ms.zip.

AMB. "Ambiquous Topsite (AMB-ambiquous.1998.02.18.nfo)," February 18, 1998. DeFacto2, warez.scene.nfo.collection.v1.0.24351.shroo.ms.zip.

Anderson, John L. "Piracy and World History: An Economic Perspective on Maritime Predation." In *Bandits at Sea: A Pirates Reader,* edited by C.R. Pennell, 82–106. New York: New York University Press, 2001.

Andersson, Jonas, and Stefan Larsson. "The Justification of Piracy: Differences in Conceptualization and Argumentation between Active Uploaders and Other File-Sharers." In *Piracy: Leakages from Modernity,* edited by Martin Fredriksson and James Arvanitakis, 217–40. Sacramento: Litwin Books, 2014.

Anemia. "Interview with The Punisher (interview with the punisher - anemia1.png)," January 1997. DeFacto2.

APC. "Apocalypse Topsite (APC-apocalypse.1999.12.10.nfo)," December 10, 1999. DeFacto2, warez.scene.nfo.collection.v1.0.24351.shroo.ms.zip.

ASP. "Alpha Storage Place Topsite (ASP-alpha.storage.place.1997.10.12.nfo)," October 12, 1997. DeFacto2, warez.scene.nfo.collection.v1.0.24351.shroo.ms.zip.

———. "Alpha Storage Place Topsite (ASP-alpha.storage.place.1998.08.27.nfo)," August 27, 1998. DeFacto2, warez.scene.nfo.collection.v1.0.24351.shroo.ms.zip.

ATL. "Atlantis Topsite (ATL-atlantis.XXXX.XX.01.nfo)," n.d. DeFacto2, warez.scene.nfo.collection.v1.0.24351.shroo.ms.zip.

ATX. "Atomic-X Topsite (ATX-atomic.x.1999.05.05.nfo)," May 5, 1999. DeFacto2, warez.scene.nfo.collection.v1.0.24351.shroo.ms.zip.

AV. "Alternate Void Topsite (AV-alternate.void.1998.11.26.nfo)," November 26, 1998. DeFacto2, warez.scene.nfo.collection.v1.0.24351.shroo.ms.zip.

AVF. "A Violent Fluid Topsite (AVF-a.violent.fluid.1997.11.18.nfo)," November 18, 1997. DeFacto2, warez.scene.nfo.collection.v1.0.24351.shroo.ms.zip.

AVL. "Avalon Topsite (AVL-avalon.XXXX.XX.00.nfo)," n.d. DeFacto2, warez.scene.nfo.collection.v1.0.24351.shroo.ms.zip.

AW. "Another World Topsite (AW-another.world.1999.07.02.nfo)," July 2, 1999. DeFacto2, warez.scene.nfo.collection.v1.0.24351.shroo.ms.zip.

AZ. "Alien Zone Topsite (AZ-alien.zone.1998.07.29.nfo)," July 29, 1998. DeFacto2, warez.scene.nfo.collection.v1.0.24351.shroo.ms.zip.

b-bstf. "Guide to Internet Piracy." *2600: Hacker Quarterly* (Summer 2004).

B2B. "Back to Babylon Topsite (B2B-back.to.babylon.1998.05.21.nfo)," May 21, 1998. DeFacto2, warez.scene.nfo.collection.v1.0.24351.shroo.ms.zip.

Babits, Lawrence E., Joshua B. Howard, and Matthew Brenckle. "Pirate Imagery." In *X Marks the Spot: The Archaeology of Piracy*, edited by Russell K. Skowronek and Charles R. Ewen, 271–81. Gainesville: University Press of Florida, 2006.

Bachmann, Michael. "Lesson Spurned? Reactions of Online Music Pirates to Legal Prosecutions by the RIAA." *International Journal of Cyber Criminology* 1, no. 2 (2007): 213–27. DOI: 10.5281/zenodo.18796.

Bale, Anthony. "Introduction." In *The Cambridge Companion to the Literature of the Crusades*, edited by Anthony Bale, 1–8. Cambridge: Cambridge University Press, 2018.

Balkin, Jack M. "Free Speech Is a Triangle." *Columbia Law Review* 118, no. 7 (2018): 2011–56. https://columbialawreview.org/content/free-speech-is-a-triangle/.

Bann, Stephen. *Concrete Poetry: An International Anthology.* London: London Magazine, 1967.

———, ed. *The Tradition of Constructivism.* London: Thames and Hudson, 1974.

BAR. "Beyond All Reality Topsite (BAR-beyond.all.reality.XXXX.XX.00.nfo)," n.d. DeFacto2, warez.scene.nfo.collection.v1.0.24351.shroo.ms.zip.

Barblan, Matthew. "Copyright as a Platform for Artistic and Creative Freedom." *George Mason Law Review* 23, no. 4 (2016): 793–809. https://ssrn.com/abstract=2776797.

BAS. "Basilica Topsite (BAS-basilica.1999.04.22.nfo)," April 22, 1999. DeFacto2, warez.scene.nfo.collection.v1.0.24351.shroo.ms.zip.

Basamanowicz, Jonathan, and Martin Bouchard. "Overcoming the Warez Paradox: Online Piracy Groups and Situational Crime Prevention." *Policy & Internet* 3, no. 2 (2011): 79–103. DOI: 10.2202/1944-2866.1125.

Basamanowicz, Jonathan R. "Release Groups & Digital Copyright Piracy." Master's thesis, Simon Fraser University, 2011.

Basilisk. "The Beginner's Guide to Ektoplazm." *Ektoplazm*, July 12, 2012. https://ektoplazm.com/blog/a-beginners-guide-to-ektoplazm.

Baskin, Brian, Dan Connelly, Michael J. Schearer, Eric S. Seagren, and Thomas Whilhelm. *Netcat Power Tools.* Edited by Jan Kanclirz. Burlington: Syngress Publishing, Inc., 2008.

Bauder, Don. "Chairman of San Diego GOP Co-Founded International Piracy Ring, Says Online News Website." *San Diego Reader,* April 29, 2008. https://www.sandiegoreader.com/weblogs/financial-crime-politics/2008/apr/29/chairman-of-san-diego-gop-co-founded-international/.

BB. "Busy Beavers Topsite (BB-busy.beavers.1999.03.25.nfo)," March 25, 1999. DeFacto2, warez.scene.nfo.collection.v1.0.24351.shroo.ms.zip.

———. "The Bleach Box Topsite (BBX-bleach.box.1996.10.17.nfo)," October 17, 1996. DeFacto2, warez.scene.nfo.collection.v1.0.24351.shroo.ms.zip.

———. "The Bleach Box Topsite (BBX-bleach.box.1996.12.19.nfo)," December 19, 1996. DeFacto2, warez.scene.nfo.collection.v1.0.24351.shroo.ms.zip.

BB2. "Brand Beer 2 Topsite (BB2-brand.beer.two.1998.07.02.nfo)," July 2, 1998. DeFacto2, warez.scene.nfo.collection.v1.0.24351.shroo.ms.zip.

BDZ. "Beat Diz Topsite (BDZ-beatdiz.2000.11.20.nfo)," November 20, 2000. DeFacto2, warez.scene.nfo.collection.v1.0.24351.shroo.ms.zip.

Berman, Geoffrey S. "United States of America v. George Bridi," August 1, 2020.

———. "United States of America v. Jonatan Correa a/k/a 'Raid,'" August 1, 2020.

———. "United States of America v. Umar Ahmad a/k/a 'Artist,'" August 1, 2020.

BF. "Black Forge Topsite (BF-black.forge.1998.05.01.nfo)," May 1, 1998. DeFacto2, warez.scene.nfo.collection.v1.0.24351.shroo.ms.zip.

Bhaskar, Michael. *The Content Machine: Towards a Theory of Publishing from the Printing Press to the Digital Network.* New York: Anthem Press, 2013.

Bhushan, A.K. "File Transfer Protocol." *Internet Engineering Task Force,* April 16, 1971. https://tools.ietf.org/html/rfc114.

BL. "Black Lotus Topsite (BL-black.lotus.1997.06.12.nfo)," June 12, 1997. DeFacto2, warez.scene.nfo.collection.v1.0.24351.shroo.ms.zip.

BLD. "The Blade Topsite (BLD-the.blade.1998.03.23.nfo)," March 23, 1998. DeFacto2, warez.scene.nfo.collection.v1.0.24351.shroo.ms.zip.

Bliendbos. "Zijn hier ook nog ouwe fxp-ers?" *FOK!forum,* November 19, 2016. https://forum.fok.nl/topic/1831163/1/999.

BLIZ. "Blizzard Topsite (BLIZ-blizzard.1997.06.02.nfo)," June 2, 1997. DeFacto2, warez.scene.nfo.collection.v1.0.24351.shroo.ms.zip.

———. "Blizzard Topsite (BLIZ-blizzard.1997.12.06.nfo)," December 6, 1997. DeFacto2, warez.scene.nfo.collection.v1.0.24351.shroo.ms.zip.

BM. "Byte Me Topsite (BM-byte.me.1999.04.15.nfo)," April 15, 1999. DeFacto2, warez.scene.nfo.collection.v1.0.24351.shroo.ms.zip.

Bodó, Balázs. "Coda: A Short History of Book Piracy." In *Media Piracy in Emerging Economies,* edited by Joe Karaganis, 399–413. New York: Social Science Research Council, 2011.

———. "Library Genesis in Numbers: Mapping the Underground Flow of Knowledge." In *Shadow Libraries: Access to Educational Materials in Global Higher Education,* edited by Joe Karaganis, 53–78. Cambridge: MIT Press, 2018.

———. "The Genesis of Library Genesis: The Birth of a Global Scholarly Shadow Library." In *Shadow Libraries: Access to Educational Materials in Global Higher Education,* edited by Joe Karaganis, 25–52. Cambridge: MIT Press, 2018.

Bodó, Balázs, and Zoltán Lakatos. "Piracy Cultures| P2P and Cinematographic Movie Distribution in Hungary." *International Journal of Communication* 6 (2012). https://ijoc.org/index.php/ijoc/article/view/1261.

Bogost, Ian. "Persuasive Games: Process Intensity and Social Experimentation." *Gamasutra,* May 23, 2012. https://www.gamasutra.com/view/feature/170806/persuasive_games_process_.php.

Bourdieu, Pierre. *Outline of a Theory of Practice.* Translated by Richard Nice. Cambridge: Cambridge University Press, 1977.

BP. "Blood Pit Topsite (BP-blood.pit.1997.04.04.nfo)," April 4, 1997. DeFacto2, warez.scene.nfo.collection.v1.0.24351.shroo.ms.zip.

BPS. "Bits Per Second Topsite (BPS-bits.per.second.2000.07.03.nfo)," July 3, 2000. DeFacto2, warez.scene.nfo.collection.v1.0.24351.shroo.ms.zip.

Bradford, Ryan. "Tony Krvaric Has Always Sucked," *AwkwardSD,* September 3, 2020. https://awkwardsd.substack.com/p/tony-krvaric-has-always-sucked.

Braudel, Fernand. *The Mediterranean and The Mediterranean World in the Age of Philip II.* Vol. 2. Translated by Siân Reynolds. New York: Harper and Row, 1972.

Brooker, Joseph. *Jonathan Lethem and the Galaxy of Writing.* London: Bloomsbury Academic, 2020.

Brown, Jeffrey A. "Comic Book Fandom and Cultural Capital." *The Journal of Popular Culture* 30, no. 4 (Spring 1997): 13–31. DOI: 10.1111/j.0022-3840.1997.3004_13.x.

Brown, Wendy. *Undoing the Demos: Neoliberalism's Stealth Revolution.* New York: Zone Books, 2015.

Bruckman, Amy. "Teaching Students to Study Online Communities Ethically." *Journal of Information Ethics* 15, no. 2 (2006): 82–98. DOI: 10.3172/JIE.15.2.82.

BT. "The Beggar's Tomb Topsite (BT-the.beggars.tomb.1998.07.02.nfo)," July 2, 1998. DeFacto2, warez.scene.nfo.collection.v1.0.24351.shroo.ms.zip.

BTP. "Babylon Trading Post Topsite (BTP-babylon.trading.post.XXXX.XX.02.nfo)," n.d. DeFacto2, warez.scene.nfo.collection.v1.0.24351.shroo.ms.zip.

BULL. "The Bull Topsite (BULL-the.bull.1997.05.19.nfo)," May 19, 1997. DeFacto2, warez.scene.nfo.collection.v1.0.24351.shroo.ms.zip.

Burkart, Patrick. *Pirate Politics: The New Information Policy Contests.* Cambridge: MIT Press, 2014.

CAM. "Camelot Topsite (CAM-camelot.1998.11.13.nfo)," November 13, 1998. DeFacto2, warez.scene.nfo.collection.v1.0.24351.shroo.ms.zip.

———. "Camelot Topsite (CAM-camelot.1999.08.29.nfo)," August 29, 1999. DeFacto2, warez.scene.nfo.collection.v1.0.24351.shroo.ms.zip.

———. "Camelot Topsite (CAM-camelot.XXXX.XX.02.nfo)," n.d. DeFacto2, warez.scene.nfo.collection.v1.0.24351.shroo.ms.zip.

CC. "Crawling Chaos Topsite (CC-crawling.chaos.1998.04.06.nfo)," April 6, 1998. DeFacto2, warez.scene.nfo.collection.v1.0.24351.shroo.ms.zip.

CD. "Core Dump Topsite (CD-core.dump.1998.08.25.nfo)," August 25, 1998. DeFacto2, warez.scene.nfo.collection.v1.0.24351.shroo.ms.zip.

Cenite, Mark, Michelle Wanzheng Wang, Chong Peiwen, and Germaine Shimin Chan. "More Than Just Free Content: Motivations of Peer-to-Peer File Sharers." *Journal of Communication Inquiry* 33, no. 3 (2009): 206–21. DOI: 10.1177/0196859909333697.

CH. "Cold Hell Topsite (CH-cold.hell.1998.08.31.nfo)," August 31, 1998. DeFacto2, warez.scene.nfo.collection.v1.0.24351.shroo.ms.zip.

CH1. "Channel One Topsite (CH1-channel.one.1998.09.05.nfo)," September 5, 1998. DeFacto2, warez.scene.nfo.collection.v1.0.24351.shroo.ms.zip.

Chacksfield, Marc. "Police Arrest European File Sharers in Co-Ordinated Raids." *TechRadar,* September 7, 2010. https://www.techradar.com/news/internet/police-arrest-european-file-sharers-in-co-ordinated-raids-715004.

Charles, Christopher. "Psyculture in Bristol: Careers, Projects, and Strategies in Digital Music-Making." PhD diss., University of Bristol, 2019.

Cheng, Hsing K., Ronald R. Sims, and Hildy Teegen. "To Purchase or to Pirate Software: An Empirical Study." *Journal of Management Information Systems* 13, no. 4 (1997): 49–60. DOI: 10.1080/07421222.1997.11518142.

Choo, Kim-Kwang Raymond, and Peter Grabosky. "Cybercrime." In *The Oxford Handbook of Organized Crime*, edited by Letizia Paoli, 482–99. Oxford: Oxford University Press, 2014.

Cimpanu, Catalin. "Chrome 87 Released with Fix for NAT Slipstream Attacks, Broader FTP Deprecation." *ZDNet*, November 17, 2020. https://www.zdnet.com/article/chrome-87-released-with-fix-for-nat-slipstream-attacks-broader-ftp-deprecation/.

Cisler, Steve. "Pirates of the Pacific Rim." *Leonardo* 39, no. 4 (August 2006): 377–80. DOI: 10.1162/leon.2006.39.4.377.

Clough, Bryan, and Paul Mungo. *Approaching Zero: Data Crime and the Computer Underworld*. London: Faber & Faber, 1992.

CMG. "Cemetery Gates Topsite (CMG-cemetary.gates.1998.02.22.nfo)," February 22, 1998. DeFacto2, warez.scene.nfo.collection.v1.0.24351.shroo.ms.zip.

———. "Cemetery Gates Topsite (CMG-cemetary.gates.1998.09.21.nfo)," September 21, 1998. DeFacto2, warez.scene.nfo.collection.v1.0.24351.shroo.ms.zip.

CO. "Covert Operation Topsite (CO-covert.operations.1998.08.25.nfo)," August 25, 1998. DeFacto2, warez.scene.nfo.collection.v1.0.24351.shroo.ms.zip.

COD. "Claws of Death Topsite (COD-claws.of.death.1998.09.18.nfo)," September 18, 1998. DeFacto2, warez.scene.nfo.collection.v1.0.24351.shroo.ms.zip.

———. "Claws of Death Topsite (COD-claws.of.death.1998.11.02.nfo)," November 2, 1998. DeFacto2, warez.scene.nfo.collection.v1.0.24351.shroo.ms.zip.

Coleman, Gabriella. *Coding Freedom: The Ethics and Aesthetics of Hacking*. Princeton: Princeton University Press, 2012.

Coleman, Sarah, and Nick Dyer-Witheford. "Playing on the Digital Commons: Collectivities, Capital and Contestation in Videogame Culture." *Media, Culture & Society* 29, no. 6 (2007): 934–53. DOI: 10.1177/0163443707081700.

Condry, Ian. "Cultures of Music Piracy: An Ethnographic Comparison of the US and Japan." *International*

Journal of Cultural Studies 7, no. 3 (2004): 343–63. DOI: 10.1177/1367877904046412.

CONG. "Cong Topsite (CONG-cong.1997.09.21.nfo)," September 21, 1997. DeFacto2, warez.scene.nfo.collection.v1.0.24351.shroo.ms.zip.

Conolly, Oliver, and Bashshar Haydar. "The Good, The Bad and The Funny." *The Monist* 88, no. 1 (2005): 121–34. DOI: 10.5840/monist20058817.

Cook, Deborah. *The Culture Industry Revisited: Theodor W. Adorno on Mass Culture.* Lanham: Rowman and Littlefield, 1996.

Cooper, Jon, and Daniel M. Harrison. "The Social Organization of Audio Piracy on the Internet." *Media, Culture & Society* 23, no. 1 (2001): 71–89. DOI: 10.1177/016344301023001004.

Cornish, Derek B., and Roland V. Clarke. "Analyzing Organized Crimes." In *Rational Choice and Criminal Behaviour: Recent Research and Future Challenges,* edited by Alex R. Piquero and Stephen G. Tibbetts, 41–64. New York: Routledge, 2002.

Coupland, Douglas. *Microserfs.* London: Flamingo, 1995.

Cowan, Rosie. "Jail for Net Pirates Who Saw Themselves as Robin Hoods." *The Guardian,* May 7, 2005. http://www.theguardian.com/technology/2005/may/07/crime.uknews.

Cowen, Tyler. *In Praise of Commercial Culture.* Cambridge: Harvard University Press, 2000.

CPX. "The Complex Topsite (CPX-the.complex.1997.01.03.nfo)," January 3, 1997. DeFacto2, warez.scene.nfo.collection.v1.0.24351.shroo.ms.zip.

Craig, Paul. *Software Piracy Exposed.* Rockland: Syngress, 2005.

CRC. "Castle Rock County Topsite (CRC-castle.rock.county.1997.04.03.nfo)," April 3, 1997. DeFacto2, warez.scene.nfo.collection.v1.0.24351.shroo.ms.zip.

Crisp, Virginia. "Access and Power: Film Distribution, Re-Intermediation and Piracy." In *The Routledge Companion to World Cinema,* edited by Rob Stone, Paul Cooke, Stephanie Dennison, and Alex Marlow-Mann, 445–54. London: Routledge, 2018.

———. "'BLOODY PIRATES!!! *Shakes Fist*': Reimagining East Asian Film Distribution and Reception through Online Filesharing Networks." *Journal of Japanese and Korean Cinema* 3, no. 1 (2012): 65–72. DOI: 10.1386/jjkc.3.1.65_1.
———. *Film Distribution in the Digital Age: Pirates and Professionals*. London: Palgrave Macmillan, 2017.
———. "Release Groups & The Scene: Re-Intermediation and Competitive Gatekeepers Online." *Cinéma & Cie* 17, no. 29 (Fall 2017): 67–79. https://riviste.unimi.it/index.php/cinemaetcie/article/view/16570.
———. "The Piratical Is Political." *Soundings* 55 (2013): 71–80. https://muse.jhu.edu/article/531188/pdf.
———. "To Name a Thief: Constructing the Deviant Pirate." In *Piracy: Leakages from Modernity,* edited by Martin Fredriksson and James Arvanitakis, 39–54. Sacramento: Litwin Books, 2014.
CV. "Cash Vault Topsite (CV-cash.vault.1998.08.25.nfo)," April 3, 1997. DeFacto2, warez.scene.nfo.collection.v1.0.24351.shroo.ms.zip.
CWS. "Courier Weektop ScoreCard 001 (cws001.txt)," February 9, 1998. DeFacto2.
D. "Daedalus Topsite (D-daedalus.1998.01.05.nfo)," January 5, 1998. DeFacto2, warez.scene.nfo.collection.v1.0.24351.shroo.ms.zip.
DA. "Dark Ambitions Topsite (DA-dark.ambitions.XXXX.XX.00.nfo)," n.d. DeFacto2, warez.scene.nfo.collection.v1.0.24351.shroo.ms.zip.
Davies, William. *The Limits of Neoliberalism: Authority, Sovereignty and the Logic of Competition*. Thousand Oaks: SAGE Publications, 2014.
Dawdy, Shannon Lee, and Joe Bonni. "Towards a General Theory of Piracy." *Anthropological Quarterly* 85, no. 3 (Summer 2012): 673–99. DOI: 10.1353/anq.2012.0043.
DBZ. "Divide By Zero Topsite (DBZ-divide.by.zero.2000.01.21.nfo)," January 21, 2000. DeFacto2, warez.scene.nfo.collection.v1.0.24351.shroo.ms.zip.

———. "Divide By Zero Topsite (DBZ-divide.by.zero.XXXX.XX.01.nfo)," n.d. DeFacto2, warez.scene.nfo.collection.v1.0.24351.shroo.ms.zip.

DC. "Digital Corruption Topsite (DC-digital.corruption.1998.02.12.nfo)," February 12, 1998. DeFacto2, warez.scene.nfo.collection.v1.0.24351.shroo.ms.zip.

———. "Digital Corruption Topsite (DC-digital.corruption.1998.03.18.nfo)," March 18, 1998. DeFacto2, warez.scene.nfo.collection.v1.0.24351.shroo.ms.zip.

———. "Digital Crossroads Topsite (DC-digital.crossroads.1998.09.02.nfo)," September 2, 1998. DeFacto2, warez.scene.nfo.collection.v1.0.24351.shroo.ms.zip.

———. "Dream Castle Topsite (DC-dream.castle.1999.03.29.nfo)," March 29, 1999. DeFacto2, warez.scene.nfo.collection.v1.0.24351.shroo.ms.zip.

DD. "Dark Data Topsite (DD-dark.data.1998.11.02.nfo)," November 2, 1998. DeFacto2, warez.scene.nfo.collection.v1.0.24351.shroo.ms.zip.

DDT. "Deadeloth Topsite (DDT-deadeloth.1997.11.17.nfo)," November 17, 1997. DeFacto2, warez.scene.nfo.collection.v1.0.24351.shroo.ms.zip.

de Campos, Augusto, Decio Pignatari, and Harold de Campos. "Pilot Plan for Concrete Poetry." In *Concrete Poetry: A World View*, edited by Mary Ellen Solt, 71–72. Bloomington: Indiana University Press, 1968.

de Souza, Philip. *Piracy in the Graeco-Roman World*. Cambridge: Cambridge University Press, 1999.

Décary-Hétu, David. "Police Operations 3.0: On the Impact and Policy Implications of Police Operations on the Warez Scene." *Policy & Internet* 6, no. 3 (September 2014): 315–40. DOI: 10.1002/1944-2866.POI369.

Décary-Hétu, David, Carlo Morselli, and Stéphane Leman-Langlois. "Welcome to the Scene: A Study of Social Organization and Recognition among Warez Hackers." *Journal of Research in Crime and Delinquency* 49, no. 3 (2012): 359–82. DOI: 10.1177/0022427811420876.

DeFacto2. "Wanted Uploads." *GitHub,* March 25, 2019. https://github.com/Defacto2/defacto2.net.

Delaney, Erin. "Searching for Constitutional Meaning in Institutional Design: The Debate Over Judicial Appointments in the United Kingdom." *International Journal of Constitutional Law* 14, no. 3 (2016): 752–68. DOI: 10.1093/icon/mow044.

Demers, Joanna Teresa. *Steal This Music: How Intellectual Property Law Affects Musical Creativity.* Athens: University of Georgia Press, 2006.

Denegri-Knott, Janice. "Sinking the Online 'Music Pirates': Foucault, Power and Deviance on the Web." *Journal of Computer-Mediated Communication* 9, no. 4 (2004). DOI: 10.1111/j.1083-6101.2004.tb00293.x.

dennison. "DENNISON'S GAME REVIEW." *Netmonkey Weekly Report* (nwr78.txt), March 29, 2000. DeFacto2.

Dent, Alexander Sebastian. "Introduction: Understanding the War on Piracy, Or Why We Need More Anthropology of Pirates." *Anthropological Quarterly* 85, no. 3 (2012): 659–72. https://www.jstor.org/stable/41857266.

Devine, Kyle. "Nightmares on Wax: The Environmental Impact of the Vinyl Revival." *The Guardian,* January 28, 2020. http://www.theguardian.com/music/2020/jan/28/vinyl-record-revival-environmental-impact-music-industry-streaming.

DF. "DaFat of the Land Topsite (DF-da.fat.1998.02.23.nfo)," February 23, 1998. DeFacto2, warez.scene.nfo.collection.v1.0.24351.shroo.ms.zip.

———. "DaFat of the Land Topsite (DF-da.fat.1998.09.16.nfo)," September 16, 1998. DeFacto2, warez.scene.nfo.collection.v1.0.24351.shroo.ms.zip.

DF2. "DaFat of the Land 2 Topsite (DF2-da.fat.two.1998.10.14.nfo)," October 14, 1998. DeFacto2, warez.scene.nfo.collection.v1.0.24351.shroo.ms.zip.

DF3. "DaFat of the Land 3 Topsite (DF3-da.fat.three.1999.06.05.nfo)," June 5, 1999. DeFacto2, warez.scene.nfo.collection.v1.0.24351.shroo.ms.zip.

DGB. "DagoBah System Topsite (DGB-dagobah.1998.11.19.nfo)," November 19, 1998. DeFacto2, warez.scene.nfo.collection.v1.0.24351.shroo.ms.zip.
DI. "Distorted Illusions Topsite (DI-distorted.illusions.XXXX.XX.01.nfo)," n.d. DeFacto2, warez.scene.nfo.collection.v1.0.24351.shroo.ms.zip.
Dibley, Sam. "Former Leader of Razor 1911, the Oldest Game Software Piracy Ring on the Internet, Sentenced." *US Department of Justice,* June 6, 2003. https://www.justice.gov/archive/criminal/cybercrime/press-releases/2003/pitmanSent.htm.
DIP. "Digital Information Playground Topsite (DIP-digital.information.playground.1998.02.28.nfo)," February 28, 1998. DeFacto2, warez.scene.nfo.collection.v1.0.24351.shroo.ms.zip.
DIS. "Disaster Topsite (DIS-disaster.1997.02.13.nfo)," February 13, 1997. DeFacto2, warez.scene.nfo.collection.v1.0.24351.shroo.ms.zip.
DK. "Digital Kingdom Topsite (DK-digital.kingdom.1999.08.25.nfo)," August 25, 1999. DeFacto2, warez.scene.nfo.collection.v1.0.24351.shroo.ms.zip.
———. "Digital Kingdom Topsite (DK-digital.kingdom.1999.11.17.nfo)," November 17, 1999. DeFacto2, warez.scene.nfo.collection.v1.0.24351.shroo.ms.zip.
DL. "Dark Land Topsite (DL-dark.land.1999.01.13.nfo)," January 13, 1999. DeFacto2, warez.scene.nfo.collection.v1.0.24351.shroo.ms.zip.
———. "DreamLand Topsite (DL-dream.land.1999.01.21.nfo)," January 21, 1999. DeFacto2, warez.scene.nfo.collection.v1.0.24351.shroo.ms.zip.
———. "DreamLand Topsite (DL-dream.land.1999.04.27.nfo)," April 27, 1999. DeFacto2, warez.scene.nfo.collection.v1.0.24351.shroo.ms.zip.
DLM. "Delerium Topsite (DLM-delirium.1998.05.20.nfo)," May 20, 1998. DeFacto2, warez.scene.nfo.collection.v1.0.24351.shroo.ms.zip.

DLS. "Darklands Topsite (DLS-darklands.2000.03.26.nfo)," March 26, 2000. DeFacto2, warez.scene.nfo.collection.v1.0.24351.shroo.ms.zip.
DM. "Dream Machine Topsite (DM-dream.machine.1997.10.14.nfo)," October 14, 1997. DeFacto2, warez.scene.nfo.collection.v1.0.24351.shroo.ms.zip.
DN. "Damn Nation Topsite (DN-damn.nation.1998.08.25.nfo)," August 25, 1998. DeFacto2, warez.scene.nfo.collection.v1.0.24351.shroo.ms.zip.
DO. "Digital Overload Topsite (DO-digital.overload.1998.04.19.nfo)," April 19, 1998. DeFacto2, warez.scene.nfo.collection.v1.0.24351.shroo.ms.zip.
DOPE. "Department of Pure Ecstacy Topsite (DOPE-department.of.pure.ecstacy.1999.03.31.nfo)," March 31, 1999. DeFacto2, warez.scene.nfo.collection.v1.0.24351.shroo.ms.zip.
DPT-d. "D.-.P.A.R.T.M.E.N.T Topsite (DPT-d.partment.1999.03.12.nfo)," March 12, 1999. DeFacto2, warez.scene.nfo.collection.v1.0.24351.shroo.ms.zip.
DPX. "The Duplex Topsite (DPX-duplex.1997.04.01.nfo)," April 1, 1997. DeFacto2, warez.scene.nfo.collection.v1.0.24351.shroo.ms.zip.
DPZ. "Dropzone Topsite (DPZ-dropzone.2000.09.25.nfo)," September 25, 2000. DeFacto2, warez.scene.nfo.collection.v1.0.24351.shroo.ms.zip.
Drucker, Johanna. *Figuring the Word: Essays on Books, Writing, and Visual Poetics.* New York: Granary Books, 1998.
———. *Graphesis: Visual Forms of Knowledge Production.* Cambridge: Harvard University Press, 2014.
———. *The Visible Word, Experimental Typography and Modern Art, 1909–1923.* Chicago: University of Chicago Press, 1997.
DS. "The Dark Side Topsite (DS-the.dark.side.1998.08.19.nfo)," August 19, 1998. DeFacto2, warez.scene.nfo.collection.v1.0.24351.shroo.ms.zip.

DST. "Dismal Surrection Topsite (DST-dismal.surrection.1999.07.27.nfo)," July 27, 1999. DeFacto2, warez.scene.nfo.collection.v1.0.24351.shroo.ms.zip.

DTO. "Ditto Topsite (DTO-ditto.1998.10.01.nfo)," October 1, 1998. DeFacto2, warez.scene.nfo.collection.v1.0.24351.shroo.ms.zip.

Durham, Blake. "Circulatory Maintenance: The Entailments of Participation in Digital Music Platforms." *American Music* 38, no. 2 (Summer 2020): 197–216. DOI: 10.5406/americanmusic.38.2.0197.

dustie. "some little notes." *Front Line Scene Release Report* (frontline_week_010.txt), July 7, 1999. DeFacto2.

DV. "Diamond Valley Topsite (DV-diamond.valley.1998.07.27.nfo)," July 27, 1998. DeFacto2, warez.scene.nfo.collection.v1.0.24351.shroo.ms.zip.

DXL. "Dixieland Topsite (DXL-dixieland.1999.02.22.nfo)," February 22, 1999. DeFacto2, warez.scene.nfo.collection.v1.0.24351.shroo.ms.zip.

Dyer-Witheford, Nick. "E-Capital and the Many Headed Hydra." In *Critical Perspectives on the Internet,* edited by Greg Elmer, 129–63. Lanham: Rowman & Littlefield Publishers, 2002.

DZ. "Danger Zone Topsite (DZ-danger.zone.XXXX.XX.00.nfo)," n.d. DeFacto2, warez.scene.nfo.collection.v1.0.24351.shroo.ms.zip.

DZL. "The Dragonz Lair Topsite (DZL-the.dragonz.lair.1998.02.05.nfo)," February 5, 1998. DeFacto2, warez.scene.nfo.collection.v1.0.24351.shroo.ms.zip.

E999. "East 999 Topsite (E999-east.999.1997.05.03.nfo)," May 3, 1997. DeFacto2, warez.scene.nfo.collection.v1.0.24351.shroo.ms.zip.

EB. "Echo Base Topsite (EB-echo.base.1999.03.11.nfo)," March 11, 1999. DeFacto2, warez.scene.nfo.collection.v1.0.24351.shroo.ms.zip.

EC. "Eternal Chaos Topsite (EC-eternal.chaos.1999.05.19.nfo)," May 19, 1999. DeFacto2, warez.scene.nfo.collection.v1.0.24351.shroo.ms.zip.

ECLI:NL:GHDHA:2013:BZ6496, voorheen LJN BZ6496, 22-004070-11 (Gerechtshof Den Haag April 8, 2013).

ECLI:NL:RBROT:2011:BR5610, voorheen LJN BR5610, 10/600129-08 (Rechtbank Rotterdam August 24, 2011).

ED. "The Evil Drome Topsite (ED-evil.drome.1998.07.26.nfo)," July 26, 1998. DeFacto2, warez.scene.nfo.collection.v1.0.24351.shroo.ms.zip.

Edwards, Adam, and Michael Levi. "Researching the Organization of Serious Crimes." *Criminology & Criminal Justice* 8, no. 4 (2008): 363–88. DOI: 10.1177/1748895808097403.

EE. "Evil Echo Topsite (EE-evil.echo.1999.06.18.nfo)," June 18, 1999. DeFacto2, warez.scene.nfo.collection.v1.0.24351.shroo.ms.zip.

Eijk, Nico van, Joost Poort, and Paul Rutten. "Legal, Economic and Cultural Aspects of File Sharing." *Communications & Strategies* 77, no. 1 (2010): 35–54.

Eliot, T.S. *The Sacred Wood: Essays on Poetry and Criticism.* New York: Alfred A. Knopf, 1921.

EMP. "The Emporium Topsite (EMP-the.emporium.1997.05.28.nfo)," May 28, 1997. DeFacto2, warez.scene.nfo.collection.v1.0.24351.shroo.ms.zip.

END. "Endurance Topsite (END-endurance.1998.03.01.nfo)," March 1, 1998. DeFacto2, warez.scene.nfo.collection.v1.0.24351.shroo.ms.zip.

English, James F. *The Economy of Prestige: Prizes, Awards, and the Circulation of Cultural Value.* Cambridge: Harvard University Press, 2005.

EOE. "Essence of Earth Topsite (EOE-essence.of.earth.2000.09.26.nfo)," September 26, 2000. DeFacto2, warez.scene.nfo.collection.v1.0.24351.shroo.ms.zip.

———. "The Ends of the Earth Topsite (EOE-endz.of.the.earth.1997.09.19.nfo)," September 19, 1997. DeFacto2, warez.scene.nfo.collection.v1.0.24351.shroo.ms.zip.

EOS. "Edge of Sanity Topsite (EOS-edge.of.sanity.1997.11.01.nfo)," November 1, 1997. DeFacto2, warez.scene.nfo.collection.v1.0.24351.shroo.ms.zip.

ER. "Escape Reality Topsite (ER-escape.reality.1997.08.25.nfo)," August 25, 1997. DeFacto2, warez.scene.nfo.collection.v1.0.24351.shroo.ms.zip.

Eriksson, Maria. "A Different Kind of Story: Tracing the Histories and Cultural Marks of Pirate Copied Film." *Tecnoscienza: Italian Journal of Science & Technology Studies* 7, no. 1 (2016): 87–108. http://www.tecnoscienza.net/index.php/tsj/article/view/254/168.

ET. "Etirnity Topsite (ET-etirnity.1996.08.10.nfo)," August 10, 1996. DeFacto2, warez.scene.nfo.collection.v1.0.24351.shroo.ms.zip.

Eve, Martin Paul. "Lessons from the Library: Extreme Minimalist Scaling at Pirate Ebook Platforms." *Digital Humanities Quarterly* (2022), forthcoming.

———. *Password*. New York: Bloomsbury Academic, 2016.

———. *Pynchon and Philosophy: Wittgenstein, Foucault and Adorno*. London: Palgrave Macmillan, 2014.

———. *The Digital Humanities and Literary Studies*. Oxford: Oxford University Press, 2022.

———. "The Great Automatic Grammatizator: Writing, Labour, Computers." *Critical Quarterly* 59, no. 3 (October 2017): 39–54. DOI: 10.1111/criq.12359.

EVN. "Evasion Topsite (EVN-evasion.1998.10.26.nfo)," October 26, 1998. DeFacto2, warez.scene.nfo.collection.v1.0.24351.shroo.ms.zip.

Ewing, Tom. "Run-DMC vs Jason Nevins – 'It's Like That.'" *FreakyTrigger*, May 4, 2014. http://freakytrigger.co.uk/popular/2014/05/run-dmc-vs-jason-nevins-its-like-that/.

F. "Flash Topsite (F-flash.1999.04.18.nfo)," April 18, 1999. DeFacto2, warez.scene.nfo.collection.v1.0.24351.shroo.ms.zip.

F2. "Foundation Two Topsite (F2-foundation.two.1997.04.26.nfo)," April 26, 1997. DeFacto2, warez.scene.nfo.collection.v1.0.24351.shroo.ms.zip.

Favale, Marcella, Neil MacDonald, Shamal Faily, and Christos Gatzidis. "Human Aspects in Digital Rights Management:

The Perspective of Content Developers." *SSRN Electronic Journal* (2016). DOI: 10.2139/ssrn.2729199.

FB. "Flashback Topsite (FB-flashbak.1998.08.25.nfo)," August 25, 1998. DeFacto2, warez.scene.nfo.collection.v1.0.24351.shroo.ms.zip.

FB2. "The Fat Babe Two Topsite (FB2-the.fat.babe.two.1997.07.12.nfo)," July 12, 1997. DeFacto2, warez.scene.nfo.collection.v1.0.24351.shroo.ms.zip.

FE. "Fatal Error Topsite (FE-fatal.error.1997.03.02.nfo)," March 2, 1997. DeFacto2, warez.scene.nfo.collection.v1.0.24351.shroo.ms.zip.

Federici, Silvia Beatriz. *Caliban and the Witch: Women, the Body, and Primitive Accumulation.* New York: Autonomedia, 1997.

Ferrer, Mercè Molist. *Hackstory.es: La Historia Nunca Contada del Underground Hacker en la Península Ibérica.* Spain: published by the author: 2014.

FF. "Fire Fox Topsite (FF-fire.fox.1999.06.28.nfo)," June 28, 1999. DeFacto2, warez.scene.nfo.collection.v1.0.24351.shroo.ms.zip.

FH. "FalseHood Topsite (FH-false.hood.1998.02.26.nfo)," February 26, 1998. DeFacto2, warez.scene.nfo.collection.v1.0.24351.shroo.ms.zip.

———. "FalseHood Topsite (FH-false.hood.1998.08.27.nfo)," August 27, 1998. DeFacto2, warez.scene.nfo.collection.v1.0.24351.shroo.ms.zip.

Finley, Klint. "The Average Webpage Is Now the Size of the Original Doom." *Wired,* April 23, 2016. https://www.wired.com/2016/04/average-webpage-now-size-original-doom/.

Fiormonte, Domenico. "Towards a Cultural Critique of the Digital Humanities." *Historical Social Research / Historische Sozialforschung* 37, no. 3 (2012): 59–76. https://www.jstor.org/stable/41636597.

FK. "Foo.Keen Topsite (FK-foo.keen.1999.09.07.nfo)," September 7, 1999. DeFacto2, warez.scene.nfo.collection.v1.0.24351.shroo.ms.zip.

———. "Foo.Keen Topsite (FK-foo.keen.XXXX.XX.01.nfo)," n.d. DeFacto2, warez.scene.nfo.collection.v1.0.24351.shroo.ms.zip.

FL. "Frag Land Topsite (FL-frag.land.1998.05.15.nfo)," May 15, 1998. DeFacto2, warez.scene.nfo.collection.v1.0.24351.shroo.ms.zip.

———. "Fungus Land Topsite (FL-fungus.land.1998.08.12.nfo)," August 12, 1998. DeFacto2, warez.scene.nfo.collection.v1.0.24351.shroo.ms.zip.

Fletcher, J. "The Painful Sting of Serious Sam 3's Anti-Piracy Protection." *Engadget*, December 7, 2011. https://www.engadget.com/2011-12-07-the-painful-sting-of-serious-sam-3s-anti-piracy-protection.html.

Fontaine, Marcel, and Filip De Ly. *Drafting International Contracts: An Analysis of Contract Clauses.* Ardsley: Transnational Publishers, 2006.

FOS. "Fortress of Solitude Topsite (FOS-fortress.of.solitude.1998.02.10.nfo)," February 10, 1998. DeFacto2, warez.scene.nfo.collection.v1.0.24351.shroo.ms.zip.

———. "Fortress of Solitude Topsite (FOS-fortress.of.solitude.1998.12.23.nfo)," December 23, 1998. DeFacto2, warez.scene.nfo.collection.v1.0.24351.shroo.ms.zip.

FP. "Floating Point Topsite (FP-floating.point.1997.06.08.nfo)," June 8, 1997. DeFacto2, warez.scene.nfo.collection.v1.0.24351.shroo.ms.zip.

FS. "Fire Site Topsite (FS-fire.site.2000.09.14.nfo)," September 14, 2000. DeFacto2, warez.scene.nfo.collection.v1.0.24351.shroo.ms.zip.

———. "Fuckin Stoned Topsite (FS-fuckin.stoned.1997.10.30.nfo)," October 30, 1997. DeFacto2, warez.scene.nfo.collection.v1.0.24351.shroo.ms.zip.

FSN. "Fusion Topsite (FSN-fusion.XXXX.XX.00.nfo)," n.d. DeFacto2, warez.scene.nfo.collection.v1.0.24351.shroo.ms.zip.

FUBAR. "Fucked Up Beyond All Recognition Topsite (FUBAR-fucked.up.beyond.all.recognition.1997.01.20.nfo),"

January 20, 1997. DeFacto2, warez.scene.nfo.collection. v1.0.24351.shroo.ms.zip.

Fukuyama, Francis. *Trust: The Social Virtues and the Creation of Prosperity.* New York: Free Press, 1995.

Furnell, S.M. "Categorising Cybercrime and Cybercriminals." *Journal of Information Warfare* 1, no. 2 (2020): 35–44. https://www.jstor.org/stable/26486092.

Ganesh, Bharath. "The Ungovernability of Digital Hate Culture." *Journal of International Affairs* 71, no. 2 (2018): 30–49. https://www.jstor.org/stable/26552328.

Gantz, John, and Jack B. Rochester. *Pirates of the Digital Millennium: How the Intellectual Property Wars Damage Our Personal Freedoms, Our Jobs, and the World Economy.* Upper Saddle River: Prentice Hall, 2005.

Garcia, Antero, and Greg Niemeyer. "Introduction." In *Alternate Reality Games and the Cusp of Digital Gameplay,* edited by Antero Garcia and Greg Niemeyer, 1–28. New York: Bloomsbury Academic, 2017.

Garrett, Ben. "Online Software Piracy of the Last Millennium," April 27, 2004. DeFacto2. http://www.defacto2.net/file/download/a53981.

Gellaerts, Sander. "Watermerken als juridisch bewijsmiddel: Een onderzoek naar de effectiviteit van digitale watermerken als juridisch bewijsmiddel." PhD diss., Tilburg University, 2015.

GF. "General Failure Topsite (GF-general.failure.1997.01.04.nfo)," January 4, 1997. DeFacto2, warez.scene.nfo.collection. v1.0.24351.shroo.ms.zip.

GH. "Guru Heaven Topsite (GH-guru.heaven.1998.05.04.nfo)," May 4, 1998. DeFacto2, warez.scene.nfo.collection. v1.0.24351.shroo.ms.zip.

Gibson, Joel. "Kookaburra Sits on a Small Fortune: Ruling on Down Under Royalties." *The Sydney Morning Herald,* July 6, 2010. https://www.smh.com.au/entertainment/music/kookaburra-sits-on-a-small-fortune-ruling-on-down-under-royalties-20100706-zy5l.html.

glftpd. "Yet Another Traffic Bouncer." 2020. https://github.com/glftpd/yatb.

GM. "Guru Meditation Topsite (GM-guru.meditation.1997.03.07.nfo)," March 7, 1997. DeFacto2, warez.scene.nfo.collection.v1.0.24351.shroo.ms.zip.

GNS. "Genesis Topsite (GNS-genesis.1999.07.05.nfo)," July 5, 1999. DeFacto2, warez.scene.nfo.collection.v1.0.24351.shroo.ms.zip.

Goldberg, Daniel. "'We Might be Old, but We're Still the Elite.'" *Computer Sweden,* April 20, 2012. https://computersweden.idg.se/2.2683/1.444716/we-might-be-old-but-were-still-the-elite.

Goldman, Eric. "A Road to No Warez: The No Electronic Theft Act and Criminal Copyright Infringement." *Oregon Law Review* 82 (2003): 369–432. https://scholarsbank.uoregon.edu/xmlui/handle/1794/4613.

———. "The Challenges of Regulating Warez Trading." *Social Science Computer Review* 23, no. 1 (2005): 24–28. DOI: 10.1177/0894439304271531.

———. "Warez Trading and Criminal Copyright Infringement." *SSRN Electronic Journal* (2004). DOI: 10.2139/ssrn.487163.

Goode, Sigi. "Exploring the Supply of Pirate Software for Mobile Devices: An Analysis of Software Types and Piracy Groups." *Information Management & Computer Security* 18, no. 4 (2010): 204–25. DOI: 10.1108/09685221011079171.

Goode, Sigi, and Sam Cruise. "What Motivates Software Crackers?" *Journal of Business Ethics* 65, no. 2 (May 2006): 173–201. DOI: 10.1007/s10551-005-4709-9.

Goodin, Dan. "Wikileaks Judge Gets Pirate Bay Treatment." *The Register,* February 21, 2008. https://www.theregister.com/2008/02/21/wikileaks_bulletproof_hosting/.

Gottschalk, Peter. *Entrepreneurship and Organized Crime: Entrepreneurs in Illegal Business.* Cheltenham: Edward Elgar, 2009.

Grafton, Anthony. *The Footnote: A Curious History.* Cambridge: Harvard University Press, 1999.

Grayson, Nathan. "Interview: Bohemia Interactive's CEO on Fighting Piracy, Creative DRM." *PC Gamer,* November 17, 2011. https://www.pcgamer.com/interview-bohemia-interactives-ceo-on-fighting-piracy-creative-drm/.

Greene, Viveca S. "'Deplorable' Satire: Alt-Right Memes, White Genocide Tweets, and Redpilling Normies." *Studies in American Humor* 5, no. 1 (2019): 31–69. DOI: 10.5325/studamerhumor.5.1.0031.

greyline. "glFTPD Configuration File Examples (glftpd-LNX-2.04_1.0.1e-2+deb7u3_x86_docs/glftpd.conf-EXAMPLES.txt)." mewbies.com, 2014. http://mewbies.com/glftpd-LNX-2.04_1.0.1e-2+deb7u3_x86_docs/glftpd.conf-EXAMPLES.txt.

———. "glftpd-LNX-2.04_1.0.1e-glFTPD TLS README (2+deb7u3_x86_docs/README.TLS.txt)." mewbies.com, 2014. http://mewbies.com/glftpd-LNX-2.04_1.0.1e-2+deb7u3_x86_docs/README.TLS.txt.

GS. "Green Skull Topsite (GS-green.skull.1997.05.25.nfo)," May 25, 1997. DeFacto2, warez.scene.nfo.collection.v1.0.24351.shroo.ms.zip.

H. "Hades Topsite (HDS-hades.1998.06.12.nfo)," June 12, 1998. DeFacto2, warez.scene.nfo.collection.v1.0.24351.shroo.ms.zip.

H2. "Hemispheres Two Topsite (H2-hemispheres.two.1998.05.27.nfo)," May 27, 1998. DeFacto2, warez.scene.nfo.collection.v1.0.24351.shroo.ms.zip.

———. "Hemispheres Two Topsite (H2-hemispheres.two.1998.07.28.nfo)," July 28, 1998. DeFacto2, warez.scene.nfo.collection.v1.0.24351.shroo.ms.zip.

H2H. "Highway 2 Hell Topsite (H2H-highway.2.hell.2000.08.27.nfo)," August 27, 2000. DeFacto2, warez.scene.nfo.collection.v1.0.24351.shroo.ms.zip.

Hall, Gary. *Pirate Philosophy: For a Digital Posthumanities.* Cambridge: MIT Press, 2016.

Harford, Tim. "High-Frequency Trading and the $440m Computer Glitch." *BBC News,* August 11, 2012. https://www.bbc.co.uk/news/magazine-19214294.

Harrison, K. David, and Gregory Anderson. "Review of Proposal for Encoding Warang Chiti (Ho Orthography) in Unicode,." *Unicode.org,* April 22, 2007.

Harwick, Cameron. "Cryptocurrency and the Problem of Intermediation." *The Independent Review* 20, no. 4 (Spring 2016): 569–88. DOI: 10.2139/ssrn.2523771.

HCN. "Holocron Topsite (HCN-holocron.XXXX.XX.00.nfo)," n.d. DeFacto2, warez.scene.nfo.collection.v1.0.24351.shroo.ms.zip.

Hebdige, Dick. *Subculture: The Meaning of Style.* London: Routledge, 2002.

Hesmondhalgh, David. "Subcultures, Scenes or Tribes? None of the Above." *Journal of Youth Studies* 8, no. 1 (2007): 21–40. DOI: 10.1080/13676260500063652.

HF. "Hard Floor Topsite (HF-hard.floor.1999.09.20.nfo)," September 20, 1999. DeFacto2, warez.scene.nfo.collection.v1.0.24351.shroo.ms.zip.

———. "Hell Fire Topsite (HF-hell.fire.1997.05.16.nfo)," May 16, 1997. DeFacto2, warez.scene.nfo.collection.v1.0.24351.shroo.ms.zip.

HH. "The Happy Hippo Topsite (HH-the.happy.hippo.1998.10.25.nfo)," October 25, 1998. DeFacto2, warez.scene.nfo.collection.v1.0.24351.shroo.ms.zip.

Hicks, Mar. *Programmed Inequality: How Britain Discarded Women Technologists and Lost Its Edge in Computing.* Cambridge: MIT Press, 2018.

Higgins, Charlotte. "China Miéville: Writers Should Welcome a Future Where Readers Remix Our Books." *The Guardian,* August 21, 2012. http://www.theguardian.com/books/2012/aug/21/china-mieville-novels-books-anti-piracy.

Hinduja, Sameer. *Music Piracy and Crime Theory.* New York: LFB Scholarly Pub., 2006.

———. "Neutralization Theory and Online Software Piracy: An Empirical Analysis." *Ethics and Information Technology* 9, no. 3 (2007): 187–204. DOI: 10.1007/s10676-007-9143-5.

Hobsbawm, Eric. *Bandits.* New York: Pantheon Books, 1981.

HOE. "Hades on Earth Topsite (HOE-hades.on.earth.1999.01.20.nfo)," January 20, 1999. DeFacto2, warez.scene.nfo.collection.v1.0.24351.shroo.ms.zip.

Hogan, Marc. "Is Vinyl's Comeback Here to Stay?" *Pitchfork,* January 22, 2018. https://pitchfork.com/features/article/is-vinyls-comeback-here-to-stay/.

HOL. "Hall of Illusions Topsite (HOL-hall.of.illusions.1999.10.28.nfo)," October 28, 1999. DeFacto2, warez.scene.nfo.collection.v1.0.24351.shroo.ms.zip.

Holm, Peter. "Piracy on the Simulated Seas: The Computer Games Industry's Non-Legal Approaches to Fighting Illegal Downloads of Games." *Information & Communications Technology Law* 23, no. 1 (2014): 61–76. DOI: 10.1080/13600834.2014.899770.

Holsapple, Clyde W., Deepak Iyengar, Haihao Jin, and Shashank Rao. "Parameters for Software Piracy Research." *The Information Society* 24, no. 4 (2008): 199–218. DOI: 10.1080/01972240802189468.

Holt, Thomas J. "Subcultural Evolution? Examining the Influence of On- and Off-Line Experiences on Deviant Subcultures." *Deviant Behavior* 28, no. 2 (2007): 171–98. DOI: 10.1080/01639620601131065.

HOM. "House of Music Topsite (HOM-house.of.music.2000.10.05.nfo)," October 5, 2000. DeFacto2, warez.scene.nfo.collection.v1.0.24351.shroo.ms.zip.

Horkheimer, Max, and Theodor W. Adorno. "The Culture Industry: Enlightenment as Mass Deception." In *Dialectic of Enlightenment: Philosophical Fragments,* edited by Gunzelin Schmid Noerr, translated by Edmund Jephcott, 95–136. Stanford: Stanford University Press, 2002.

HOW. "Hall of Warez Topsite (HOW-hall.of.warez.1997.05.24.nfo)," May 24, 1997. DeFacto2, warez.scene.nfo.collection.v1.0.24351.shroo.ms.zip.

Hui, Yuk. *On the Existence of Digital Objects.* Minneapolis: University of Minnesota Press, 2016.

Huizing, Ard, and Jan A. van der Wal. "Explaining the Rise and Fall of the Warez MP3 Scene: An Empirical Account from the Inside." *First Monday* 19, no. 10 (2014). DOI: 10.5210/fm.v19i10.5546.

Humphries, Jane. "Enclosures, Common Rights, and Women: The Proletarianization of Families in the Late Eighteenth and Early Nineteenth Centuries." *The Journal of Economic History* 50, no. 1 (1990): 17–42. DOI: 10.1017/S0022050700035701.

HW. "Hard Wired Topsite (HW-hard.wired.1997.03.27.nfo)," March 27, 1997. DeFacto2, warez.scene.nfo.collection.v1.0.24351.shroo.ms.zip.

———. "Hard Wired Topsite (HW-hard.wired.1998.08.27.nfo)," August 27, 1998. DeFacto2, warez.scene.nfo.collection.v1.0.24351.shroo.ms.zip.

IC. "Identity Crisis Topsite (IC-identity.crisis.1999.03.31.nfo)," March 31, 1999. DeFacto2, warez.scene.nfo.collection.v1.0.24351.shroo.ms.zip.

IMP. "The Imperium Topsite (IMP-imperium.1998.07.19.nfo)," July 19, 1998. DeFacto2, warez.scene.nfo.collection.v1.0.24351.shroo.ms.zip.

———. "The Imperium Topsite (IMP-imperium.XXXX.XX.01.nfo)," n.d. DeFacto2, warez.scene.nfo.collection.v1.0.24351.shroo.ms.zip.

iNCiTE. "007 GoldenEye 1995 iNTERNAL DVDRip XviD (incite-goldeneye-xvid.nfo)," March 23, 2005. srrDB.

INF. "Infinity Topsite (INF-infinity.1998.04.10.nfo)," April 10, 1998. DeFacto2, warez.scene.nfo.collection.v1.0.24351.shroo.ms.zip.

Ingblad, Frederick. "Tillslag Mot Fildelningsnätverk." *Åklagarmyndigheten*, September 8, 2010. https://web.archive.org/web/20100908084809/https://www.aklagare.se/Media/Nyheter/Tillslag-mot-fildelningsnatverk1/.

IP. "Internet Protocol Topsite (IP-internet.protocol.1999.10.05.nfo)," October 5, 1999. DeFacto2, warez.scene.nfo.collection.v1.0.24351.shroo.ms.zip.

Irwin, John. *Scenes*. Thousand Oaks: SAGE Publications, 1977.

ISLE. "The Isle Topsite (ISLE-the.isle.1997.06.10.nfo)," June 10, 1997. DeFacto2, warez.scene.nfo.collection.v1.0.24351.shroo.ms.zip.

IST. "Insanity Storm Topsite (ISTORM-insanity.storm.1998.08.13.nfo)," August 13, 1998. DeFacto2, warez.scene.nfo.collection.v1.0.24351.shroo.ms.zip.

———. "Insanity Storm Topsite (ISTORM-insanity.storm.1998.09.19.nfo)," September 19, 1998. DeFacto2, warez.scene.nfo.collection.v1.0.24351.shroo.ms.zip.

IX. "Intoxicated Topsite (IX-intoxicated.1999.12.26.nfo)," December 26, 1999. DeFacto2, warez.scene.nfo.collection.v1.0.24351.shroo.ms.zip.

Jeffries, Fiona. "Reading 'Caliban and the Witch' Politically." *Gender, Place & Culture* 25, no. 9 (2018): 1322–28. DOI: 10.1080/0966369X.2018.1462772.

Jie, You. "Cultural Resistance or Corporate Assistance: Disenchanting the Anti-Capitalist Myth of Digital Piracy." In *Piracy: Leakages from Modernity*, edited by Martin Fredriksson and James Arvanitakis, 195–215. Sacramento: Litwin Books, 2014.

JNG. "The Jungle Topsite (JNG-the.jungle.1998.08.18.nfo)," August 18, 1998. DeFacto2, warez.scene.nfo.collection.v1.0.24351.shroo.ms.zip.

———. "The Jungle Topsite (JNG-the.jungle.XXXX.XX.00.nfo)," n.d. DeFacto2, warez.scene.nfo.collection.v1.0.24351.shroo.ms.zip.

Johns, Adrian. *Piracy: The Intellectual Property Wars from Gutenberg to Gates*. Chicago: University of Chicago Press, 2011.

———. "Pop Music Pirate Hunters." *Daedalus* 131, no. 2 (2002): 67–77. https://www.jstor.org/stable/20027761.

K. "Kane Topsite (K-kane.XXXX.XX.01.nfo)," n.d. DeFacto2, warez.scene.nfo.collection.v1.0.24351.shroo.ms.zip.

K2. "K2 Topsite (K2-k2.1998.03.21.nfo)," March 21, 1998. DeFacto2, warez.scene.nfo.collection.v1.0.24351.shroo.ms.zip.

Karkov, Catherine E., Anna Kłosowska, and Vincent W.J. van Gerven Oei, eds. *Disturbing Times: Medieval Pasts, Reimagined Futures.* Earth: punctum books, 2020.

Kaufman, Amy S., and Paul B. Sturtevant. *The Devil's Historians: How Modern Extremists Abuse the Medieval Past.* Toronto: University of Toronto Press, 2020.

Keery, Justin. "Special Report on Electronic Gifts: Teenage Pirates and the Junior." *The Independent,* December 11, 1992. https://www.independent.co.uk/news/science/special-report-on-electronic-gifts-teenage-pirates-and-the-junior-underworld-parents-should-know-that-children-can-buy-or-sell-illegal-copies-of-video-games-and-sex-writes-justin-keery-1562928.html.

Kendall, Lori. "Nerd Nation: Images of Nerds in US Popular Culture." *International Journal of Cultural Studies* 2, no. 2 (1999): 260–83. DOI: 10.1177/136787799900200206.

Kevelson, Morton. "Isepic." *Ahoy!,* October 1985, 71–73. https://archive.org/details/ahoy-magazine-22/page/n69/mode/2up.

Kiberd, Roisin. "The Minecraft Server That Will Kill You 1,000 Times." *Newsweek,* September 15, 2016. https://www.newsweek.com/2016/09/23/minecraft-anarchy-server-2b2t-will-kill-you-498946.html.

KK. "Kalles Kaviar Topsite (KK-kalles.kaviar.1999.09.15.nfo)," September 15, 1999. DeFacto2, warez.scene.nfo.collection.v1.0.24351.shroo.ms.zip.

Kline, Stephen, Nick Dyer-Witheford, and Greig De Peuter. "Workers and Warez: Labour and Piracy in the Global Game Market." In *Digital Play: The Interaction of Technology, Culture, and Marketing,* 197–217. Montreal: McGill-Queen's University Press, 2003.

Klug, Patrick. "What Happens When Pirates Play a Game Development Simulator and Then Go Bankrupt Because of Piracy?" *Greenheart Games,* April 29, 2013. https://www.greenheartgames.com/2013/04/29/what-happens-when-pirates-play-a-game-development-simulator-and-then-go-bankrupt-because-of-piracy/.

Knight Lightening and Taran King. "Phrack Pro-Phile 3: Featuring: User Groups and Clubs." *Phrack Magazine,* June 10, 1986. http://phrack.org/issues/6/2.html.

Kozinets, Robert V. *Netnography: Ethnographic Research in the Age of the Internet.* Thousand Oaks: SAGE Publications, 2010.

KRAD. "KRAD Topsite (KRAD-krad.1997.06.29.nfo)," September 15, 1999. DeFacto2, warez.scene.nfo.collection.v1.0.24351.shroo.ms.zip.

Krawczyk, Michał, Joanna Tyrowicz, Anna Kukla-Gryz, and Wojciech Hardy. "'Piracy Is Not Theft!' Is It Just Students Who Think So?" *Journal of Behavioral and Experimental Economics* 54 (2015): 32–39. DOI: 10.1016/j.socec.2014.11.003.

KRIB. "The Krib Topsite (KRIB-the.krib.1997.07.30.nfo)," July 30, 1997. DeFacto2, warez.scene.nfo.collection.v1.0.24351.shroo.ms.zip.

KRYNN. "Krynn Topsite (KRYNN-krynn.1997.11.25.nfo)," November 25, 1997. DeFacto2, warez.scene.nfo.collection.v1.0.24351.shroo.ms.zip.

KSH. "Kashmir Topsite (KSH-kashmir.1997.02.22.nfo)," February 22, 1997. DeFacto2, warez.scene.nfo.collection.v1.0.24351.shroo.ms.zip.

KTS. "Kinetics Topsite (KTS-kinetics.1997.01.15.nfo)," January 15, 1997. DeFacto2, warez.scene.nfo.collection.v1.0.24351.shroo.ms.zip.

Ku, Raymond Shih Ray. "The Creative Destruction of Copyright: Napster and the New Economics of Digital Technology." *The University of Chicago Law Review* 69, no. 1 (Winter 2002): 263–324. DOI: 10.2307/1600355.

Kugelberg, Johan, and Jon Savage. *Punk: An Aesthetic.* New York: Rizzoli, 2012.

LA. "Lunatic Asylum Topsite (LA-lunatic.asylum.1995.04.21.nfo)," April 21, 1995. DeFacto2, warez.scene.nfo.collection.v1.0.24351.shroo.ms.zip.

Lamer. "TNT." *The Unbiased DOX Report* (DR200510.TXT), July 11, 2005. DeFacto2.

Lasica, J.D. *Darknet: Hollywood's War against the Digital Generation.* Hoboken: Wiley, 2005.

Lawson, Stuart. "Open Access Policy in the UK: From Neoliberalism to the Commons." PhD diss., Birkbeck, University of London, 2019. https://hcommons.org/deposits/item/hc:23661/.

Leisure. Cubby, Inc. v. CompuServe, Inc., No. 776 F Supp 135 (United States District Court, S.D. New York October 29, 1991).

Lessig, Lawrence. *Free Culture: The Nature and Future of Creativity.* New York: Penguin Books, 2004.

———. *Remix: Making Art and Commerce Thrive in the Hybrid Economy.* New York: Penguin Books, 2008.

lester. "Deep Thoughts." *Netmonkey Weekly Report* (nwr17.txt), August 16, 1998. DeFacto2.

———. "Stories from the Watercooler." *Netmonkey Weekly Report* (nwr47.txt), May 11, 1999. DeFacto2.

———. "The Art of Good Trading." *Netmonkey Weekly Report* (nwr28.txt), December 22, 1998. DeFacto2.

———. "Which Ftpd Is Right for You?" *Netmonkey Weekly Report* (Nwr36.Txt), February 22, 1999.

Levi, Michael. "Organized Crime." In *The Oxford Handbook of Criminology,* edited by Mike Maguire, Rodney Morgan, and Robert Reiner. 3rd edn. New York: Oxford University Press, 2002.

Levin, Aron M., Mary Conway Dato-on, and Kenneth Rhee. "Money for Nothing and Hits for Free: The Ethics of Downloading Music from Peer-to-Peer Web Sites." *Journal of Marketing Theory and Practice* 12, no. 1 (2004): 48–60. DOI: 10.1080/10696679.2004.11658512.

Limayem, Moez, Mohamed Khalifa, and Wynne W. Chin. "Factors Motivating Software Piracy: A Longitudinal Study." *IEEE Transactions on Engineering Management* 51, no. 4 (November 2004): 414–25. DOI: 10.1109/TEM.2004.835087.

Linebaugh, Peter, and Marcus Rediker. *The Many-Headed Hydra: Sailors, Slaves, Commoners, and the Hidden History of the Revolutionary Atlantic.* Boston: Beacon Press, 2003.

LIS. "Lost in Space Topsite (LIS-lost.in.space.1997.08.13.nfo)," August 13, 1998. DeFacto2, warez.scene.nfo.collection. v1.0.24351.shroo.ms.zip.

Lithgow, Timothy. "Sci-Fi Unveils the 'Geek Pound.'" *MediaWeek,* June 27, 2005. https://www.campaignlive.co.uk/article/sci-fi-unveils-geek-pound/510998.

Liu, Alan. *The Laws of Cool: Knowledge Work and the Culture of Information.* Chicago: University of Chicago Press, 2004.

LL. "Low Lands Topsite (LL-low.lands.1999.09.08.nfo)," September 8, 1999. DeFacto2, warez.scene.nfo.collection. v1.0.24351.shroo.ms.zip.

Lobato, Ramón. *Shadow Economies of Cinema: Mapping Informal Film Distribution.* London: Palgrave Macmillan, 2012.

Lobato, Ramon, and Julian Thomas. "An Introduction to Informal Media Economies." *Television & New Media* 13, no. 5 (2012): 379–82. DOI: 10.1177/1527476412443565.

Logan, Lucas. "The IPR GPR: The Emergence of a Global Prohibition Regime to Regulate Intellectual Property Infringement." In *Piracy: Leakages from Modernity,* edited by Martin Fredriksson and James Arvanitakis, 137–56. Sacramento: Litwin Books, 2014.

Lomuto, Sierra. "White Nationalism and the Ethics of Medieval Studies." *In the Middle,* December 5, 2016. https://www.inthemedievalmiddle.com/2016/12/white-nationalism-and-ethics-of.html.

Lord Rameses. "Interview with hodd of VOLiTiON." *Courier Weektop Scorecard* (CwS-116.txt), September 3, 2000. DeFacto2.

———. "Interview with Seraph of XCRYPT." *Courier Weektop Scorecard* (CwS-118.txt), September 17, 2000. DeFacto2.

LS. "CWS News." *Courier Weektop Scorecard* (CWS-80.txt), January 1, 1999. DeFacto2.

———. "Lost Shrine Topsite (LS-lost.shrine.1998.05.28.nfo)," May 28, 1998. DeFacto2, warez.scene.nfo.collection. v1.0.24351.shroo.ms.zip.

———. "SCENE NEWS." *Courier Weektop Scorecard* (CwS-102.txt), June 3, 2000. DeFacto2.

———. "SiTE OPS AND TRADERS READ BELOW." *Courier Weektop Scorecard* (CwS-137.txt), February 3, 2001. DeFacto2.

———. "The Last Stand Topsite (LS-the.last.stand.1998.01.22.nfo)," January 22, 1998. DeFacto2, warez.scene.nfo.collection.v1.0.24351.shroo.ms.zip.

LTZ. "Less Than Zero Topsite (LTZ-less.than.zero.1997.11.02.nfo)," November 2, 1997. DeFacto2, warez.scene.nfo.collection.v1.0.24351.shroo.ms.zip.

Lunt, Steven J. "FTP Security Extensions." *Internet Engineering Task Force,* October 1997. https://tools.ietf.org/html/rfc2228.

Luther, William J. "Bitcoin and the Future of Digital Payments." *The Independent Review* 20, no. 3 (Winter 2015/2016): 397–404. DOI: 10.2139/ssrn.2631314.

LW. "The Lost World Topsite (LW-the.lost.world.1997.10.25.nfo)," October 25, 1997. DeFacto2, warez.scene.nfo.collection.v1.0.24351.shroo.ms.zip.

LXL. "Linux Unleashed Topsite (LXL-linux.unleashed.1999.06.29.nfo)," June 29, 1999. DeFacto2, warez.scene.nfo.collection.v1.0.24351.shroo.ms.zip.

LYNX. "Lynx Topsite (LYNX-lynx.1997.10.08.nfo)," October 8, 1997. DeFacto2, warez.scene.nfo.collection.v1.0.24351.shroo.ms.zip.

MacLellan, Rory. "Far-Right Appropriations of the Medieval Military Orders." *The Mediaeval Journal* 9, no. 1 (2019): 175–98. DOI: 10.1484/J.TMJ.5.119916.

MAD. "Mutually Assured Destruction Topsite (MAD-mutually.assured.destruction.1999.01.29.nfo)," January 29, 1999. DeFacto2, warez.scene.nfo.collection.v1.0.24351.shroo.ms.zip.

Madrigal, Alexis C. "The Lost Ancestors of ASCII Art." *The Atlantic,* January 30, 2014. https://www.theatlantic.com/technology/archive/2014/01/the-lost-ancestors-of-ascii-art/283445/.

Maher, Jimmy. "A Pirate's Life for Me, Part 2: The Scene." *The Digital Antiquarian,* January 1, 2016. https://www.filfre.net/2016/01/a-pirates-life-for-me-part-2-the-scene/.

———. *The Future Was Here: The Commodore Amiga.* Cambridge: MIT Press, 2012.

Manjoo, Farhad. "Were DrinkOrDie Raids Overkill?" *Wired,* December 13, 2001. https://www.wired.com/2001/12/were-drinkordie-raids-overkill/.

MantiCore. "AW: SQL scannen lohnt sich das noch?" *raid.rush,* May 3, 2010. https://raidrush.net/threads/sql-scannen-lohnt-sich-das-noch.711040/.

Margolin, James, and Nicholas Biase. "Acting US Attorney Announces Federal Charges and International Operation To Dismantle Online Piracy Group." *US Department of Justice,* August 26, 2020. https://www.justice.gov/usao-sdny/pr/acting-us-attorney-announces-federal-charges-and-international-operation-dismantle-0.

Marshall, Lee. "For and Against the Record Industry: An Introduction to Bootleg Collectors and Tape Traders." *Popular Music* 22, no. 1 (2003): 57–72. DOI: 10.1017/S0261143003003040.

Marsio, Leena. "Demoscene, Musical Saw Playing and Horsemanship of the Roma – 12 New Elements Inscribed on the National Inventory of Living Heritage." *Museovirasto,* September 4, 2020. https://www.museovirasto.fi/en/articles/demoskene-sahansoitto-ja-romanien-hevostaidot-elavan-perinnon-kansalliseen-luetteloon-12-uutta-kohdetta.

Martin, John D. "Piracy, Public Access, and Preservation: An Exploration of Sustainable Accessibility in a Public Torrent Index." *Proceedings of the Association for Information Science and Technology* 53, no. 1 (2016): 1–6. DOI: 10.1002/pra2.2016.14505301123.

Marx, Karl. *Capital: A Critique of Political Economy.* Translated by Ben Fowkes, 1–146. Vol. 1. London: Penguin Books, 1992.

Maxwell, Andy. "Alleged SPARKS Member 'Raid' Pleads Not Guilty to Piracy Charges." *TorrentFreak,* September 8, 2020.

https://torrentfreak.com/alleged-sparks-member-raid-pleads-not-guilty-to-piracy-charges-200908/.

———. "Inside Yesterday's European Warez Piracy Raids." *TorrentFreak,* September 8, 2010. https://torrentfreak.com/inside-yesterdays-european-warez-piracy-raids-100908/.

———. "New 'Scene' Security Notice: 'SPARKS' Piracy Raids Busted Dozens of Sites." *TorrentFreak,* September 1, 2020. https://torrentfreak.com/new-scene-security-notice-sparks-piracy-raids-busted-dozens-of-sites-200901/.

———. "Police in File-Sharing Raids Across Europe, WikiLeaks Host Targeted." *TorrentFreak,* September 7, 2010. https://torrentfreak.com/police-in-file-sharing-raids-across-europe-wikileaks-host-targeted-100907/.

———. "SPARKS Piracy Busts: Facts, Rumors & Fear Point to Something Huge." *TorrentFreak,* August 27, 2020. https://torrentfreak.com/sparks-piracy-busts-facts-rumors-fear-point-to-something-huge-200827/.

———. "The Scene: A Stress Headache That Most Pirates Can Do Without." *TorrentFreak,* September 6, 2020. https://torrentfreak.com/the-scene-a-stress-headache-that-most-pirates-can-do-without-200906/.

———. "US Indictments and Raids of Piracy Group Members in 'The Scene' Throw Top-Tier Piracy World into Chaos." *TorrentFreak,* August 26, 2020. https://torrentfreak.com/us-indictments-and-raids-of-piracy-group-members-in-the-scene-throw-top-tier-piracy-world-into-chaos-200826/.

MBZ. "Menzoberranzan Topsite (MBZ-menzoberranzan.1999.01.03.nfo)," January 3, 1999. DeFacto2, warez.scene.nfo.collection.v1.0.24351.shroo.ms.zip.

———. "Menzoberranzan Topsite (MBZ-menzoberranzan.1999.02.12.nfo)," February 12, 1999. DeFacto2, warez.scene.nfo.collection.v1.0.24351.shroo.ms.zip.

———. "Menzoberranzan Topsite (MBZ-menzoberranzan.XXXX.XX.00.nfo)," n.d. DeFacto2, warez.scene.nfo.collection.v1.0.24351.shroo.ms.zip.

McArthur, J.A. "Digital Subculture: A Geek Meaning of Style." *Journal of Communication Inquiry* 33, no. 1 (January 2009): 58–70. DOI: 10.1177/0196859908325676.

McCain, Jessica, Brittany Gentile, and W. Keith Campbell. "A Psychological Exploration of Engagement in Geek Culture." *PLOS ONE* 10, no. 11 (2015). DOI: 10.1371/journal.pone.0142200.

McCandless, David. "Warez Wars." *Wired,* April 1, 1997. https://www.wired.com/1997/04/ff-warez/.

McGonigal, Jane. "'This Is Not a Game': Immersive Aesthetics and Collective Play." In *Melbourne DAC 2003 Streamingworlds Conference Proceedings.* Melbourne: Royal Melbourne Institute of Technology University, 2003.

McNultey, Paul J. "Warez Leader Sentenced to 46 Months." *US Department of Justice,* May 17, 2002. https://www.justice.gov/archive/criminal/cybercrime/press-releases/2002/sankusSent.htm.

MDK. "Murder Death Kill Topsite (MDK-murder.death.kill.XXXX.XX.00.nfo)," n.d. DeFacto2, warez.scene.nfo.collection.v1.0.24351.shroo.ms.zip.

Meese, James. "The Pirate Imaginary and the Potential of the Authorial Pirate." In *Piracy: Leakages from Modernity,* edited by Martin Fredriksson and James Arvanitakis, 19–38. Sacramento: Litwin Books, 2014.

MERC. "Mercure Topsite (MERC-mercure.1998.01.16.nfo)," January 16, 1998. DeFacto2, warez.scene.nfo.collection.v1.0.24351.shroo.ms.zip.

———. "Mercure Topsite (MERC-mercure.1999.02.21.nfo)," February 21, 1999. DeFacto2, warez.scene.nfo.collection.v1.0.24351.shroo.ms.zip.

MF. "Magnetic Fields Topsite (MF-magnetic.fields.2000.06.05.nfo)," June 5, 2000. DeFacto2, warez.scene.nfo.collection.v1.0.24351.shroo.ms.zip.

MFT. "Manifest Topsite (MFT-manifest.1997.10.21.nfo)," October 21, 1997. DeFacto2, warez.scene.nfo.collection.v1.0.24351.shroo.ms.zip.

MG. "Midgaard Topsite (MG-midgaard.2000.08.22.nfo)," August 22, 2000. DeFacto2, warez.scene.nfo.collection.v1.0.24351.shroo.ms.zip.
MH. "Madhaus Topsite (MH-madhaus.1997.09.22.nfo)," September 22, 1997. DeFacto2, warez.scene.nfo.collection.v1.0.24351.shroo.ms.zip.
MI. "Monkey Island Topsite (MI-monkey.island.1998.02.06.nfo)," February 6, 1998. DeFacto2, warez.scene.nfo.collection.v1.0.24351.shroo.ms.zip.
MIH. "Made in Heaven Topsite (MIH-made.in.heaven.1999.05.21.nfo)," May 21, 1999. DeFacto2, warez.scene.nfo.collection.v1.0.24351.shroo.ms.zip.
Miracle. "USA Retail Shipment Speeds (USA shops and speed.txt)," n.d. DeFacto2.
Mitchell, David. *Utopia Avenue.* London: Sceptre, 2020.
MM. "Major Malfunction Topsite (MM-major.malfunction.1999.07.29.nfo)," July 29, 1999. DeFacto2, warez.scene.nfo.collection.v1.0.24351.shroo.ms.zip.
———. "Mental Meltdown Topsite (MM-mental.meltdown.1997.04.26.nfo)," April 26, 1997. DeFacto2, warez.scene.nfo.collection.v1.0.24351.shroo.ms.zip.
MNS. "Midnight Sun Topsite (MNS-midnight.sun.1999.01.23.nfo)," January 23, 1999. DeFacto2, warez.scene.nfo.collection.v1.0.24351.shroo.ms.zip.
MO. "Mount Olympus Topsite (MO-mount.olympus.1998.10.23.nfo)," October 23, 1998. DeFacto2, warez.scene.nfo.collection.v1.0.24351.shroo.ms.zip.
Montola, Markus, and Jaakko Stenros. "Case B: The Beast." In Markus Montola, Jaakko Stenros, and Annika Wærn, *Pervasive Games: Theory and Design*, 25–30. Boston: Morgan Kaufmann Publishers, 2009.
Montola, Markus, Jaakko Stenros, and Annika Wærn. *Pervasive Games: Theory and Design.* Amsterdam: Morgan Kaufmann, 2009.
Moore, Samuel. "Common Struggles: Policy-Based vs. Scholar-Led Approaches to Open Access in the Humanities." PhD

diss., King's College London, 2019. https://hcommons.org/deposits/item/hc:24135/.

Moore, Samuel, Cameron Neylon, Martin Paul Eve, Daniel Paul O'Donnell, and Damian Pattinson. "'Excellence R Us': University Research and the Fetishisation of Excellence." *Palgrave Communications* 3 (2017). DOI: 10.1057/palcomms.2016.105. https://www.nature.com/articles/palcomms2016105.

Morris, Jeremy Wade. *Selling Digital Music, Formatting Culture.* Berkeley: University of California Press, 2015.

Morselli, Carlo, and Tom Vander Beken. "Opportunistic Structures of Organized Crime." In *The Oxford Handbook of Organized Crime,* edited by Letizia Paoli, 288–302. Oxford: Oxford University Press, 2014.

Morselli, Carlo, Mathilde Turcotte, and Valentina Tenti. "The Mobility of Criminal Groups." *Global Crime* 12, no. 3 (2011): 165–88. DOI: 10.1080/17440572.2011.589593.

MOS. "Mos Eisley Topsite (MOS-mos.eisley.1998.03.25.nfo)," March 25, 1998. DeFacto2, warez.scene.nfo.collection.v1.0.24351.shroo.ms.zip.

Moshirnia, Andrew V. "Giant Pink Scorpions: Fighting Piracy with Novel Digital Rights Management Technology." *DePaul Journal of Art, Technology & Intellectual Property Law* 23, no. 1 (2012): 1–67. https://ssrn.com/abstract=3031273.

MRG. "Mirage Topsite (MRG-mirage.1997.08.03.nfo)," August 3, 1997. DeFacto2, warez.scene.nfo.collection.v1.0.24351.shroo.ms.zip.

MS. "Mile Stone Topsite (MS-mile.stone.1997.07.04.nfo)," July 4, 1997. DeFacto2, warez.scene.nfo.collection.v1.0.24351.shroo.ms.zip.

MSV. "Moonshine Vision Topsite (MSV-moonshine.vision.1998.08.26.nfo)," August 26, 1998. DeFacto2, warez.scene.nfo.collection.v1.0.24351.shroo.ms.zip.

Muggleton, David, and Rupert Weinzierl. *The Post-Subcultures Reader.* New York: Berg, 2003.

MW. "Mist World Topsite (MW-mist.world.1998.06.04.nfo)," June 4, 1998. DeFacto2, warez.scene.nfo.collection.v1.0.24351.shroo.ms.zip.
MXP. "Maximum Power Topsite (MXP-maximum.power.1998.02.06.nfo)," February 6, 1998. DeFacto2, warez.scene.nfo.collection.v1.0.24351.shroo.ms.zip.
Mytton, David. "Cloudflare, Free Speech and the Rule of Law." *David Mytton,* August 15, 2019. https://davidmytton.blog/cloudflare-free-speech-and-the-rule-of-law/.
Nash, Jennifer C. *The Black Body in Ecstasy: Reading Race, Reading Pornography.* Durham: Duke University Press, 2014.
Naylor, R.T. "Towards a General Theory of Profit-Driven Crimes." *The British Journal of Criminology* 43, no. 1 (2003): 81–101. https://www.jstor.org/stable/23638918.
NBM. "Niobium Topsite (NBM-niobium.1999.02.14.nfo)," February 14, 1999. DeFacto2, warez.scene.nfo.collection.v1.0.24351.shroo.ms.zip.
NCT. "Nocturne Topsite (NCT-nocturne.1998.12.06.nfo)," December 6, 1998. DeFacto2, warez.scene.nfo.collection.v1.0.24351.shroo.ms.zip.
ndetroit. "ndetroit's sites and stats section." *Netmonkey Weekly Report* (nwr47.txt), May 11, 1999. DeFacto2.
———. "The Scene News." *Netmonkey Weekly Report* (nwr55.txt), August 2, 1999. DeFacto2.
———. "The Truth about GLFTPD." *Netmonkey Weekly Report* (nwr39.txt), March 17, 1999. DeFacto2.
ndetroit and lester. "Interview with metaray." *Netmonkey Weekly Report* (nwr56.txt), September 8, 1999. DeFacto2.
NEI. "New Evil Incarnate Topsite (NEI-new.evil.incarnate.1997.11.29.nfo)," November 29, 1997. DeFacto2, warez.scene.nfo.collection.v1.0.24351.shroo.ms.zip.
Newman, James. *Videogames.* London: Routledge, 2013.
NF. "Near Future Topsite (NF-near.future.1999.08.26.nfo)," August 26, 1999. DeFacto2, warez.scene.nfo.collection.v1.0.24351.shroo.ms.zip.

———. "Near Future Topsite (NF-near.future.1999.11.08.nfo)," November 8, 1999. DeFacto2, warez.scene.nfo.collection.v1.0.24351.shroo.ms.zip.

NF2K. "Near Future 2000 Topsite (NF2K-near.future.2000.10.12.nfo)," October 12, 2000. DeFacto2, warez.scene.nfo.collection.v1.0.24351.shroo.ms.zip.

NGS. "Neon Genesis Topsite (NGS-neon.genesis.XXXX.XX.00.nfo)," n.d. DeFacto2, warez.scene.nfo.collection.v1.0.24351.shroo.ms.zip.

NHL. "Nihil Topsite (NHL-nihil.1997.03.02.nfo)," March 2, 1997. DeFacto2, warez.scene.nfo.collection.v1.0.24351.shroo.ms.zip.

NKS. "Narkos Topsite (NKS-narkos.XXXX.XX.00.nfo)," n.d. DeFacto2, warez.scene.nfo.collection.v1.0.24351.shroo.ms.zip.

NMS. "Nemesis Topsite (NMS-nemesis.1998.09.08.nfo)," September 8, 1998. DeFacto2, warez.scene.nfo.collection.v1.0.24351.shroo.ms.zip.

Noble, Safiya Umoja. *Algorithms of Oppression: How Search Engines Reinforce Racism.* New York: New York University Press, 2018.

NOS. "Nos Topsite (NOS-nos.1998.05.17.nfo)," May 17, 1998. DeFacto2, warez.scene.nfo.collection.v1.0.24351.shroo.ms.zip.

NPT. "Noptarus Topsite (NPT-noptarus.1999.02.03.nfo)," February 3, 1999. DeFacto2, warez.scene.nfo.collection.v1.0.24351.shroo.ms.zip.

NUD. "Nuclear Dust Topsite (NUD-nuclear.dust.2000.08.22.nfo)," August 22, 2000. DeFacto2, warez.scene.nfo.collection.v1.0.24351.shroo.ms.zip.

———. "Nuclear Dust Topsite (NUD-nuclear.dust.XXXX.XX.01.nfo)," n.d. DeFacto2, warez.scene.nfo.collection.v1.0.24351.shroo.ms.zip.

NXS. "Nexus Topsite (NXS-nexus.1998.05.07.nfo)," May 7, 1998. DeFacto2, warez.scene.nfo.collection.v1.0.24351.shroo.ms.zip.

O5. "Orbit Five Topsite (O5-orbit.five.1997.02.14.nfo)," February 14, 1997. DeFacto2, warez.scene.nfo.collection.v1.0.24351.shroo.ms.zip.

Oberholzer-Gee, Felix, and Koleman Strumpf. "File Sharing and Copyright." *Innovation Policy and the Economy* 10, no. 1 (2010): 19–55. DOI: 10.1086/605852.

Oliveira, Thaiane Moreira de. "'Ingress': A Restructuring of the ARG or a New Genre? An Ethnography of Enlightened and Resistance Factions in Brazil." In *Alternate Reality Games and the Cusp of Digital Gameplay,* edited by Antero Garcia and Greg Niemeyer, 288–310. New York City: Bloomsbury Academic, 2017.

OM. "Omerta Topsite (OM-omerta.1999.12.31.nfo)," December 31, 1999. DeFacto2, warez.scene.nfo.collection.v1.0.24351.shroo.ms.zip.

———. "Operation Mindcrime Topsite (OM-operation.mindcrime.1997.12.29.nfo)," December 29, 1997. DeFacto2, warez.scene.nfo.collection.v1.0.24351.shroo.ms.zip.

ON. "Origin Topsite (ON-origin.1997.12.04.nfo)," December 4, 1997. DeFacto2, warez.scene.nfo.collection.v1.0.24351.shroo.ms.zip.

OON. "Outskirts of Nowhere Topsite (OON-outskirts.of.nowhere.1998.12.15.nfo)," December 15, 1998. DeFacto2, warez.scene.nfo.collection.v1.0.24351.shroo.ms.zip.

Osborn, Don. *African Languages in a Digital Age: Challenges and Opportunities for Indigenous Language Computing.* Cape Town: HSRC Press, 2010.

Osipovich, Alexander. "High-Frequency Traders Push Closer to Light Speed with Cutting-Edge Cables." *Wall Street Journal,* December 15, 2020. https://www.wsj.com/articles/high-frequency-traders-push-closer-to-light-speed-with-cutting-edge-cables-11608028200.

OT. "Obscure Transmissions Topsite (OT-obscure.transmissions.1997.12.07.nfo)," December 7, 1997. DeFacto2, warez.scene.nfo.collection.v1.0.24351.shroo.ms.zip.

OU. "Origin Underground Topsite (OU-origin.underground.1997.10.25.nfo)," October 25, 1997. DeFacto2, warez.scene.nfo.collection.v1.0.24351.shroo.ms.zip.

———. "Origin Underground Topsite (OU-origin.underground.1998.01.13.nfo)," January 13, 1998. DeFacto2, warez.scene.nfo.collection.v1.0.24351.shroo.ms.zip.

OX. "Oxide Topsite (OX-oxide.1997.07.15.nfo)," July 15, 1997. DeFacto2, warez.scene.nfo.collection.v1.0.24351.shroo.ms.zip.

P1. "Pier One Imports Topsite (P1-pier.one.imports.1996.10.29.nfo)," October 29, 1996. DeFacto2, warez.scene.nfo.collection.v1.0.24351.shroo.ms.zip.

Paoli, Letizia. "Introduction." In *The Oxford Handbook of Organized Crime,* edited by Letizia Paoli, 1–10. Oxford: Oxford University Press, 2014.

Paoli, Letizia, and Tom Vander Beken. "Organized Crime: A Contested Concept." In *The Oxford Handbook of Organized Crime,* edited by Letizia Paoli, 13–31. Oxford: Oxford University Press, 2014.

PB. "Point Break Topsite (PB-point.break.1998.12.12.nfo)," December 12, 1998. DeFacto2, warez.scene.nfo.collection.v1.0.24351.shroo.ms.zip.

PBOX. "Pandora's Box Topsite (PBOX-pandoras.box.1999.02.15.nfo)," February 15, 1999. DeFacto2, warez.scene.nfo.collection.v1.0.24351.shroo.ms.zip.

———. "Pandora's Box Topsite (PBOX-pandoras.box.2000.07.23.nfo)," July 23, 2000. DeFacto2, warez.scene.nfo.collection.v1.0.24351.shroo.ms.zip.

PC. "Pirate's Cove Topsite (PC-pirates.cove.1997.03.02.nfo)," March 2, 1997. DeFacto2, warez.scene.nfo.collection.v1.0.24351.shroo.ms.zip.

PD. "Plastik Dreams Topsite (PD-plastik.dreams.1996.11.12.nfo)," November 12, 1996. DeFacto2, warez.scene.nfo.collection.v1.0.24351.shroo.ms.zip.

———. "Playboys Dreams Topsite (PD-playboys.dream.1998.10.25.nfo)," October 25, 1998. DeFacto2, warez.scene.nfo.collection.v1.0.24351.shroo.ms.zip.

———. "Playboys Dreams Topsite (PD-playboys.dream.1999.10.21.nfo)," October 21, 1999. DeFacto2, warez.scene.nfo.collection.v1.0.24351.shroo.ms.zip.

———. "Psychadelic Dreams Topsite (PD-psychadelic.dreams.1997.09.30.nfo)," September 30, 1997. DeFacto2, warez.scene.nfo.collection.v1.0.24351.shroo.ms.zip.

PDX. "Paradox Topsite (PDX-paradox.1999.01.20.nfo)," January 20, 1999. DeFacto2, warez.scene.nfo.collection.v1.0.24351.shroo.ms.zip.

———. "Paradox Topsite (PDX-paradox.1999.02.26.nfo)," February 26, 1999. DeFacto2, warez.scene.nfo.collection.v1.0.24351.shroo.ms.zip.

Pennell, C.R. "Introduction." In *Bandits at Sea: A Pirates Reader,* edited by C.R. Pennell, 2–24. New York: New York University Press, 2001.

Perea, Manuel, Jon Andoni Duñabeitia, and Manuel Carreiras. "R34D1NG W0RD5 W1TH NUMB3R5." *Journal of Experimental Psychology: Human Perception and Performance* 34, no. 1 (2008): 237–41. DOI: 10.1037/0096-1523.34.1.237.

Perice, Glen A. "Rumors and Politics in Haiti." *Anthropological Quarterly* 70, no. 1 (January 1997): 1–10. DOI: 10.2307/3317797.

Perloff, Marjorie. *Radical Artifice: Writing Poetry in the Age of Media.* Chicago: University of Chicago Press, 1991.

———. *The Poetics of Indeterminacy: Rimbaud to Cage.* Princeton: Princeton University Press, 1981.

———. *Unoriginal Genius: Poetry by Other Means in the New Century.* Chicago: University of Chicago Press, 2010.

PG. "Project Genocide Topsite (PG-project.genocide.1998.07.07.nfo)," July 7, 1998. DeFacto2, warez.scene.nfo.collection.v1.0.24351.shroo.ms.zip.

———. "Project Genocide Topsite (PG-project.genocide.1998.08.21.nfo)," August 21, 1998. DeFacto2, warez.scene.nfo.collection.v1.0.24351.shroo.ms.zip.

PH. "Pirates' Hideout Topsite (PH-pirates.hideout.XXXX.XX.00.nfo)," n.d. DeFacto2, warez.scene.nfo.collection.v1.0.24351.shroo.ms.zip.

Philip, Kavita. "What Is a Technological Author? The Pirate Function and Intellectual Property." *Postcolonial Studies* 8, no. 2 (2005): 199–218. DOI: 10.1080/13688790500153596.

PL. "Paradise Lost Topsite (PL-paradise.lost.1997.11.25.nfo)," November 25, 1997. DeFacto2, warez.scene.nfo.collection.v1.0.24351.shroo.ms.zip.

———. "Pirate Lair Topsite (PL-pirate.lair.1999.08.03.nfo)," August 3, 1999. DeFacto2, warez.scene.nfo.collection.v1.0.24351.shroo.ms.zip.

———. "Primary Link Topsite (PL-primary.link.1996.11.03.nfo)," November 3, 1996. DeFacto2, warez.scene.nfo.collection.v1.0.24351.shroo.ms.zip.

———. "Primary Link Topsite (PL-primary.link.1997.03.02.nfo)," March 2, 1997. DeFacto2, warez.scene.nfo.collection.v1.0.24351.shroo.ms.zip.

———. "Primary Link Topsite (PL-primary.link.1997.12.19.nfo)," December 19, 1997. DeFacto2, warez.scene.nfo.collection.v1.0.24351.shroo.ms.zip.

PM. "Prime Mover Topsite (PM-prime.mover.1998.05.10.nfo)," May 10, 1998. DeFacto2, warez.scene.nfo.collection.v1.0.24351.shroo.ms.zip.

———. "Prime Mover Topsite (PM-prime.mover.1998.08.13.nfo)," August 13, 1998. DeFacto2, warez.scene.nfo.collection.v1.0.24351.shroo.ms.zip.

Pogue, David. "Some Warez over the Rainbow." *MacWorld,* October 1997. https://cdn.preterhuman.net/texts/computing/macintosh/Macintosh.txt.

Polgár, Tamás. *Freax: The Brief History of the Computer Demoscene.* Winnenden: CWS-Verlag, 2008.

Poort, Joost, Jorna Leenheer, Jeroen van der Ham, and Cosmin Dumitru. "Baywatch: Two Approaches to Measure the Effects of Blocking Access to The Pirate Bay." *Telecommunications Policy* 38, no. 4 (May 2014): 383–92. DOI: 10.1016/j.telpol.2013.12.008.

PP. "Pelos Portal Topsite (PP-pelos.portal.1998.04.22.nfo)," April 22, 1998. DeFacto2, warez.scene.nfo.collection.v1.0.24351.shroo.ms.zip.

———. "Piper's Pit Topsite (PP-pipers.pit.1999.10.21.nfo)," October 21, 1999. DeFacto2, warez.scene.nfo.collection.v1.0.24351.shroo.ms.zip.

———. "Pussy Power Topsite (PP-pussy.power.XXXX.XX.00.nfo)," n.d. DeFacto2, warez.scene.nfo.collection.v1.0.24351.shroo.ms.zip.

PR. "Phoenix Rising Topsite (PR-phoenix.rising.1999.10.12.nfo)," October 12, 1999. DeFacto2, warez.scene.nfo.collection.v1.0.24351.shroo.ms.zip.

Prince, Brian. "Tracking the Crackers – A Look at Software Piracy." *EWEEK*, November 14, 2008. https://www.eweek.com/security/tracking-the-crackers-a-look-at-software-piracy.

PS. "Parasite Topsite (PS-parasite.1998.03.11.nfo)," March 11, 1998. DeFacto2, warez.scene.nfo.collection.v1.0.24351.shroo.ms.zip.

———. "Progressive Topsite (PS-progressive.1997.03.11.nfo)," March 11, 1997. DeFacto2, warez.scene.nfo.collection.v1.0.24351.shroo.ms.zip.

PSR. "Possible Reality Topsite (PSR-possible.reality.XXXX.XX.00.nfo)," n.d. DeFacto2, warez.scene.nfo.collection.v1.0.24351.shroo.ms.zip.

PST. "Prosperity Topsite (PST-prosperity.1999.07.25.nfo)," July 25, 1997. DeFacto2, warez.scene.nfo.collection.v1.0.24351.shroo.ms.zip.

PT. "Pzykotik Thoughts Topsite (PT-pzykotik.thoughts.1997.05.19.nfo)," May 19, 1997. DeFacto2, warez.scene.nfo.collection.v1.0.24351.shroo.ms.zip.

"Pub-Crackin 101." *PC-FXP.* http://pc-fxp.tripod.com/pc101.htm.

PWH. "Pre Whore House Topsite (PWH-pre.whore.house.2000.09.01.nfo)," September 1, 2000. DeFacto2, warez.scene.nfo.collection.v1.0.24351.shroo.ms.zip.

QC. "QuadCon Topsite (QC-quadcon.1998.02.09.nfo)," February 9, 1998. DeFacto2, warez.scene.nfo.collection.v1.0.24351.shroo.ms.zip.

QR. "Quantum Reality Topsite (QR-quantum.reality.1998.05.23.nfo)," May 23, 1998. DeFacto2, warez.scene.nfo.collection.v1.0.24351.shroo.ms.zip.

RA. "Restricted Area Topsite (RA-restricted.area.1999.06.13.nfo)," June 13, 1999. DeFacto2, warez.scene.nfo.collection.v1.0.24351.shroo.ms.zip.

Raftery, Miriam. "San Diego GOP Chairman Co-Founded International Piracy Ring." *The Raw Story,* April 29, 2009.

Rancière, Jacques. *The Politics of Aesthetics: The Distribution of the Sensible.* Edited and translated by Gabriel Rockhill. London: Bloomsbury Academic, 2018.

RAY. "Rebellion Authority Topsite (RAY-rebellion.authority.1999.03.18.nfo)," March 18, 1999. DeFacto2, warez.scene.nfo.collection.v1.0.24351.shroo.ms.zip.

Raymond, Eric S. *The Cathedral and the Bazaar: Musings on Linux and Open Source by an Accidental Revolutionary.* Cambridge: O'Reilly Media, 2001.

RBL. "The Rebellion Topsite (RBL-the.rebellion.1997.02.19.nfo)," February 19, 1997. DeFacto2, warez.scene.nfo.collection.v1.0.24351.shroo.ms.zip.

RC. "Random Chaos Topsite (RC-random.chaos.1997.09.05.nfo)," September 5, 1997. DeFacto2, warez.scene.nfo.collection.v1.0.24351.shroo.ms.zip.

Readings, Bill. *The University in Ruins.* Cambridge: Harvard University Press, 1996.

Rebel Chicken. "That Wasn't You?" *Reality Check Network* (RCN-20.txt), 1996. DeFacto2.

Rehn, Alf. "Electronic Potlatch: A Study on New Technologies and Primitive Economic Behaviors." PhD diss., Royal Institute of Technology, Stockholm, 2001.

———. *Ordered Misbehavior: The Structuring of an Illegal Endeavor.* Stockholm: Royal Institute of Technology, 2003.

———. "The Politics of Contraband: The Honor Economies of the Warez Scene." *The Journal of Socio-Economics* 33, no. 3 (July 2004): 359–74. DOI: 10.1016/j.socec.2003.12.027.

RELIC. "The Relic Topsite (RELIC-the.relic.1997.12.29.nfo)," December 29, 1997. DeFacto2, warez.scene.nfo.collection.v1.0.24351.shroo.ms.zip.

Reunanen, Markku. "Computer Demos—What Makes Them Tick?" Master's thesis, Aalto University, 2010.

Reunanen, Markku, Patryk Wasiak, and Daniel Botz. "Crack Intros: Piracy, Creativity and Communication." *International Journal of Communication* 9 (2015): 798–817. https://ijoc.org/index.php/ijoc/article/view/3731/.

RFLUX. "Reality Flux Topsite (RFLUX-reality.flux.1998.03.03.nfo)," March 3, 1998. DeFacto2, warez.scene.nfo.collection.v1.0.24351.shroo.ms.zip.

———. "Reality Flux Topsite (RFLUX-reality.flux.1998.07.03.nfo)," July 3, 1998. DeFacto2, warez.scene.nfo.collection.v1.0.24351.shroo.ms.zip.

RH. "Ratz Hole Topsite (RH-ratzhole.1999.08.14.nfo)," August 14, 1999. DeFacto2, warez.scene.nfo.collection.v1.0.24351.shroo.ms.zip.

Rimini, Francesca da, and Jonathan Marshall. "Piracy Is Normal, Piracy Is Boring: Systemic Disruption as Everyday Life." In *Piracy: Leakages from Modernity,* edited by Martin Fredriksson and James Arvanitakis, 323–44. Sacramento: Litwin Books, 2014.

RiSC. "Ethics (risc.ethics.txt)," n.d. DeFacto2.

———. "Guidelines (risc.guidelines.txt)," n.d. DeFacto2.

ROC. "Realms of Chaos Topsite (ROC-realms.of.chaos.1998.11.23.nfo)," November 23, 1998. DeFacto2, warez.scene.nfo.collection.v1.0.24351.shroo.ms.zip.

Rodman, Gilbert B., and Cheyanne Vanderdonckt. "Music for Nothing or, I Want My MP3: The Regulation and Recirculation of Affect." *Cultural Studies* 20, nos. 2–3 (2006): 245–61. DOI: 10.1080/09502380500495734.

Roman. "Q&A with DeFacto2: The NFO File," January 22, 2013. DeFacto2. https://defacto2.net/file/detail/ac2b81.

Rosenblat, Alex. *Uberland: How Algorithms Are Rewriting the Rules of Work.* Berkeley: University of California Press, 2018.
Rosnow, Ralph L., and Gary A. Fine. *Rumor and Gossip: The Social Psychology of Hearsay.* Amsterdam: Elsevier, 1976.
RP. "Relentless Pipeline Topsite (RP-relentless.pipeline.1998.10.02.nfo)," October 2, 1998. DeFacto2, warez.scene.nfo.collection.v1.0.24351.shroo.ms.zip.
RUHEBITTE. "The Truth About Warez Seller Since aka Kartus aka Styler (The.truth.about.warez.seller.Since.aka.Kaktus.aka.Styler-RUHEBITTE)," c. -2010 2006. DeFacto2, warez-scene-notices-2006-2010.
Ryason55. "DRM Scorpions," May 11, 2014. https://steamcommunity.com/sharedfiles/filedetails/?id=259074771&searchtext=.
RZ. "RZ Soft Topsite (RZ-rzsoft.1997.12.22.nfo)," December 22, 1997. DeFacto2, warez.scene.nfo.collection.v1.0.24351.shroo.ms.zip.
SA. "Secured Area Topsite (SA-secured.area.1997.02.22.nfo)," February 22, 1997. DeFacto2, warez.scene.nfo.collection.v1.0.24351.shroo.ms.zip.
SAD. "Satan's Dome Topsite (SAD-satans.dome.1998.07.29.nfo)," July 29, 1998. DeFacto2, warez.scene.nfo.collection.v1.0.24351.shroo.ms.zip.
———. "Satan's Dome Topsite (SAD-satans.dome.1998.08.30.nfo)," August 30, 1998. DeFacto2, warez.scene.nfo.collection.v1.0.24351.shroo.ms.zip.
Saint Tok. "Interview with The Crazy Little Punk." *DeFacto2* (df2-02.txt), February 1997. DeFacto2.
SANI. "Sanitarium Topsite (SANI-sanitarium.1997.06.13.nfo)," June 13, 1997. DeFacto2, warez.scene.nfo.collection.v1.0.24351.shroo.ms.zip.
———. "Sanitarium Topsite (SANI-sanitarium.1998.01.08.nfo)," January 8, 1998. DeFacto2, warez.scene.nfo.collection.v1.0.24351.shroo.ms.zip.
SB. "San Bruno Topsite (SB-san.bruno.1998.07.01.nfo)," July 1, 1998. DeFacto2, warez.scene.nfo.collection.v1.0.24351.shroo.ms.zip.

SBC. "San Bruno Club Topsite (SBC-san.bruno.club.1999.12.27.nfo)," December 27, 1999. DeFacto2, warez.scene.nfo.collection.v1.0.24351.shroo.ms.zip.

———. "San Bruno Club Topsite (SBC-san.bruno.club.2000.02.26.nfo)," February 26, 2000. DeFacto2, warez.scene.nfo.collection.v1.0.24351.shroo.ms.zip.

Scarfone, Karen, Wayne Jansen, and Miles Tracy. *Guide to General Server Security: Recommendations of the National Institute of Standards and Technology*. Gaithersburg: National Institute of Standards and Technology, 2008.

Schwartz, Hillel. *Culture of the Copy: Striking Likenesses, Unreasonable Facsimiles.* New York: Zone Books, 2014.

Sciannamblo, Mariacristina. "The Internet between Politics and the Political: The Birth of the Pirate Party." In *Piracy: Leakages from Modernity,* edited by Martin Fredriksson and James Arvanitakis, 177–94. Sacramento: Litwin Books, 2014.

SD. "Solid Disruption Topsite (SD-solid.disruption.1998.06.27.nfo)," June 27, 1998. DeFacto2, warez.scene.nfo.collection.v1.0.24351.shroo.ms.zip.

———. "Surface Defect Topsite (SD-surface.defect.1998.06.06.nfo)," June 6, 1998. DeFacto2, warez.scene.nfo.collection.v1.0.24351.shroo.ms.zip.

———. "Surface Defect Topsite (SD-surface.defect.1998.09.25.nfo)," September 25, 1998. DeFacto2, warez.scene.nfo.collection.v1.0.24351.shroo.ms.zip.

SDK. "The Sandokan's Dome Topsite (SDK-the.sandokans.dome.1998.02.25.nfo)," February 25, 1998. DeFacto2, warez.scene.nfo.collection.v1.0.24351.shroo.ms.zip.

SE. "Savage Exile Topsite (SE-savage.exile.1997.10.25.nfo)," October 25, 1997. DeFacto2, warez.scene.nfo.collection.v1.0.24351.shroo.ms.zip.

———. "Sonic Empire Topsite (SE-sonic.empire.1998.01.03.nfo)," January 3, 1998. DeFacto2, warez.scene.nfo.collection.v1.0.24351.shroo.ms.zip.

Seeborg, Richard. "United States of America v. Chirayu Patel, Aka Nebula, Aka Nabwrk, Aka Aluben, Aka Notneb, Aka Aluben: Warrant for Arrest," June 28, 2005.

Seppala, Timothy J. "'The Sims 4' Turns into a Pixelated Mess If You Pirate It." *Engadget*, September 5, 2014. https://www.engadget.com/2014-09-05-sims-4-pirate-pixelation.html.

Seuss, Geisel Theodor. *If I Ran the Zoo.* New York: Random House for Young Readers, 1950.

Sewell, Amanda. "How Copyright Affected the Musical Style and Critical Reception of Sample-Based Hip-Hop." *Journal of Popular Music Studies* 26, nos. 2–3 (2014): 295–320. DOI: 10.1111/jpms.12078.

SEX. "Silicon Exchange Topsite (SEX-silicon.exchange.1999.05.24.nfo)," May 24, 1999. DeFacto2, warez.scene.nfo.collection.v1.0.24351.shroo.ms.zip.

SF. "Springfield Topsite (SF-springfield.1997.04.06.nfo)," April 6, 1997. DeFacto2, warez.scene.nfo.collection.v1.0.24351.shroo.ms.zip.

SG. "Shadow Gate Topsite (SG-shadow.gate.1999.04.21.nfo)," April 21, 1999. DeFacto2, warez.scene.nfo.collection.v1.0.24351.shroo.ms.zip.

Sharma, Amita, and J.W. August. "Video Resurfaces Featuring Images of Hitler and Local GOP Party Chair Tony Krvaric." *KPBS*, August 21, 2020. https://www.kpbs.org/news/2020/aug/21/video-surfaces-images-hitler-and-tony-krvaric/.

SheepNet, LocalNet, OneNET, Nuclear, ZoNeNET, FRENCHNET, Gotmilk, et al. "Nuke Council Rules (nfo_2008_NC.nfo)." *Scenerules.org*, November 8, 2008. scenerules.org.

Shields, David. *Reality Hunger: A Manifesto.* London: Hamish Hamilton, 2011.

SHK. "Shike Topsite (SHK-shike.1997.05.28.nfo)," May 28, 1997. DeFacto2, warez.scene.nfo.collection.v1.0.24351.shroo.ms.zip.

Sihvonen, Tanja. *Players Unleashed!: Modding The Sims and the Culture of Gaming.* Amsterdam: Amsterdam University Press, 2011.

Silvast, Antti, and Markku Reunanen. "Multiple Users, Diverse Users: Appropriation of Personal Computers by Demoscene Hackers." In *Hacking Europe: From Computer Cultures to*

Demoscenes, edited by Gerard Alberts, 151–63. New York: Springer, 2014.

Simpson, Penny M., Debasish Banerjee, and Claude L. Simpson. "Softlifting: A Model of Motivating Factors." *Journal of Business Ethics* 13, no. 6 (1994): 431–38. DOI: 10.1007/BF00881451.

skimp. "Interview with glimerman of RiSC." *Courier Weektop Scorecard* (CwS-137.txt), February 3, 2001. DeFacto2.

———. "Interview with Redbone of RTS." *Courier Weektop Scorecard* (CwS-130.txt), December 16, 2000. DeFacto2.

Skowronek, Russell K. "X Marks the Spot – Or Does It?" In *X Marks the Spot: The Archaeology of Piracy,* edited by Russell K. Skowronek and Charles R. Ewen, 282–98. Gainesville: University Press of Florida, 2006.

SL. "Sand Land Topsite (SL-sand.land.1997.10.29.nfo)," October 29, 1997. DeFacto2, warez.scene.nfo.collection.v1.0.24351.shroo.ms.zip.

Slowinska, Maria A. *Art/Commerce: The Convergence of Art and Marketing in Contemporary Culture*. Bielefeld: Transcript Verlag, 2014.

SLR. "The Cellar Topsite (SLR-the.cellar.1998.09.07.nfo)," September 7, 1998. DeFacto2, warez.scene.nfo.collection.v1.0.24351.shroo.ms.zip.

———. "The Cellar Topsite (SLR-the.cellar.1998.11.08.nfo)," November 8, 1998. DeFacto2, warez.scene.nfo.collection.v1.0.24351.shroo.ms.zip.

SOC. "Socrates Topsite (SOC-socrates.1997.11.12.nfo)," November 12, 1997. DeFacto2, warez.scene.nfo.collection.v1.0.24351.shroo.ms.zip.

Sockanathan, Andrew. "Digital Desire and Recorded Music: OiNK, Mnemotechnics and the Private BitTorrent Architecture." PhD diss., Goldsmiths, University of London, 2011.

SOH. "South of Heaven Topsite (SOH-south.of.heaven.1998.08.27.nfo)," August 27, 1998. DeFacto2, warez.scene.nfo.collection.v1.0.24351.shroo.ms.zip.

Sökefeld, Martin. "Rumours and Politics on the Northern Frontier: The British, Pakhtun Wali and Yaghestan." *Modern Asian Studies* 36, no. 2 (2002): 299–340. DOI: 10.1017/S0026749X02002020.

Solove, Daniel J. *The Future of Reputation: Gossip, Rumor, and Privacy on the Internet.* New Haven: Yale University Press, 2007.

Solt, Mary Ellen, ed. *Concrete Poetry: A World View.* Bloomington: Indiana University Press, 1970.

Sonnad, Nikhil. "A Eulogy for 'What.CD', the Greatest Music Collection in the History of the World—Until It Vanished." *Quartz,* November 18, 2016. https://qz.com/840661/what-cd-is-gone-a-eulogy-for-the-greatest-music-collection-in-the-world/.

SP. "Secret Paradise Topsite (SP-secret.paradise.1998.08.30.nfo)," August 30, 1998. DeFacto2, warez.scene.nfo.collection.v1.0.24351.shroo.ms.zip.

SPADE. "The Spade Topsite (SPADE-the.spade.1999.01.23.nfo)," January 23, 1999. DeFacto2, warez.scene.nfo.collection.v1.0.24351.shroo.ms.zip.

SQB. "Could a Hard Drive Actually Have Been Erased as Described in 'Cryptonomicon'?" Physics Stack Exchange, May 1, 2014. https://physics.stackexchange.com/questions/110870/could-a-hard-drive-actually-have-been-erased-as-described-in-cryptonomicon.

SR. "Shattered Reality Topsite (SR-shattered.reality.1998.10.05.nfo)," October 5, 1998. DeFacto2, warez.scene.nfo.collection.v1.0.24351.shroo.ms.zip.

SS. "Silly Symphonies Topsite (SS-silly.symphonies.1998.05.13.nfo)," May 13, 1998. DeFacto2, warez.scene.nfo.collection.v1.0.24351.shroo.ms.zip.

Stahl, Geoff. "Tastefully Renovating Subcultural Theory: Making Space for a New Model." In *The Post-Subcultures Reader,* edited by David Muggleton and Rupert Weinzierl, 27–40. Oxford: Berg, 2003.

Stallman, Richard. “Did You Say ‘Intellectual Property’? It’s a Seductive Mirage.” *gnu.org*, April 20, 2015. https://www.gnu.org/philosophy/not-ipr.en.html.

Star, Susan Leigh. “The Ethnography of Infrastructure.” *American Behavioral Scientist* 43, no. 3 (1999): 377–91. DOI: 10.1177/00027649921955326.

Starkey, David J. “Pirates and Markets.” In *Bandits at Sea: A Pirates Reader*, edited by C.R. Pennell, 107–24. New York: New York University Press, 2001.

Stephenson, Neal. *Cryptonomicon*. New York: Random House, 2012.

Sterling, Bruce. *The Hacker Crackdown: Law and Disorder on the Electronic Frontier*. New York: Bantam Books, 1992.

Sterne, Jonathan. *MP3: The Meaning of a Format*. Durham: Duke University Press, 2012.

STH. “Stairway to Heaven Topsite (STH-stairway.to.heaven.1997.02.16.nfo),” February 16, 1997. DeFacto2, warez.scene.nfo.collection.v1.0.24351.shroo.ms.zip.

———. “Stairway to Heaven Topsite (STH-stairway.to.heaven.1998.03.04.nfo),” March 4, 1998. DeFacto2, warez.scene.nfo.collection.v1.0.24351.shroo.ms.zip.

———. “Stairway to Heaven Topsite (STH-stairway.to.heaven.1999.08.27.nfo),” August 27, 1999. DeFacto2, warez.scene.nfo.collection.v1.0.24351.shroo.ms.zip.

Strangelove, Michael. *The Empire of Mind: Digital Piracy and the Anti-Capitalist Movement*. Toronto: University of Toronto Press, 2005.

Straw, Will. “Systems of Articulation, Logics of Change: Communities and Scenes in Popular Music.” *Cultural Studies* 5, no. 3 (1991): 368–88. DOI: 10.1080/09502389100490311.

Suber, Peter. *Open Access*. Cambridge: MIT Press, 2012.

Sugarbaker, Mike. “What Is a Geek?” *Gazebo (The Journal of Geek Culture)*, 1998. http://www.gibberish.com/gazebo/articles/geek3.html.

SUN. "Sun Topsite (SUN-sun.1999.11.09.nfo)," November 9, 1999. DeFacto2, warez.scene.nfo.collection.v1.0.24351.shroo.ms.zip.
SW. "Spice World Topsite (SW-spice.world.1998.06.21.nfo)," June 21, 1998. DeFacto2, warez.scene.nfo.collection.v1.0.24351.shroo.ms.zip.
SYN. "Syn City Topsite (SYN-syncity.1996.11.04.nfo)," November 4, 1996. DeFacto2, warez.scene.nfo.collection.v1.0.24351.shroo.ms.zip.
———. "Syn City Topsite (SYN-syncity.1998.08.27.nfo)," August 27, 1998. DeFacto2, warez.scene.nfo.collection.v1.0.24351.shroo.ms.zip.
SZ. "Storm Zone Topsite (SZ-storm.zone.1999.09.17.nfo)," September 17, 1999. DeFacto2, warez.scene.nfo.collection.v1.0.24351.shroo.ms.zip.
Szulborski, Dave. *This Is Not a Game: A Guide to Alternate Reality Gaming.* Macungie: New-Fiction Publishing, 2005.
TA. "The Armageddon Topsite (TA-the.armageddon.1998.08.05.nfo)," August 5, 1998. DeFacto2, warez.scene.nfo.collection.v1.0.24351.shroo.ms.zip.
TAL. "Talinc Topsite (TAL-talinc.1999.12.28.nfo)," December 28, 1999. DeFacto2, warez.scene.nfo.collection.v1.0.24351.shroo.ms.zip.
TAR. "The Ancient Ruins Topsite (TAR-the.ancient.ruins.1998.03.25.nfo)," March 25, 1998. DeFacto2, warez.scene.nfo.collection.v1.0.24351.shroo.ms.zip.
Taylor, Astra. "Serfing the Net." *The Baffler* 2, no. 1 [18] (2010): 20–26. https://www.jstor.org/stable/43307607.
TBB. "The Black Box Topsite (TBB-the.black.box.1999.05.27.nfo)," May 27, 1999. DeFacto2, warez.scene.nfo.collection.v1.0.24351.shroo.ms.zip.
TBC and rgba. "elevated (elevated.nfo)," 2009. pouet.net.
TBF. "Tera-Bit-Fit Topsite (TBF-tera.bit.fit.1999.01.15.nfo)," January 15, 1999. DeFacto2, warez.scene.nfo.collection.v1.0.24351.shroo.ms.zip.

TBL. "Turbulence Topsite (TBL-turbulence.1998.08.11.nfo)," August 11, 1998. DeFacto2, warez.scene.nfo.collection.v1.0.24351.shroo.ms.zip.

TBP. "The Bottomless Pit Topsite (TBP-the.bottomless.pit.1998.07.05.nfo)," July 5, 1998. DeFacto2, warez.scene.nfo.collection.v1.0.24351.shroo.ms.zip.

TBR. "The Boxer Rebellion Topsite (TBR-the.boxer.rebellion.1997.12.09.nfo)," December 9, 1997. DeFacto2, warez.scene.nfo.collection.v1.0.24351.shroo.ms.zip.

———. "The Boxer Rebellion Topsite (TBR-the.boxer.rebellion.1998.08.23.nfo)," August 23, 1998. DeFacto2, warez.scene.nfo.collection.v1.0.24351.shroo.ms.zip.

TC. "The Center Topsite (TC-the.center.1997.10.24.nfo)," October 24, 1997. DeFacto2, warez.scene.nfo.collection.v1.0.24351.shroo.ms.zip.

———. "Trash City Topsite (TC-trash.city.1998.01.23.nfo)," January 23, 1998. DeFacto2, warez.scene.nfo.collection.v1.0.24351.shroo.ms.zip.

———. "Trash City Topsite (TC-trash.city.1998.03.02.nfo)," March 2, 1998. DeFacto2, warez.scene.nfo.collection.v1.0.24351.shroo.ms.zip.

TCD. "The Corner Deli Topsite (TCD-the.corner.deli.1998.01.31.nfo)," January 31, 1998. DeFacto2, warez.scene.nfo.collection.v1.0.24351.shroo.ms.zip.

TD. "The Dome Topsite (TD-the.dome.1998.08.31.nfo)," August 31, 1998. DeFacto2, warez.scene.nfo.collection.v1.0.24351.shroo.ms.zip.

TDA. "The Digital Afterlife Topsite Ring (TDA-the.digital.afterlife.1997.01.20.nfo)," January 20, 1997. DeFacto2, warez.scene.nfo.collection.v1.0.24351.shroo.ms.zip.

TDD. "The Dragons Den Topsite (TDD-the.dragons.den.1997.07.15.nfo)," July 15, 1997. DeFacto2, warez.scene.nfo.collection.v1.0.24351.shroo.ms.zip.

———. "The Dragons Den Topsite (TDD-the.dragons.den.1997.07.17.nfo)," July 17, 1997. DeFacto2, warez.scene.nfo.collection.v1.0.24351.shroo.ms.zip.

TDH. "The Dawg House Topsite (TDH-the.dawg.house.1997.05.25.nfo)," May 25, 1997. DeFacto2, warez.scene.nfo.collection.v1.0.24351.shroo.ms.zip.

———. "The Digital Harm Topsite (TDH-the.digital.harm.1997.10.25.nfo)," October 25, 1997. DeFacto2, warez.scene.nfo.collection.v1.0.24351.shroo.ms.zip.

TDI. "The Desert Inn Topsite (TDI-the.desert.inn.1999.07.21.nfo)," July 21, 1999. DeFacto2, warez.scene.nfo.collection.v1.0.24351.shroo.ms.zip.

TDL. "The Dead Land Topsite (TDL-the.dead.lands.1998.05.25.nfo)," May 25, 1998. DeFacto2, warez.scene.nfo.collection.v1.0.24351.shroo.ms.zip.

TDM. "The Diamond Mine Topsite (TDM-the.diamond.mine.1997.01.10.nfo)," January 10, 1997. DeFacto2, warez.scene.nfo.collection.v1.0.24351.shroo.ms.zip.

TDP. "The Dawg Pound Topsite (TDP-the.dawg.pound.1998.05.02.nfo)," May 2, 1998. DeFacto2, warez.scene.nfo.collection.v1.0.24351.shroo.ms.zip.

———. "The Dawg Pound Topsite (TDP-the.dawg.pound.XXXX.XX.00.nfo)," n.d. DeFacto2, warez.scene.nfo.collection.v1.0.24351.shroo.ms.zip.

———. "The Devil's Pit Topsite (TDP-the.devils.pit.1999.01.07.nfo)," January 7, 1999. DeFacto2, warez.scene.nfo.collection.v1.0.24351.shroo.ms.zip.

TDS. "The Dark Site Topsite (TDS-the.dark.site.1997.06.29.nfo)," June 29, 1997. DeFacto2, warez.scene.nfo.collection.v1.0.24351.shroo.ms.zip.

TDZ. "The Drop Zone Topsite (TDZ-the.drop.zone.1997.11.03.nfo)," November 3, 1997. DeFacto2, warez.scene.nfo.collection.v1.0.24351.shroo.ms.zip.

TE. "The Enterprise Topsite (TE-the.enterprise.1998.05.13.nfo)," May 13, 1998. DeFacto2, warez.scene.nfo.collection.v1.0.24351.shroo.ms.zip.

———. "Total Eclipse Topsite (TE-total.eclipse.1998.01.11.nfo)," January 11, 1998. DeFacto2, warez.scene.nfo.collection.v1.0.24351.shroo.ms.zip.

TE3. "The Third Total Eclipse Topsite (TE3-total.eclipse.three.1999.07.09.nfo)," July 9, 1999. DeFacto2, warez.scene.nfo.collection.v1.0.24351.shroo.ms.zip.

TEC. "The Electric Circus Topsite (TEC-the.electric.circus.1998.08.27.nfo)," August 27, 1998. DeFacto2, warez.scene.nfo.collection.v1.0.24351.shroo.ms.zip.

TEL. "Trans Electric Light Topsite (TEL-trans.electronic.light.1997.07.16.nfo)," July 16, 1997. DeFacto2, warez.scene.nfo.collection.v1.0.24351.shroo.ms.zip.

TEMP. "The Temple Topsite (TEMP-the.temple.1997.09.21.nfo)," September 21, 1997. DeFacto2, warez.scene.nfo.collection.v1.0.24351.shroo.ms.zip.

TEN. "The Ether Net Topsite (TEN-the.ether.net.XXXX.XX.00.nfo)," n.d. DeFacto2, warez.scene.nfo.collection.v1.0.24351.shroo.ms.zip.

Tenen, Dennis. *Plain Text: The Poetics of Computation.* Stanford: Stanford University Press, 2017.

Tetzlaff, David. "Yo-Ho-Ho and a Server of Warez." In *The World Wide Web and Contemporary Cultural Theory: Magic, Metaphor, Power,* edited by Andrew Herman and Thomas Swiss, 99–126. New York: Routledge, 2000.

TF. "The Flash Topsite (TF-the.flash.1997.01.17.nfo)," January 17, 1997. DeFacto2, warez.scene.nfo.collection.v1.0.24351.shroo.ms.zip.

TFR. "The Fried Rabbit Topsite (TFR-the.fried.rabbit.1998.09.09.nfo)," September 9, 1998. DeFacto2, warez.scene.nfo.collection.v1.0.24351.shroo.ms.zip.

TG. "The Gateway Topsite (TG-the.gateway.1999.01.10.nfo)," January 10, 1999. DeFacto2, warez.scene.nfo.collection.v1.0.24351.shroo.ms.zip.

———. "The Gateway Topsite (TG-the.gateway.XXXX.XX.00.nfo)," n.d. DeFacto2, warez.scene.nfo.collection.v1.0.24351.shroo.ms.zip.

TH. "The Haven Topsite (TH-the.haven.1998.08.30.nfo)," August 30, 1998. DeFacto2, warez.scene.nfo.collection.v1.0.24351.shroo.ms.zip.

Thomas, Douglas. *Hacker Culture.* Minneapolis: University of Minnesota Press, 2002.

———. "Innovation, Piracy and the Ethos of New Media." In *The New Media Book,* edited by Dan Harries, 82–91. London: British Film Institute Publishing, 2004.

Thornton, Sarah. *Club Cultures: Music, Media and Subcultural Capital.* Cambridge: Polity Press, 1995.

TK. "Tragic Kingdom Topsite (TK-tragic.kingdom.1997.06.06.nfo)," June 6, 1997. DeFacto2, warez.scene.nfo.collection.v1.0.24351.shroo.ms.zip.

———. "Tragic Kingdom Topsite (TK-tragic.kingdom.1997.06.24.nfo)," June 24, 1997. DeFacto2, warez.scene.nfo.collection.v1.0.24351.shroo.ms.zip.

TLT. "The Toilet Topsite (TLT-the.toilet.1998.12.13.nfo)," December 13, 1998. DeFacto2, warez.scene.nfo.collection.v1.0.24351.shroo.ms.zip.

TM. "Terrible Mistake Topsite (TM-terrible.mistake.1999.02.13.nfo)," February 13, 1999. DeFacto2, warez.scene.nfo.collection.v1.0.24351.shroo.ms.zip.

———. "The Matrix Topsite (TM-the.matrix.1999.09.25.nfo)," September 25, 1999. DeFacto2, warez.scene.nfo.collection.v1.0.24351.shroo.ms.zip.

TMS. "The Mother Superior Topsite (TMS-the.mother.superior.1999.02.13.nfo)," February 13, 1999. DeFacto2, warez.scene.nfo.collection.v1.0.24351.shroo.ms.zip.

TNB. "The Number of the Beast Topsite (TNB-the.number.of.the.beast.1997.10.21.nfo)," October 21, 1997. DeFacto2, warez.scene.nfo.collection.v1.0.24351.shroo.ms.zip.

TNF. "The New Forge Topsite (TNF-the.new.forge.1997.06.12.nfo)," June 12, 1997. DeFacto2, warez.scene.nfo.collection.v1.0.24351.shroo.ms.zip.

TNL. "The Neverland Topsite (TNL-the.neverland.1999.02.12.nfo)," February 12, 1999. DeFacto2, warez.scene.nfo.collection.v1.0.24351.shroo.ms.zip.

———. "The Neverland Topsite (TNL-the.never.land.1999.04.14.nfo)," April 14, 1999. DeFacto2, warez.scene.nfo.collection.v1.0.24351.shroo.ms.zip.

TNT. "The Nympho Temple Topsite (TNT-the.nympho.temple.1997.07.12.nfo)," July 12, 1997. DeFacto2, warez.scene.nfo.collection.v1.0.24351.shroo.ms.zip.

TO. "Technology Overload Topsite (TO-technology.overload.1998.02.10.nfo)," February 10, 1998. DeFacto2, warez.scene.nfo.collection.v1.0.24351.shroo.ms.zip.

———. "Technology Overload Topsite (TO-technology.overload.1998.02.25.nfo)," February 25, 1998. DeFacto2, warez.scene.nfo.collection.v1.0.24351.shroo.ms.zip.

TonikGin. "IRC XDCC Hacking Exposed." September 11, 2002. http://www.madchat.fr/reseau/IRC_XDCC_Hacking_Exposed.htm.

TOS. "The Orion Syndicate Topsite (TOS-the.orion.syndicate.1999.03.29.nfo)," March 29, 1999. DeFacto2, warez.scene.nfo.collection.v1.0.24351.shroo.ms.zip.

Toshkov, Dimiter. "The 'Global South' Is a Terrible Term. Don't Use It!" *RE-DESIGN*, November 11, 2018. http://re-design.dimiter.eu/?p=969.

TOT. "Temple of Torture Topsite (TOT-temple.of.torture.1999.04.24.nfo)," April 24, 1999. DeFacto2, warez.scene.nfo.collection.v1.0.24351.shroo.ms.zip.

TP. "The Prophecy Topsite (TP-the.prophecy.1997.08.01.nfo)," August 1, 1997. DeFacto2, warez.scene.nfo.collection.v1.0.24351.shroo.ms.zip.

———. "The Prophecy Topsite (TP-the.prophecy.1998.03.11.nfo)," March 11, 1998. DeFacto2, warez.scene.nfo.collection.v1.0.24351.shroo.ms.zip.

———. "The Prophecy Topsite (TP-the.prophecy.XXXX.XX.00.nfo)," n.d. DeFacto2, warez.scene.nfo.collection.v1.0.24351.shroo.ms.zip.

———. "The Pyramid Topsite (TP-the.pyramid.1999.12.13.nfo)," December 13, 1999. DeFacto2, warez.scene.nfo.collection.v1.0.24351.shroo.ms.zip.

———. "The Pyramid Topsite (TP-the.pyramid.2000.04.28.nfo)," April 28, 2000. DeFacto2, warez.scene.nfo.collection.v1.0.24351.shroo.ms.zip.

TPH. "The Pharmacy Topsite (TPH-the.pharmacy.1998.07.27.nfo)," July 27, 1998. DeFacto2, warez.scene.nfo.collection.v1.0.24351.shroo.ms.zip.
TR. "The River Topsite (TR-the.river.1997.05.29.nfo)," May 29, 1997. DeFacto2, warez.scene.nfo.collection.v1.0.24351.shroo.ms.zip.
———. "The Rock Topsite (TR-the.rock.1998.08.14.nfo)," August 14, 1998. DeFacto2, warez.scene.nfo.collection.v1.0.24351.shroo.ms.zip.
———. "The Rock Topsite (TR-the.rock.1999.03.13.nfo)," March 13, 1999. DeFacto2, warez.scene.nfo.collection.v1.0.24351.shroo.ms.zip.
Treverton, Gregory F., Carl Matthies, Karla J. Cunningham, Jeremiah Goulka, Greg Ridgeway, and Anny Wong. "The Shape of Counterfeiting and the Example of Film Piracy." In *Film Piracy, Organized Crime, and Terrorism*, 27–38. Santa Monica: RAND Corporation, 2009.
TRM. "The Raging Monkey Topsite (TRM-the.raging.monkey.1997.09.18.nfo)," September 18, 1999. DeFacto2, warez.scene.nfo.collection.v1.0.24351.shroo.ms.zip.
———. "The Rising Sun Topsite (TRS-the.rising.sun.XXXX.XX.00.nfo)," n.d. DeFacto2, warez.scene.nfo.collection.v1.0.24351.shroo.ms.zip.
TRS. "The Rising Sun Topsite (TRS-the.rising.sun.1998.01.18.nfo)," August 18, 1998. DeFacto2, warez.scene.nfo.collection.v1.0.24351.shroo.ms.zip.
TS. "The Site Topsite (TS-the.site.XXXX.XX.00.nfo)," n.d. DeFacto2, warez.scene.nfo.collection.v1.0.24351.shroo.ms.zip.
———. "The Tombstone Topsite (TS-the.tombstone.1998.12.24.nfo)," December 24, 1998. DeFacto2, warez.scene.nfo.collection.v1.0.24351.shroo.ms.zip.
TSG. "The Sadistic Granddaughter Topsite (TSG-the.sadistic.granddaughter.1999.04.20.nfo)," April 20, 1999. DeFacto2, warez.scene.nfo.collection.v1.0.24351.shroo.ms.zip.

TT. "Titty Twister Topsite (TT-titty.twister.1999.03.19.nfo)," March 19, 1999. DeFacto2, warez.scene.nfo.collection.v1.0.24351.shroo.ms.zip.

———. "Titty Twister Topsite (TT-titty.twister.1999.12.31.nfo)," December 31, 1999. DeFacto2, warez.scene.nfo.collection.v1.0.24351.shroo.ms.zip.

TTD. "The Toxic Dump Topsite (TTD-the.toxic.dump.1998.02.04.nfo)," February 4, 1998. DeFacto2, warez.scene.nfo.collection.v1.0.24351.shroo.ms.zip.

TUR. "The Unknown Realm Topsite (TUR-the.unknown.realm.1998.09.16.nfo)," September 16, 1998. DeFacto2, warez.scene.nfo.collection.v1.0.24351.shroo.ms.zip.

Turner, Fred. "Where the Counterculture Met the New Economy: The WELL and the Origins of Virtual Community." *Technology and Culture* 46, no. 3 (2005): 485–512. DOI: 10.1353/tech.2005.0154.

TV. "Tar Valon Topsite (TV-tar.valon.1998.09.28.nfo)," August 28, 1998. DeFacto2, warez.scene.nfo.collection.v1.0.24351.shroo.ms.zip.

———. "Terminal Velocity Topsite (TV-terminal.velocity.1998.12.27.nfo)," December 27, 1998. DeFacto2, warez.scene.nfo.collection.v1.0.24351.shroo.ms.zip.

———. "Terminal Velocity Topsite (TV-terminal.velocity.1999.01.29.nfo)," January 29, 1999. DeFacto2, warez.scene.nfo.collection.v1.0.24351.shroo.ms.zip.

TVD. "The Void Topsite (TVD-the.void.XXXX.XX.00.nfo)," n.d. DeFacto2, warez.scene.nfo.collection.v1.0.24351.shroo.ms.zip.

TVP. "The Vanishing Point Topsite (TVP-the.vanishing.point.1998.09.15.nfo)," September 15, 1998. DeFacto2, warez.scene.nfo.collection.v1.0.24351.shroo.ms.zip.

TWH. "The Wolves House Topsite (TWH-the.wolves.house.1997.03.21.nfo)," March 21, 1997. DeFacto2, warez.scene.nfo.collection.v1.0.24351.shroo.ms.zip.

———. "The Wolves House Topsite (TWH-the.wolves.house.1998.02.15.nfo)," February 15, 1998. DeFacto2, warez.scene.nfo.collection.v1.0.24351.shroo.ms.zip.

———. "The Wolves House Topsite (TWH-the.wolves.house.1999.12.30.nfo)," December 30, 1999. DeFacto2, warez.scene.nfo.collection.v1.0.24351.shroo.ms.zip.

TWI. "Twilight Topsite (TWI-twilight.1999.12.02.nfo)," December 2, 1999. DeFacto2, warez.scene.nfo.collection.v1.0.24351.shroo.ms.zip.

———. "Twilight Topsite (TWI-twilight.XXXX.XX.02.nfo)," n.d. DeFacto2, warez.scene.nfo.collection.v1.0.24351.shroo.ms.zip.

TWL. "The Waste Land Topsite (TWL-the.waste.land.1997.05.22.nfo)," May 22, 1997. DeFacto2, warez.scene.nfo.collection.v1.0.24351.shroo.ms.zip.

———. "The Waste Land Topsite (TWL-the.waste.land.1998.07.29.nfo)," July 29, 1998. DeFacto2, warez.scene.nfo.collection.v1.0.24351.shroo.ms.zip.

TX. "Terra X Topsite (TX-terra.x.1998.02.14.nfo)," February 14, 1998. DeFacto2, warez.scene.nfo.collection.v1.0.24351.shroo.ms.zip.

u/shrine. "Charitable Seeding Update: 10 Terabytes and 900,000 Scientific Books in a Week with Seedbox.Io and UltraSeedbox." *Reddit,* 2019. https://www.reddit.com/r/seedboxes/comments/e3yl23/charitable_seeding_update_10_terabytes_and_900000/.

———. "Library Genesis Project Update: 2.5 Million Books Seeded with the World, 80 Million Scientific Articles Next." *Reddit,* 2020. https://www.reddit.com/r/DataHoarder/comments/ed9byj/library_genesis_project_update_25_million_books/.

u/skoyern. "R/Networking—What Happened to FXP?," Reddit, 2016. https://www.reddit.com/r/networking/comments/499d1z/what_happened_to_fxp/.

UC. "Unhuman Creations Topsite (UC-unhuman.creations.1998.08.27.nfo)," August 27, 1998. DeFacto2, warez.scene.nfo.collection.v1.0.24351.shroo.ms.zip.

———. "United Centre Topsite (UC-united.centre.1998.08.21.nfo)," August 21, 1998. DeFacto2, warez.scene.nfo.collection.v1.0.24351.shroo.ms.zip.

UD. "Unconquered Dreams Topsite (UD-unconquered.dreams.1999.01.28.nfo)," January 28, 1999. DeFacto2, warez.scene.nfo.collection.v1.0.24351.shroo.ms.zip.

———. "Unconquered Dreams Topsite (UD-unconquered.dreams.XXXX.XX.01.nfo)," n.d. DeFacto2, warez.scene.nfo.collection.v1.0.24351.shroo.ms.zip.

ULS. "Unleashed Topsite (ULS-unleashed.1999.03.26.nfo)," March 26, 1999. DeFacto2, warez.scene.nfo.collection.v1.0.24351.shroo.ms.zip.

———. "Unleashed Topsite (ULS-unleashed.1999.09.14.nfo)," September 14, 1999. DeFacto2, warez.scene.nfo.collection.v1.0.24351.shroo.ms.zip.

Underwood, Ted. *Distant Horizons: Digital Evidence and Literary Change.* Chicago: University of Chicago Press, 2019.

United Kingdom Government. Theft Act 1968. https://www.legislation.gov.uk/ukpga/1968/60/contents.

United States Pirate Party. *No Safe Harbor: Essays about Pirate Politics.* n.p.: CreateSpace, 2012.

UNV. "Universe Topsite (UNV-universe.XXXX.XX.00.nfo)," n.d. DeFacto2, warez.scene.nfo.collection.v1.0.24351.shroo.ms.zip.

Urbas, Gregor. "Cross-National Investigation and Prosecution of Intellectual Property Crimes: The Example of 'Operation Buccaneer.'" *Crime, Law and Social Change* 46, nos. 4–5 (December 2006): 207–21. DOI: 10.1007/s10611-007-9060-x.

US Attorney's Office. "Florida Man Who Participated in Online Piracy Ring Is Sentenced." *FBI,* May 6, 2009. https://www.fbi.gov/newhaven/press-releases/2009/nh050609a.htm.

US Department of Justice. "60th Felony Conviction Obtained in Software Piracy Crackdown 'Operation Fastlink.'" March 6, 2009. https://www.justice.gov/opa/pr/60th-felony-conviction-obtained-software-piracy-crackdown-operation-fastlink.

UT. "Utwente Topsite (UT-utwente.2001.07.17.nfo)," July 17, 2001. DeFacto2, warez.scene.nfo.collection.v1.0.24351.shroo.ms.zip.

UW. "Under World Topsite (UW-under.world.1999.02.15.nfo)," February 15, 1999. DeFacto2, warez.scene.nfo.collection.v1.0.24351.shroo.ms.zip.

———. "Under World Topsite (UW-under.world.1999.05.06.nfo)," May 6, 1999. DeFacto2, warez.scene.nfo.collection.v1.0.24351.shroo.ms.zip.

V. "Valhalla Topsite (V-valhalla.2000.07.17.nfo)," July 17, 2000. DeFacto2, warez.scene.nfo.collection.v1.0.24351.shroo.ms.zip.

V13. "Vault Thirteen Topsite (V13-vault.thirteen.1998.08.01.nfo)," August 1, 1998. DeFacto2, warez.scene.nfo.collection.v1.0.24351.shroo.ms.zip.

Vaidhyanathan, Siva. *Copyrights and Copywrongs: The Rise of Intellectual Property and How It Threatens Creativity*. New York: New York University Press, 2003.

Van der Sar, Ernesto. "Scene Bust Triggered Historic Drop in 'Pirate' Releases." *TorrentFreak,* September 4, 2020. https://torrentfreak.com/scene-bust-triggered-historic-drop-in-pirate-releases-200904/.

———. "'What.CD' Debuts Lightweight Tracker for Its 5 Million Peers." *TorrentFreak,* October 14, 2010. https://torrentfreak.com/what-cd-debuts-lightweight-tracker-for-its-5-million-peers-101014/.

Varese, Federico. "Introduction." In *Organized Crime: Critical Concepts in Criminology,* edited by Federico Varese, 1–35. London: Routledge, 2010.

VDR. "Virtual Dimension Research Lake Topsite (VDR-vdr.lake.1997.05.16.nfo)," May 16, 1997. DeFacto2, warez.scene.nfo.collection.v1.0.24351.shroo.ms.zip.

———. "Virtual Dimension Research Lake Topsite (VDR-vdr.lake.1997.06.06.nfo)," June 6, 1997. DeFacto2, warez.scene.nfo.collection.v1.0.24351.shroo.ms.zip.

———. "Virtual Dimension Research Lake Topsite (VDR-vdr.lake.1998.02.09.nfo)," February 9, 1998. DeFacto2, warez.scene.nfo.collection.v1.0.24351.shroo.ms.zip.

———. "Virtual Dimension Research Lake Topsite (VDR-vdr.lake.1998.04.02.nfo)," April 2, 1998. DeFacto2, warez.scene.nfo.collection.v1.0.24351.shroo.ms.zip.

VERTEX. "1000 Password Plus v1.1.0 (vertex.nfo)," November 1, 2007. DeFacto2.

VF. "Vision Factory Topsite (VF-vision.factory.1999.03.18.nfo)," March 18, 1999. DeFacto2, warez.scene.nfo.collection.v1.0.24351.shroo.ms.zip.

VI. "Violent Illusions Topsite (VI-violent.illusions.1999.06.11.nfo)," June 11, 1999. DeFacto2, warez.scene.nfo.collection.v1.0.24351.shroo.ms.zip.

———. "Violent Illusions Topsite (VI-violent.illusions.1999.09.18.nfo)," September 18, 1999. DeFacto2, warez.scene.nfo.collection.v1.0.24351.shroo.ms.zip.

Virilio, Paul. *The Information Bomb.* Translated by Chris Turner. London: Verso, 2005.

VL. "Vampyre's Lair Topsite (VL-vampyres.lair.1997.10.21.nfo)," October 21, 1997. DeFacto2, warez.scene.nfo.collection.v1.0.24351.shroo.ms.zip.

W10. "Warp Factor Ten Topsite (W10-warp.factor.ten.1997.09.30.nfo)," September 30, 1997. DeFacto2, warez.scene.nfo.collection.v1.0.24351.shroo.ms.zip.

———. "Warp Factor Ten Topsite (W10-warp.factor.ten.1997.11.07.nfo)," November 7, 1997. DeFacto2, warez.scene.nfo.collection.v1.0.24351.shroo.ms.zip.

———. "Warp Factor Ten Topsite (W10-warp.factor.ten.XXXX.XX.00.nfo)," n.d. DeFacto2, warez.scene.nfo.collection.v1.0.24351.shroo.ms.zip.

WALMART. "WALMART Anti-P2P Statement (tairlthan-walmart.nfo)," 2007. DeFacto2.

Wasiak, Patryk. "'Illegal Guys': A History of Digital Subcultures in Europe during the 1980s." *Zeithistorische Forschungen/Studies in Contemporary History* 9 (2012): 257–76. DOI: 10.14765/ZZF.DOK-1595.

———. "Telephone Networks, BBSes, and the Emergence of the Transnational 'Warez Scene.'" *History and Technology* 35, no. 2 (2019): 177–94. DOI: 10.1080/07341512.2019.1652432.

Waters, Florence. "Film Buyers Fooled by Sony's 'The Girl with the Dragon Tattoo' DVD Joke." *The Telegraph,* March 21, 2012. https://www.telegraph.co.uk/culture/film/film-news/9158437/Film-buyers-fooled-by-Sonys-The-Girl-with-the-Dragon-Tattoo-DVD-joke.html.

Watson, Jeff. "Games Beyond the ARG." In *Alternate Reality Games and the Cusp of Digital Gameplay,* edited by Antero Garcia and Greg Niemeyer, 187–210. New York: Bloomsbury Academic, 2017.

WD. "Wet Dreams Topsite (WD-wet.dreams.1999.04.25.nfo)," April 25, 1999. DeFacto2, warez.scene.nfo.collection.v1.0.24351.shroo.ms.zip.

———. "Wet Dreams Topsite (WD-wet.dreams.1999.05.27.nfo)," May 27, 1999. DeFacto2, warez.scene.nfo.collection.v1.0.24351.shroo.ms.zip.

werner. "FLT Busts." Theisonews, May 2, 2004. https://www.theisonews.com/forums/index.php/topic,117995.msg1559546.html?#msg1559546.

WFZ. "Warez Free Zone Topsite (WFZ-warez.free.zone.1999.07.10.nfo)," July 10, 1999. DeFacto2, warez.scene.nfo.collection.v1.0.24351.shroo.ms.zip.

WH. "White House Topsite (WH-white.house.1998.03.15.nfo)," March 15, 1998. DeFacto2, warez.scene.nfo.collection.v1.0.24351.shroo.ms.zip.

———. "White House Topsite (WH-white.house.1998.09.09.nfo)," September 9, 1998. DeFacto2, warez.scene.nfo.collection.v1.0.24351.shroo.ms.zip.

What.CD. Project Gazelle. *GitHub,* 2020. https://github.com/WhatCD/Gazelle.

———. "Project Gazelle: Classes/Rules.Class.php." *GitHub,* November 8, 2016. https://github.com/WhatCD/Gazelle.

———. "Project Gazelle: Sections/Schedule/Index.php." *GitHub,* January 8, 2016. https://github.com/WhatCD/Gazelle.

Williams, J. Patrick. "Authentic Identities: Straightedge Subculture, Music, and the Internet." *Journal of*

Contemporary Ethnography 35, no. 2 (2006): 173–200. DOI: 10.1177/0891241605285100.

Williams, Raymond. *Keywords: A Vocabulary of Culture and Society.* Oxford: Oxford University Press, 2014.

Willinsky, John. *The Intellectual Properties of Learning: A Prehistory from Saint Jerome to John Locke.* Chicago: University of Chicago Press, 2017.

WL. "Wonder Land Topsite (WL-wonderland.XXXX.XX.00.nfo)," n.d. DeFacto2, warez.scene.nfo.collection.v1.0.24351.shroo.ms.zip.

WND. "The Windmill Topsite (WND-the.windmill.1997.06.19.nfo)," June 19, 1998. DeFacto2, warez.scene.nfo.collection.v1.0.24351.shroo.ms.zip.

WOC. "World of Chaos Topsite (WOC-world.of.chaos.1998.07.05.nfo)," July 5, 1998. DeFacto2, warez.scene.nfo.collection.v1.0.24351.shroo.ms.zip.

Woo, Benjamin. "Alpha Nerds: Cultural Intermediaries in a Subcultural Scene." *European Journal of Cultural Studies* 15, no. 5 (2012): 659–76. DOI: 10.1177/1367549412445758.

WOPR. "Wouldn't You Prefer A Good Game of Chess? Topsite (WOPR-wopr.1998.08.14.nfo)," August 14, 1998. DeFacto2, warez.scene.nfo.collection.v1.0.24351.shroo.ms.zip.

WS. "Warez Sector Topsite (WS-warez.sector.1997.04.17.nfo)," April 17, 1997. DeFacto2, warez.scene.nfo.collection.v1.0.24351.shroo.ms.zip.

WT. "Watch Tower Topsite (WT-watch.tower.1998.03.02.nfo)," March 2, 1998. DeFacto2, warez.scene.nfo.collection.v1.0.24351.shroo.ms.zip.

WTC. "World Trade Center Topsite (WTC-world.trade.center.1998.07.07.nfo)," July 7, 1998. DeFacto2, warez.scene.nfo.collection.v1.0.24351.shroo.ms.zip.

WW. "Wild West Topsite (WW-wild.west.1998.09.04.nfo)," September 4, 1998. DeFacto2, warez.scene.nfo.collection.v1.0.24351.shroo.ms.zip.

XF. "X Filez Topsite (XF-x.filez.1997.07.25.nfo)," July 25, 1997. DeFacto2, warez.scene.nfo.collection.v1.0.24351.shroo.ms.zip.

———. "X Filez Topsite (XF-x.filez.1997.08.15.nfo)," August 15, 1997. DeFacto2, warez.scene.nfo.collection.v1.0.24351.shroo.ms.zip.

XNS. "Xenosis Topsite (XNS-xenosis.1998.05.18.nfo)," May 18, 1998. DeFacto2, warez.scene.nfo.collection.v1.0.24351.shroo.ms.zip.

———. "Xenosis Topsite (XNS-xenosis.1998.06.10.nfo)," June 10, 1998. DeFacto2, warez.scene.nfo.collection.v1.0.24351.shroo.ms.zip.

XQZ. "Xquizit Topsite (XQZ-xquizit.1998.03.25.nfo)," March 25, 1998. DeFacto2, warez.scene.nfo.collection.v1.0.24351.shroo.ms.zip.

———. "Xquizit Topsite (XQZ-xquizit.1999.07.24.nfo)," July 24, 1999. DeFacto2, warez.scene.nfo.collection.v1.0.24351.shroo.ms.zip.

XZONE. "X Zone Topsite (XZONE-x.zone.1998.03.01.nfo)," March 1, 1998. DeFacto2, warez.scene.nfo.collection.v1.0.24351.shroo.ms.zip.

———. "X Zone Topsite (XZONE-x.zone.XXXX.XX.00.nfo)," n.d. DeFacto2, warez.scene.nfo.collection.v1.0.24351.shroo.ms.zip.

Yglesias, Matthew. "Piracy Is a Form of Theft, and Copyright Infringement Is Neither." *Slate Magazine,* December 15, 2011. https://slate.com/business/2011/12/piracy-is-a-form-of-theft-and-copyright-infringement-is-neither.html.

ZEUS. "Zeus Topsite (ZEUS-zeus.1998.11.20.nfo)," November 20, 1998. DeFacto2, warez.scene.nfo.collection.v1.0.24351.shroo.ms.zip.

ZL. "Z Land Topsite (ZL-zland.1998.12.02.nfo)," December 2, 1998. DeFacto2, warez.scene.nfo.collection.v1.0.24351.shroo.ms.zip.

ZLA. "Zilla Topsite (ZLA-zilla.1998.08.09.nfo)," August 9, 1998. DeFacto2, warez.scene.nfo.collection.v1.0.24351.shroo.ms.zip.

———. "Zilla Topsite (ZLA-zilla.1999.02.17.nfo)," February 17, 1999. DeFacto2, warez.scene.nfo.collection.v1.0.24351.shroo.ms.zip.

———. "Zilla Topsite (ZLA-zilla.1999.06.30.nfo)," June 30, 1999. DeFacto2, warez.scene.nfo.collection.v1.0.24351.shroo.ms.zip.

Made in the USA
Coppell, TX
05 November 2026

11327620R00245